'Glen O'Hara has brought his rigo_ _____
the biggest and most important acto_
tural history: the sea that surrounds th_W_ _____ _ incorrigible
landlubber will be educated and fascinat_ _____ original book.'
—Niall Ferguson, Laurence A. Ti___ _rofessor of History, Harvard
University, and author of *Empire: How Britain Made the Modern World*

In this first full-scale treatment of Britain's relationship with the surrounding oceans, Glen O'Hara examines the history of British people's maritime lives and, in turn, the formation of British cultural identities. A lens through which to view British life, *Britain and the Sea* spans more than 400 years, beginning in 1600 and taking us through to the present day. Tying together every aspect in the development of Great Britain, from state formation, industrialisation and modernisation, through to histories of transport, migration, slavery, warfare and crime, this book illustrates how the rich tapestry of Britain's narrative was decided not among the fields of the 'green and pleasant land', but out at sea.

Glen O'Hara is Senior Lecturer in Modern History at Oxford Brookes University. He is the author of *From Dreams to Disillusionment: Economic and Social Planning in 1960s Britain* and the joint editor, with Helen Parr, of *The Modernisation of Britain? Harold Wilson and the British Labour Governments of 1964–1970.*

Britain and the Sea

Since 1600

Glen O'Hara

First published 2010 by
PALGRAVE MACMILLAN

Palgrave Macmillan in the UK is an imprint of Macmillan Publishers Limited, registered in England, company number 785998, of Houndmills, Basingstoke, Hampshire RG21 6XS.

Palgrave Macmillan in the US is a division of St Martin's Press LLC, 175 Fifth Avenue, New York, NY 10010.

Palgrave Macmillan is the global academic imprint of the above companies and has companies and representatives throughout the world.

Palgrave® and Macmillan® are registered trademarks in the United States, the United Kingdom, Europe and other countries.

ISBN-13: 978–0–230–21828–4 hardback
ISBN-13: 978–0–230–21829–1 paperback

This book is printed on paper suitable for recycling and made from fully managed and sustained forest sources. Logging, pulping and manufacturing processes are expected to conform to the environmental regulations of the country of origin.

A catalogue record for this book is available from the British Library.

A catalog record for this book is available from the Library of Congress.

10   9   8   7   6   5   4   3   2   1
19 18 17 16 15 14 13 12 11 10

Printed in China

*This book is dedicated to my A-Level History tutors,
Jon Cook and Martin Cross.*

Contents

Acknowledgements

Any work of synthesis inevitably builds up a huge number of debts: to readers for suggesting new works to consult, to friends who agree to plough through the text, and to colleagues who are willing to take on duties while others are busy in the library. But though many hands assisted in the creation of *Britain and the Sea*, all errors and inaccuracies remain my own.

I have in particular to single out the continuing support of two academic mentors, Niall Ferguson and Kathleen Burk, who have once again provided encouragement, friendship and advice at times when this project – and much else – looked in doubt. Kate Haines of Palgrave Macmillan continued to believe in this project when it looked perhaps more prudent not to. Among the most important readers and critics have been, in alphabetical order: Joanne Bailey, Laura Beers, Martin Conway, Tom Crook, Virginia Crossman, Anne-Marie Kilday, Angela McShane, David Nash, Sarah Pearsall, Laura Sandy, Richard Sheldon, Andrew Spicer, Isobel Urquhart and three anonymous referees for the publishers. They all did sterling work.

Successive cohorts of undergraduates who took my Oxford Brookes Advanced Level course, 'Blue, White and Green Nation: Britain and the Sea since 1600', made suggestions and raised issues that have made this book immeasurably better than it would otherwise have been.

The support of my partner, Lyndsay Grant, has been once more vital. None of this would have been possible without her.

Finally, for getting me interested in history in the first place, and for helping me piece together the ways in which Britain fits into the world, I must record my lifelong debts to the best A-Level History tutors any student could hope to have: Jon Cook and Martin Cross. This book is dedicated to them.

I must down to the seas again, to the lonely sea and the sky,
And all I ask is a tall ship and a star to steer her by,
And the wheel's kick and the wind's song and the white
    sail's shaking,
And a grey mist on the sea's face, and a grey dawn breaking.

I must down to the seas again, for the call of the running tide
Is a wild call and a clear call that may not be denied;
And all I ask is a windy day with the white clouds flying,
And the flung spray and the blown spume, and the sea-gulls crying.

I must down to the seas again, to the vagrant gypsy life,
To the gull's way and the whale's way where the wind's like
    a whetted knife;
And all I ask is a merry yarn from a laughing fellow-rover
And quiet sleep and a sweet dream when the long trick's over.

taken from 'Sea-Fever' by John Masefield

1

Histories

The last two decades have transformed British maritime history. Concerns central to non-maritime scholarship have colonised this field, which has then allowed oceanic history to influence other areas of study in its turn. Economics, trading and business once dominated the history of the sea, but the sub-discipline has been transformed under the pressure of globalisation. At least six new areas of study are noticeable in this respect, and they constitute themes that will then be pursued through the rest of the book. The first is the manner in which oceanic traders' contacts and routes increasingly came to resemble those 'networks' that, contemporary social scientists and philosophers are convinced, characterise late twentieth- and early twenty-first-century societies in the developed world. The second major development is a renewed interest in the nature of oceanic regions, appropriate perhaps in a world grouping itself into political and trading *blocs*. Third, the 'new' maritime history is critically concerned with divisions of labour and social histories of those 'below decks', an understandable development in a globalising world often criticised for deepening international class divides through the free movement of capital without any concomitant liberalisation of migration laws. Fourth, this chapter will go on to describe the influence of recent cultural studies on maritime history, evident in historiographies focussing on sexual, criminal or ideological 'transgressions' of perceived norms. Fifth, this introduction will then discuss recent histories of travel and tourism, which reflect a world in which such movement has become an accepted part of life for the citizens of many rich countries. The sixth and perhaps most pressing area of recent innovation has been in the field of environmental history – a development which reflects the climactic emergency of overfishing and climate change that threaten finally to wipe out many of Britain's fish stocks and inundate her coastal regions. This explosion of interest, and these multifarious literatures, means that it is often difficult to keep track of Britons' contact with the sea. It has certainly become harder to integrate all these different elements. It will finally be suggested here that the formation of 'Britishness' itself, and narratives of British engagements with the sea, may provide an analytical category that will help such understandings develop.

The renaissance of British maritime history

British maritime history has recently been enjoying something of a renaissance. Collections of essays and special editions of academic journals on this subject have poured from the presses. In 2001, a special edition of *The William and Mary Quarterly* looked anew at the Atlantic slave trade, and included new quantitative and qualitative estimates of its scale and significance, as well as some new assessments of how both Europeans and black Africans perceived and experienced the trade.[1] The same journal published a special issue in July 2005 on 'the Atlantic economy in an era of revolutions', and contained a forum looking 'beyond the Atlantic' in October 2006. Both volumes lit up the North Atlantic basin in particular, and allowed the eighteenth-century English-speaking maritime world to be seen as a systemic whole. No longer were the great upheavals and revolutions to be seen only as 'internal independence movements'; they were now part of the 'deeply entwined' 'economies of multiple nations', created in part by 'the communication of merchants and sailors, exchange of commodities, extension of credit, and enriched consumer cultures of island and mainland settlements in the Western Hemisphere'.[2]

But how were these 'communications' managed? The role of oceanic passenger and merchant traffic, allowing news, rumour, peoples and goods to flow around the world, was to the fore. As Peter Coclanis put it in the 'beyond the Atlantic' forum: 'the sea is very much in these days. We have Atlantic historians and historians of the Indian Ocean world . . . . Some scholars are studying the world of the North Sea, and there are Pacific basinites and rimmers galore.'[3] Not to be outdone by *The William and Mary Quarterly*, *The American Historical Review* published a forum on 'oceans of history' in its third issue for 2006. Kären Wigen opened it thus: 'maritime scholarship seems to have burst its bounds; across the discipline, the sea is swinging into view.' The contributors included Alison Games on the Atlantic world, making clear both how 'desirable' and how elusive an inclusive, totalising and explanatory trans-oceanic history might prove, and Peregrine Horden and Nicholas Purcell insisting that histories of particular oceans and seas had to take connections with other regions into account.[4] The online journal *History in Focus* had already covered some of the same ground, though much more briefly, in a 2005 collection that included essays on popular views of sailors, women's wait for their husbands and lovers to come home, dockers' lives and the British seaside holiday.[5]

Two recent edited collections have summed up the influence of this maritime history. David Armitage and Michael Braddick's 2002 book, *The British Atlantic World*, has already become a classic of the genre. Their 'inter-hemispheric system' was not exclusively maritime, to be sure: it embraced Canada and the American 'mainland' as well as British ports, Caribbean islands and the high seas. But the themes covered – trade, transfer and migration – and the evocation of 'waters . . . crowded with British traders engaged in all sorts of illegal operations' constantly called to mind seafaring, sea power and transgression.[6] In 2007, David Cannadine brought together an extremely august set of contributors, including Maxine Berg, Catherine Hall and Simon Schaffer, for a lecture series and edited volume on *Empire, the Sea and Global History*.[7]

There is at least one extremely powerful analytical explanation for the recent interest in the British maritime world, and that is late twentieth- and early twenty-first-century globalisation. This has, in A.G. Hopkins' formulation, become 'the catch-word of the day'.[8] But it has also provided many historians with a strong framework for many of the most exciting and ground-breaking developments in global and maritime history. Miles Ogborn's recent book *Global Lives*, which takes on the enormous subject of 'Britain and the World, 1550–1800', begins with just this sense of history's contemporary relevance:

> Social theorists and media commentators have propounded views of a new glob-alised economy, society and culture emerging in the late twentieth century. At the same time those concerned with the past have engaged in efforts to put these contemporary forms of globalisation into a longer-term – and sometimes very long-term indeed – history of modes of global connection. Globalisation, it is stressed, has a past. It has a history.[9]

It is this renewed interest in globalisation that has transformed the historiography of the sea. For what are the hallmarks of a 'globalising' world? In a very brief and inadequate characterisation, we could outline six major trends. In economic terms, one of globalisation's hallmarks has been a massive boom in international trade, creating evermore complex networks of physical and seaborne commerce. The threat of chaos in ungoverned markets, and the need to negotiate on more-or-less equal terms between different trading *blocs*, has led to a second development: trade has increasingly tended to take place within regional political frameworks. The rise of groupings such as the European Union and the North American Free Trade Association are good examples.[10] The trade boom and its regional nature have in themselves sparked debates in a third area: about the appropriate international division of labour and the possibilities for increased exploitation and income inequality in global markets.[11]

In political and social terms, this globalised world is marked, fourthly, by an increased awareness of overlapping and uncertain international jurisdictions. This trend runs in parallel with a sense of an increasingly 'weightless', 'floating' or kaleidoscopic world: the critic Noreena Hertz, turning positive imaginings of that world on their head, has imagined it as 'confused, contradictory and mercurial', a world full of a 'litany of doubts'.[12] The geographer David Harvey has demonstrated how massive increases in trade and communications, alongside deepening regionalisation, might require the fusion of theories of location and power: of how, when and why places and spatial meanings are constructed.[13] This might be joined by a fifth trend: a sense of the importance of marginalised genders, sexual groups and races among protestors and the academy.[14] Sixth and last, increases in free time, travel and leisure, at least for citizens of the privileged developed world, have commodified, packaged and aestheticised the tourist experience.[15]

British maritime historians have been grappling with a very similar list of problems, and areas of historiographical innovation clearly observable in the literature closely mirror contemporary developments.[16] These might be summarised, firstly, as histories of trading and other networks, personified by merchants and their cargoes – a trend reinforced by the increasing importance of regional histories within the discipline.[17] Secondly, maritime 'mapping' and ideas of oceanic space have also become the subject of intense historical interest. This work owes a great deal to Bernard Bailyn's long-standing innovations within, and advocacy of, histories of the Atlantic – though historians working this field tend to emphasise ideological and cultural identities, rather than just economic ties, in their work.[18] A third area of current concern is the social character and composition of plebeian crews 'down below', often conjoined with a fourth theme – 'difference' or 'otherness', embodied in transgressions of crime, race and gender. Markus Rediker's famous 1987 work, *Between the Devil and the Deep Blue Sea*, has unquestionably been the most influential text in this regard.[19] Fifth and last, leisure, spectacle and the seaside holiday form a sixth and final research agenda central to the new histories of the sea.[20] These categories do not exhaust the possibilities of the 'new' maritime history. But they do give us a strong clue as to their roots in contemporary history and political economy.

For each area is central to the new globalised world that historians cannot escape; and every one has become central to the renewed historical lives of the ocean. These trends will be to the fore in the following pages.

Environmental danger and human history

Even more pressing than historiographical trends, and much more vital in terms of public policy, is the last reason for historians' rejuvenated interest in the sea: the environmental emergency presently underway in the world's oceans. The worsening situation seems constantly to forestall even the new environmental history's attempts to grapple with its implications for the past. The destruction of fish stocks is only the most obvious example. One recent study has calculated that two-thirds of the near-surface fish in the North Atlantic disappeared in the second half of the twentieth century.[21] There has probably been a 90 per cent reduction in the numbers of large predatory fish that humans like to eat – cod and tuna, for instance – since the onset of industrialised fishing.[22] The losses may be most ominous in the evolutionary 'hotspots' where different species and environmental systems interact: these sensitive areas might very quickly be decimated if one part of the food chain is removed.[23] The oceanic law expert John Kunich has argued that this amounts to the 'decimation of life on earth; a Mass Extinction-level episode in human history, and one that is happening without most citizens even noticing'.[24]

Other environmental dangers may be even more lethal to the planet's oceans. The combination of man-made global warming, rising acidity levels associated with hotter climates, 'red tides' of algae caused by fertilisers and huge whirlpools of discarded plastic recently caused even the usually sober *Economist* to conclude: 'man is assaulting the oceans. They will smite him if he does not take care.'[25] The periodical included a special report on the sea in January 2009, calling for more marine reserves, transferable fishing permits rather than 'quotas' that cause perfectly good fish to be thrown overboard, and US ratification of the UN Law of the Sea. As of 2009, the USA still has not signed the treaty – though the Obama Administration has pledged to do so.[26]

Sea level rises associated with global warming mean that many low-lying areas of Britain, especially but not exclusively in East Anglia, may eventually have to be abandoned to the sea. In 2004 the Government launched *Making Space for Water*. This declared that there was simply no point spending billions on flood defences that might only last for a couple of decades.[27] A more 'holistic' approach, emphasising better planning for sustainability, more resilient buildings and a better flood warning system, might be part of a strategy of managed retreat.[28] Lord Smith of Finsbury, who became head of the Environment Agency in 2008, announced then that the Agency was looking at the areas that would have to be given up over the next 100 years. 'We are almost certainly not going to be able to defend absolutely every bit of coast – it would simply be an impossible task.'[29]

In this situation, it is not surprising that the last few years have witnessed the emergence of an environmental historiography – a development that has been vital in fixing maritime history's new and more prominent position within the academy.[30] It is, perhaps, the last and one of the most interesting of our 'globalised' themes. 'Ecology', indeed, is now often itself analysed 'as a science of empire' and European maritime expansion rather than as an inherited 'given' – ideas that owe a great deal to the pioneering work of Alfred Crosby, who made clear just how much Europeans had shaped and changed the environments around them.[31] By connecting man's industry and trade with their presence on the oceans, such work may offer future researchers a new way to link historical realities *at* sea with past imaginings *of* the sea. Morten Karnøe Søndergaard has recently tracked the collapse of North American mackerel stocks in the late nineteenth century, and its knock-on effects for the numbers of fish remaining in European waters.[32] The new emphasis on the environment, obvious in the globalised politics of the twenty-first century, is so pervasive that it can be found in areas as apparently unlikely as the history of international maritime diplomacy.[33]

This is, once more, not an entirely new development, and it has roots in both maritime and non-maritime historical thought. Fernand Braudel's work was seminal in terms of the landscape's importance to human history, an approach that also stressed the importance of the coastline and the ocean.[34] Harold Innis' interwar work on the Canadian fur trade and cod fisheries was informed by a Marxist concern for the expropriation of seaborne resources.[35] But humans' interaction with the natural world has now moved centre stage, and voyages previously and straightforwardly celebrated for their role as 'discovery and exploration' have thus been re-examined. R.H. Grove has detected 'the beginnings of global environmentalism' in the presence of the polymath Sir Joseph Banks on Captain Cook's *Endeavour*, and of the German naturalists Johann Reinhold Forster and Georg Forster on Cook's second voyage of discovery.[36] Richard Drayton's history of Kew Gardens as a site of 'imperial improvement' has also been enormously important here. One of Drayton's central themes is the 'new imperialism of the Enlightenment' and how it 'hoisted the Royal Botanic Gardens at Kew on to the stage of world history' as a centre of horticulture, seeding, science and natural history.[37] The circulation of environmental ideas, the shipment of fragile plants, and past societies' views of nature seem more than ever appropriate in an age of 'globalisation' that threatens the climate and the seas more acutely than ever.

Merging green and blue histories

Taken together, these developments have effected a fundamental change in maritime history. N.A.M. Rodger has gone so far as to term the last few years of the twentieth century a 'golden age' of naval history, and the word 'naval' could easily be replaced by 'maritime'.[38] As late as 1978, Ralph Davis argued that this sub-discipline was concerned with 'the history of men in ships and boats and of those who employed, directed, or served them'.[39] That sentence could never be written now, for the momentum for change is coming from surprising and unexpected sources. The emphasis on economic and social history alone held true only until the late 1980s, when new histories influenced by cultural studies, the linguistic turn towards *meaning* rather than *events*, and historians of 'otherness' and the environment began to colonise the field. This is clearly now a judgement that belongs in the past.

Recent globalisations, and the concomitant shift in the academy's world-view, help to explain this revolution in British maritime studies.[40] It is an influence that does not stop at some vague or generic impulse, for as we have seen, specific non-maritime historiographies have been crucial in providing inspiration. The sea and the coast have moved closer together, a testament to hydrography's interest in changing views and ideas of the ocean. Land has termed this a 'coastal' history, in which blue and green histories have to be considered as parts of one coherent whole: 'coastlines would not exist without their proximity to the ocean, but their character is not determined solely by the ocean's action.'[41]

It is a fitting image, for as we have seen new histories of the sea have rested on ideas, tools and techniques adopted from the discipline as a whole, as well as on specifically maritime approaches. One source for this new 'fusion' of land and sea, for instance, can be found in recent archaeological approaches to the development of island societies. Paul Rainbird has drawn on linguistic and physical evidence in his work 'fusing [the] land and people' of early Micronesia; Cyprian Broodbank relies on more traditional (and land-based) physical evidence in the ancient Aegean.[42] But both emphasise equally just how much humankind has utilised the seas, as well as the extent to which the seascape changed the societies they are investigating.[43] The 'ocean's action', once more, is twofold: it acts to form and shape societies, before people change the waters themselves in turn.

Even so, self-confidence within maritime studies *per se* still remains elusive. This is partly because of the multifaceted methodological inheritances inherent in Isaac Land's 'coastal' history, but also to some extent because oceanic histories must often be written using evidence based on 'dry land'. Even novel environmental histories, in the hands of innovative historians such as W. Jeffrey Bolster's work on sixteenth- to eighteenth-century fish stocks, have to still rely on records made on land: in Bolster's case, on colonial authorities competing or co-operating with native peoples over fishing rights.[44] As Seán McGrail has noted, archaeologists working on ships' remains are much more likely to work in estuaries, on riverbanks, near ports and on land than they are in the deep ocean.[45]

Even so, more coherent and more integrated histories of Britons' relationship with the seas are required, and they might focus around the idea of maritime contact and national identity. Linda Colley has provided one route by which this may be possible, showing how cultural and social history may be brought to bear on the vexed question of the formation of British national identity overall. Her most recent book, *Captives*, at least hints at the way in which British 'freedom' was defined as trade and service on the high seas, as distinct from Moorish captivity.[46] The future may then reside in utilising two of the major traditions we have analysed here – the history of the state and the cultures of its peoples, those two sides of nation-building – in harness. We would not then have to pick between class, the central organising category of Rediker and the new social historians, nation, so central to histories of mapping and meaning, and culture, however defined – plebeian, transgressive or carnivalesque. We might be able to treat them as part of the same experience.

Some historians have already suggested what might be possible in an overall treatment of this theme, for instance, on Bethamite reform in the dockyards or the Royal Navy's role as one of the central tropes of 'Britishness'.[47] Ken Lunn and Ann Day have offered a short but penetrating list of interconnections between national identity and the sea, embodied in 'Jolly Jack' the patriotic sailor, supposedly good relations between officers and men in the Royal Navy, as well as the romantic heroism of Drake and Nelson.[48] Three recent books point the way further towards a history of Britain and the sea. The first two focus on the Royal Navy: Timothy Jenks' *Naval Engagements* looks at the navy's symbolic role in forming and reforming notions of patriotism during the Napoleonic Wars; Jan Rüger's *The Great Naval Game* picks up similar themes for the late Victorian and Edwardian periods.[49] In terms of economic and social history more broadly, Christopher Harvie's recent and extraordinary evocation of the waters between Britain and Ireland as an 'inland sea' has imagined the sea as connecting the Scottish, Irish, Welsh and Northern English more than it divided them.[50]

But treatments of the subject of nation-making and the sea as a whole have in general been brief and descriptive, rather than analytical: these recent works are the exception, rather than the rule. There is a cursory glance at the subject in Robert Colls' *Identity of England*, where it is argued that in the eighteenth and nineteenth centuries, 'the sea became the further extreme of British territory. It was their most intimate and their most objective defining characteristic.'[51] There are scattered references elsewhere, for instance, the characteristically excellent concise summary of seventeenth- and eighteenth-century views of state, government and the sea in Raphael Samuel's classic *Patriotism*.[52] But the idea has not been consistently pursued or used consistently to uncover the relationships between the British peoples, their ideas, the British state and the oceanic context. Perhaps the twentieth century – the age of mass armies, continental powers, European engagement and Frank Newbould's rural wartime vision of 'deep England' – was not the time for understanding such cross-currents.[53]

Such an awareness might allow us to tell a richer and more complex story about Britons' engagement with the world than politicians' musings on 'Britishness' allow, and which maritime anniversaries and celebrations encourage. What follows in these pages can only constitute a few steps in that direction. No attempt is made to be comprehensive, or even to claim that most of the story and its implications can be covered in a single volume. The following pages will, rather, gather together just some of the many threads and themes evident in the maritime past, and attempt to integrate them within the wider context of British and world history. The diversity and richness of recent maritime history is indeed daunting. But seen through the lens of lives conducted and choices made at or around the sea, and synthesised with and allied to a sense of state formation and national cultures, those oceanic narratives may provide one key to understanding British history – and Britons' lives – within both their and our rapidly globalising world.

Part I
The Flowing Tide

2

Merchants

This chapter investigates Britain's rise to world maritime commercial, trading and shipbuilding predominance. At the outbreak of the First World War, ships registered in the United Kingdom carried 40 per cent of all seaborne trade, and Britons owned one-third of the world's merchant marine. This was an extraordinary transformation for the nations of the British Isles, which in 1600 were politically divided and economically weak, traded mainly with Scandinavia, the Netherlands and the Iberian Peninsula and, for the most part, exported only cloth in return for luxury consumables. How had this change occurred? It will be suggested here that it had four main components. An increasingly aggressive assertion of state power, as embodied in chartered companies and the seventeenth-century Navigation Acts, attacked Spanish and Dutch influence both in the Atlantic and in Asia. Secondly, Britain's deep and secure western harbours, and a geographical position that made it relatively simple and quick to sail to the Americas, allowed the British to establish a plantation culture in the New World. Goods from these settlements then helped to foster a culture of consumption, novelty and fashion back at home. Thirdly, and most noticeably during the eighteenth century, a dense network of canals linked Britain's ports with its industrial heartlands and helped forge a new type of world economy: one based on the processing of goods transported across the world's oceans, which were then shaped into manufactures in Britain's factories. They also gave Britain a rich and tight-knit merchant class, often identified with minority religious or racial groups. This helped to bring together the interest of coaster trades, for instance, in coal, and long-distance merchants, as well as supporting local shipbuilding industries in, most notably, Glasgow. In the fourth and last stage of this ascent to economic dominance, an immensely powerful economy forged by state power, geographical position, consumerism, transport links, urban infrastructure and an 'interested' business class was freed from mercantilist restrictions. This helped the British state force free trade, not only on reluctant agriculturalists within Britain itself, but upon other countries who feared that the uniquely strong British economy built up behind tariff walls and cultural barriers might overwhelm their own native production. And so it proved, at least for most of the nineteenth century. Together, these four stages of maritime economic development transformed life in the British Isles, changing its very nature from a backwater to the powerhouse of the global economy. Britain became the world's foremost entrepôt, transport hub, consumer of last resort and shipbuilding centre, as well as enforcing the economic and cultural 'norms' of free trade and the freedom of the seas. This was the meaning of Charles II's remark that the country 'could only be considerable [through] our trade and power by sea'.

Nations on the edge of Europe

Any rational sixteenth-century observer, examining trade in and out of the British Isles, would hardly have identified that archipelago as a potential economic superpower. For one thing, in the early seventeenth century she relied a great deal on just one product – cloth, exports of which had boomed under Henry VII, and which replaced wool as England's main export during the sixteenth century. Cloth exports more than doubled between the 1470s and the 1550s, mostly passing through London on their way to be traded at Antwerp. Gloucester, Wiltshire and East Somerset broadcloths, for instance, might be sold on from there to markets as diverse as Portugal, Central Europe, Germany or the Baltic.[1] In 1515 one of Cardinal Wolsey's correspondents told him that Antwerp was 'now one of the wonders of the world, of which the English merchants were the greatest cause, drawing many other merchants thither, as they would probably find out if Englishmen resorted elsewhere'.[2] The list of England's imports – velvet, silk, sugar, dates, prunes, almonds, currants, pepper, grain, pitch, tar, flax, canvas, iron, wax and wine – was much longer than her export monoculture.[3]

While the Spanish were busy conquering the New World, and bringing back fleets of silver and spices, the English were struggling to maintain their existing trade with Europe. Even an assertive king such as Henry VIII had to throw the ports open to foreign trade in 1539, as he searched for allies and supplies during his wars with France and the Holy Roman Empire. War with Spain in the late 1500s did not help either. Iberian luxuries had been one of the staple trades of cities such as Bristol, bringing in wine, port and silks; that inevitably dried up during hostilities in the 1580s and 1590s. The first years of peace under James I were good ones, during which cloth exports rose from 100,000 pieces in 1600 to 127,000 in 1614. But the 1620s saw the trade depressed, especially after the deadly mix of plague and poverty in 1625. War then paralysed trade in 1629, and another prolonged export slump, from which the old cloth industries would not recover, followed in the 1630s. Cloth exports slumped amid English inflation and increasing continental competition. The white, undressed cloth industries of Wiltshire, Gloucestershire, Worcestershire, Somerset and Oxford all experienced deep distress.[4]

England's answer was to develop what were becoming known as the 'new draperies'. East Anglia, Lancashire, Devon and Kent were at the forefront of this, along with most of the large towns on the coast from Yarmouth all the way round to Plymouth. Inflation and competition were less important factors in this sector. The new bays, says, camlets and fustians, twilled cloths and cut fabrics that often felt like velvet or silk were cheaper to produce and used less wool. This made market conditions considerably easier than in the 'old' draperies, especially for smaller manufacturers. And the Statute of Artificers, which laid down conditions of work and apprenticeship, did not apply to these new industries, since they had not existed when it was enacted in 1563: this meant that the new draperies could compete on cost, and react quickly to rapid market changes. Up to and including the eighteenth century, the popularity of these novel materials meant that woollens remained England's biggest single group of home-manufactured exports, though not the largest segment of her trade overall.[5]

Despite this eventually vigorous response to the crisis of the woollen industries, it was the Dutch, not the British, who were masters of the trading oceans from the 1640s until at least the 1680s.[6] They could build a 300-ton 'flyboat' for £1300–£1400, whereas the same ship would cost £2200–£2400 in England.[7] The wars of the 1620s, the need for well-defended ships on the East India run and conservative state policy that encouraged ships that would be useful in wartime meant that the greatest width of English ships came not at or near the waterline, but some 3–5 feet higher at the gun-deck, in order to allow a better range for firing.[8] The sides tapered sharply to the keel, making the ship more manoeuvrable but foregoing room for cargo. The Dutch *fluitschip*, or flyboat in English, became the pride of the Dutch merchant marine following its debut in the 1590s; they were light, slight, but practicable, easily manoeuvred, with one deck, but longer than usual, and with a flat bottom, gaining cargo capacity at their bulging bows and stern.

This was partly because they had to pass the Sound into the Baltic off Jutland, which could be dangerous to deep-hulled shipping. So although English ships could compete in very profitable smaller cargoes, such as spices from the East, the Dutch were able to corner the market for carrying bulkier cargoes such as Baltic timber.[9]

When Bernard de Mandeville, who had been born in Rotterdam, came to write his *Fable of the Bees* in 1714, he reflected on the consequences of this commercial success. He reported of the Dutch that 'in pictures and marble they are profuse; in their buildings and gardens they are extravagant to folly. In other countries you may meet with stately courts and palaces ... but in all Europe you shall find no private buildings so sumptuously magnificent.'[10] By 1670, 735 Dutch ships were regularly sailing into the Baltic and North Sea, even excluding fishing and small coasting craft. Such large numbers of ships, amounting to perhaps only half the Dutch merchant fleet, on their own outnumbered all English ships two to one. Even in the Asian trade, the Dutch still sent out nearly twice as many ships as the English in the 1690s.[11]

The Scots, meanwhile, traded mostly with the Baltic and Northern Europe, by virtue of both their geographical position and their very small merchant fleet. Until the prolonged slump that began in the mid-sixteenth century, the majority of their trade was also in wool, and most of it passed through Edinburgh and Leith. One source of profit was the re-export of English cloth; another was fishing, especially after Scotland's annexation of the Shetlands in 1469. This trade left behind a significant movement of people, as well as goods. Scots were particularly attracted to Poland, and the port city of Gdansk. One of Gdansk's suburbs had even been named after them, as *Szkoty*, or *Schottland*, since the Middle Ages. During the seventeenth century, there were probably 400–500 Scottish traders and soldiers in the city at all times. At least one of them, William Robertson, appears to have been just as much a banker as a trader. His 1670 will expressed the wish to be buried inside the Church of Saints Peter and Paul, an option only open to the well-to-do.[12]

Trade, power and the Navigation Acts

Political elites everywhere watched such developments with great interest and concern, for the great majority of sixteenth- and seventeenth-century political thinkers saw trade and commerce as simply one element of the constant struggle for power between states. 'Whenever we lose our trade', wrote the seventeenth-century thinker Charles Davenant, 'we must bid farewell to that wealth and strength which have hitherto enabled us to preserve our liberties, against the designs of Spain and France.' In an age before the establishment of professional navies, trading vessels could easily be turned into fighting ships; and at a time when government was small, private chartered companies could conduct diplomacy and spread countries' influence.[13]

The great monopolistic trading companies of this time were one expression both of the struggle for survival and of the increasing self-confidence. The Muscovy Company, reformed in 1555; the Eastland Company, set up in 1579; the Levant Company of 1583, reorganised in 1592; and of course the East India Company, initially granted a 15-year monopoly in 1600, are all examples of this trend. Most of these were set up by importers trying to avoid the hostility of Spanish and Portuguese middlemen, trying to exclude both commercial rivals and Protestant interlopers: as such they were funded by some very rich and powerful backers indeed. Of the original 12 patentees of the 1581 Turkey Company, 6 were London Aldermen, and 3 were MPs. Their average subsidy payment was £216 at a time when only 49 other residents of the City paid as much to the Crown.[14] The East India Company was easily the most successful, despite being expelled from the East Indies themselves by the Dutch in their war of 1618–19. They fell back on their base at Surat, at India, and continued their very successful search for profits. The Company's third fleet alone made a profit of 234 per cent on an investment of £20,000, with their cloves, costing them only £2048 to buy in the East, selling in London for £36,287. The cottons of Gujarat in India also helped to make up for the loss of the spice trade of the Indies: the Company also established Fort St George in Madras (today's Chennai) in 1641, from where they later developed new settlements at Balasore and Hooghly. It had taken the East India Company only 50 years to establish its highly lucrative trade shipping cotton from Gujarat, silks from Persia and Bengal, indigo from Lahore, pepper from the Malabar ports and saltpetre and sugar from Bengal.[15]

These monopolistic ideas culminated in the Navigation Acts of 1650–51, clarified and strengthened in legislation passed at the time of the Restoration in 1660 and 1662. The 1650–51 laws stipulated that all goods should be brought directly from the country where they were produced, and that they had to be moved either in English ships or in vessels registered in the country where the goods were coming from. The 1660–62 laws were slightly more realistic, for it was obviously absurd to expect every captain to list all the goods he had in his hold. Instead, a list of enumerated goods was drawn up, mainly of bulky produce such as salt, pitch, tar, hemp, flax and strategic naval stores. These amounted to less than half the value of England's foreign trade, so lightening the load of the previous Act. But the intention was still to throttle the entrepôt trade of the Netherlands, since even in the 1660–62 legislation *all* importation of the enumerated items was banned from Holland or northern Germany, while building up England's own merchant fleet by encouraging bigger ships and controlling naval supplies.[16] On one level, the new Navigation Acts simply strengthened legislation dating back to Richard II's time, when laws were passed forbidding trade in non-English ships. However, legislation passed under Henry VII in 1485 and 1489, though reiterating such ideas, seemed to allow merchants to use foreign ships, so long as there were no English rivals simultaneously in port. Although confusing, widely abused and ignored, the new Acts exerted a much stronger control over English (and, after 1707, British) trade than ever before: following clarifying Acts in 1663 and 1696, all trade both to and from her colonies had to be carried in British ships at least two-thirds manned by British and Irish sailors.[17]

Foreign ships were prohibited from carrying coal around Britain's coasts, a law nearly as important as the Navigation Acts themselves in making Britain a nursery for shipping. Shipping tonnage on the coal run from Newcastle tripled during Elizabeth's reign, and tripled again before the Civil War, with 200–400 coal-bearing ships coming into the Thames on every tide; the city's collier tonnage perhaps rose from 28,000 tons to 71,000 tons between 1615 and 1660.[18] The West Cumberland port of Whitehaven, which for a while in the late seventeenth and early eighteenth century threatened to rival Bristol and Liverpool, started as a commercial outlet for the coal of her developers, the colliery-owning Lowther family. As the local merchant Sir John Lowther pointed out in the 1690s, 'where ships are, the whole world is the market.'[19] Colliers made themselves famous as the nurseries of seafaring talent. The young James Cook learnt his trade moving coal from the North East, since he was apprenticed in 1746, at the age of 18, to Whitby shipowners. His first known voyages were on Whitby coal ships, bringing that precious fuel down to London.[20]

It is difficult to be precise about the actual date when British ports and shipping became more important than those of the Netherlands, but the final years of the seventeenth century, and the first decades of the eighteenth, saw a definite shift in the centre of economic gravity. The Dutch wars of 1652–54, 1665–67 and 1673–74 all saw the English fleet take large Dutch shipping prizes, meaning that about one-third to one-half of English shipping in the later seventeenth century had begun its life in the Netherlands. This allowed home shipbuilders to copy Dutch methods, with collier workshops on the Tyne and Tees adopting Dutch models most comprehensively.[21]

With the Dutch state exhausted by war, with the French as well as the English between 1672 and 1678, port duties and import taxes went up; there was a failure to develop world-class port facilities; and shipbuilders increasingly turned to constructing smaller vessels to trade with Germany and the European interior, rather than on the oceans. When the Baltic trade to St Petersburg soared in the second half of the eighteenth century, the Dutch were unable to secure a large share of it. It was the British nations that made the critical breakthrough towards an economy based on transoceanic trade and its profits and commodities. Imports increased by a third between 1663 and 1701, and exports went up by more than 50 per cent. In 1640 between 80 and 90 per cent of London's exports had been woollens; by 1699–1701 this had been reduced to 47 per cent. Nearly a third of the goods exported at that latter date were American and Asian products re-exported to Europe: 82,000 tons of British shipping left the country for Caribbean, American and Asian destinations during 1686, but by 1771–72 that number was 182,000 tons.[22] Something essential had transformed British trade, and consequently her place in the world.

The triumph of the western orientation

One of the reasons the British could shoulder the Dutch aside was their 'western orientation' – their gradual domination of trade in the North Atlantic. Most famously, this began with the voyage of the Italian, John Cabot, from Bristol in 1497. Henry VII initially granted Cabot a royal licence because the discovery of new trade routes might allow England to circumvent Venetian and Spanish rivals in the spice trades with the East, and his merchant backers in Bristol were certainly more interested in profit than exploration. Cabot spent 2 or 3 weeks exploring North America, first sighting land perhaps at Newfoundland or Cape Breton Island. Cabot was followed in 1501 by Bristol merchants including Richard Ward, Thomas Ashurst and John Thomas, and in 1509 by his own son, Sebastian. Their shared aim was simple: to seek a passage around the north and north-west of Canada, thus discovering a new way to get to the Indies and its rich spice trade.[23]

It was only much later, when Bartholomew Gosnold brought back the medicinal herb sassafras from Maine in 1602, and the Bristol councillor and sheriff John Guy sought to set up a colony in Newfoundland from 1610, that thoughts of permanent settlement in the Americas really took hold. But by the 1700s, the Americas were quickly becoming one of the main elements in Britain's trading system. They provided 21 per cent of English and Welsh imports in 1700–01, 33 per cent in 1750–51 and 38 per cent of the British total in 1797–98. In return, the British shipped woollens, linen and, increasingly, manufactures across the Atlantic. By the 1770s more than half her exports were going to the Empire, and 15 per cent of her entire output of woollen garments was being sold in the Thirteen Colonies.[24]

As western trade and colonies developed, London, for so long the only really serious trading city in the British Isles, now had to cede ground to Bristol, Liverpool, Glasgow and even the upstart Whitehaven, closer to the sea-lanes that would take ships to the Americas. London handled 43 per cent of English trade in 1702, but that total fell to 28 per cent by 1751. Bristol was the busiest of these outports until late in the eighteenth century, when its oceangoing trade was overtaken by Liverpool. The presence elsewhere of large, deep harbours with which the Avon could not compete caused foreign shipping increasingly to desert Bristol, which could boast only what the businessman William Campion called 'the present contemptible channel' leading into the city centre. Bristol's new floating harbour, diverting the Avon at Totterdown for 2 miles and building the Bathurst Basin to increase shipping capacity, was not completed until 1809 – rather too late to win back most of this business – and was extremely expensive. The city docks could not pay a dividend to its shareholders until 1823. Completely new and modern docks at Avonmouth and Portishead, avoiding the need to navigate the higher reaches of the river, were not opened until the 1870s.[25] Liverpool had its first 4-acre docks on the Mersey as early as 1715, though the dock wall was not ready until 1719.[26]

Scots also began to loosen their trading links with northern Europe, and turned towards England and the Atlantic. They first tried to take advantage of England's plantations in the Americas, with the Virginia collector of customs complaining in the 1600s that 'I find that in these three years past there has not been above five ships trading legally in these rivers . . . above 20 Scots, Irish and New England vessels within these eight months have sailed out . . . with their loadings of tobacco . . . and the man of war has not discovered one of them.'[27] There was even an abortive attempt to establish a Scottish colony at Darien, on the Isthmus of Panama, between 1698 and 1699 – though it ended in disaster through disease, poor management and English and Spanish opposition. The Navigation Acts, which Scotland's merchants unsuccessfully lobbied to be excluded from, made life even more difficult. Still, half of Scotland's trade was with her powerful southern neighbour in 1700, and most of the cattle, coal, salt, linen and grain that she exported to England were carried on by sea. This became easier after the Act of Union in 1707, partly necessitated by English promises to pay for the losses incurred at Darien.[28]

Given the Union, Scotland now came within England's previously discriminatory tariff walls, and industry was encouraged by bounties for linen producers after 1742. Scotland's linen exports thereafter boomed, and one of the main markets for it was Ireland. Good quality Scottish linen production gradually replaced her earlier coarse linen trade with finer goods from the 1720s, and the trade grew very quickly from the 1740s: by the early 1780s good quality 'kentings' represented 31 per cent of her total exports, and 60 per cent of domestic exports to Ireland.[29] Her linen exports doubled again between 1780 and 1800, and formed 13 per cent of exports by the end of the century even as the wider textiles market, notably cotton, boomed as well.[30]

The importation of raw commodities, whether for consumption at home or for re-export, was at the heart of this dynamic trade. Maxine Berg has recently emphasised just how important they were in the creation of an 'economy extolling the virtues of quality, delight, fashion and taste'.[31] Sugar refining began in Bristol in 1612, and the first tobacco to come into that city was landed only slightly later. Sugar had in fact been available from the Middle East since the Arab expansion of the seventh and eighth centuries, and the Crusaders had popularised its use back in Europe. More recently, the Portuguese and Spanish had used their Atlantic island possessions, such as the Canaries, to cultivate sugar cane closer to home. But with the settlement of Barbados in 1627, and the Cronwellian seizure of Jamaica and its rich sugar plantations in 1655, the English forced their way into the market for sugar.[32] It could sell for very high prices in Europe. Even during the 1650s, when sugar prices dipped a little, businessmen could make £37 net return per acre on sugar plantations, four times the return on industrial crops in England.[33] Between 1750, when it passed linen in importance, and about 1825, when raw cotton passed it in turn and the sugar industry began to stagnate, sugar was Britain's most important and lucrative import. Total sugar exports to Britain, the USA and Canada from the British West Indies went up from 1.89 million tons to 1.96 million tons between 1770 and 1787. Total British exports to the West Indies went up in their turn from £1.26 million to £1.48 million between 1763–75 and 1784–89.[34] French competition – and before the Seven Years' War and the Revolutionary and Napoleonic Wars they owned most of the Caribbean's sugar islands – then wiped out British sugar sales on the continent. But behind the Imperial tariff wall, the sweet-toothed peoples of the British Isles consumed 11 lb. of sugar a year each, while the French ate perhaps 2 lb.[35] Those tastes made sugar a very good investment.

The addictive habit of smoking soon caught on in Britain, and indeed across Europe. The first English smokers may well have been members of Hawkins' slave-trading and piracy mission around the Caribbean in 1562; Drake was probably the next man to bring tobacco to England, as he had been given 'feathers and bags of tobacco' by the natives of what is now San Francisco in 1579.[36] Its price inevitably fell as supplies became more plentiful, and its use spread to labouring people: from a very expensive 3d a pipeful in 1600, it only cost 3d per lb. by the 1670s, and was increasingly imported not from the Portuguese colony of Brazil, but from Barbados and Jamaica. This opened up a myriad of commercial opportunities, especially in the early years of the eighteenth century, when the weed's popularity shot ahead. In 1660, 10 m lb. of tobacco were imported into England in 1660, rising to 36 m in the 1680s, and 100 m lb. by 1770. Much of this was re-exported to the continent: on the eve of the American Revolution one-quarter of English tobacco imports went directly to France from English ports.[37] In just 7 years, between 1704 and 1711, Liverpool's imports of tobacco rose from 600 to 1600 tons a year.[38]

Scotland's merchants, with their long experience of trying to circumvent England's Navigation Acts, now became the most important single group in the tobacco trade. By the 1690s trade between the Americas and the Clyde had become quite extensive: in 1693–94, 13 ships chartered by Scots merchants arrived in Virginia and Maryland, while 27 were listed as doing so in 1695–96. In 1701, about 894,000 lb. of tobacco went to Scotland from the Americas; by 1707 that had risen to over 2 million lb., increasing to 2.5 million lb. by 1715, to 7.25 million lb. in 1728 and to a vast 47 million lb. in 1771. This was more than half the total of British imports, and also constituted more than half of Scotland's outward trade as she re-exported that tobacco to England and Europe. The tobacco trade helps to explain the extraordinary performance of Scottish merchants in the American trades, since between 1755 and 1774 they were bringing in goods equal to 40 per cent of England's: a remarkable advance for a much smaller and poorer country.[39] Tobacco imports added to the great rivalry between Port Glasgow and Greenock, both upriver from Glasgow itself and more accessible to shipping. Port Glasgow's authorities built the first dry dock in Scotland there in 1762, to challenge the more successful Greenock, while the latter added more harbour facilities, and later, in 1786, built their own dry dock.[40]

This commodity trade was only one part of the original mercantilist design. Colonies were supposed to act as protected stores of raw materials, buying British manufactures with the income they received from selling commodities. So long as they lasted, a wall of punitive trade taxes ensured that system's survival. Duties on foreign sugar ran at 270 per cent above the rates levied on colonial sugar between 1661 and 1705, and 340 above them between 1705 and 1747.[41] During the fierce controversy over whether to allow free trade with the new United States of America, William Knox, previously Under-Secretary for America, put his opposition thus: 'it was better to have no colonies at all, than not to have them subservient to the maritime structure and commercial interest of Great Britain.'[42]

The authorities therefore attempted to outlaw the woollen industry in the colonies in 1699, and steel and ironworking was banned outside the mother country in 1750, regulations were widely abused or ignored. Since the Navigation Acts encouraged Scandinavian shipowners and merchants to keep the Baltic trades for themselves rather than supply wood for Britain, the British authorities encouraged the production of pitch, tar, hemp and timber for masts in North America. Combined with the natural cost advantage conferred by easily available timber, this often meant that British ships were built there, even after the loss of the Thirteen Colonies in 1783. In the early years of the nineteenth century it was estimated that half of Liverpool's merchants were running ships built in Canada.[43]

Seaborne trade and the development of Britain's economy in the eighteenth century

The eighteenth century saw Britain transformed into a world commercial superpower. Between 1699 and 1774, English combined imports and exports grew 132 per cent, while her population 'only' increased by 33 per cent. About 7000 civil vessels were registered in Britain by that time.[44] She even recovered very quickly from the damage the American Revolution did to the Imperial trading system, and indeed commerce with the new United States grew and thrived. Most of the commercial ties built up over 150 years were not permanently disrupted, since they were so deeply rooted. Britain imposed high dock charges on US ships and tried to stop Americans trading with Canada and the Caribbean, but even so, the USA tended to get most of her woollens and manufactures from Britain; in return, Britain continued to import most of her tobacco and rice from the USA. Under 'Jay's Treaty' of 1794, US Chief Justice John Jay managed to convince the British to give up their ban on US trade with British colonies. What is more, the Canadian colonists were still importing some key manufactures from the mother country, including nails, boots and shoes, saddlery, harnesses and textiles. Britain's shipping tonnage continued to surge ahead, from 900,000 just before the American Revolution, to 1.7 million tons in the early 1790s.[45]

Britain's waterways allowed goods to get quickly and cheaply in and out of industrial centres. The Thames, Severn, Trent, Yorkshire Ouse and Great Ouse connected inland producers with the ports: Sheffield steel used the Don, Yorkshire cloth the Aire and Calder and Lancashire textiles the Mersey. One early writer called the rivers 'the cherishing veins of the body of every country, Kingdom and Nation'.[46] Once the rivers were supplemented by canals during the canal-building manias of the 1770s and 1790s, the entire interior was linked to the dockside. Liverpool was most famously linked closely to the flourishing industrial economy of Manchester in the 1770s, when the Duke of Bridgewater's canal was connected to the Mersey. The Trent and Mersey Canal allowed goods to flow directly between Britain's east and west coasts by linking those two rivers together from 1777, though the Leeds-Liverpool canal, which linked east and west with most of Yorkshire and Lancashire's manufacturing districts, was not complete until 1816. Canals halved transport costs for distances up to 50 miles, from 1s per ton-mile to 6d per ton-mile, especially important for low value, high bulk raw materials, for instance coal, needed by Yorkshire's and Lancashire's growing factories.[47]

These new commercial arteries encouraged industrial specialisation in a number of trades that flourished in the midst of a spider's web of waterways: these included Sheffield steel, Birmingham guns and locks and Manchester cotton. Reductions in transport costs allowed 'old' industrial centres not only to survive, but also to entrench their dominance as they adapted to new techniques, and this local and provincial renaissance is important in terms of our understanding of industrialisation. One of the reasons modern economic historians who focus on *national* output miss some of the revolutionary impact of the new industries is because they aggregate the whole country together. The problem with that approach is that the convulsive changes occurring in these centres, sucking in labour and capital from their hinterlands, might not dominate the overall numbers.[48] An agricultural survey of Hampshire complained in 1804 that 'Portsmouth and the shipyards of the coast afford a constant market for all the prime and picked labourers of the country, leaving little behind but feebleness and debility to carry forward the common labours.' British cities received a huge economic windfall from the sailors who made land in them. Dockyards became hugely important employers, and three-quarters of the population of Portsmouth and Portsea, though hardly typical, worked in the docks.[49]

Port towns could also cash in on the more fleeting demands of sailors. Consumer goods were always in great demand, since individual seamen usually had to provision themselves, and were always hungry for any luxury they could afford and get their hands on. In 1699 John Hedley of the *Joseph and Jacob* called on his brother to help fit him out with brandy and sugar to make punch, as well as cheese, pepper and mustard to enhance his onboard diet.[50] Port cities' wholesalers thrived on the import business. London's eighteenth-century tobacco and coal merchants, 'silkmen' and food wholesalers disposed of huge amounts of working capital. Just among the dairy traders, in 1733 Abraham Daking sold about one-fifth of all the butter traded on the London market in addition to having his own very large cheese business.[51]

It is the extraordinary range and variety of the trade that strikes the observer. Voyages might be as short as 2- or 3-day trips up and down the coast, they might take up a few days on the shuttle across to Norway for timber or they might take captains further into the Baltic for a few weeks, to buy bar-iron, flax, hemp, tar and pitch. On the other hand, trading might take as long as the 6 months required to reach the West Indies and return, to the year taken up by a full-scale triangular voyage, or the more than a year an East Indiamen took to get to India and back to Britain. Nor should one write off the importance of the coasting trade, which allowed businessmen to move bulky goods around the kingdom much more freely than would otherwise have been the case. As Adam Smith said, 'by means of water carriage a more extensive market is opened to every sort of industry than what land carriage alone can afford it.'[52] Among Liverpool ships in the 1750s, 106 vessels traded with the West Indies and North America, 88 were in the African trade, 28 went back and forth to Europe, and there were 125 ships – admittedly much smaller – in the Irish and coasting trades.[53] The short run between the West of Scotland and Ireland was also important. Scottish coal exports to Ireland dominated some of the smaller ports in the eighteenth century, for instance, at Ayr, Irvine and Saltcoats. Coal ships leaving Ayr represented 20–30 per cent of Scottish tonnage by the 1770s and 1780s, and this had the knock-on effect of lowering freight costs for other goods: 86 ships leaving Irvine with coal in 1764 carried textiles as well as coal.[54] Daniel Defoe witnessed the importance of small coasters while writing his *Complete English Tradesman* in 1726, watching 'multitudes of people employed [on] ... barges and boats for carriage in the rivers, and ships and barks for carrying by sea, and all for the circulating [of] ... manufactures'.[55]

But despite the continued importance of the coasting and short-distance trade, by the late eighteenth century the 'triangular' route between Britain, West Africa and the Americas involved between 700 and 900 ships annually, averaging about 250 tons. It was worth a huge amount of money, as we shall see in Chapter 4: a West Indiaman and its cargo might be covered for anything up to £60,000, over £17 million at a very rough guess in modern prices. Direct trade with Britain's colonies was also highly varied, and West Indiamen might take out goods as diverse as clothes, building materials, food, drink, silver goods, tea urns and other pottery, furniture and clocks. One ship leaving Bristol for Jamaica in 1776 contained Taunton ale and Gloucester cheese, textiles, household goods, stationery and 'volumes of entertaining history'.[56] At the same time, trade with southern and south eastern Europe – that previously monopolised by the Levant Company – stagnated or fell away from the 1730s onwards. French competition, and the fashion for Bengal rather than Middle Eastern silk, helped to accelerate its decline.[57]

Trade with India, monopolised by the East India Company, was even more profitable. During the eighteenth century, it was increasingly able to diversify from Indian textiles to consumer goods, such as tea. Every time the Government's heavy duties were lifted from tea, demand for the drink boomed. When Prime Minister William Pitt slashed duties in 1784, the 6 million lb. officially imported every year in the early 1780s leapt to over 16 million in 1785, and 20 million by 1786.[58] The monopoly was so successful that at a time when Liverpool slave shippers were touting for cargo at £5 a ton, the East India Company was demanding and obtaining £25. Atlantic freight rates fell by a third in the eighteenth century, but the East India Company was able to double its prices. In the 1750s the Company's new ships began to breach the 500-ton mark regularly, above which they were obliged by law to carry a chaplain; by the 1770s their *standard* size was equal to the 'great ships' of the Stuart monarchs' seventeenth-century navy, and the Company could regularly put 800-ton ships to sea; the *Nottingham*, *Ceres* and *Boddam*, all employed in 1787, were over 1000 tons.[59] By 1801 East India cargoes probably averaged between £250,000 and £300,000, and in that year 77 ships cleared Britain for India: the average in the first 10 years of the eighteenth century had been 12. The Company by that time had 122 vessels averaging 870 tons in displacement. In no other trade was there such a concentration or wealth of profit.[60]

The key role of imported consumables

The import of raw materials was clearly at the centre of this system, and the first of those industries to attract the British out to sea had been the rich Atlantic fisheries. Indeed, the historian Harold Innis was moved to conclude in his seminal 1940 work on *The Cod Fisheries* that 'cod was the lever by which she [England] wrested her share of the riches of the New World from Spain.'[61] Cod was highly coveted for its size and bulk, and the reported abundance of that fish had caused Cabot's friends to rejoice back in 1497. Edward Misselden in his 1623 *Circle of Commerce* called the sea 'a Mine of Gold': because of fishing, 'the Mine is deep, the veins are great, the Ore is rare, the Gold is pure, the extent unlimited, the wealth unknown, the worth invaluable.'[62] The problem in the early seventeenth century was that foreign sailors tended to dominate fishing even very near to Britain's coasts. 'French, Hollanders, Emdeners, Bremeners, Hamburgers, and others . . . do beat upon all his Majesty's coasts for fish,' complained John Keymer in the early years of that century, '[and] with great ships take and carry away innumerable riches, when our little boats . . . dare not look out at sea but in fair weather'.[63] It became all the more vital to develop fishing grounds that were not already popular and overcrowded.

The most important grounds were the Iceland fishery, growing to a peak out of East Anglian ports before 1600, and the Newfoundland trade out of Devon and Dorset, which later became Britain's most important fishery. Over 300 ships were going there every year by the 1620s.[64] Fish were New England's most valuable export throughout the colonial period. John Smith, one of the original Virginian colonists at Jamestown, wrote in his *Description of New England* that 'herring, cod, and ling is that triplicate that makes their wealth and shipping multiplicies [*sic*] such as it is.'[65] Smith himself brought back 7000 green cod from one of his voyages, which he sold in England, and 40,000 stockfish, which he sold to Malaga, while the Massachusetts Bay Company brought 300,000 cod to the world market in 1640. One of Boston's Puritan Ministers, Francis Higgenson, aptly noted in 1629 that 'the abundance of sea fish are almost beyond believing.'[66]

Other fisheries had their days as well, particularly the whaling grounds south of Iceland, and off Greenland in the 1780s following the disruption of the American War of Independence. Britain's cities needed oil, for street lamps if nothing else; it was also used on machinery making woollens. There were only 44 British whalers in those waters in 1782; by 1778–88 there were 250, weighing in at 73,000 tons in total and employing 10,000 men. To put that investment in perspective, those ships probably cost more than £1 million, and every single one of them was probably worth more than David Dale's contemporaneous, and much more famous, New Lanark Mills. They also appear to have made a profit of between 8 and 11 per cent on the investment, higher than in most other industries. The rise of gas lighting, over-fishing off Greenland and the replacement of whale oil by rapeseed oil in industry spelled a long, slow and painful decline for the nineteenth-century whaling trade; but for a time, it made its main centres, particularly Hull and Aberdeen, very wealthy.[67]

Salt, too, proved a very profitable business. As one observer put it in the 1790s: 'the Salt Trade is generally acknowledged to have been the Nursing Mother, and to have contributed more to the first rise, gradual increase, and present flourishing state of the Town of Liverpool, than any other Article of Commerce.'[68] Liverpool's early advances were indeed not governed by imports of novelties, but rather by the export of salt and coal: these in turn also stimulated the flow of capital back out from Liverpool to the Cheshire salt mines and the Lancashire coalfield. Cheshire had been yielding salt from brine at Northwich since before Roman times, but from the 1670s this was replaced by ever much plentiful finds of rock salt under the property of landowners such as John Jackson and Sir Thomas Warburton. This made its mining and export extremely attractive. Salt was good ballast for ships on their outward journey, but was also essential for the Newfoundland cod fisheries. Salted fish was then taken to the West Indies or the Mediterranean and there sold or exchanged for sugar, coffee, wine or fruit, which was then imported from those areas. From the 1730s Liverpool's salt refineries were located next to the second wet dock, which therefore became known as the Salthouse dock: between 1732 and 1752, the annual quantities of salt shipped down the River Weaver increased from 7954 tons to 14,359 tons.[69]

The expansion of trade caused a great increase in maritime manpower. This was one of the reasons politicians, economists and clergy alike praised their Imperial role so heartily – as long as they behaved as soberly as manners dictated. In 1770, a customs report estimated that there might be 50,000 British merchant seamen, of whom 20,000 worked in the inshore fishing or carrying trade; there had been perhaps only 30,000 in 1660. One anonymous writer estimated in 1792 that there might be '121,000 seafaring men who were liable to serve the Crown in time of war'. In the same year, the first figures from the Register General of Shipping put us on safer statistical ground, with a Great Britain total of seamen at 101,060, including 13,491 Scots.[70] Whatever the precise numbers, there can be no doubt that more labour was being demanded by the seaborne trades even during Britain's rapid industrialisation: their numbers might have doubled even as the country experienced what economic historians used to call the 'take off' into self-sustaining growth.

None of these markets should be seen as hermetically sealed off from the others. The logs of one ship, the *Cadiz Merchant*, have survived, and they show that in 1675–83 she went to Newcastle, Amsterdam, Hamburg, Portugal, Norway, the Baltic, Jamaica and the Spanish Main, as well as undertaking two long trips to the West Indies and Mediterranean. Despite all those efforts, she made a loss of £251 for the whole period, mainly because her captain died on her last voyage, and West Indian planters and merchants refused to trust his son and replacement with their precious sugar. Another example will demonstrate how even small ports could be involved in vast trade networks. The Bideford shipowner Thomas Burnard, born in 1769, was the son of a minor local merchant: at various times between 1786 and 1849 his family held shares in 102 vessels and were outright owners of a further 32. Their ships gained increasingly far-flung employment, carrying goods between London and Ireland, commerce direct to Ireland from the South West of England and trading with the Spanish and Portuguese, as well as running the little 37-ton *Roebuck* on the coasting trade. By 1827 there were 400 seamen and 100 vessels around Bideford and Appledore, serving not only to the British Isles and the Atlantic coastline but also engaged in the Canadian lumber trade, as well as travelling to the Azores and Mediterranean.[71]

The complexities of world trade also necessitated the creation of some sophisticated business machines, of which the East India Company was one of the most impressive. The Company could not really control the costs of war, insurance or wages; but they could cut overheads through shortening the turnaround period in foreign ports. This could be a high proportion of costs: charges on the time spent sitting empty in port made up over 10 per cent of the costs of the Company ship *Winchester*'s voyage in 1746. As the Company's directors, governors and agents took increasing notice and control of what happened in distant outports, procedures were increasingly standardised. By the second half of the eighteenth century, shipping costs to different Company ports varied very little. Bombay (Mumbai), Calcutta (Kolkata), Madras and Canton (Guangzhou) cost similar amounts per ton shipped through them – though the losses due to delays tended to rise as individual captains made detours for their own profit along the way.[72] Coming home from China in 1770, Captain Waddell of the Company ship *Plassey* moved his ship out of territorial waters so that he could transfer 'his' illegal cut of more than 60 chests – at £18 a box – to a cutter alongside, while revenue officers on a nearby schooner were forced to watch.[73]

The development of a rich mercantile class

The merchant classes that forged Britain's maritime hegemony tended to be clannish, intermarried and jealous of their rights. Historians could provide a list for any port city in the United Kingdom. Very early on in Liverpool, rich landowners – the Derbys of Knowsley, the Molyneux of Croxteth (Earls of Sefton from 1771) and the Blundells of Crosby Hall – were first attracted to shipping by the huge profits to be made from property speculation around the docks. The tobacco trade also made small groups of men very rich indeed, and the Glaswegian 'tobacco lords' in particular kept the business very close to their chest. In late 1742, two-thirds of the tobacco imported was brought into the port by four family syndicates: the Dunlops, Bogles, Oswalds and McCalls. Most of the rest was handled by only six other associations. This was, to be sure, no ultra-rich caste of chartered Elizabethan monopolists. Trade was expanding extremely quickly, and could be risky: new entrants were always likely to make their way into such a profitable business. Forty-three per cent of the tobacco merchants' fathers had been in Glasgow's foreign trades, but that meant that more than half had not. Only a small number involved in the trade in the 1740s, when it took off, were still there in the 1790s.[74]

Other cities had their own elites. Hull's trade, too, was dominated by just a few families. In 1702, 116 merchant companies were making shipments from Hull, but 94 of those companies shifted fewer than 10 cargoes: the remaining 22 were the really big players. These included such long-lived merchants names as the Beilbys, Scotts, Mowlds, Crowles, Wilkinsons and Carlills, though as in Glasgow, there were opportunities for 'new' men. The Somerscales, leading timber importers in the first half of the century, came from Grimsby; William Wilberforce senior, grandfather of the famous slave trade Abolitionist, came from Beverley – just a few miles from Hull proper. The first William Wilberforce of Hull married into another prosperous Hull family in the Baltic trade, the Thorntons, and had two sons and two daughters; his eldest son, also William, married his first cousin Hannah Thornton and then joined his father-in-law, an important merchant in the Russia trade, in London.[75] Thomas Thompson, the Wilberforce's clerk, was in turn able to buy his way into the company and was put in effective charge of Wilberforce and Smith while his master pursued his political ambitions.[76] A small group of merchants, each with more than £3000 at their behest, dominated London's trade with the Baltic in the late seventeenth century. The most important 108 among them had £176,449 of the trade in 1699, and were responsible for over 90 per cent of the bulk imports from the Baltic.[77]

Before 1708, when East India Company directors were prohibited from being shipowners, they made vast amounts of money commissioning their own ships – and they made smaller, but still very tidy profits until the government and non-Company shipbuilders forced them to accept totally open tendering in 1799.[78] The names of the Company's ships in the late seventeenth century gave the game away. *The Berkeley Castle*, the *Bedford*, the *Tavistock*, the *Beaufort* and the *Massingbird* were named after the men involved: William Russell, Marquis of Tavistock and Duke of Bedford; the Duke of Beaufort and his brother, the Marquis of Worcester, Charles II's godson; the Earl of Berkley, one of the six peers who asked Charles II to return in 1660, and married to John Massingbird's daughter.[79] Not all of the Company's leaders were large landowners or aristocrats, however. Sir Josiah Child started as a brewer and victualling contractor who bought £12,000 of East India stock by 1673, becoming the largest single shareholder with £17,000 in holdings by 1680; he was a director, until his death in 1699, for all but one year. These men were often highly influential within government. Child was included in the new Board of Trade when it was re-created in 1695.[80]

Further down the social ladder, a 'new' class of technical men emerged to conduct specialist maritime work, becoming shipbrokers, underwriters, insurance brokers and wholesalers: they were helped by the very goods they traded in, meeting as they often did in coffee houses. The Jamaica coffee house became a common port of call for men in the West Indian trade, while Jonathan's was the equivalent of the modern stock exchange.[81] Such men equipped themselves with a highly developed sense and language of honour. One acquaintance summed up James Lowther, the Whitehaven coal and port owner, in 1742: 'I think there is nothing (except money) he is more desirous of possessing than the respect, dependence and almost adoration of his friends and relations; and to have ... insinuated with seriousness his riches, power and abilities.'[82] This sense of probity was partly helped to commit other merchants to paying their debts over long distances and time-periods, and to some extent because they consciously saw themselves as a new and dynamic elite, who would modernise and reform Britain and its colonies. When the Leeds firm of Ibbetson and Koster had to explain to a correspondent that one bill supposed to be drawn on another merchant, Henry Uhthoff, would probably be returned unpaid, they still assured him that someone who owed them in Amsterdam or Ghent would 'pay it for the honour of the drawer or endorser'.[83]

This sense of pooled honour – and the shared risks that went with it – helps to explain why small religious minorities and families, who had no one to trust but one another, did so well in seventeenth- and eighteenth-century business. One Liverpool slave trader made clear that 'the right sort of credit made the wheel turn,' and family links clearly helped: Scots, Jews and Quakers often pooled their credit, knowledge and even families by marriage, so as to advance their maritime interests.[84] Transatlantic swaps and visits among these tight-knit communities became increasingly important. The young Quaker Jabez Maud Fisher came to Britain with his father in 1775 to look at Britain's metalware technology, as well as hardware and textiles, and he kept a notebook on the best commercial contacts for his father's dry goods business on the resumption of peace. His brother made similar tours in 1767–68 and 1783–84, ordering goods on the first visit in the North of England. He spent time, during his second tour, noting down the techniques of hosiery manufacturers at Nottingham and Manchester, as well as glove makers at Worcester.[85] Hull merchant families such as the Wilberforces, Maisters, Henworths, Mowlds and Fearnleys placed at least one family member at their Baltic trading posts at all times.[86]

Business connections frequently lent money to one another, since this spread their risks, or from landowners of their acquaintance: the Hull merchant Hugh Mason borrowed £1000 from his business partner John Thornton in 1728. The growing complexity and scale of trade in the mid-eighteenth century caused more and more families to formalise their links with other trading private empires: in Hull, the Williamsons combined with the Wallers, Maisters with Rennard and Parkers, Stephensons with Fearnleys, Terrys with Wrights and so on.[87] The multifarious connections which British traders had forged were personal and ideological, as well as profitable and physical: they fostered the emergence of merchant elites dedicated to the country's economic dominance on the high seas.

Free trade and the heyday of Britain's maritime commercial dominance

The mercantilist system could not outlast the various challenges of easier communications, Enlightenment economics and philosophy and the increasingly important interests of domestic manufacturers. For a long time the state did continue to intervene, for instance, banning the import of cotton calicoes in 1700 and 1721; but 'sumptuary' legislation, which governed what people could wear, was increasingly seen as politically beyond the pale.[88] The chartered companies lost much of their influence in the early years of the Restoration, and had more of their privileges stripped away in the 'Glorious Revolution' of 1688.[89] Only the East India Company, dealing with indigenous and local peoples over vast distances, was any longer seen as strictly necessary. Even that Company had to relinquish its trade monopoly in 1793, rights which were formally repealed in 1813; in 1834 it lost its monopoly of the China trade, after which it virtually ceased to buy and sell in its own right, limiting itself to regulating the trading system.[90]

Meanwhile, the intellectual case for free trade was growing in strength all the time. Pitt the Younger spent the 1780s trying to open up trade with France and Ireland; as early as 1808 the merchant banker Alexander Baring called the idea 'a generally accepted principle'.[91] William Huskisson, as president of the Board of Trade during the 1820s, oversaw more and more liberalisation. The Reciprocity of Duties Act of 1823, for instance, gave the Government the right to allow foreign ships to trade direct with Britain, subject only to the same duties as their British counterparts.[92] The economic crises and trade depressions of the late 1830s and early 1840s quickened the pace, making it seem as if nothing would save British industry if free trade were not granted. Only this would allow her manufacturers to import raw materials, and for working people to 'recruit their exhausted strength with abundant and untaxed food', as the Conservative Prime Minister Robert Peel put it.[93] That was exactly the appeal of the free traders involved in the Anti-Corn Law League. As they argued: why should farmers make money off the backs of industrialists and the working people? As Richard Cobden, one of their leaders, put it: 'most of us entered upon the struggle with the belief that we had some distinct class interest in the question.'[94]

Partly because he was intellectually convinced of the case, to some extent because he wanted to offset protests at bringing back the income tax, and also because he feared the social consequences of further resistance, Peel cut tariffs again and again during the 1840s. During the Irish famine, these culminated in the repeal of the great Corn Laws themselves in 1846. Taken with the repeal of the Navigation Acts in 1849 by the subsequent administration, this meant that the entire mercantilist structure had been torn down and a free trade system erected in its place. Dockside investment, canals, personal contacts, maritime experience and manpower then paid off: Britain's trade surged ahead in the decades to come.[95]

This new departure was to have far-reaching consequences for national identity. The Free Trade issue upon which Peel broke his party in two – especially over the repeal of the Corn Laws – eventually became another part of British self-fashioning, right up until the inception of protectionism in the Depression of the early 1930s. Cheryl Schonhardt-Bailey has shown how Free Traders 'nationalised' their appeal to non-believers. In the hands of the Anti-Corn Law League, and most politicians, freedom to trade on the high seas became a matter of national prosperity, anti-monopoly policy, class unity and simple morality.[96] Frank Trentman has stressed how 'Free Trade managed to build a democratic culture … [it was] once a vibrant and powerful democratic force … [that] appealed to the ethics of fairness and international understanding'. It promised order, in place of chaos; a world of rules, instead of naked competition; and transparent openness, rather than selfish national or sectional interests. Given the defeat of Edwardian tariff reformers, 'Free Trade … seemed at the root of a very British form of civilization.' One populist Free Trade song opined that 'we'll still trust the old well-tried BANNER / FREE TRADE for the ISLE of the SEA.'[97]

More prosaically, earnings from the shipping boom that followed were vital in preserving Britain's trading equilibrium. For almost every 5-year period we can analyse during the nineteenth century, income from shipping proved one key element in Britain's balance of payments that made the difference between credit and deficit. In the period 1815–20 shipping earnings averaged a net £9.92 million per annum, while the balance of payments was £7.22 million in the black, while in 1841–45 the figures were £11.7 million and £5.9 million; as late as 1876–80 they were £54.2 million as against £24.9 million. Shipping payments were positive in every single year during the nineteenth century, and they 'failed' to be large enough to lend Britain a positive balance of payments in only 25 years during that period.[98] Put simply, shipping was earning Britain the money which she needed to import both raw materials and exotic luxuries.

Britain's carrying trade was so dominant because she continued to be the world's entrepôt, buying in raw materials, selling them on and profiting from manufactures to pay for them. Raw cotton, brought in through Liverpool for Lancashire to spin and weave into clothes, was one of the key commodities moved by Britain's merchant marine. Cotton made up 40 per cent of that port's total imports in the 1850s, though its share had fallen to 30 per cent by 1913 as food – wheat, barley, frozen meat – poured in to feed Britain's growing population. In 1820, 110,000 tons of cotton came into Liverpool, a figure which had more than tripled to 360,000 by 1850. And even at the turn of the century, cotton yarn, piece goods and other textiles were by far the Imperial port's most important single group of exports, accounting for roughly half of them in 1901.[99]

Scotland's economy was even more radically transformed, as a relatively small European country suddenly became one of the great players on the world industrial scene. More than a third of her coal was shipped abroad or along Britain's coasts to be used in factories and locomotives. Dundee grew rich by processing and selling spun jute in order to make the bags to hold that cotton and coffee that British merchants were sending round the world. A cargo and passenger transport boom allowed central Glasgow to be redeveloped, bringing to an end the historic rivalry between Port Glasgow and Greenock, and putting the city centre right at the heart of its shipping industry. The early nineteenth-century redevelopment of the Broomielaw, and the addition of Steamboat and Anderston Quays to the west of it, brought central Glasgow's quay length up to 1543 yards, and the harbour to 14 acres: by 1851 there were 51 acres of enclosed water, and 3591 yards of quay. By that time there were 81 Glasgow-registered steamers grossing 29,371 tons, one half of the entire Scottish steam fleet.[100]

Fishing, too, grew in the late nineteenth century to be one of the most 'industrialised' of commercial endeavours. The rapid growth of the 'new' fishing ports of Hull, Grimsby and North Shields demonstrated the importance of fishing to the late Victorian economy: each of them to some extent reflected the rise of the trawler in the 1840s and 1850s. Dragging huge nets behind them on the sea bed, these revolutionised the process of catching fish in Britain. In 1854, 1571 tons of fish were landed at Hull, but a decade later that total had risen tenfold to 10,782 tons.[101] The growth of the herring fisheries caused the massive growth of ports at Fraserburgh and Peterhead on the east coast of Scotland in the 1820s. Some towns were reputed to be almost empty in the summer as women followed their menfolk by land as they followed the southwards migration of the herring; labour was sucked in from as far as the Western Isles of Lewis and Harris.[102]

Larger and larger fishing vessels were from the 1860s equipped with many more of the new, lighter and more flexible cotton nets that replaced the old hempen nets at that time. Some Scarborough ships now mounted as many as 130 nets at once.[103] The 1870s and 1880s also saw the spread of steamship trawling, which provided ever greater economies of scale and scope. Larger ports such as Aberdeen, traditionally in the shade of nearby, much smaller and more specialist Fraserburgh and Peterhead until the 1880s, became centres of both white and herring fisheries. The city became home to its first steam trawler, the *Toiler*, in 1882.[104] The new railways – in Aberdeen and elsewhere – then made the distribution of their catch much easier from about the 1840s; by the early 1860s they were handling a total of 100,000 tons of fish a year.[105] Billingsgate fish market in London received its first supplies by rail in 1846, but for a decade or more most of the fish coming in from Grimsby and other Yorkshire ports was relatively high-quality salmon. By 1863 the Yorkshire ports had become major suppliers of fresh fish of all sorts to the capital.[106]

This new world of industrialised fishing affected British tastes, and then the country's diet itself. Even before this massive influx from ports outside London, the social investigator Henry Mayhew estimated in the late 1840s that Billingsgate was receiving a total of 450 million lb. of fish a year, about half of it in herring. If only half this total was eaten by Londoners (Billingsgate was a distribution centre as well as a local market), that would mean that per capita fish consumption in the capital was 90 lb. per head per year – more than the individual meat consumption of perhaps 75 lb. per year, and enough to show just how important fish had become to the average Briton's diet.[107] Herring, though, was a fish for export *par excellence*, and was far outstripped in Britons' tastes by larger, 'meatier' fish.[108] White fried fish such as cod, served along with fried potatoes, became the signature dish of the nation, especially among the northern working class. 'Fish and chip' shops were relatively rare in the 1860s; by the dawn of the twentieth century they were ubiquitous.[109] Britain's ability to sustain its fast-rising population, and its very cultural identity as embodied in fish and chip 'suppers', came to some extent from the sea. On the eve of the First World War there were 125,000 British fishermen, catching a total of 1.25 million tons of fish a year in 3000 large steamboats and an assorted mix of 10,000 other 'second class' but dedicated fishing boats.[110]

Just as most other Britons had made good use of their seafaring ability, the Scots already had the skills required to adapt to constant technical innovation and industrial change: the knowledge that built steam engines for mines and factories could easily be turned to manufacturing steamships on the Clyde, where the first – Henry Bell's *Comet* – had begun Europe's first successful passenger steam service as early as 1812. River steamers were based at the central Broomielaw until the George V Bridge opened in 1928, at which point they moved to the south side of the river. Glaswegians developed a particularly close romantic attachment to them, whether they were running one-day pleasure cruises in the holidays, or steaming to and from Ireland.[111]

Less than 5 per cent of British shipping had been launched on the Clyde in 1813–14, but this position was soon transformed by Scottish shipbuilders' mastery of the new steam techniques. Engineer-shipbuilders such as David Napier and his cousins James and Robert pioneered the use of condensers and tubular boilers that increased the pressure within the steam engine, as well as building more efficient paddles. Screw propellers and compound engines were also first applied commercially on the Clyde.[112] The rest of Britain struggled to keep up, with two-thirds of the country's iron ships launched around Glasgow in the 1860s and 1870s. That city alone produced more ships than every German shipyard added together.[113] London's shipbuilding industry, which had in past ages provided Britain with much of its shipping, collapsed following financial crises in 1857 and 1866. The Thames builders were used to wood, employing teams of highly skilled men in smaller private yards; they were far from easy supplies of coal and metals; their costs were high, driven up by the very crowded and expensive city around them. David Napier argued after his retirement that 'London will never be a place for building steamers on account of everything connected with their production being higher there than in the North.'[114] Only one firm, the Thames Ironwork Company, attempted to adopt large-scale northern methods in the capital, and by the 1870s London was relegated to specialist and repair work.[115]

The USA had threatened to challenge Glasgow's dominance for a time in the first half of the nineteenth century. The American Donald Mackay launched the *Flying Cloud* in 1848, a massive 'clipper' sailing ship which, at 1783 tons, was much bigger than the average British ship at around 1000 tons. In steam technology, too, the Americans were highly competitive: with long, navigable rivers, they had many more river steamers than even Britain in the 1820s. However, their collapse into civil war, followed by the long, hard slog of reconstruction, as well as Britain's early lead in iron and steel, relegated the USA into second place until the 1920s and 1930s, even taking their river and lake tonnage into account.[116] This is reflected in the overall shipping figures. The tonnage clearing British ports jumped by 97 per cent in the decade after the end of the Navigation Acts, while British shipping's own clearances grew by 'only' 35 per cent. But in the 1870s, freed from American competition, the number of British ships leaving home ports went up by 85 per cent while total clearances rose by 'only' 56 per cent.[117]

Britain's shipbuilders mainly constructed ships for British merchants, and since the latter dominated world shipping, with 40 per cent of all seaborne trade and one-third of the world's merchant marine – the USA was second at 22 per cent in 1910 – they had a huge market to satisfy.[118] Shipbuilders also profited from the gradual shift-over from sail to steam: steamers passed their sail predecessors in terms of ships being built in 1870, and in terms of tonnage overtook them in the 1880s. Given the cost and scale of such ships, this technological advance provided a huge windfall to British manufacturers, and shipbuilding alone was estimated to provide 3 per cent of Britain's entire industrial output in 1907.[119] Even in the Edwardian era, during which in other respects Britons began to fret about their industrial and technical lead, shipping and shipbuilding at least seemed secure.

Conclusions: trade, power and the sea

It has recently been fashionable to downplay the impact of trade and new factory industries on Britain's economic revolution – and especially to stress the limited impact of cotton, that remarkable source of Manchester and Liverpool's early nineteenth-century economic energy. Exports overall amounted to less than 10 per cent of national output in 1700, and although spectacularly dynamic, they still made up less than a fifth of Britain's production at their apogee in the 1850s. As such, highly productive industries such as cotton cannot have contributed as much to Britain's relatively rapid economic growth as contemporaries thought.[120] There is a great deal to be said for this argument, at least so far as *overall* national economic growth goes; and it is clear that the maritime economy was very small by modern standards. In no eighteenth-century European economy did transatlantic trade add up to more than 2 per cent of GNP; all Atlantic shipping tonnage in 1800 could fit into two modern supertankers.[121]

But in fact Britain's maritime orientation was fundamental to her economic transformation. It was no accident in this respect that the seventeenth century, during which Britain began to aspire to maritime commercial dominance, witnessed the first attempts to synthesise a language of political economy. The change in Britons' fortunes was so spectacular, so unexpected, that it required a whole new language to articulate it. Imperial trade had ceased to threaten liberty, as classically trained politicians familiar with the fall of the Roman Republic had once feared. Now, as the natural philosopher and administrator Sir William Petty among others reasoned, trade seemed poised to secure freedom, for Britons at least.[122] Britain's merchants had built and nurtured a trading system that had fulfiled all of Richard Hakluyt's plans and John Dee's dreams, and they had created the first truly global maritime trading empire, sustained by a merchant marine and a seafaring labour force unrivalled in history.

Prepared for power by decades of mercantilist protection, and then loosed upon a world subjugated by British arms as well as goods, Britain's merchants spread her influence, and made money, more efficiently even than her governments. They made Britain into a great bellows, sucking in raw materials and exotic consumer goods, and blowing out manufactures to pay for them: and as we shall see when we consider the power of the Royal Navy, they helped her avoid continental entanglements which might have allowed other European powers to throttle her economy. Without her ports, Britannia's subjects would never have enjoyed the range of fashionable luxuries to which the better sort became accustomed, and her growing industrial population could never have been fed. Her markets would have been smaller, investment lower, coal less plentiful, transport costs higher, the balance of payments in deficit. In summary, everything that by 1914 made her economically pre-eminent depended on maritime trade. As Charles II once wrote to his sister, the country 'could only be considerable [through] our trade and power by sea'.[123]

Timeline of events

1497	John Cabot sails from Bristol to 'Newfoundland'
1539	Henry VIII forced to open English ports to foreign trade
1555	Muscovy Company reformed
1577–78	John Dee publishes *The Art of Navigation* and writes *The Limits of the British Empire*
1579	Eastland Company set up

1579	Drake given tobacco on the West Coast of the Americas
1580s–90s	War with Spain constricts wine, port and silk trade
1581	Turkey Company established
1583	Levant Company established
1589	Richard Hakluyt publishes *The Principal Navigations, Voyages and Discoveries of the English Nation*
1592	Levant Company reorganised
1600	East India Company granted initial monopoly
1606	Virginia Company established
1612	Sugar refining begins in Bristol
1623	Edward Misselden publishes his *Circle of Commerce*
1624	Virginia Company dissolved: Virginia becomes a Crown Colony
1620s–30s	Depression in traditional cloth industry
1650–51	Navigation Acts passed
1652–54	First Dutch War
1655	English forces seize Jamaica
1659	First clear evidence of sale of chocolate in London
1660–63	Navigation Acts reconfirmed and reformed
1665–67	Second Dutch War
1670s	Rock salt mining becomes increasingly profitable
1673–74	Third Dutch War
1695–96	Charles Davenant publishes *An Essay on Ways and Means of Supplying the War* and his *Essay on the East-India Trade*
1698–99	Scottish attempt to colonise 'Darien' on the Isthmus of Panama
1700	English ban on import of printed cotton calicoes; dyers simply colour them in England
1707	Act of Union between England and Scotland
1708	East India Company directors prohibited owning Company ships
1721	Renewed and more effective ban on import of all cotton calicoes in Britain
1742	Bounties introduced for linen manufacture in Scotland and Ireland

c.1750	Sugar becomes Britain's most important traded commodity
1776	Duke of Bridgewater's canal connected to the Mersey
1784	Pitt reduces tea duties from 119 per cent to 12.5 per cent in Commutation Act
1793	Britain at war with Revolutionary France
1793	East India Company trade monopoly removed
1806–07	Napoleon attempts to blockade British trade by establishing the 'Continental System' of boycotts
1813	East India Company trade monopoly formally repealed
1823	Reciprocity of Duties Act gives government right to establish free trade with other nations
c.1825	Cotton passes sugar as Britain's most important traded commodity
1834	East India Company loses monopoly on China trade
1841–45	Sir Robert Peel's Conservative government reduces or abolishes most tariffs
1846	Abolition of the Corn Laws
1849	Abolition of the Navigation Acts
1850s	Tonnage leaving British ports doubles in a decade
1910	Britain carries 40 per cent of all seaborne trade and owns one-third of the world's merchant marine

3

Renegades

Between the 1660s and the 1720s, the so-called golden age of piracy saw many thousands of Britons fighting as renegades, not – as they later posed – as law-givers and benevolent peacekeepers. They had for centuries imagined pirates as 'corsairs' – Muslim privateers who seized thousands of Europeans in the eastern Atlantic or in the Mediterranean, and then sold them on into slavery. Britons who joined the corsairs were condemned as both religious and national traitors. Now that picture changed as Britain's own pirates roamed the sea-lanes, at first striking at Spanish treasure routes on the lines of Elizabethan privateers, but gradually turning their attentions to any shipping that came within their grasp. This world was characterised by constant movement in and out of the realm of 'legality', as well as by the sudden and often-vicious application of violence. The Victorians' invention of later romantic figures such as Captain Hook, excitingly evil as they are made to seem, distracted from much of this given the exotic nature of the villains. But the reality was usually more prosaic. Merchant captains would become privateers, fighting under crown commissions but primary for profit, and then – failing to secure employment at the peace – turn to piracy as a way of continuing to make quick and easy money in attacks on merchant shipping. The seas were vast, in a world where sailing ships took many months to reach India or the Americas; peacetime and even wartime navies were relatively small, certainly by later standards; colonial politicians and officials would often connive with the pirates for their own economic or ideological ends. In this situation it was little wonder that piracy gained a hold. Recent historians have divined a set world of rules within these tight-knit communities, often bound together by family ties as well as blood. They were resisting early attempts to assert British Imperial authority in the sea-lanes; they often divided their spoil equally; and they could be a 'motley crew' of different peoples, races and classes. Though this case is probably overstated, and in some part anachronistic, it is certainly the case that they were challenging the authority of Britain's commercial and political elites, both in London and in the colonies. By the early 1700s powerful interests, including the East India Company and the Government, resolved that growing state power and the increasing threat to profits meant that they both could and should do something about the 'pirate menace'. Thus began a concerted state campaign finally to extirpate all pirates, which by the 1730s had succeeded in killing or driving underground most of its opponents. All that remained were the well-publicised but essentially one-sided nineteenth-century campaigns to defeat North African pirates once and for all.

Piracy in a world of legal and political uncertainty

Pirates usually inhabited an uncertain world between the legal and the illegal, an alegal space opened up by poor communications, overlapping jurisdictions and constant intra-European warfare. Letters of marque, which pirates such as William Kidd often used to justify their campaigns, were fighting commissions from monarchs, and were usually issued in wartime alone for action against enemy fleets – the very definition of 'privateering' as distinct from simple piracy. Kidd himself was sent out to fight piracy by well-placed politicians: Lord Bellomont, a strong supporter of the ruling Whigs and Governor of New York and Massachusetts Bay, along with other members of the regime such as Lords Somers, Orford, Romney and Shrewsbury.[1] But the distinction between 'legal' and 'illegal' actions, especially so far from those issuing the letters of marque, was a rather fine one. It left a huge space for confusion and manipulation, as indeed Kidd hoped when he sailed forth into the Indian Ocean in January 1697 and started a violent campaign against merchant shipping in his own right. Movement in and out of this shadowy semi-legal world, especially during or just after the end of wars, was commonplace – as we shall see.[2] But by 1701, when Kidd was executed in London for his crimes, brute force was being deployed against the outlaws in a manner that would bring the pirates' 'golden age' to an end. Once powerful Indians and the East India Company – whose ships Kidd raised – as well as the resurgent Tories back in London were set against Kidd, the divide between crime and state policy mattered less than the sheer amount of power ranged against him. At his trial, Kidd was rather pathetically reduced to pleading that if only the court could see his letters of marque from Bellomont, he would be acquitted. It was a forlorn hope.[3]

The question of neutral shipping is another good example of the slippery nature of oceanic legality as seafarers moved between what was 'legal' and 'illegal'. In one case in 1590, the Italian merchant Filippo Corsini represented his fellow countrymen when English ships seized their cargoes coming out of Portugal. He managed to obtain a court order for the arrest of the goods in question, but found that one of the cargoes had been split up before it even arrived at Weymouth. The eventual decision of the Privy Council in favour of the Italians, delivered 2 years later, was of little help to them in obtaining their goods.[4] The location of any fighting was also important in this confused situation. Traditionally, the 1494 Treaty of Tordesillas had divided the world between Spanish and Portuguese zones. The Spanish thereafter attempted to ban any other settlement and trade in their zone of the western hemisphere. But Caribbean waters were not explicitly included in the grant, and British freebooters of all sorts used the ambiguity, indeed non-existence, of formal maritime law to do as they pleased there – 'beyond the line', as they would have phrased it. Despite England and Scotland's neutrality in the Thirty Years' War of 1619–48, English and Scottish captains seized enough gold to help undermine Spain's war effort.[5]

In any case, the question of which sovereign had issued any captains' orders could be a moot one. It was hardly unknown for letters of marque to be faked, extended or re-written at sea. And if one monarch would not issue commissions, another surely would. English and Spanish authorities had faced this conundrum as they drifted towards war in the 1560s and 1570s. Protestant corsairs would go to the King of Navarre or to the Prince of Orange if the Queen of England would not help them. The problem did not go away after the peace of 1603, for privateers such as Peter Easton continued their private war against Spain by serving under Dutch letters of marque. Easton eventually came under the protection of the Duke of Villefranche in 1613, commanding four ships and 900 men. He cemented his position by marrying an heiress and converting to Catholicism, by which time his progression to respectability was complete. The seventeenth-century privateer Henry Morgan conspired with the French when British ships could not serve his interests. Legal opinions were divided as to whether the laws that held on land extended out into international waters. The great Dutch jurist Hugo Grotius believed there was no lawful capture outside a state of war; the Italian Alberico Gentili, writing in Oxford, held that sovereigns could indeed legitimate such actions. 'The late accident in America', the phrase that the English government grasped at to explain Morgan's attack on Panama in July 1668, was 'beyond the line' in more senses than one.[6]

These were legal gaps that everyone could sail a warship through, should they be so minded. Ships became 'islands of law', one reason why mutiny was punished so severely: tiny specks of legal jurisdiction carrying their national orders with them. Since pirate ships tended to be so multi-racial, they posed an ideological as well as a practical threat, a tiny lawless germ in the empty waters. One ship captured around 1700 had 43 Englishmen aboard, 50 Frenchmen and a scattering of Danes, Dutch and Swedes. Head-counts of the pirate hideout at New Providence Island between 1715 and 1725 have estimated that just over a third of the pirates quarter were from Britain, slightly fewer were American colonials, while a fifth came from the West Indian colonies, mostly Jamaica, Barbados and the Bahamas; 10 per cent were Scottish, and 8 per cent Welsh.[7]

The English authorities in the Caribbean often felt they had little choice but to lean on tolerated mercenaries such as Morgan. Hard pressed by the Spanish, they wanted to press every able-bodied man they could. In December 1679 Rowland Powell, clerk of the Jamaican Council, wrote to Harry Coventry, England's Secretary of state, in just this vein:

> Necessity in these parts is the mother of privateering, which is occasioned and initiated by the unneighbourliness of the Spaniard, and maintained by their plenty and pusillanimity, and without consortship of both Crowns and a good force at sea not to be suppressed, they being an experienced, courageous but ungovernable sort of people.[8]

The years between the English seizure of Jamaica in 1655, and the end of Morgan's active piracy in 1671, witnessed the peak of these 'ungovernable' acts. In just 16 years, English privateers sacked 18 cities, four towns and more than 35 villages. Governor Modyford of Jamaica turned a blind eye to Morgan's excesses because he had already learnt that private violence worked: privateer expeditions had won St Eustatius and Saba from the Dutch in 1665.[9] This was, to be sure, no new phenomenon, for British politicians of all sorts had long thought of privateers as auxiliary forces to summon up in the event of war. John Dee had praised them in his *General and Rare Memorials Pertaining to the Perfect Art of Navigation*. 'Good account is to be made of their bodies', he wrote, 'already hardened to the seas; and chiefly of their courage and skill for good service to be done at the sea'.[10]

It was only as the Royal Navy became powerful enough so as not to rely on these men, and to destroy the enemy shipping that they would have preyed on in any case, that privateering activities finally began to seem less relevant. During the Seven Years' War (1756–63), there were periods of extremely slim pickings indeed for privateers as French ships were progressively destroyed or captured by His Majesty's Ships. And the Government was lukewarm about private naval warfare, since the Elder Pitt as Secretary of State responsible for Foreign Affairs had to take care that he did not overly affront neutral trading powers. Although privateers did make a significant contribution to victory, their endeavours of the late eighteenth century – including the War of American Independence – put them at the centre of the naval picture for the last time. Even during that war, two letters of marque were revoked – one for piracy – and the smaller Channel privateers were prevented from giving full vent to their violent ambitions. There were 1679 privateering ships in total during the Seven Years' War, and 2676 during the War of the American Independence, but that marked the zenith of their formal influence on British strategy and tactics.[11]

The pirate 'other' and the Victorian imagination

Kidd's semi-legal world of ruthless politics and brutal punishments is a long way from the common image of piracy. Kidd's treasure, always rumoured to be buried on the American seaboard and to be worth much more than it actually amounted to, was mythologised in Edgar Allan Poe's 'The Gold-Bug', published in 1843.[12] Elsewhere, the very word 'pirate' summons up images of wooden legs, parrots on shoulders, 'yo ho ho and a bottle of rum'. All these clichés, of course, entered the mainstream via Robert Louis Stevenson's 1883 boy's classic *Treasure Island*. Long John Silver, the ship's cook who eventually seizes the *Hispaniola* during its treasure hunt, leaps off the page in a way that Captain Smollett, the Doctor, the Squire and even young Jim do not. He is 'deep', 'ready', 'clever', or at least devious enough to fool the treasure-hunters into letting him run the ship. 'He had good schooling in his young days'; 'all the crew respected and even obeyed him'; his physical resilience, leaping over stockades and running through woods, belies his missing leg.[13]

Silver has become one of the most popular fictional characters that Britain has given the world. *Treasure Island* made an immediate impact. Gladstone is rumoured to have stayed up until two in the morning to finish it; Gerard Manley Hopkins thought that 'Stevenson shows more genius in a page than Scott in a volume.'[14] The book became the template for pirate literature, translated not only into almost every European language but into Gujarati, Vietnamese and Swahili, with a Persian version following in 1986 even after the Iranian Revolution. At least five film versions have been released. Everything else that we think we know about pirates, from the BBC's Captain Pugwash to Johnny Depp in *Pirates of the Caribbean*, can trace its ancestry to *Treasure Island*.

Silver is ruthless, devious and extremely violent, but even his brutality carries the excitement of shock fiction, rather than the terror of true violence. When one of the pirates defies him, he strikes back with stunning violence, right between the shoulders in the middle of his back. His hands flew up, he gave a kind of gasp, and fell . . . the murderer minded him not a whit, cleansing his blood-stained knife the while upon a wisp of grass.[15]

The effect is as intended: thrilling, rather than dreadful. Silver even comes to an uneasy truce with the crew he betrayed and plotted to murder, and is provided with some sort of happy ending. Escaping from the *Hispaniola*, and taking some of its treasure with him, he 'perhaps still lives in comfort' with his girlfriend and his parrot.[16]

Silver did not spring entirely out of nowhere, for he owed a great deal to Captain Johnson's monumental *General History of the Pyrates*, originally published in 1724. Johnson's work was extremely popular, and indeed became the basis for many of the clichés that Stevenson introduced to the public. The book went through four print runs within 2 years, prompting the publication of a second edition in 1728.[17] Many of the really striking details from *Treasure Island* have more than a grain of truth in them, partly because Stevenson drew on Johnson's book. There were enough pirates with a wooden leg to give Silver's peg a ring of authenticity. When the East India Companyman John Macrae was taken by pirates off Madagascar in 1720, he was reprieved by 'a fellow with a terrible pair of whiskers, and a wooden leg'. This pirate had served with him before, and attested to the fact that Macrae was 'an honest fellow'.[18] Captain Skyrm, commander of one of Bartholomew Roberts' pirate ships, had his leg shot off in battle, while Israel Hynde, boatswain of the *Ranger*, lost his arm in the same action. Long John Silver's service as the *Hispaniola*'s cook is also quite close to the 'truth', since cooks were often seamen with missing limbs. Many seamen owned parrots as well, talking or not.[19]

Whatever the truth or otherwise of Stevenson's vision, the Victorians did create the modern image of piracy. J.M. Barrie's *Peter Pan* is another example of this myth-making in action. Captain Hook has taken as much of a hold of the popular imagination as Long John Silver: Boris Karloff, Alastair Sim, Donald Sinden and Dustin Hoffman have all played him on screen. By the time of *Pan*'s publication in novel form in 1911, all the components of piracy in children's fiction we are so familiar with were in place. Hook's piracy is exciting: it is only when the children are told that there might be pirates on their voyage that John exclaims: 'let us go at once!' And there is something of a children's game to the battles on the island: 'the lost boys were out looking for the lost boys, the redskins were out looking for the pirates, and the beasts were out looking for the redskins.'[20] The Hook of Barrie's novel puts Peter, Tinker Bell and Wendy completely in the shade. He is very much like Silver, since he is 'most polite . . . the truest test of breeding' that his public school education has given him; this, 'no less than the distinction of his demeanour, showed him one of a different cast from his crew'. He retains his brave, cruel fighting spirit when his men desert him, just like Silver; he is a 'fell genius', 'a dark and solitary enigma'; a 'not wholly unheroic figure'. Altogether, it is no surprise that 'to the boys, there was at least some glamour in the pirate calling.'[21]

The 'fell genius' was so attractive to Victorians because he was so different to the maritime exemplars they were used to reading about. Nelson was usually taken as the model for nineteenth-century gentlemen. By then men wishing to be thought exciting, admirable and attractive had to be patriotic, like Britain's most famous Admiral. Matthew Barker argued in his 1836 *Life of Nelson* that the great man's biographers should pay attention only to 'his ardent love of country, his fervent attachment to his profession, and his acute skill and accurate judgement in nautical affairs'.[22] Real men had 'character' – as the Tory historian James Anthony Froude said in 1850, 'the only education worth anything is an education of character' – and they used all the experiences gained in full, busy, crowded lives to serve their country. The catalogue of the National Maritime Museum lists 135 naval biographies published between 1830 and 1914, and 28 of them were of Nelson. He was meant to be one model among many, as one anonymous author put it in 1876: 'Lives of great men all remind us / We may make our lives sublime'.[23] Since this was to be an age of dutiful hagiography, and because pirates had mainly been cleared from the sea-lanes in any case, the renegades were reduced to comic-opera villainy. Without patriotism, love, selflessness, skilful detachment and a deep concern for their crew, pirates' earlier rank populism disappeared. Now any sneaking admiration turned to comic memory, disgust or – what would have felt far worse had Morgan been around to feel it – ridicule.

Muslim corsairs and English turncoats

'All the world about has heard / Of Danseker and Captain Ward / And of their proud adventures every day': so the popular balladeer sang of John Ward, an English privateer who defected to Islam in the early seventeenth century. Ward was probably born in Kent, and had gone to Plymouth to try to make his fortune; he joined the navy, and served on the Channel Guard named the *Lion's Whelp*, probably in 1602 or 1603. There he spent his time lamenting the passing of the old age of privateering, 'when we might sing, drab, swear and kill men as freely as your cakemakers do flies; when the whole sea was our empire where we robbed at will'.[24] Seizing a French ship off the Scilly Isles, he and his crew renamed her the *Little John*, testament to their view of themselves as latter-day Robin Hoods. They took her to Algiers, and decided to take their chances with the Barbary corsairs. Though Ward originally worked with Danseker, a Dutchman, the two men fell out over their ill-gotten gains, leaving Danseker based at Algiers, and Ward at Tunis. From Tunis Ward pursued his campaign of piracy against European shipping, ranging from Ireland in the west to Greece in the east, seizing English, French and Venetian ships at will.[25]

Ward was important because he brought modern sailing technology to the 'Moors', North African pirates who were notorious for seizing European Christians and selling them on as slaves. 'Sallee Rovers' alone, based on the west coast of Morocco, took 6000 slaves on their own account in the first years of the seventeenth century. Before Ward arrived, Captain John Smith of Virginian and Pocohontas fame noted that 'the Moors scarcely knew how to sail a ship.' Ward introduced them to the larger, rounder European sailing ship, armed with broadsides of iron guns, and replacing their galleys. He made his fortune – and was able to build a palace at Tunis – when he seized the Venetian galeasse *Reneira e Soderina* in 1607. He not only made this huge 1500-ton ship his flagship, but sold her cargo for 70,000 crowns.[26]

Given Ward's influence, Muslim pirates' tactics grew bolder and more dangerous. There were 4500 British captives in Algiers and Sallee by 1626, and their threat extended to the coast of Britain itself. The political pressure to do something about them contributed to Charles I's decision to levy Ship Money, that disastrous and unpopular maritime tax, across the country. In March 1637 the Royal ships *Expedition*, *Providence*, *Leopard*, *Antelope*, *Hercules* and the *Great Neptune* attacked the corsair port of Sallee. Rainsborough, the leader of the expedition, received vital help when representatives of Sallee's Old Town arrived and offered to help him against the rovers who had brought the city to this pass. By July the New Town's resistance had collapsed as the English ships continuously bombarded the harbour, though it took four ships to transport all the freed captives. Before long the Moroccan ambassador was being processed down Whitehall to see Charles' *Sovereign of the Seas*, probably the biggest warship in the world at that time. The *Sovereign* had three decks and over 100 large cannon. Her lumbering frame would probably have been useless in any real combat, but the political message was hardly lost on the Moroccans.[27]

Any Britons serving with the 'corsairs' were thought particularly villainous back at home. One playwright called Algiers 'the cage of unclean birds of prey, the habitation of sea-devils, the receptacle of Renegadoes of God, and traitors to their country'. Elaborate ceremonies were held to welcome back Christian penitents who had been forced to embrace Islam; Samuel Purchas published a number of collections in the early 1600s that denounced Algiers as 'a theatre of all cruelties' where 'about five hundred [a year] become Mahumetan apostates'.[28] Another – Robert Daborne in his 1612 play *A Christian Turned Turk* – showed how the 'Moors' would eventually turn on Ward. Daborne used Ward's imagined fall to demonstrate the wages of treason, that 'heart itself of villainy'.[29] Balladeers might well have celebrated Ward's fame, but they also pointed out how transient they might prove: 'his honours we shall find / Shortly blown up with the wind, / Or prove like letters written in the sand'. His death from plague in 1622 was perhaps not what the balladeer had in mind, but we can be sure that European sea-men in the Mediterranean did not trouble themselves about the cause of his death.[30] England's Ambassador to Venice called Ward 'beyond doubt the greatest scoundrel that ever sailed from England'.[31] Ward's apostacy – his 'treason' – shows once more the permeable boundary between legality and illegality. Seize Muslim ships, or Frenchmen and Spaniards at times of war, and one was celebrated; attack Christians and 'turn Turk', and one had passed beyond the pale.

Traders, privateers, pirates and the ending of wars

It was not only the ability to project violence that attracted British politi-cians, officials and merchants to privateering. Valuable information, and a great deal of money, might be secured as well. The Frenchman Alexandre Exquemeling, who sailed with Morgan, filled his account with descriptions of the places Morgan looted, and 'exact descriptions and maps of South Seas ports, harbours, rivers, creeks, islands, rocks, towns and cities'. Another good example of the buccaneer as cartographer is William Dampier, who three times sailed around the world under British and French letters of mar-que in search of Spanish treasure ships. Dampier claimed that he wrote his account out of a 'hearty zeal for the promoting of useful knowledge and of any thing that many never so remotely tend to my country's advantage'.[32]

Dampier's *New Voyage Around the World*, published in 1697, went through five editions, and was supplemented with two more volumes by 1703. Huge amounts of natural history and detail were included. This was partly an appeal to those in scientific and official circles who saw the opportunity of using that knowledge to expand Britain's intellectual reach, as well as her military and commercial influence. Dampier's works brought him to the attention of the Royal Society, and allowed him to complete his transfor-mation from semi-legal fighter to man of science. He argued that he always wanted 'to indulge my curiosity [rather] than ... get wealth'. His patrons, Sir Robert Southwell and Charles Montague, both presidents of the Royal Soci-ety, introduced him to the First Lord of the Admiralty, who then sponsored Dampier's exploration of the coast of 'New Holland'.[33] Dampier was able to retire from private warmaking as a rich man, who could reinvent himself as an explorer. His personal history is another sign of the constant move-ment between the semi-legal and respectable worlds of seventeenth- and eighteenth-century 'society'. He was separated from William Kidd's fate only by opportunity, luck and a greater measure of judgement.

Despite Dampier's denials, semi-legal aggression was a potential treasure trove of cash, since during the sixteenth to the eighteenth centuries Spanish trade was particularly vulnerable. It cost a great deal to equip a privateering expedition – Woodes Rogers' preparations in 1708 cost £13,188 – and commensurate profits were required.[34] Huge stores of gold and silver were coming out of South America, financing and helping to justify Spain's Atlantic Empire; but Spanish ships had to pass through pinch-points where British sailors could simply sit and wait for them. These included the Straits of Florida, the Windward Passage, the Galleon's Passage north of Trinidad, as well as the Guadeloupe, Dominica, Martinique and St Vincent Passages. There was another highly exposed land route the Spaniards found difficult to protect, the overland mule-trail and river route that connected Nombre de Dios and then Porto Bello with Panama and the Pacific. There were rich pickings to be had in the sixteenth and seventeenth centuries. The treasure fleet that sailed from the Spanish Main, at Porto Bello or Cartagena, might typically involve a convoy of five to eight men-of-war, with between 40 and 50 guns, and a fleet of merchantmen of varying size. By 1589 Christopher Newport, better known for later efforts to settle Virginia, led a privateer squadron that raided both Puerto Cabalos and Trujillo on the Honduran coast. Attacks were so numerous that Spain's West Indian treasure convoy was ordered to stay in Havana.[35]

The sixteenth-century English state had to rely on privatising warfare, and thus on privateers. Royal pockets were very shallow, while the seas swarmed with English fighters looking for a haul of Spanish money. Queen Elizabeth's total concurrent income did not reach above £300,000 per year at a time when Francis Drake's West Indian raid of 1585 had a total stock of £60,400.[36] There were 236 operating at the peak of the war between 1589 and 1591, declining to under a hundred by the end of the century. They took £300,000 in prizes in the former period alone, and about £40,000 even in the quieter year.[37] Sir Walter Raleigh and his brother Carew, Lord Cumberland and the Queen were partners in the biggest seizure of this period, the *Madre de Dios*. The ship was captured off the Azores in 1592, with a cargo worth £150,000, including the jewels, spices, silks and cottons found on board.

But these men were very difficult to control, even during wartime. Secretary of State Sir Robert Cecil abandoned the caution of his father, Lord Burghley, and started reaping his own profits from such voyages. He began to finance one Richard Gifford, but his captain continuously abandoned his brief and seized anyone who crossed his path. This was exceedingly embarrassing, and Cecil was eventually forced to condemn Gifford by proclamation.[38] Not that the authorities were always embarrassed when privateers exceeded their brief. Modyford wrote home to London that anyone who had invested in Morgan's attack on Porto Bello would 'double, nay treble, [their] money without any hazard'.[39]

Privateers' seizures help to explain at least one puzzle, for it must have taken huge investments to develop Jamaica's sugar plantations. One historian has put the requisite investment at more than half a million pounds, and the true figure is probably much higher. Very few settlers arrived with enough capital to carve out a plantation, and some of the shortfall was at least made up through privateering profits. It was said at the time that Morgan's men came back with £60 each, which given that there were 300 of them must have brought in at least £1800 from those men alone. The raid on Porto Bello, including Morgan's enormous share of the profits, was rumoured to have brought in £75,000, more than seven times Jamaica's income from sugar exports at that time. Illegal and illicit trade with the Spaniard probably made up much of the rest of Jamaica's capital shortfall.[40]

Another part of the Caribbean's wealth was governed by simple reality at the least legal end of this spectrum of warlike activities: pirates needed somewhere to sell their goods and buy provisions, and the quieter the better. The pirate Henry Mainwaring observed that as early as the sixteenth century 'whole towns' in the Caribbean subsisted by trading with the pirates.[41] Port Royal, Jamaica's main English town in the early years of settlement, was destroyed by an earthquake on 7 June 1692. So wicked was it thought to be, so dissolute its inhabitants, that many contemporaries thought that it had got what it deserved. One visitor called it 'the Sodom of the New World', a place full of 'pirates, cutthroats, whores and some of the vilest persons in the whole of the world'.[42] Irish towns such as Baltimore, Crookhaven and Leamcon were markets and supply centres for seventeenth-century Atlantic pirates.[43] A string of 'alehouses' sprang up along the southern Irish coast, really serving as shops and markets for the pirates. Closer to the ever-shifting boundary between legality and criminality, Franco-Irish business elites were prominent among the financiers of late-seventeenth-century Jacobite privateering. John Aylward and his brother-in-law, John Porter of Rouen, had long been involved in the historic export trade of Breton linens to Cadiz, as well as in the shipment of French provisions to the West Indies. They were some of the first names approached by Jacobite fighters on the outbreak of war with France.[44]

Contemporaries both understood, and sometimes celebrated, the two-way traffic between trade and piracy. In Thomas Heywood and William Rowley's play *Fortune by Land and Sea* (1607–09), the pirates Purser and Clinton not only reminisce about their martial exploits, but are given a way out. 'Clinton, I know thee,' one of their victims says, demonstrating that Clinton, at least, had been a merchant seaman before he decided to go 'on the account': Clinton's captive offers to help him 'if now thou do'st me a good office'. The audience was left in no doubt that, whatever the reasons that a man swapped trading for piracy, there were still routes back.[45] Even Daniel Defoe, that great defender of merchant capitalism, could see how pirates might get sucked into that illegal world, and how they might be redeemed. *Captain Singleton*, published in 1720, is the memoir of a reformed pirate, and a man of extreme ambition and resourcefulness at that. Bob Singleton falls into piracy when he is marooned off Madagascar, following a mutiny on his ship. 'I'll be a pirate', one of the company says, 'or anything, nay, I'll be hanged for a pirate, rather than starve here'. The company then build canoes to attack any European ships that pass by, so that they can attempt sailing back home.[46]

The ambiguities do not end there. Singleton's accompanying outlaw, William, is a Quaker, a sect famous for their business acumen, but also for their morality. William prevents Singleton and his fellow pirates torturing a shipload of black slaves to find out what happened to the white crew – though he sells them on instead, for an enormous profit. And he helps save Bob from his own piracy. 'Did you ever know a pirate repent?' Singleton asks him, and William replies: 'at the gallows, I have one before, and I hope thou wilt be the second'.[47] Throughout the book there is a sense, even for Defoe, that there might be little difference between a trader and a pirate.[48] Singleton and William eventually manage to fall in with legal Dutch traders, and fence their 'ill-gotten wealth' in Basra, Baghdad and Agra. Singleton returns to England to marry William's sister, 'with whom I am much more happy than I deserve'.[49] The permeable boundary between legal and illegal activities as well as the grace of God save Bob Singleton. Even pirates, it seemed, could enjoy happy endings.

This is the same Daniel Defoe who, just a year before, had published *Robinson Crusoe*, with its terrifying account of being taken at sea by Moroccan raiders from Sallee. The Sallee captain 'entered sixty men upon the decks and rigging', Crusoe tells us:

> We plied them with small shot...powder chests, and such like, and cleared our deck of them twice. However...our ship being disabled, and three of our men killed and eight wounded, we were obliged to yield, and were carried all prisoners into Sallee, a port belonging to the Moors.

Even this does not turn out too badly for the captured Englishmen. He is put to work by the pirate captain as a domestic servant, doing 'the common drudgery of slaves about his house', and eventually running his master's fishing boat.[50] There is an ambiguity here, a space for movement, from Heywood down to Defoe. Perhaps piracy is not worth condemning in too lurid a tone, these authors attest: perhaps it is profitable, softer than reported, even sometimes justified. This literary background helps to explain the Victorians' glamorisation of pirates.

The problem was what to do with privatised forces once peace was declared, for it was no accident that the peaks of British piracy between 1603 and 1616, 1697 and 1701 and again between 1714 and 1726, came at the close of great wars. Many men who had earned their bread by killing simply knew no other life. As the colonial entrepreneur Sir Ferdinando Gorges, founder of Maine, told the Earl of Salisbury in 1611: 'these peaceable times afford no means of employment to the multitude of people that daily do increase and many are enforced (by necessity) to seek some way to sustain themselves.'[51] Many 'pirates' were privateers going into business for themselves: displaced men circulated freely around the Caribbean as islands and territories changed hands. When the English part of St Christopher fell to the French in 1666, one French historian fixed the exodus from that island at 8000. New Providence, which became the buccaneers' base after the War of the Spanish Succession, had three times been attacked and laid waste by the French and Spanish during the war.[52] The Belize buccaneers who took St George's Cay as their base, perhaps as early as the sixteenth century, were attacked and driven off by the Spanish in 1695 and 1779, and again – unsuccessfully this time – in 1798. The devastating attack of 1779 destroyed the logging and dye industries that the British had set up, as well as their church and houses. The inhabitants were held captive until they were allowed to flee to Jamaica in 1782.[53]

Displaced settlers could end up anywhere, and move between legal trade and illegal fighting with bewildering speed. The famous buccaneer John Coxon set a course for Jamaica once Morgan became its Lieutenant Governor (1675–81), so that he could resume his semi-legal campaign against the Spanish. Upon Morgan's later retirement, he tried to diversify into the logwood trade, but was seized again for piracy in 1686. Escaping from custody, Coxon then carved out a new career as the leader of the Campeachy logwood cutters in modern-day Mexico, though he occasionally resumed his personal war against the Spaniards, sending them to Jamaica only for embarrassed colonial governors to release them into Spanish custody. The authorities simply lacked the means to stop him. As the Jamaican government wrote home: 'after this exploit, he strengthened his personal guard with about 80 more . . . the persons . . . employed for the seizing of him could neither find the opportunity nor the assistance they required for the doing of it.'[54] Coxon's career is a good example of the whirlpool of Caribbean trade, privateering and piracy, in which thousands of displaced, unattached men were buying, selling – and fighting – for survival.

Extinguishing the pirate threat

The pirate Bartholomew Roberts liked the thrill and daring of command. As Captain Johnson tells us, he had once 'sailed in an honest employ' as a second mate out of London, but 'what he did not like as a private man he could reconcile to his conscience as a commander'.[55] He had been seized on a trip to the Guinea coast, as had so many other future outlaws, and became a pirate in his turn. Though he did not initially take to the life, it had certain compensations. He very quickly rose to be captain in his turn, sailing to the West Indies in search of prizes in 1719. Here he had the good fortune to stumble upon a Portuguese treasure fleet. Looking out upon one of the largest ships, far bigger than theirs, Roberts' men were in 'no ways dismayed', for 'they were Portuguese, they said, and immediately steered away for him'. Despite the overwhelming odds, fighting their way into a fleet of 42 Portuguese ships, they were able to make off with their prize. They found the ship 'exceeding rich', full of gold, 'chains and trinkets... particularly a cross set with diamonds, designed for the King of Portugal'.[56]

Sailing back across the Atlantic, Roberts seized the Royal African Company's *Onslow*, renaming it the *Royal Fortune* and replacing his old French flagship, the *Ranger*. By 1721 he was the head of a formidable fleet of ships, and he may well have felt royally fortunate to be sitting inside a flagship with 40 guns. But the pirates' luck was hardly likely to go on forever. They knew that HMS *Weymouth* and HMS *Swallow*, the two Royal Navy ships that were supposed to hunt down pirates on the West African coast, would be gone for most of the rest of 1721. But getting wind of the pirates' menacing cruises up and down the coast, the *Swallow* managed to surprise Roberts' fleet off Cape Lopez in West Africa during February 1722. The pirates, many of whom were drunk, thought they would surprise and fire on a ship they did not recognise, but the *Ranger* got a shock when 'all turned sour in an instant.' The Navy ship opened fire, hit their mast and flag and failed to turn and run as they expected her to. Within 2 hours the *Ranger*'s captain had had his leg blown off in the mêlée, and the crew had surrendered. Just under a week later it was Roberts' turn to be surprised, as a blast of grapeshot ripped his throat out in the *Swallow*'s first attack on his ship. Now the pirates' reliance on charismatic leadership failed them, for as Johnson records, 'he had been the life and soul of the gang.' Without him, 'their spirits sunk; many deserted their quarters; and all stupidly neglected any means for defence or escape.'[57] The fight was over.

Roberts' death signalled the end of an era – the 'golden age' of piracy, during which huge numbers of pirates flooded the Atlantic sea-lanes. The best recent estimate is that a peak of 2400 men faced merchant shipping between 1716 and 1718.[58] The Council of Trade and Plantations in London was told by a Virginia correspondent in 1700 that 'all the news of America is, the swarming of pirates not only on these coasts, but all the West Indies over'.[59] This 'golden age' was a period of unparalleled naval robbery and violence, when not only Roberts, but Edward Teach ('Blackbeard'), 'Calico Jack' Rackham and Charles Vane, raided and killed apparently at will. The sheer numbers involved exasperated many citizens in both Britain and the Thirteen Colonies. Balladeers lionised Teach's nemesis – the Royal Navy captain who killed him in 1718 – as 'Brave Maynard', and 'when the story told / How they killed the pirates many, they'd applause from young and old'.[60] Morgan was a hero; Ward admired, as a fighter if not as a Christian; Roberts and Teach were drawing on the very last drops of public sympathy as the frontier became less and less lawless.

The explosion of pirate activity had been prompted not so much by the coming of peace in 1714 – the first couple of years had been relatively uneventful – but by the riches promised by salvage from a Spanish treasure fleet that was wrecked off Florida in July 1715. Henry Jennings and a band of ex-privateers joined up to go 'a-wrecking': theoretically helping with recovery, but in reality enjoying yet another thin excuse to attack Spanish interests. They attacked the Spanish storehouses on the Florida coast where the salvage was being held, making off with 120,000 pieces of eight – silver Spanish dollars. But Jennings and his mates heard that they were being called 'pirates' while they were out fighting, as they saw it, for King and country. Instead of returning to Jamaica they went to the Bahamas and joined up with Benjamin Hornigold and his small community of other pirates on New Providence. Before long they were joined by English logwood-cutters who had recently been driven by the Spaniards from their 'illegal' settlements in Campeche and Honduras. The peak of piracy's 'golden age' can be explained by the Bahamas thus coming under the pirates' sway. Outlaw raiding redoubled, with perhaps 30 crews operating from New Providence alone.[61]

A flood of complaints came in from colonial governors and foreign governments. Both were angry, not only at the numbers involved, but also over the illicit encouragement that local administrators such as Antigua's Governor Archibald Hamilton were giving to semi-legal 'privateers' that turned pirate as soon as they left his shores. George I was moved to send out Woodes Rogers, once a privateer himself but by now wise enough to paint himself as an explorer and privateer, to stop them. Rogers was himself from an established Bristol merchant family. He had taken two ships fitted out by his Bristol trader friends – the *Duke* and the *Duchess* – around the world between 1708 and 1711, to great acclaim at home. Since Britain was at war with France and Spain, his behaviour on the voyage was patriotic, rather than piratical. He took Guayaquil on the South American island of Puna, and seized a Manila treasure ship worth £800,000. He had to settle for less ransom than he would have liked after taking hostages from Guayaquil, but the seizure of the Manila ship more than made up for that.[62]

Rogers' *Cruising Voyage Around the World* is in fact an account with eerie echoes of both Dampier's *Journals* – Dampier was one of Rogers' captains on his round-the-world voyage – and Johnson's treatment of Roberts' exploits. Rogers' book was full of ethnographic and geographic descriptions, just as Dampier's had been. The city of Guayaquil, for instance, was described as 'about a mile and a half long...divided into old and new, joined by a wooden bridge above half a mile in length'. The narrative concerning their seizure of the Manila ship was uncannily like Roberts' account of his attack on the Portuguese in 1719: 'we gave her several broadsides, plying our small arms very briskly, which they retuned as thick a while, but did not ply their great guns half so fast as we...[once they were subdued] we sent our pinnace aboard, and brought the captain with the officers away.'[63] Rogers was also a very a rich man by the time the authorities asked him to tackle Atlantic piracy. He had by this point invested in other ships to do his privateering for him – he was one of the owners of the *Whetstone Galley* out of Bristol, at 130 tons, carrying 30 men and mounting 16 guns, no tiny raft herself.[64] Given his experience, Rogers – like Kidd – was clearly the thief set to catch a thief.

Rogers was sent out in 1718 with news of a general pardon, as well as the Governorship of the Bahamas in his pocket. This was to encourage pirates to give themselves up, a common tactic of the naval establishment. The idea of an amnesty was familiar from James I's general pardon of 1611–12; another had been issued in 1701. Pirates who gave themselves up were again pardoned in 1744, so long as they took up arms in the War of the Austrian Succession. Six captains and around 450 men took up the Crown's offer on this occasion, which greatly reduced the pressure on the authorities in the western Atlantic.[65] Though Rogers succeeded in his immediate mission, many pirates simply scattered to the African and American coasts, where they could hide until the storm had passed. Some of them went back to their old bases in Madagascar, where about 10 per cent of them – perhaps 250 pirates, along with some families and servants – were hiding in the early 1700s.[66] By the early 1720s, they had become an extremely frightening menace to the shipping of the Thirteen Colonies. The offer of a general pardon had isolated the really violent hard-core raiders from the rest, and the war at sea became ever more brutal. This, together with their continuing force in numbers, helps to explain why the authorities now reacted so harshly.

Official and respectable opinion had long since shifted against the pirates – the Governor of Virginia in 1699 called them 'a vermin in a commonweal [who] ought to be dangled up like polecats or weasels in a warren' – but now the contrary flow turned into a flood.[67] Speaking to pirates on the gallows in November 1717, the famous preacher Cotton Mather told them: 'all nations agree to treat your tribe, as the common enemies of mankind, and [to] extirpate them out of the world.'[68] The law was tightened in 1721, laying down the death penalty for anyone cooperating with pirates, and stipulating 6 months' imprisonment for sailors who declined to defend their ships.[69]

Naval forces in the area were successively increased. Until the late seventeenth century, only fifth- and sixth-rate ships were regularly used against the Caribbean pirates, with a maximum of 40 guns. These ships were not nearly big enough to attack outlaw ships with any confidence, and some pirates handsomely outgunned and outmanned them. The North American colonies had no naval protection at all. The end of the Nine Years' War in 1697 meant that the Royal Navy could pay more attention to this theatre of operations, and more ships were committed to the fight. Six vessels now patrolled off North America, while in the Caribbean there were normally two ships each on station off Jamaica, the Leewards and Barbados. In 1721 the British and French authorities in the Lesser Antilles even agreed to coordinate their military efforts against the pirates.[70]

This campaign gradually had the desired effect. Blackbeard, who defied Rogers' offer of a pardon and even blockaded Charlestown in May 1718, was killed later that year. The *Boston News Letter* recorded what happened:

> One of Maynard's men being a Highlander, engaged Teach with his broad sword, who gave Teach a cut on the neck, Teach saying, well done lad; the Highlander replied, if it is not well done, I'll do it better. With that he gave him a second stroke, which cut off his head, laying it flat on his shoulder.[71]

Late in 1720 Jack Rackham was captured, joined a few weeks later by Charles Vane, who had dared to scorn Rogers when he arrived in the Bahamas, and had tried to burn his ship. Both were hanged in chains.[72] Such was the significance of the campaign of violence that brought the outlaw world to heel and led to Roberts' death off West Africa: it sent a signal that the 'golden age' was over.

Piracy as a world of rules

Piracy had rules. Though individual pirates could be − and often were − ruthless killers, and were certainly best appeased rather than crossed, for the most part they served under what they saw as their own 'laws of the sea'. They spent months or years together, beyond the law; they had to impose their own regulations, or chaos would ensue. Pirate captains were usually elected as the chief military officer on board; Quartermasters were elected under them, as civil officers, to protect 'the interest of the crew'. Captains and quartermasters were usually entitled to between one-and-a-half and two shares of any booty, which was a radical departure from Royal Navy practice, under which officers took almost all the spoils. 'Councils of war' were usually held before major engagements, to consider the potential risks and rewards of any attack. Bartholomew Roberts and his crew were supposed to abide by 12 major rules, which included the promise that 'every man [was] to be called fairly in turn, by list, on board of prizes', to pick out what they wanted to steal. 'No person [was] to game at cards or dice for money'; 'every man's quarrels [were] to be settled on shore, at sword and pistol'; 'the captain and quartermaster [were] to receive two shares of a prize; the master, boatswain and gunner, one share and a half; and other officers one and a quarter.'[73]

These rules to some extent emerged from pirates' previous history, for many pirates were fleeing from ill-treatment or worse at the hands of the authorities. Many civilian sailors were 'pressed' like those in the navy – forced on board, either by violence and threats, or by promises of rewards that never actually transpired.[74] Merchant ships seethed with resentment about treatment once on board, and in that situation joining the pirates might come to seem an attractive option. Henry Avery, for instance, had begun his career as a pirate when a privately financed trade mission for the Spanish – and by implication against the French – went wrong. Sitting at La Coruña in Galicia, by the spring of 1694 the men had not been paid for 8 months; their food was running low; their Admirals had even ignored a wives' petition to ease their plight. When they finally received their orders to sail to the West Indies, a virtual charter to continue their ill-treatment, Avery and his men simply renamed their ship the *Fancy*, and set sail for the Indian Ocean.[75]

Captains thought particularly harsh could lose their crew, or worse. Defoe's Singleton and his fictional pirate crew were joined at the Cape by East India Companymen because their captain 'had starved the men, and used them like dogs... if the rest of the men knew they should be admitted... two thirds of them would leave the ship'.[76] Pirates often held mock trials once they had seized a captain, to hear how he had treated his men. Anyone thought too merciless could expect little mercy in their turn. Merchant captains petitioned their governors for help, since 'we are sure to suffer all the tortures w[hi]ch... a... crew can invent, upon the least intimation of our striking any of our men.'[77]

Privateers had rules as well. Dampier called them 'laws', amounting to what the French in St Domingue knew as the 'custom of the coast'. This gave privateers, many of whom of course went on to become pirates, a corpus of practices which held their imagination well into the eighteenth century. 'Riflinge' – cheating the owners of some of their share of the booty – was one of these practices. There was also, once more, a very detailed set of rules as to who was to get what when loot was handed out.[78] Pirates' councils were foreshadowed, perhaps prefigured, by privateers who met in just the same way before attacking the bigger prizes. Before his attack on Guayaquil, Woodes Rogers' captains and chief officers met to agree to attack the city: though this did not involve all of the men, it was more democratic than practice in the navy. Rogers' crew also settled how prizes would be doled out in the event of any seizures. Most goods would 'be divided equally amongst the men of each ship, with their prizes, whether aboard or ashore, according to the whole shares' granted to each ship.[79]

Pirates often banded together in packs, which should also caution us against seeing them purely as ruthless and ungovernable killers. They at least saw their aims in a different light, binding them together in a common, equal endeavour to which they committed their all, and which helped to explain why many of their codes stipulated that they should 'take no Married Man'. Oaths were often taken to cement this feeling of communality, as demonstrated by Edward Davis' confession in 1718. 'In a short time the *New Men* being sworn to be faithful', he swore, 'they all consulted and acted together with great unanimity, and no distinction was made between *Old* and *New*.'[80]

Even so, the outlaws often grouped together so that they might better employ tactics designed to frighten and overawe their targets. This was the meaning of the black flags the pirates adopted at some point in the early eighteenth century. The skull with crossed bones beneath it had been a symbol of death, scratched, for instance, into the walls of churches, since medieval times. Captains at sea had often used it in their logs to denote the death of a crewman. Pirates now appropriated the same symbol, to show they laughed in the face of death, but also to strike fear in the hearts of their victims. When Roberts' men attacked Trepassi in Newfoundland, they 'entered the harbour . . . with their black flags flying, drums beating, and trumpets sounding'.[81] Costume and display were part of these tactics of sudden astonishment. Few corsair captains were without a costume: Kit Oloard, for one, cut a spectacular figure 'dressed in black velvet trousers and jacket, crimson silk socks, black felt hat, brown beard, and shirt collar embroidered in black silk'.[82]

These pirate bands often thought of themselves as primitive democrats, resisting and exposing the hypocrisy of a merchant order that thieved from seamen every time they were beaten or refused their wages. 'They vilify us, the scoundrels so', pointed out one pirate captain, 'when there is only this difference: *they* rob the poor under the cover of law, forsooth, and *we* plunder the rich under the protection of our own courage'.[83] The eighteenth-century pirate Samuel Bellamy held similar views, as he told one captain who refused to join up. 'You are a devilish Conscience Rascal, d–n ye', Bellamy told him: 'I am a free Prince and I have as much Authority to make War on the whole World as he who has a hundred Sail of Ships at Sea, and an army of 100,000 men in the Field.'[84] Many pirates of the 'golden age' saw themselves, often quite consciously and deliberately, as social rebels trying to construct an excitingly rebellious, fairer and more democratic social order.

Race did not seem to matter so much to the pirates as did profit, and their ships often did contain black crew members. John Bowen, whose *Speaking Trumpet* was wrecked off Mauritius in 1702, had several black men in his crew, and they were thought to be useful men in a fight, 'very cunning and well trained in the use of arms'.[85] But this did not mean that pirates were any more sensitive to Africans' rights or views than anyone else. The *Princes Galley*, taken off Barbados on 14 September 1723, had 11 black slaves on board. When the outlaws brought them up from the hold, they were simply moved across to the pirate ship in chains, since they were valued at about £500.[86] Bowen was happy to sell some of his black crewmen when he had to. When Bartholomew Roberts' slave dealings were frustrated by a particularly recalcitrant merchant off Whydah, he simply had the ship set on fire. The black slaves inside were still chained to each other, and were faced with 'the miserable choice of perishing by fire or water; those who jumped over board from the flames were seized by sharks . . . and, in their sight, torn limb from limb alive'. Eighty black Africans died in this manner.[87]

Democratic views were also probably scant comfort for those crews the pirates seized, for pirate outcasts often felt themselves 'forced' to resort to terror in order to overturn the social order. Indeed, this often became the goal in and of itself, as high ideals were subsumed in the manner of achieving them. The search for booty could be exceedingly violent, as Morgan's victims had found. Pirates usually preferred to get hold of the captain first, hoping that he would know where treasure was hidden, and that his capitulation would knock the fight out of the rest of the crew. When Aaron Smith was captured as First Mate of the *Zephyr* in 1822, the crew was immediately 'ordered . . . to lower our stern boat and send the captain on board of her'.[88] Torture would be used to extract information about any treasure still hidden, just as Morgan had beaten and kidnapped to get his way in the 1660s and 1670s. Smith's captain, a Mr Lumsden, was called before the pirate captain who had seized his ship, and repeatedly asked 'what money he had on board'. When he countered that he had none, he was told that the pirate captain 'would burn her [Lumsden's ship] with every soul belonging to her'. Lumsden continued his resistance, but the *Zephyr's* children were then thrown in the hold, and 'combustibles' stacked up around them. This at last extracted a satisfactory confession.[89] The seventeenth-century pirate Wiliam Baughe was particularly ruthless when told that £3000 was somewhere on a captive Flemish ship. He got hold of one of the crew and 'sawed his throat with a dagger until the blood ran down'.[90] Proceedings might sometimes be even less orderly. When Captain Samuel Cary of the *Samuel* was taken by Bartholomew Roberts in July 1720, Roberts' crew acted like 'a parcel of furies'. The pirates were full of 'madness and rage', tearing the ship to pieces, taking what they wanted, throwing what they did not into the sea and threatening, cursing and blaspheming the whole time.[91]

The next step was to carry off any human cargo that might be useful. Navigators, carpenters and surgeons were all useful additions to a pirate crew, and could expect to face the choice between going 'on the account' and death. Aaron Smith was taken 'as a captive, to navigate the ship', since he had his naval charts and instruments with him.[92] In the seventeenth century, one Captain Stephenson offered a carpenter the choice of joining his crew, or being 'shot off in a piece of ordnance'.[93] Skilled men from the *Princes Galley* were forced to join the pirates. William Gibbons, the surgeon's mate, and James Sedgwick, the carpenter's mate, were carried off at gunpoint.[94]

No one should be fooled into thinking that pirates' sense of a communal identity, their insistence on rules and their cooperation one with another meant that they had built some kind of primitive utopia. Their rough and ready democracy meant that captains could expect a dagger in the back if they failed to deliver 'the goods': Captain John Johnson was so scared of his own men that he locked up their muskets in the ship's bread-room, to which only he had the key.[95] Benjamin Hornigold was overthrown by his own crew in 1717 when he refused to attack English ships.[96] Aaron Smith witnessed one bandit's fate when he was thought to be plotting against the captain. He was stripped and tied at the side of a mangrove swamp, for the burning sun and the sandflies to 'make him confess'. There was little point. Within half an hour 'his body began to swell, and he appeared one complete blister from head to foot . . . in a very short time . . . his face had become so swollen that not a feature was distinguishable.'[97] Pirate methods were often cruel, far beyond the limits of the threats needed to secure compliance or information, partly because they could expect no quarter from the authorities if they were caught. All the more need, then, for rules to steer by.

Pirates were, indeed, resisting the expansion of mercantilist European power; but they took advantage of its weakness as well. The lack of Royal Navy ships in the western hemisphere allowed them to thrive, and when the state did decide to take a much tougher line, pirates' days were numbered. Nor did they seem entirely wedded to a truly new and more egalitarian society. Many among their leaders turned into respectable landowners and merchants just about as soon as they could: plenty were willing to take Woodes Rogers' offer of a pardon. Above all, sailors' culture was riven with divisions. 'Crimps' and 'spirits' at the waterfront lured men to their fates; pirates' drinking and fighting were as much an attempt to put a brave face on a bad situation as they were a positive rejection of authority. 'Brother Tars', willing at the first hint of weakness to throw off their savage captains, were often opposed by sailors who stayed loyal.[98] Pirates may have had rules: but that was scarce comfort to some of their victims, or even to those among their own number who fell from favour.

Conclusions: the attack on Algiers and the end of the pirate world

On 27 August 1816 Edward Pellew, Lord Exmouth, attacked Algiers with a force of five ships of the line. He demanded the end of all slavery, the release of all Christian captives and a promise that Algerian ships would stop seizing European ships. The flagship, the *Queen Charlotte*, mounted 100 guns; she was accompanied by the *Impregnable*, of 98 guns, three other warships, a two-decker of 50 guns, four frigates and several gunboats. Receiving no answer from Algiers' ruler, the Dey, he began firing after hearing the first shots from the defenders, which rang out just before 3 o'clock in the afternoon. Exmouth had sailed straight into the harbour, so close to the defenders, and the gawping crowds, that he could wave his hat at them to warn them out of the way. Within a few minutes, the air was full of smoke; within a few more, most of the shore batteries had been destroyed, and the Algerian frigate trying to block the harbour's entrance had been boarded and blown up. One Royal Navy officer thought that the Algerian gunboats trying to attack *Queen Charlotte* and *Impregnable* 'might as well have tried to board the moon'. Though the subsequent bombardment of the city itself was relatively ineffective, and the British in fact soon ran out of ammunition, the Dey had seen enough. Within a week, he had acceded to Exmouth's demands.[99]

Exmouth's 1816 operation showed that, despite the end of *British* piracy as such, there were still plenty of pirates to menace British shipping. But the end of the long wars with France in 1815 freed the Royal Navy finally to clear the seas. Though the bombardment of Algiers settled little – the Dey's subjects soon went back to seizing European ships – attitudes and ideas were changing quickly. Though the high days of British piracy were long past, British shipping was still menaced by pirates from other nations, and the Admiralty was now determined to bring this situation to an end. In 1815 Persian Gulf pirates had taken a small East India Company ship and massacred its crew; the Company's 14-gun sloop *Aurora* had to fight to protect a Company convoy from pirate dhows in the Gulf. In response, during 1819 British ships mounted a week-long siege of the pirate base at Ras-el-Khyma on the Straits of Hormuz, killing 300 pirates in the process of taking the town. The British signed a treaty with most of the Gulf rulers for the suppression of piracy, and left behind a naval base on the Straits of Hormuz. Though this did not finally extinguish Middle Eastern piracy, it certainly signalled the beginning of the end.[100]

At the same time, hundreds of privateers were employed in Spain's war with her rebellious South American colonists, and they took a great deal of time off in the early 1820s to attack British, and especially American, ships. Britain's Foreign Secretary George Canning, though more cautious about extirpating the pirates than his US colleagues, resolved that he could not leave Caribbean waters purely to the Americans. In 1822 British warships were ordered to warn off Spanish privateers operating in Jamaican waters; some were boarded and inspected. When the British schooner *Swift* was taken by an uncommissioned Spanish 'privateer', and moored at St Jago de

Cuba, the local commander on the spot in HMS *Tyne* sailed into the harbour, liberated *Swift* and demanded compensation. The political situation in Europe was difficult, since conservative opinion was bent on intervening in Spain to reverse its liberal revolution; Britain, alone of the great powers, was prepared to let the situation develop without outside interference. This meant that Canning found it hard to take a firm military stand, since he could not push his liberal stance too far. Even so, in 1823 a further squadron was despatched to the Caribbean, and cooperation among local British and American commanders meant that there were few places for the pirates to hide by the late 1820s.[101]

The age of piracy, wherever it flourished and whoever was behind it, was coming to an end. The sometimes democrats, a vast rag-bag of fugitives ranging from the most gentlemanly to the most grotesquely violent, were a breed of the past. They had, nonetheless, left an indelible mark on the British maritime imagination, and indeed had helped to make Britain the pre-eminent naval power that she had become by 1815. Without auxiliary killers such as Morgan, there would have been no seaborne British empire; the Spanish would have strangled it at birth, or the French would have been quite happy to have it fall into their laps. Without the need to police the seas, the peacetime Royal Navy of the eighteenth and nineteenth centuries would have been even smaller than it was. Lacking men trained and experienced in combat, it is doubtful whether the Royal Navy could have been so bitterly aggressive, or so heedless of danger. But there was another legacy, almost as dark as that left by the trade in human slaves. For the British Empire possessed an unacknowledged dark side, founded as it was on the jurisdictional chaos of the high seas, rather than its legal exploration; partly built with outlaw money; reliant on imagining that the 'fey genius' of a fictional character like Hook was entirely different to the courage of a Nelson or a Drake; and dependent on exterminating men who had once seemed eminently useful. It was, by the Victorian era, easier to laugh at Silver and Hook than it was to look this truth in the face.

Timeline of events

1494	Treaty of Tordesillas divides the world into Spanish and Portuguese spheres
1562–68	John Hawkins' three voyages to West Africa and South America
1589	Christopher Newport raids Puerto Cabalos and Trujillo on the Honduran coast
1592	Walter Raleigh seizes the *Madre de Dios* off the Azores

1602–03	John Ward seizes the *Little John* off the Scillies
1603–16	'First wave' of British piracy
1611–12	First general pardon offered for piracy
1613	English privateer Peter Easton comes under the protection of the Duke of Villefranche
1622	John Ward dies in Tunis
1630	English colony of Tortuga founded off the northwest coast of Hispaniola
1637	Royal Navy assault on the corsair port of Sallee
1665	Privateer expeditions seize St Eustatius and Saba from the Dutch
July 1668	Morgan's privateering attack on Panama
1671	Henry Morgan ends career of outright piracy
1692	James II begins to issue privateering commissions from exile in France
June 1692	Port Royal earthquake
October 1695	William Kidd commissioned to fight Indian Ocean pirates
1697–1701	'Second wave' of British piracy
1697	William Dampier publishes his *New Voyage Around the World*
1697–98	Kidd's campaign of piracy in the Indian Ocean
July 1699	Kidd arrested
1701	Second general pardon offered for piracy
May 1701	Kidd hanged at Wapping
1708–11	Woodes Rogers takes the *Duke* and the *Duchess* on global circumnavigation
1714–26	'Third wave' of British piracy
July 1715	Spanish treasure fleet wrecked off Florida attracts pirates and privateers
1716–18	Probable peak of British pirate attacks on merchant shipping
1718	Woodes Rogers sent to the Bahamas to offer a general pardon there
1718	Edward Teach or 'Blackbeard' killed in action against the Royal Navy

1719	Bartholomew Roberts seizes Portuguese pirate fleet
1720	Daniel Defoe publishes *Captain Singleton*
1720	Jack Rackham and Charles Vane captured and executed
1721	Death penalty stipulated for anyone cooperating with pirates
February 1722	Royal Navy defeats and kills Roberts off Cape Lopez in West Africa
1724	Publication of Captain Johnson's *General History of the Pirates*
1744	Third general pardon for piracy offered
August 1816	Royal Navy attack on Algiers ends Muslim corsair threat in Mediterranean
1843	Publication of Edgar Allan Poe's short story 'The Gold Bug'
1883	Publication of Robert Louis Stevenson's *Treasure Island*
1901	First performance of the stage version of *Peter Pan*
1911	First publication of the novel version of *Peter Pan*

4

Slavers

For nearly 200 years Britain was the world's pre-eminent slaving power. British ships transported over three million enslaved black Africans across the Atlantic, mainly to work on plantations in the Caribbean and South America. The entire Atlantic economy that the British built in the eighteenth century, including that of the 13 mainland American colonies, was built around this trade. There were few products that were moved across the oceans, and few ports, that were not implicated in the shipment of captive peoples. West Africa, from whence most of the slaves came, became a key outlet for British manufactures and commodities in the early years of industrialisation within Britain itself. The slaves helped to build up enormous fortunes for the planter classes of the New World – and for many of the maritime trading elites who built Britain's port cities. Although the profits of the trade itself were not as high as previous generations of historians estimated, the classic 'triangular trade' and its various offshoots and guises formed one vital component of Britain's trading system. A constant stream of human misery was carried on the seas: beatings and abuse were rife, conditions were appalling and suicides were common. Even the white (and sometimes free black) sailors who manned the ships were ill-treated, and often succumbed to tropical diseases after their risky journey on a ship full of chained Africans. It proved impossible to keep clean these wooden ships full of the unwilling: they were an obvious breeding ground for disease and hardship. By the eighteenth century the Abolitionist movement had begun to organise to abolish this trade. This was the first truly 'modern' political consumer movement, using trade boycotts, 'shaming' companies and organising petitions and campaigns against the enslavement of Africans. It eventually paid off, for a mix of reasons including genuine humanitarianism, the fact that British statesmen wanted to lock other European powers out of the western hemisphere, and the economistic view that free labour would be more efficient than slaves. The slave trade was abolished in the British Empire in 1807, and slavery itself prohibited by statute in 1833, a law that took effect in 1837. By this point liberal Abolitionism had become a mark of faith in 'Britishness' itself, and the Royal Navy's long campaign against the slave trade was closely watched and constantly celebrated at home. The undoubted dangers of that long war against slavery were often thought to have gone some way to expiating Britain's original guilt: indeed, for many, it was explicitly designed to wash those crimes away. Even so, Britons continued to enjoy slave sugar and cotton for many years after Abolition: and by the 1860s 'Britishness' had become identified even more closely with 'whiteness'. Abolition seemed, paradoxically, to have in part reinforced the established social and political order.

The scale and scope of the British slave trade

The British came to the slave trade rather late, at least as compared with the Portuguese and Spanish. John Hawkins had traded in slaves as far back as the 1560s, but it was only after the capture of St Kitts and Barbados in 1624–25 that English planters grew the tobacco and sugar that might profit from mass imports of cheap black labour.[1] In the 1640s, attention on Barbados turned to the enormous profitability of the latter crop, and the labour force was transformed. Where once they had been worked by indentured labour, the fields were now full of labouring slaves, 50,000 in number by 1700. The seizure of Jamaica from Spain in 1655 accelerated this trend towards a British Caribbean dependent on slave labour, and that larger and geographically varied island had imported 42,000 slaves by the early eighteenth century. As the tobacco trade moved increasingly to the Chesapeake on the North American mainland, there were a further 145,000 slaves by 1750. The British North Atlantic plantation economy, which rose to international primacy in just those years, had created the demand for hundreds of thousands of unfree black labourers.[2] It was fully backed by the state, from Prince Rupert's backing for the Royal Adventurers into Africa, to the Duke of York's role as chief shareholder and governor Royal African Company, which held a monopoly on the West African trade between 1672 and 1698.[3]

The numbers transported overall were, and are, truly staggering. The most recent estimates are that the British moved 3.11 million slaves across the Atlantic between the sixteenth and the early nineteenth centuries, a trade which peaked in the 1750s and 1760s. Only 25,000 had been forcibly displaced by 1650, confirming the importance of Jamaica in the trade: for over the next 50 years 358,000 were moved. The trade was given a further boost in 1713, when the Treaty of Utrecht forced to Spain to issue Britain with an *asiento*, or contract, for the importation of slaves to Spanish South America. The South Sea Company now had exclusive rights over that trade – at least in theory. The scramble for its shares, and the war with Spain that interrupted the *asiento* between 1718 and 1721, helps to explain the famous 'South Sea Bubble', and the crash of 1720.[4] At the same time, the increasing hunger of planters for more and more labour meant that the 50 years from 1700 saw 871,000 black Africans shipped across the Atlantic.[5] The carrying trade operated for other powers (as well as the dearth of complete records) means it is difficult to be absolutely precise about the numbers of slaves carried to different locations in British ships, but approximate figures may be given. Between 1676 and 1700 about 10,000 black Africans were transported to North America, while 182,000 were forced to work in the Caribbean. By the years between 1751 and 1775, there was a little less disparity in that trade, and the numbers were 117,000 and 635,000 respectively.[6] In the 1790s one slave ship left Britain for Africa every other day.[7]

A typical slaving voyage might set off from Bristol, or from Liverpool after that port superseded its south-western rival in the early eighteenth century: by 1740 there were 33 slave voyages out of Liverpool every year. Seasonal patterns were important here, with a typical voyage setting off in the British winter, so as to get in and out of the Caribbean after its cane sugar had been harvested, but before the coming of the autumnal hurricane season.[8] Upon leaving British waters, such a ship would then proceed via the Canary Islands or the Cape Verde Islands, make African landfall as quickly as possible and then skirt the Guinea coast looking for buying and selling opportunities – unless the ship was headed south-eastwards to Gabon or what is now Angola. Once off the coast of Africa, the process of loading slaves for the New World could begin. Then the captain would strike out directly for South West Africa or the New World, perhaps calling at the Portuguese island of São Tomé *en route*.[9] But the reality is that there was no 'typical slaving voyage', despite the textbook insistence of a 'triangular trade' between Britain, West Africa and the Caribbean or the American 'mainland': this was a complex, multilinear system that tied together Asian and British markets as much as Britain, African and the Americas.[10]

It was at this stage that Europeans might begin their own suffering. Cape Coast Castle in Ghana was one of Britain's premier slave fortresses in the eighteenth century, imprisoning slaves in its dungeons until they could be transferred to ships waiting off the coast. Yet there was a mean life expectancy among the officers serving in the African Service of only 4–5 years. On average, a funeral took place within the Castle every 10 days, and the men in the ranks suffered just as much: out of the 48 soldiers who arrived in February 1769, 40 had died by the end of May. Malaria and yellow fever, two of the main killers, accounted for as much morbidity as mortality. More than two-thirds of the Castle's men were laid up in August 1801, for instance.[11] Many men tried to desert at this stage, often encouraged by their fellow crew members and local Africans. Edward Shiddefield, Daniel Lake and Sampson Hardy deserted from the Bristol *Antelope* in 1750, with at least the tacit support of the rest of the crew. They were never found, much to the Admiralty courts' frustration.[12] Before the *Bloom* sailed in 1787 the merchant Robert Bostock wrote to Captain Peter Burne warning him that the men might try to seize a boat and escape, an event which had 'overset' many slaving expeditions.[13]

Now the negotiations had to begin, however many desertions there were. This might take anything from 2 months to a year while the right contacts were made and contracts drawn up. British slavers would be trying to offload as many textiles (often Indian), exotic commodities and manufactures as they could, as evidenced by this inventory of the Bristol *Pilgrim* in 1790:

> 1858 bars English iron . . . 65 chests muskets, 23 casks felt hats, 11 casks gun flints, 1 cast wrought iron knives, 5 butts cotton, 4 tubs 10 casks brass manufacture, 3 crates 500 pieces earthenware . . . 12 butts 1 trunk East India goods, 4 chests bugles, 12 cases calicoes, 2 puncheon rum, 15 dozen bottles wine.

But it was not enough simply to bring the right goods. Meeting the right wholesalers was particularly important, and building up networks of trust and familiarity were absolutely vital in doing business on the West African coast. Some of the bigger companies even established their own commercial agents on the coast.[14] Since cultural traditions were so different, and because there were no blood ties to exploit, personal relationships became even more vital than at home in Britain.[15]

Once bought on the coast, black slaves would be loaded onto the ships, and shackled two by two, the right wrist and ankle of one to the left wrist and ankle of another.[16] Captains now had to transport their slaves across the Atlantic to the Caribbean or North America, conditions during which voyage we will consider below; and then try to sell their slaves when they got to their final destination. Captains faced another host of problems at this stage. The first was that, in the West Indies at least, the plantocracy of sugar producers was in control of the legislatures, and the law was being increasingly interpreted in favour of debtors, buying on account, rather than their creditors – likely to be the merchants bringing slaves to the local estate owners. The Antiguan legislature reduced their maximum legal rate of interest from

10 to 6 per cent in 1738, cutting the value of slave purchase debts to merchants trading in Africans. The planters were also in a good position to bid up the price of their crop while merchants rode in harbour, a position that perhaps reached its apogee in the third quarter of the eighteenth century. This was especially so if it was late in the year and most of the crop had already been sent to Britain. The inevitable delays in selling slaves made this situation all the more likely.[17] It also made the haggling all the more frightening for the slaves: the abolitionist Alexander Falconbridge saw one group of slaves terrified at their West Indian unloading, climbing over the fence of the dock and running about town in a panic.[18] Many slaves thought they were about to be eaten, partly, perhaps, because they associated cannibalism with witchcraft and evil in Africa.[19] It was a fitting and not entirely inaccurate comment on both their treatment and their ultimate fate.

The profits of slavery

And what, we may ask, of the profits that were made? A lively debate has continued for decades as to their extent and significance. Eric Williams, who was later to become prime minister of Trinidad and Tobago, argued in the 1940s that 'the triangular trade made an enormous contribution to Britain's industrial development. The profits from this trade fertilized the entire productive system of the country.'[20] Many other historians have argued the gains from slavery and the slave trade were indeed central to early British industrial investment; others that the profitability of the Caribbean and North American plantations provided an outlet for British goods that would not otherwise have been available; and still others that the cheap raw materials and food that poured into Britain from the colonies accelerated her economic growth.[21] We have already encountered some elements of the third case, in Chapter 2, and found that the *culture* of exotic consumption fostered by this trade was indeed important in the forging of Britain's economic lead. As for the other points, there seems little doubt that the profits of slavery and American markets did *aid* British industrialisation, a significant enough finding in and of itself. But there is a much bigger question mark about any more central role in transforming the British economy as a whole.

We may start with the trade in slaves themselves, a business in which individual fortunes were, indeed, there for the taking. The subscribers to the Duke of York's Royal African Company read like a merchants' list of connection and authority. There was Sir George Carteret, commissioner for trade and plantations; the peer and director Lord Berkeley; 15 of the lord mayors of London in the years between the Restoration and the Glorious Revolution; as well as 25 sheriffs of London. A century later, 28 of the 50 slaving voyages out of London in 1789–91 were accounted for by only three partnerships and one individual: Anthony Calvert, Thomas King and William Camden; Richard Miles and J.B. Weuves; John and Alexander Anderson; and William Collow. Over two-thirds of Liverpool slaving ships were owned by just a third of the owners in 1790.[22]

Bristol Members of Parliament, representing as they did a city whose early wealth was bound up with the slave trade, usually had a hand in it during the seventeenth and eighteenth centuries. In 1713 the city's two MPs, Joseph Earle and Thomas Edwards Jr, were respectively a privateer and slaving investor, and the part-owner of a Bristol slaving ship.[23] Such men clearly did not expect to make a loss – the average cost of a slaving expedition by the end of the century has been put at £8534, a large outlay that needed to be outdone to make a profit.[24] Later in the trade, in the 'golden age' of extraordinary growth in the Americas between the Seven Years' War and the American Revolution, the price of slaves inevitably rose quite quickly. They probably cost just over £30 each at the start of that period, rising to £40.70 on the eve of the Declaration of Independence. A 25 per cent rise in gross profits presented plenty of opportunities.[25]

It does not, however, appear that their profits were as high as some mid-twentieth-century historians supposed. Roger Anstey estimated in the mid-1970s that, taking overheads into account, a profit of 10 per cent may have been typical in the late eighteenth century. It was a good return, in general – certainly better than investing in government securities, for example. But it was hardly a spectacular bonanza vis-à-vis the national economy. If all of these profits had been invested back at home, Anstey reckoned it would have accounted for 1.59 per cent of all national investment.[26] This has latterly been disputed, by Joseph Inikori and Barbara Solow among others: the latter's equivalent figure is more like 8 per cent.[27] These figures, of course, depend on very unstable estimates for the numbers of slaves imported into the Americas, their cost and the quantity of British industrial investment itself. And Williams, in fact, suggested that slavery made its crucial contribution in the 1720s and 1730s, before the period covered by Anstey's data.[28] But whatever the total, it marks only the absolute upper bounds of slavery's significance in terms of investment. We would have to make very unlikely assumptions to think that all this money did indeed go into manufacturing.[29] Slavers certainly did not invest all their money in British industry. Such men liked country houses: Thomas Leyland of Liverpool built Walton Hall near that city. Various estates around Bristol – Blaise Castle, Redland Court, Cleve Hill, Ashton Court – were also bought by slave traders and owners.[30] Only some among them put their money in industry: Brian Blundell of Liverpool and Lyonel Lyde of Bristol, for instance, invested in coal or iron respectively.[31]

The number of ships, even at the height of the slave trade, was never quite enough to convince that slaving was a vital part of the shipping industry.

Between 1798 and 1802, with the trade still near its height, 204 vessels, with a capacity of 38,099 tons, left the country on slaving missions. There were 14,334 vessels totalling 1.44 million tons registered in the country at that time, meaning that the slave trade accounted for less than 1.5 per cent of British ships, and less than 3 per cent of the tonnage. This same worry about scale would seem to hold in terms of the more general economic significance of the sugar industry. Even if we expand our range to consider the import of the whole West Indian sugar 'system', iron, woollen, cotton, sheep farming and linen textiles all outstripped its output on the eve of the abolition of the slave trade. But no one argues for the special or transformative role of, for instance, the Ulster or Scots linen trade.[32] This dynamism in the other sectors of the Imperial economy poses yet another problem for the alleged economic importance of the traffic and use of human beings. For it is not enough for Williams and those who sympathise with his line of argument to show that large amounts of capital were flowing through these markets. They would have to show that the money would not have been used, profitably, elsewhere: and this seems unlikely given the vigour of the metals and textiles trades.[33]

This is not to say that the slave trade played no role in British economic growth: this would be all too comforting a conclusion for a nation that was later to turn its face against human trafficking. Attempts to argue that no profits were made overall by *any* European nation, given the competitive nature of the market and the near-perfect supply of everything needed to maintain it, seem some way wide of the mark.[34] The trade should rather be seen as one part of an Atlantic *system*, essential to the connections and trade routes outlined in Chapter 2. As David Richardson has argued, 'the slave trade and slavery should be viewed not as some peculiar promoter of industrial expansion and change in Britain, but rather as integral though subordinate components of a growing North Atlantic economy.' At a crucial moment in what used to be thought of as Britain's 'take off' into sustained industrial growth – the 1750s and 1760s – the Americas and Africa provided Britain with 70 per cent of her outlet for textiles, which amounted to half the total worth of her goods sent abroad. The ships carrying them were also taking slaves across the Atlantic.[35] Together, these two regions were Britain's single biggest market by the early 1770s.[36] By 1805–06 the West Indies alone were Britain's most important customer for British brass and copper (at 37 per cent of exports), iron and steel (also at 37 per cent), as well as for fish, hats, leather goods and linen.[37] The other side of the equation was British commodity imports from the American colonies, and these grew exponentially in the late eighteenth century. France's imports from her colonies grew nowhere near as quickly, which suggests one economic difference between the two powers, and one reason for their very different growth paths.[38] If we add together the total profits of the entire system, including plantations and the other trades carried on cheek by jowl with the traffic in slaves, we *might* get enough to equal between a fifth and a half of all British investment in the 1770s.[39]

In the end all this might rather miss the point. It may be, as David Eltis has argued, that 'economic paradigms have limited usefulness in explaining the ending of slavery.' Economic investigation might also have limited analytical purchase on its rise and extent. It is – for instance – clearly the case that a limited supply of white and indigenous American labour, coupled with falling transport costs for slaves, helps to explain the rise of New World Slavery. But such an explanation fails to answer the counterfactual question: why were black Africans not recruited as indentured servants? And why were white Europeans not enslaved? Explicitly racial, ideological and political modes of thinking must have been involved in excluding those possibilities.[40] It is probably better to see the rise and fall of Atlantic slave trading as explained by what Seymour Drescher has termed its 'social peculiarity' within 'a highly differentiated intercontinental system': a patchwork quilt of legal jurisdictions, politics and policy that allowed it to thrive for decades, but which ultimately the authorities in the metropole refused to let continue.[41] Anything else threatens to commit the economistic fallacy of thinking that slavery was *primarily* or *only* an economic institution. This might in turn make its end a comforting fable: as David Davis once put it, it would convey 'the comfortable assurance that slavery was doomed by impersonal laws of historical progress'.[42]

So the slave trade relied essentially on selling manufactures and luxury goods to Africans, buying slaves, transporting them to plantations and then coming home with North American commodities. This much is clear, even obvious. But what is less clear in some treatments is how risky this was. Disease, storms, a lack of commercial contacts, poor market conditions and sheer bad luck, either in West Africa or in the Americas, were endured for profits that, for the great majority of slavers, were good but not spectacular even in successful years. It is a tragic conclusion, but even in terms of Europeans' own profit-and-loss accounts, all the suffering could be for nothing.

The daily realities of the slave trade

The trade was as unremittingly grim as it was risky. Most of these ships were small, as the great majority of them would have displaced less than 200 tons. Close analysis of the characteristics of slaving ships reveals that, in the mid-eighteenth-century Virginian trade, a third were 'snows', of less than 100 tons. And 44 per cent were classified as 'ships', but that still meant they displaced less than 180 tons. Nearly 6 per cent of the ships were 'brigs', of only about 50 tons.[43] One ship – the aptly named *Little Ben* – could claim only 27 tons when it sailed out of Liverpool in 1791.[44] Most of them would originally have been prizes or 'normal' cargo ships, and would then have been hastily and haphazardly converted to their new task. That hardly made for well-designed berths, had there been the inclination to provide them at all – which there usually was not.[45]

Life below deck on these cramped and ill-adapted vessels was consequently appalling. When the Royal Navy inspected ships in Liverpool Harbour for the House of Commons' 1788 inquiry, they found that each slave was confined to a space 6 feet long by 16 inches wide.[46] The slaves might be taken out every morning joylessly to 'dance' for their masters while still in chains; and the shortest passage from the Gambia River to Barbados might take only 3 weeks by the mid-eighteenth to late eighteenth century. But when the weather was bad, or the seas high, the ventilation panels down below were shut. Falconbridge took careful note of the consequences: 'the negroes' rooms very soon become intolerably hot. The confined air, rendered noxious by the effluvia exhaled from their bodies and by being repeatedly breathed, soon produces fevers and fluxes which generally carries off great numbers of them.'[47] As Falconbridge knew very well, disease took an appalling toll on the slaves, with gastrointestinal disorders known as the 'bloody flux' to the fore. Since the slaves were lying in their own faeces, and the sick were left to suffer where they lay, the spread of such contagions was not surprising.[48] It is, to be sure, difficult to be completely precise about the numbers of black slaves who never made it to their destination. But one sample of nine voyages, randomly picked out between 1766 and 1780, came up with a mortality rate of 6.5 per cent; the Privy Council's own investigation settled on a figure of 12.5 per cent, which was in line with official French estimates.[49]

These conditions, along with the force applied to get the slaves on board, brought with them other consequences. We now know that about 10 per cent of slaving ships experienced some form of slave revolt, though very few were able to take over their ships. If any crew grew too small, quarrelled with one another or let down their guard, many slaves were ready to take the chances of armed or unarmed rebellion.[50] Given the armaments of the crew, and the large numbers of sailors employed by slavers worried about just such insurrections, their chances of success were usually slim. The figure for crew per ton on 252 ships that left Liverpool for Africa in the 1780s was 0.17, whereas it was only 0.09 for ships aiming straight for the Caribbean.[51] One captain on a 1693–94 voyage noted that 'to prevent [revolts] ... we always keep centinels upon the hatchways, and have a chest full of small arms, ready loaden and prim'd, constantly lying at hand upon the quarter-deck'.[52] The slave trader, John Newton – who later turned Abolitionist and wrote the anti-slavery hymn *Amazing Grace* – stocked his deck with four blunderbusses: they would, he hoped, 'be sufficient to intimidate ye slaves from any thoughts of an insurrection'.[53] About 25 slaves were killed on average in such incidents, or about 10 per cent of those captives on board.[54] But successful revolts were not vanishingly unlikely: of 186 vessels lost on the African coast between 1741 and 1807, and recorded as such in *Lloyd's List*, 79 cases were due to conflicts with slaves or coastal Africans.[55]

The last form of resistance was suicide. William Barry of the *Dispatch* of Bristol was told in 1725 that, as soon as he left Africa, he should 'keep [the slaves] shackled & hand bolte[d] fearing their rising or Leaping Overboard'.[56] One woman on the *Elizabeth* managed to find some rope yarn and hang herself on the armourer's vice: she was found dead the next morning. These were not isolated incidents, and the slave, and writer Olavdah Equaino recorded them as faithfully as everything else he observed. As he wrote, 'one day, when we had a smooth sea...two of my wearied countrymen, who were chained together...preferring death to such a life of misery, somehow made through the nettings, and jumped into the sea; immediately another quite dejected fellow, who, on account of his illness, was suffered to be out of irons, also followed their example'.[57] 'Dejected' was the right word; Dr Isaac Wilson, the *Elizabeth*'s surgeon, identified a type of 'fixed melancholy' that he believed might lead not only to suicide, but a higher likelihood of giving way to disease.[58]

This depression was an eerie echo of European experiences in West Africa, since many believed, with the former slave ship surgeon Henry Meredith, that Europeans who allowed themselves to worry and fret were more likely to fall ill.[59] And indeed the crews – nearly always, but not exclusively, white – did suffer in their own ways. They might sometimes be treated nearly as badly as their cargo; the surgeon serving on board the *Albion*, for instance, at one point made very clear that he was 'only paid for attending the slaves' and would not look at the men. The Abolitionist Thomas Clarkson reckoned that sailors' relative mortality was actually *higher* than that of the slaves.[60] Though captains were prevented by law from killing the crew, they could effectively sentence them to death: by clapping them in irons while sick, for example. Flogging was used incessantly: Falconbridge remembered that one man was whipped every day, until he jumped overboard in his turn.[61] There were other, more invidious effects. Newton thought that 'treating the Negroes with rigour gradually brings a numbness upon the heart and renders those who are engaged in too indifferent to the sufferings of their fellow-creatures.' As he remembered, 'there is no trade in which seamen are treated with so little humanity.'[62]

Sailors were expected to check, feed and wash the slaves and their quarters continuously. Vinegar and lime juice was commonly given in the morning to prevent scurvy.[63] Newton's logs are full of references to such chores: 'wash'd the slaves with fresh water and rub'd them with Bees wax and Florence oil' is one typical entry.[64] David Tuohy issued very specific instructions to his captain, William Spurs, in command of the *Ranger*. The captain was told to make sure of 'washing the beams and over the slaves heads with vinegar three times a week ... while the slaves are twined up'. Other witnesses reported sailors 'scraping the slave rooms, smoking with tar, tobacco and brimstone for two hours, afterwards washed with vinegar'.[65] The strain very rarely let up. Quite apart from the institutional brutality of the whole system, seamen on the Middle Passage could grow even more bored, unpredictable, violent and sadistic than their captains. One man was recorded as having taken the skin off a child's swollen feet by forcing them into boiling water; every time the child refused to eat, it was beaten. When the child eventually died, the mother was asked to dump it overboard.[66] Newton described a similar scene when a child's crying disturbed one of the crew's sleep: 'he ... tore the child from the mother, and threw it into the sea ... [but] she [the mother] was too valuable to be thrown overboard, and he was obliged to hear the sound of her lamentations.'[67]

The long-term psychological effects of dealing with so much violence and repression may only be speculated upon: but if the prodigious quantities of food and alcohol downed in Cape Coast Castle are anything to go by (amounting to 20,000 gallons of brandy alone every year), there was a sense of living now, and repenting later. These coping strategies did not always work: one Mr Nixon went out into the Castle's garden and shot himself in 1803. His suicide note only said: 'it's my fire next'.[68] It was not only Newton, who turned against his former occupation in later life, who felt guilty.

The Abolitionist campaigns

The slave trade was the target of the first truly modern political and consumerist campaign, complete with boycotts of 'slave sugar' and mass petitioning. It brought together many of those people who regarded themselves as most modern, and most moral: urbanites, especially in the new manufacturing centres; evangelicals, including Quakers and Methodists; and reforming businessmen who thought that commerce would be better conducted on more peaceful lines. The London organising committee founded in 1787 contained a number of astute businessmen, including the ceramics entrepreneur Josiah Wedgwood: they fancied they knew how to run an advertising campaign, and how to abolish the dichotomy between what was right and what was profitable.[69] The Manchester committee alone spent £129 on newspaper advertisements backing Wilberforce's motion for abolition, while in London the figure was over £1100, including the costs of printing Newton's book.[70]

These well-to-do leaders were joined by many more humble campaigners. The 11,000 who signed Manchester's anti-slavery petition in December 1787 accounted for 66 per cent of the adult male population. Manchester was a seat of particular enthusiasm for the cause, but elsewhere the results were similar: in York, for instance, 40 per cent of the adult males may have signed. It was a relatively uneven 'breakthrough' in this first round of enthusiasm for Parliamentary abolition, and the Home Counties were under-represented; but this was made up for in the second round, in 1792, when every county was well represented.[71]

Women were also included in the Abolitionist campaigns, almost for the first time on an explicitly 'political' issue. Quaker women were instrumental in spreading opposition to the trade. Their preachers and speakers, for instance, Catherine Phillips of Dudley in Worcestershire and Mary Peisley of Ballymore in County Kildare, often included an account of slavery as one of those practices that was against the 'golden rule' of treating others as one would be treated. Phillips and Peisley had been to the North American colonies in the 1750s, and spoke from first-hand knowledge. Their financial backing was not inconsiderable, too. One subscription list for the Abolition Society in 1788 contains the names of 206 women, comprising around 10 per cent of total subscribers. They gave £363, more than 10 per cent of the Society's total income at that time. In Manchester over one-fifth of the subscribers were women.[72] After the abolition of the British trade itself, the women's movement grew to contain thousands of 'female societies', though women involved in these usually only met with other women. Contributing to mixed gatherings was discouraged, and female reformers often drew on their 'femininity' to highlight their concern for African 'sisters' and the effects of slavery on the nuclear family.[73] They wore anti-slavery jewellery and emblems – especially Wedgwood's – on their clothes, and in their hair; at home they discussed books of anti-slavery poems presented as 'A Subject for Conversation at the Tea-Table'.[74]

It is important to remember that many Britons continued to support the slave trade – though in later years most preferred to keep this quiet. Even Evangelicals such as George Whitefield and James Habersham owned plantation slaves in mid-eighteenth-century Georgia.[75] The radical publisher and political activist William Cobbett made his name in the nineteenth century excoriating the British governing classes. But he was happy to support slavery during his time as a Philadelphia newspaper publisher in the 1790s. Back in Britain, his weekly *Political Register* in 1804 condemned reformers' 'wild and dangerous' plans to abolish the slave trade.[76] The more overt forms of modern racism, constructing 'higher' and 'lesser' races, were still some way off. But there was anti-black prejudice in abundance. British-American courts condemned black women, among other things, for failing to 'restrain themselves in their Cloathing as the Law requires', and newspapers put miscegenation and white sexual exploitation down to such practices.[77] Jamaican planters and pro-slavery writers agreed, arguing either that black women were naturally promiscuous, or that Evangelicals and 'well-meaning' churchmen had encouraged them to 'breed' and grow stronger. Another, and much rarer view among pro-slavery writers, was that the brutalities of plantation life had made female slaves desperate – though, of course, it was then the duty of the planter class to make sure they were tutored and controlled more effectively.[78] Most of the 'West India interest' – basically, the planter classes – also defended their estates to the last. Petitions came in from islands such as Barbados, Montserrat, Jamaica and from the 'West Indies' more widely right up until Emancipation itself – though they were often addressed to the Crown, rather than Parliament, an implicit acceptance of the unpopularity of their cause back 'home'.[79]

But although West Indian sugar planting and its leaders were hardly in general or terminal decline, in the early 1800s they were experiencing deep problems associated with the war. The French fleet having been swept from the ocean after Trafalgar, and most of the French Caribbean seized, overproduction was a huge problem while the West Indian planters were shut out of their European markets by Napoleon's continental system. Rampant wartime inflation, high transport costs and falling prices owing to overproduction were at least causing many of their erstwhile allies to doubt the wisdom of continuing to produce so much sugar.[80] Still, there can be little doubt that the British anti-slave trade campaign and its moral fervour was the main reason for the eventual abolition of that trade, which came in 1807 after numerous failed attempts, notably in 1788 and 1792. Its mobilisation of mass 'opinion', almost for the first time, made numbers count as facts about the views of 'the public'; allowed women a space to express their views; allied London and Manchester businessmen with radical reformers; and brought together Quakers, Evangelicals and Anglicans. It was a prodigious achievement. As John Wesley put it, this was an argument 'upon the consideration of interest as of humanity and justice', though even he 'feared . . . that 'the former . . . would have more weight than the latter'.[81]

The trade's abolition was seen at the time as a victory for hard-headedness as well as justice and wisdom: for hard-headed and tender-hearted Britishness itself. Clarkson thought that a free West Indies would be more productive.[82] But this was a more fundamental appeal to national self-image: it did not depend on these rather suspect economic arguments. The two most famous images of the campaign were Wedgwood's famous brass medal – upon which was imprinted the image of kneeling slave entreating 'am I not a man and a brother?' – and a diagram showing just how tightly packed were the Africans on board the slave ship *Brooks*. But both images effaced the Africans' own lives and efforts, making them respectively a subject of pity and horror: as the critic Marcus Wood has pointed out, they are more about the British than the slaves.[83] J.M.W. Turner's famous painting of the *Zong* incident, *Slavers Throwing Overboard the Dead and Dying*, asked in the painter's impassioned accompanying lines: 'where is thy market now?'[84] However, and despite that sense of national guilt, the painting was still taken as but one of many studies of what Linda Colley has termed 'the past giving way before the force of British progress'. Turner put slaves' hands in the foreground – but only as they sank beneath the waves. The Lord Chancellor was not alone in picturing Britain as 'the morning star that enlightened Europe, and whose boast and glory was to . . . administer humanity and justice to all nations'.[85]

The Royal Navy and the war against the slave trade

The abolition of Britain's part in the trade was followed by a long-drawn-out battle to suppress it. On the return of peace in 1815, Europe's exhausted and defeated nations had little choice but to accede to British demands – at least for now. The French agreed to a ban on the trade; the Spanish and Portuguese to be brought out over a period of years for £400,000 and £300,000 respectively; the Dutch in return for resuming control of their territories in the East Indies.[86] But the British still had to forego perhaps 4 per cent of their national income as their sugar industries became less 'competitive' and their share of the market collapsed; and were to lose nearly 5000 lives at sea and on inland anti-slaving expeditions. The direct financial costs of suppression, suggested by the expense of keeping the Royal Navy off West Africa between 1816 and 1865, amounted to £12.4 million on their own. All this was equal to perhaps 1.8 per cent of national income over 60 years from 1808 to 1867. By way of comparison, this is nearly nine times the average amount of untied OECD development aid between the 1970s and 1990s.[87]

The campaign did not bring an immediate end to the slave trade. The numbers of slaves imported into Cuba and Brazil in fact accelerated, running at 30,000 *per annum* at Rio de Janeiro during the mid-1820s. The numbers mounted to 45,000 a year in the latter years of that decade, before hitting 60,000 in 1829 and 1830. The quarter century after 1825 saw 1.6 million slaves moved across the Atlantic, only a small drop on the previous 25 years and nearly 15 per cent of the entire numbers carried during the slave trading era.[88] Nor were the Iberian authorities particularly active in preventing this. Britain's 1817 treaty with Spain banned slaving north of the equator immediately, and at least appeared to apply 'south of the line' from 1820 onwards. But the treaty was a masterfully ambiguous document. Apparently quite clear that ships sailing out of Spanish ports were not to buy slaves and force them across the Atlantic, there was nothing to stop them arming and equipping in foreign ports, or engaging in the extremely profitable export and re-export trade within the Spanish colonies. Such evasions helped to sustain the slave trade for many decades, for slaves could be taken on in all those non-metropolitan ports. The Spanish authorities connived in this, managing to seize precisely two slave ships between 1820 and 1842.[89]

From the 1750s onwards British governments had already tried to insist that 'freedom of the seas' did not extend to neutral shipping in wartime, which might be stopped and searched for enemy goods at any time. At the Congress of Verona in 1822, the British attempted to define the slave trade as piracy to allow them to stop and search any ships that might be carrying slaves. This would have meant, again, that the Royal Navy could force their way onto any ship, of any nation, they suspected of carrying illegal cargoes. Not surprisingly, most other nations opposed and voted down this measure.[90] Legal and practical barriers hampered the British anti-slaving campaign throughout. Only when the British entered Brazilian ports under Admiral Schomberg in 1850 did the trade really begin to tail off: the Brazilians outlawed the trade the following year.[91]

It was the Royal Navy's smaller ships – its frigates, sloops, brigs and schooners – that ranged up and down the African coast hoping to catch slavers in the act. Great ships of the line were rather peripheral in such a design, and played little role in these police actions. But the British did not give up, and maintained their campaign across more than three decades. There were 14 anti-slaving patrol ships off West Africa in 1836; 32 by 1847; and 35 by the end of that decade. The Royal Navy managed to release 153,000 captives, from 1588 ships, a remarkable number that we may be sure represented only one small part of the entire industry. National heroes were made in this long maritime action, just as surely as they had been made by the campaign for abolition and emancipation. Thomas Pasley, who was later to become an admiral, was one of them, and described what he found on board one ship:

> In my life I have never witnessed anything so shocking. About 450 people were packed into that small vessel as you would pack bales of goods; and diseases of all sorts became rife with them. One hundred had died before she was taken, and they were and are still dying daily . . . some children were in the last stages of emaciation and sores. It was dreadful, and so distressing, I could have cried.[92]

This had not been an unusual picture on board British ships just a few years earlier, as we have seen; but for now, British patriots were content to hear that they were the linchpin of a naval campaign to end such 'abuses'. The campaign against the slave trade was in Britain's interest in any case, and were accompanied by what Boyd Hilton has termed 'high handed' interventions and tactics.[93] But the point is that anti-slavery became mixed up with other elements – national self-determination, free trade – that came to be seen as quintessentially British. They should therefore take their place among those 'psychological' benefits that Britons gained from their far-flung possessions and interests: an 'imaginative construct' that is difficult to capture or quantify, but which was undoubtedly important in the making and remaking of British national identity.[94]

Conclusions: slavery, Abolition and 'Britishness'

By the mid- to late nineteenth century, anti-slavery opinion was entrenched as a matter of secular faith in 'Britishness'. Almost everywhere the British took their formal Empire, often far from the Atlantic and its history of slaving, they took an attack on this trade with them. They looked down on those, like the citizens of the early USA, who still traded in slaves: 'liberators of the world', they sarcastically called them.[95] Even their informal suzerainty over non-Imperial lands, for instance, late nineteenth-century Egypt, was gradually used to make slavery less attractive. In 1877 and 1880 Conventions signed by the French, British and Egyptians pursued these aims through co-operation with the other powers; this was followed by administrative action once the British were in control after 1882, and by further conventions in 1889 and 1895. By 1877–78 at least seven Royal Navy ships and one gunboat were patrolling the Red Sea and nearby waterways, and such efforts continued well into the 1890s.[96]

But it was fear and guilt that lay behind this insistence on a particularly virtuous national character. As for the former, Britons knew that they *could* be slaves, despite the words of 'Rule Britannia'. The English and then British empires in the Americas had been stocked with white indentured servants and convicts before these had been manned by black Africans, men and women whose status was often little better than the slaves who replaced them. They were the chief labour recruits from 1618, when the entrepreneurs Thomas Smythe and Sir Edwin Sandys swept up London's street children to work in Virginia (with questionable legal authority), to the late 1600s, when black slaves became cheaper to import. These bonded labourers could be bought and sold between masters; and in the absence of much in the way of written evidence, the courts usually upheld their superiors' interpretation of the length and terms of contracts.[97] Political prisoners, for instance, defeated Royalists in the 1650s, were often sent to join bondmen in the New World.[98] The Moorish threat and the seizure of English men and women in the Channel had helped to discredit Charles I in the 1620s and 1630s, as we have already seen in Chapter 3.[99] Redemption campaigns, sermons and popular captivity narratives kept the issue of the 'Barbary captives' in the public mind.[100] A curious show at Covent Garden in 1751, in which British ex-prisoners who had been redeemed from North Africa rattled their chains and showed their rags, attracted huge audiences. What better way than song and show to ward away the nightmare of British slavery?[101]

Catherine Hall has also pointed out that, although 'in the 1830s, respectable English middle-class men supported the anti-slavery movement', their support was bound up with their own ideas of self-sufficiency, individualism and paternalism. Such men's interest in more radical calls for equality drained slowly away thereafter, and a new and more scientific idea of racial segregation took hold. By the 1860s, and the debates over the Second Reform Act, 'Britishness' was being defined as a property-holding maleness and whiteness.[102] Abolition had always had conservative as well as radical implications. It made British statesmen the arbiters of what was 'civilised' and 'uncivilised', and it allowed them to pose as reformers whatever political repression they sanctioned at home.[103] It also allowed Britain, with a nearly clear conscience, to continue to import slave-grown commodities, and if anything Britain's trade with Cuba and Brazil had continued to grow after 1815. In 1852 perhaps 22 per cent of all sugar imports coming into Britain were still slave-grown. Two-thirds of the raw cotton coming into Britain, and almost all the tobacco, also came from slave-owning areas.[104] Britons were haunted by two ideas – the fact that some of them had become slaves, and their past and present complicity with the trade. It was another part of their Empire's dark side – of a renegade, freebooting and piratical past – that nineteenth-century Britons wanted to efface. They celebrated their 'freedom' all the more loudly, for they could never quite shake off the memory of the evil in which they had been engaged.

Timeline of events

1562–67	John Hawkins trades in slaves on three West African and Caribbean voyages
1618	Thomas Smythe and Sir Edwin Sandys export London slave children to Virginia
1620s–30s	Peak of Muslim corsair threat in English home waters
1625–25	English capture of St Kitts and Barbados
1655	England seizes Jamaica from Spain
1672–98	Royal African Company enjoys monopoly in West African trade
1713	Treaty of Utrecht: Spain forced to issue the British with an *asiento* to trade slaves
1720	'South Sea Bubble' financial crash

1750s–60s	Numerical peak of the British slave trade
1759	Birth of abolitionist William Wilberforce
1772	'Somerset case': Lord Justice Mansfield rules that a slave cannot be seized in England
1781	Mass killing of African slaves on board the *Zong*
1783	Quaker petition for end of the slave trade presented to Parliament
1787	Committee for the Abolition of the Slave Trade founded
1787–88	First great Abolitionist petition organised
1791	Slave revolt on French Saint-Domingue, modern Haiti
1792	Second great Abolitionist petition organised
1794	Revolutionary France abolishes slavery
1799	Napoleon as First Consul in France; re-imposition of slavery
March 1807	Britain legislates to abolish the slave trade throughout the British Empire
1808–60	Major operations of the Royal Navy's West African squadron: 1600 ships captured
1815	Congress of Vienna: continental nations agree to abolish their own slave trades
1817	British treaty with Spain bans slaving north of the Equator immediately
1820	Supposed date set by treaty for Spain to abandon slaving south of the Equator
1825–50	Renaissance of Spanish slaving: 1.6 million slaves moved across the Atlantic
July 1833	Death of William Wilberforce
August 1833	Slavery Abolition Act passes Parliament, emancipating slaves in the British Empire
August 1834	Slavery Abolition Act comes into force, though slaves remain indentured
1838–40	Indentured 'apprenticeships' under Slavery Abolition Act begin to lapse
1840	Final indentured 'apprenticeships' completed under Slavery Abolition Act
1850	British attack on Brazil helps finally to reduce Spanish slaving

1852	British sugar imports still partly slave-grown, at about 22 per cent of total
January 1863	Emancipation Proclamation in the USA frees all slaves
1865	Passage of the Thirteenth Amendment to the US Constitution ends slavery in the USA
1877–80	French, British and Egyptian Conventions to outlaw slavery in Egypt
1877–78	British squadrons patrol Red Sea to stamp out Egyptian slavery
1889–95	Further anti-slaving conventions in Egypt under British rule
1944	Eric Williams' *Capitalism and Slavery* published

5

Migrants

For three centuries, Britain experienced Europe's most sustained long-term migration, as well as divesting itself of the most people relative to its population among the larger European powers. British migrants peopled large tracts of the world, first in the Caribbean, then in 'mainland' North America and then across the world in Britain's new acquired colonies and territories. Three hundred million people could claim descent from the peoples of the British Isles by the end of the twentieth century. Very high proportions of Canadians, Australians and New Zealanders, in particular, could trace their lineage back to British roots. Many in the early days of North American settlement emigrated out of a desire for religious redemption, though even among the 'Puritans' there were many simply searching for more and better paid jobs and cheap land. Some migrants were being driven off the land, many of them from the Highlands of Scotland and especially in the second part of the eighteenth century, or being made redundant from their recession-prone crafts, the experience of many 'Irish Scots' from Ulster's linen industry. It is these privations, quite apart from Scots' general and long-noted tendency to leave their native country for work, that help explain the presence of so of their countrymen among the British migrations. But many emigrants were actually relatively well-off, at least compared to the peasant migrations of popular histories, or Eastern Europeans fleeing from subsistence farming: skilled workmen, perhaps, or tenant farmers. This phenomenon became more pronounced as the period wore on due to the increasing influence of previous migrants writing home, of agents promoting the new lands, and the growth of popular knowledge and propaganda. Only understanding all these factors together can explain the British diaspora, for these emigrants had to endure extreme privations that must have made their destinations seem very desirable indeed. The very ports from which they embarked were full of shipping agents, hoteliers and 'porters' who were intent on parting them from their money. The ships that carried them were subject to the outbreak of deadly diseases, at least until the Navigation Acts of the early 1800s and the more efficient 'age of steam' that followed the middle of the nineteenth century. Only the ever-present fear of shipwreck, or the appalling overcrowding and bad food and water on the migrant ships, broke the boredom. They were divided places, too, often the site of racial and national conflicts, or fights between crew and passengers, and full of concerns over women's place on ships. Those complicated battles on board migrant ships mirrored emigrants' multifaceted and difficult decisions to leave Britain. Far from making a new Britishness at home or across the Empire, as some of its promoters hoped, the journey often served only to show how different Britons were from one another. As one historian has noted, this mass exodus was indeed 'untidy, fractured and complex rather than rational, purposeful and coherent'.

Counting Britain's emigrants

The British diaspora was a vast movement of human peoples, a great exodus that gradually (if unevenly) accelerated as time passed. The story begins with North America and the Caribbean: famously and first with the English colony at Jamestown in Virginia, where a settlement finally took root after several attempts in 1607. During 1607 and 1608, 864 settlers arrived at the settlement designated by the Virginia Company, some of them men with a little capital dreaming of managing their own plantations. This initial contact with new worlds was hardly auspicious. Within a year, more than half of them were dead, though the colony just managed to survive when a trading ship brought relief 2 years later.[1] It took many decades for the colony to become self-sufficient in terms of population. As late as 1625, 3000 had died there, leaving only 1200 *in situ*.[2]

Elsewhere, a literally 'New England' was planted in what is today Massachusetts during the 'busy years' of the 1630s. Around 200 vessels, each carrying perhaps 100 Englishmen and women on board, transported up to 21,000 emigrants to New England between 1630 and 1641. They had mixed motives, but the more religious among them at least saw America as a haven from material and spiritual temptation. The voyage out became a trial, a barrier like the Red Sea confronting the Israelites, that had to be undergone if the 'pilgrims' were to come out on the other side. The Puritan minister Cotton Mather later described the first emigrants to New England leaving their ships 'almost as the Family of Noah did the Ark, having a Whole World before them to be peopled'.[3] Another minister, John Cotton, believed that 'the safety of mariners' and passengers' lives ... lieth not on ropes and cables ... but in the name and hand of the lord.' The sea was a deeply frightening place, and the drama of the *rite de passage* was all the more intense for that. John Wollcott, outlining how difficult it was to attract labour to Connecticut in 1639, described how 'good workmen ... are fearful to go to sea for fear they shall not live to come to your land, but were it not for the danger of the sea you might have enough'.[4]

Puritan elites, for instance, those arriving on the *Arbella* in 1630, formed a tight-knit and confident cadre of leaders: in this case Lady Arbella Fiennes, sister of the Earl of Lincoln, in whose honour the ship has been named, as well as Isaac Jonson, her husband, and her brother, Charles Fiennes. But John Winthrop, a Suffolk lawyer and dissenter who was later to become the colony's leader, may have been a better representative of the relatively middle-aged 'middling sort' – yeomen, husbandmen, artisans, craftsmen, merchants and traders – who came to the colony. This 'Winthrop fleet' of 11 ships is indeed chiefly remembered for his presence.[5] Alison Games' analysis of the London port register for 1635 shows that 37 per cent of the emigrants leaving for New England were between 25 and 59 years of age, a higher figure than for Virginia or the Caribbean. Though London was a relatively rich source of servants, full of indigent workers looking for a job as it was, craftsmen and particularly cloth workers were pouring out of England's other ports.[6]

Thereafter, in great numbers, and from the American 'mainland' as well as the mother country, Britons began to gravitate to the Caribbean plantations. In 1601–25, 6000 Europeans moved to the American mainland, and only a negligible number to the Caribbean; but 81,000 moved to the Caribbean between 1626 and 1650, as against only 34,000 for the 'Mainland'. It took until the last years of the eighteenth century for Britain's North American colonies to recover the relative pre-eminence they had enjoyed in the early seventeenth century.[7] Overall, just under 400,000 Britons, overwhelmingly from England and Wales, had migrated to the Americas by 1700. The sugar and tobacco plantations were sucking in labour at a ferocious rate, and there were more jobs to be taken than workers to fill them: planters scrambled to bring in labour on a massive scale.[8]

There was nothing particularly new about Britons moving abroad as they looked for work or profit. Wars and technologies we associate with the eighteenth and nineteenth centuries may have intensified the sense of a 'world in motion', but they had not created it.[9] Scots, for instance, had always been famous travellers. They served across Europe as soldiers, notably, for instance, during Scandinavia's Seven Years' War between 1563 and 1570, and – as we have already seen – were commonly found as traders in Europe's northern waters.[10] In the early sixteenth century alone, between 55,000 and 70,000 Scots migrated across the North Sea to northern Germany, Scandinavia and Poland.[11] Between 55,000 and 70,000 Scots moved to Poland and Scandinavia in the years from 1600 to 1650.[12] This became a recurrent *motif* in the period under consideration here. Disbanded soldiers from Scots regiments were also noticeable among the increasing numbers of British subjects in North America after the Seven Years' War, the War of American Independence and the struggles with France between 1793 and 1815.[13]

The English had been moving to regional urban centres, or to London, for centuries: once the Atlantic was open, Bailyn has written, it 'became a highway like the Great North Road', with poorer Englishmen who would normally flow into Bristol just continuing on their way.[14] Games has promoted an Atlantic perspective on British history precisely because it allows us to see 'migration . . . as an entirely normal activity, a regular part of the life cycle, a common response to personal ambition, economic hardship, or perceived opportunities elsewhere'.[15] But what was different now was the scale of migration, as it quickened in the early seventeenth century, as well as the transoceanic distances involved.

The settling of North America and the Caribbean in the seventeenth century was followed by something of a lull, and migration from England and Wales in particular fell away as the population at home stagnated.[16] But this was followed by yet another 'peak', as between the close of the Seven Years' War in 1763 and the opening of the American Revolutionary War in 1776, 55,000 Protestant Irish, 40,000 Scots and over 30,000 Englishmen left for North America.[17] The Ulster Protestants were the single most notable group, in proportion to their total strength as well as in gross numerical terms, and their exodus had been going on since at least 1718. Land promoters and speculators encouraged the process, personified by Arthur Dobbs, from County Antrim, who became Governor of North Carolina in 1753. North Carolina had a range of schemes to attract 'poor Protestant' settlers from the North of Ireland.[18] The reasons for this exodus included successive downturns in Ulster's linen industry, dearths, the falling in of rents granted in the 1690s when landlords had been eager to secure Protestant tenants, splits within Ulster's Presbyterian churches and the promise of religious liberty in the New World.[19] The regular and relatively cheap passage of ships on trade routes between Ulster and the Americas, carrying such goods as flaxseed and potash to Ulster's linen industry and then shipping migrants back in their empty holds, was also important. [20] Scots were the next most numerous group among this wave of emigrants, so much so that one Scots Catholic priest noted in 1801 that 'we begin now to look upon America as but one of our Islands on the Coast and on the Sea that intervenes as but a little brook that divides.'[21] We shall examine their experiences more closely in due course.

These were tiny numbers by later standards: perhaps 6500 Europeans over-all moved to the Americas every year over the entire period stretching from 1500 to 1800.[22] But that number needs to be placed in context. Impe-rial Spain, at the height of her power, possibly sent 3000 migrants a year to the Americas, from a population of 8 million; France, between 1608 and 1760, managed 27,000 from 20 million. The British, from a smaller population, migrated on a much larger scale: 400,000 left in the seven-teenth century alone, and in the surge of 1763–75, 3 per cent of the entire Scottish population may have left that country for a new life overseas.[23] By 1820, about 850,000 white Europeans of all nations – but mainly the British – had peopled British North America, the USA and the British Caribbean.[24]

Nineteenth-century outflows were on an even more gigantic scale, usually focused on what became the 'white Dominions'. Nearly 9 million people left Great Britain and Ireland between the 1850s and 1900. On a slightly different time-scale, 10 million left England alone between 1875 and 1930.[25] Approaching 2 million of these went to Australia, 1.5 million alone emi-grating there in 1821–1900.[26] More than 300,000 went to New Zealand in the second half of the century.[27] There were 450,000 people of British birth in Canada in 1890, and 80,000 more were arriving every year by 1911.[28] Even in the late nineteenth century, as Mediterraneans and Eastern Euro-peans became more and more noticeable among the flood, the British made up a fifth of Europe's emigrants.[29] The huge number of migrants meant that the European shipping industry had to fight even to keep up with demand. Europe's ports dealt with 32,000 tons of shipping in 1831; by 1876 that figure was 3.3 million tons.[30]

There were two more huge 'waves' noticeable in the numbers down to the First World War, in the 1880s and then again in the first years of the twentieth century. Great Britain divested itself of a balance of 818,000 people in the former decade, and 755,000 emigrants in the years between 1901 and 1911.[31] The numbers seem to have fluctuated, at least by this point, in relation to relative unemployment at home and in receiving countries, though long-term trends were related even more strongly to relative real wages.[32] The picture is not entirely clear, even so. Regional pay differences do not seem to have narrowed for those years well covered by data, which we would expect if migration was highest due to relative real wages and those on low incomes left *en masse* from relatively deprived areas. The very large fluctuations in migrant numbers, even from year to year, were not exclusively related to unemployment and wages. And as we shall see, the role of emigration publicity has to be taken into account.[33] Even so, it seems fair to expect and to conclude that the relatively higher wages in the USA and most of the colonies seemed more attractive in times of trade recession at home. At least some of the great peaks and troughs in late-nineteenth-century emigration can be put down to economic conditions, a fact that is particularly noticeable when comparing the statistics from several European nations.[34]

Who were the migrants?

Religious motivations were supposed to be at the centre of the seventeenth-century Pilgrims' world, at least. In the hands of preachers such as Samuel Danforth, Urian Oakes or Cotton Mather, the ideas of religious commitment and faith became a rallying call for the colonists, as well as providing a stick with which to beat the unfaithful. The very journey became a salvation that paralleled the Israelites' escape from Egypt. Edward Johnson wrote in his *Wonder-Working Providence* that 'you people whom he [Christ] by the hand did lead / From *Egypt* land through Seas with watry Wall: / Apply your selves his Scriptures for to read'.[35] But the truth was, as Plymouth Colony's governor William Bradford himself knew, that there were 'sundry weighty and solid reasons' for travelling to the New World. *Good News from New England*, a Puritan pamphlet from 1648, listed land, social mobility, economic independence, earning and a thirst for novelty as among those 'solid reasons'.[36]

The religious faithful were joined by around 50,000 convicts, most of whom ended up working as indentured labourers in the Chesapeake plantation colonies of Maryland and Virginia.[37] Perhaps 36,000 of them were from England and Wales, and the rest from Ireland, not counting those of Irish origin who were transported from the 'mainland'.[38] Attempts were later made to play down this fact, so as to erase the 'convict stain' from the young American Republic: Jefferson, for instance, thought that 'the malefactors sent to America were not sufficient in number to merit enumeration.' But shipping convicts was in fact a long-established tradition. As early as 1611 Governor Thomas Dale of Virginia asked that 'all offenders out of the common gaols condemned to die' be sent to him instead.[39] Under the Transportation Act of 1718, a uniform code of practice was established that made the trade very profitable for its contractors: first and foremost Jonathan Forward, already a successful City merchant who had made his name trading in the slave markets, who handed the business on to the even less scrupulous Andrew Reid in February 1742.[40] By 1772 the trade in convicts was so profitable that the state could afford to withdraw all subsidies.[41]

The ships carrying these men and women were small – most displaced no more than 200 tons – and the convicts were tightly packed, all the better to profit from their passage. One man visiting a convict ship remembered that 'all the states of horror I ever had an idea of are much short of what I saw this poor man in; chained to a board in a hole not above sixteen feet long, more than fifty within; a collar and padlock about his neck, and chained to five of the most dreadful creatures I ever looked on.' A Virginia trader wrote to one carrier in 1767, advising that 'if ever you should send Servants [the convicts were for sale] ... again, [I] would not advise so many, for there was not room upon deck to muster them.'[42] Early Australia was of course initially peopled by convicts after Britain's loss of North America, over 160,000 of them on one count – 80,000 were transported to New South Wales, 69,000 to Van Diemen's Land and 10,000 to Western Australia. The majority of them, as with the North American convicts who preceded them, were in their twenties.[43]

We have also become used to the image, fostered by an earlier generation of historians, of the peasant migrant, who 'turned his back upon the village at the crossroads', in Oscar Handlin's words: a figure who was embarking on 'a long journey that his mind would forever mark as its most momentous experience', 'the end of peasant life in Europe'.[44] Historians of the 1940s and 1950s followed authors such as Brinley Thomas and Marcus Lee Hansen in seeing the 'expansion of Europe' as rooted in 'a fundamental reorganization of [the] rural economy in every country that was affected'.[45] Nicholas Canny has critiqued this literature as 'based on the assumption that movement across the Atlantic was the only logical course open to people in the Old World for whom economic opportunity was shrinking'.[46] The true situation was a great deal more complex than this.

Many among the migrants, to be sure, were trying to escape rural suffering. The Scots, in particular those moving in the 1760s and 1770s and in the early nineteenth century, were indeed often fleeing from agrarian distress. Migrant numbers suddenly rose to an annual average of 8000 between 1760 and 1775: the largest single group among these were Scots, many of whom were suffering from the long and hard 'Black Winter' of 1771–72.[47] Longer leases, increased rents often switched from 'kind' or labour to cash and livestock enclosure in the Highlands were all proceeding apace in the name of productivity at this time. These were long-established trends, as most recent historians have pointed out. Lairds and their tenants had been managing the consequences of such changes for decades. But the acceleration of 'modernisation' in these years, and the poor deal many crofters got out of it, was too much for many.[48] Though the profitable trade in kelp and seaweed warded off any flight from the Western Isles for some years, the close of the Napoleonic Wars saw that business collapse as well, and the ensuing crises resulted in the acceleration of migration from the Western Highlands.[49]

But most migrants were not desperate escapees. Bailyn's analysis of a worried government's survey of 9662 migrants in the years 1773 to 1775 has demonstrated that there were two major 'pools' of migrants. The first was centred on London, the Home Counties around the metropolis and the Thames Valley, and the second, 'provincial' and more rural, came from a great arc of land stretching up from the Midlands, through Yorkshire, and into Scotland, where migration numbers were densest from the West Highlands and Islands. Members of the former cluster in England's south and east were much younger, more skilled, more urban and more male than those migrants from the latter group.[50] The composition of North America's labouring immigrants, at least, gradually shifted in these last colonial years from the indigent and desperate to labouring people with trades and skills.[51]

Despite Bailyn's 1770s evidence of Highlanders moving as individuals, many leaving the Highlands and Islands of Scotland in the 1700s did travel in family groups. In one sample, two-thirds of those leaving in the second half of the eighteenth century were farmers, not labourers travelling on their own. In 1729, for instance, Hector McNeill of Lossit in Kintyre settled his West Highlanders on Cape Fear River, and 10 years later his brother Neil brought another 550 Scots from Argyll to New Campbeltown, a settlement which became known as Lafayetteville after Independence. Those travelling in such groups during the later and even more intense period of late-eighteenth-century migration included 425 clansmen, including 125 men, 100 women and 200 children, who sailed for New York from Fort William on the *Pearl* in September 1773. They were led by their lords, later to form the nucleus of Glengarry County in Canada: three brothers in the shape of John Macdonell of Leek, Allan of Collachie and Alexander of Aberchalder, and their first cousin, 'Spanish' John Macdonell of Scotus.[52]

Nineteenth-century evidence should also give us pause before we accept the stereotype of the peasant migrant and the passage only of rural labourers forced off the land. Charlotte Erickson's careful work on the figures for the census and migration to the USA in 1831 helps make the point. Agricultural workers were, if anything, *under*-represented as against their numbers at home.[53] It was only after the relative *success* of the Scottish economy became evident, from about the 1860s, that the tide of emigrants from that country peaked.[54] Statistics analysed by Dudley Baines for the second half of the nineteenth century reveal that just over one-third of migrants were born in London, the West Midlands or Lancashire, and another one-quarter in other heavily urbanised counties. Most migrants were not peasants moving off the land, despite the views of an earlier generation of historians such as Brinley Thomas. Many of them had previously been living in Britain's cities as part of a 'staged migration' that would see them carry on travelling straight through the port; but the majority were urban natives.[55] Mid-nineteenth-century migrants, for instance, those to Australia, could usually read and write: between 56 per cent and 64 per cent were capable of this by the 1850s.[56]

'Farmers' moving to the USA in 1851, another census year, were mainly younger smallholders from grain-farming areas hard-hit by agricultural recession: a Mr Birtwhistle stopped on his way to take ship at Liverpool on his way to the USA that year, and the local newspaper recorded his entirely rational and well-thought-out plans. He was, the *Doncaster Chronicle and Farmers' Journal* reported,

> a clever and skilful practical agriculturalist, and he has occupied the farm which he has just given up for upwards of twelve years, but finding that with all his energy and all his industry he could . . . scarcely 'make both ends meet', he determined to relinquish his unprofitable occupation before his capital became exhausted . . . [to] cross . . . the waters of the broad Atlantic.[57]

It was the tenant farmer, not the landless labourer, who was causing anxiety among the propertied classes by this time. In 1878 *The Times* went so far as to urge the Government to do something for him: 'his disappearance and the development of ever greater estates could be a cause for revolution,' the paper feared.[58]

The emigrant ports

Liverpool was the greatest embarkation point in the Empire during the nine-teenth century, and in the world until the great tide out of Germany in the early years of the twentieth century overtook its pre-eminence. Its railway links with Northern and Central England were very good; it had a coastwise traffic that regularly and quickly linked it to Scotland and Wales; and it had relatively efficient and modern deep-water docks. The vertiginous ascent of the port's passenger business began in the 1830s, and was accelerated by car-rying numberless victims of the Irish famine of 1846–48. By the time of the Australian gold rush of the early 1850s, 206,000 emigrants a year were being embarked at Liverpool.[59]

London had been a prime point of exit throughout most of the eighteenth century, as Bailyn's researches have revealed, but it was in Liverpool that the trade reached its apogee.[60] As late as 1891, 110,000 left Liverpool for New York, including the vast majority of the Scandinavian long-distance migrations, as against 82,000 at the city's nearest European rival, Hamburg. Glasgow, by way of a British comparison, catered for 23,000 migrants in the same year.[61] Whole areas of the biggest port in the world were given over to this trade by the 1830s, for instance, around Goree Piazza, where the slave trade had once had its offices, or on Waterloo Road, which ran northwards from the city centre past the docks, and from which 19 shipping agents or brokers operated. From here, brokers could try to match passengers to ships – entirely at the migrants' risk, for the contract was then with the shipowners, not the brokers, and it was extremely difficult to sue if things went wrong in any case. It was a huge business, estimated (probably conservatively) to be worth £581,315 in 1850. Two transatlantic brokers, actually Americans rather than Britons, may serve as an example. William and James Tapscott ran W. and J.T. Tapscott, which employed between 12 and 20 agents in Liverpool and New York in the early 1850s, and sent out 20,000 emigrants during 1851, taking perhaps £8750 as their 12.5 per cent cut of the business.[62]

Chaos would probably be the best word to describe what confronted emigrants at this stage of their journey. Even in the highly regulated state emigration depots, where 'good behaviour' was rewarded with better food and a better bedroll, waiting to go on board could be an unnerving experience. One Joseph Tarry remembered the scene at Birkenhead in 1853: 'Two or Three hundred persons were to sleep in one room – on Beds almost as hard as Stones – the scene altogether seemed very ludicrous – so unlike anything we had witnessed before – Some were laughing, others crying.'[63]

The great crush of peoples – including the majority of Irish emigrants – did not always make for an appetising mix. Liverpool contained 264 *licensed* public houses for a town of 164,000 souls in 1831; drinking, gambling and fighting were three of the main pastimes in a dock area where 'want and woe staggered arm in arm'. The American consul, Nathaniel Hawthorne, was appalled, and revealed many of his ideas about the poor when he wrote: 'the people are as numerous as maggots in cheese; you behold them, disgusting, all moving about, as when you raise a plank or log that has long lain on the ground.'[64] 'Of all the seaports in the world', Herman Melville wrote in 1849, 'Liverpool perhaps most abounds in all the variety of land-sharks, land-rats and other vermin which make the helpless mariner their pretty. In the shape of landlords, barkeepers, clothiers, crimps and boarding-house lodgers, the land-sharks devour him limb by limb.'[65]

Liverpool and Glasgow were only two ports among many where such people merchants practised their trade. To be sure, Canadian Pacific Railway ships unloaded people in Glasgow's docks, and 2.3 million Scots emigrated from that city between 1825 and 1938. This was the highest per capita emigration rate anywhere in Europe.[66] But nearly half a million people left Britain in the second half of the nineteenth century even from the relatively small ports of Devon and Cornwall. *White's Directory* of 1850 lists seven emigration agencies in Plymouth alone.[67] Britain's ports were all carrying a huge load of migrants by this stage, and Liverpool was only the most crowded among them: even so, the chaos, thievery, drinking and organised corruption of that city's docksides were the hallmarks of the single most numerically important site of emigration, and the spectacle grasped the early Victorian imagination.

Surviving the voyage

Open mourning at seeing Britain's shores recede was rare; a sense of lingering regret and loss was the more usual and dominant mood. When Rachel Hemming sailed to Australia on the *Calcutta* in 1854 she wrote back to her sister, the only member of the whole family to remain at home: '[we] watched you from the deck of the steamer on that rainy morning [of embarkation] till we were so far from the shore that we could not see you any longer.'[68] As the *David Clark* left Greenock for Australia on 15 June 1839, one passenger, John Arthur, played 'Lochaber no more' on the pipes with 'all present standing silently and experiencing deep and never to be forgotten emotion'.[69] The nineteenth-century emigrant William Wood recorded that 'it would be impossible to describe the various emotions which must have agitated the breasts of all on board': his young son added, 'his little voice echoing to each Steamer that rolled by Tah Tah'. Wood was filled with a mix of 'hilarity, grief *and* joy'.[70]

Other observers were struck by the continuation of the whirling chaos and wildly different experiences that had been so evident at the dockside. The mix of emotions, running from open weeping to cheerful contemplation of the opportunities ahead, was ably described by a young governess named Sophie Eyre, on her way to Australia on board the *David Scott* in the 1830s:

> The scene became painfully interesting from the number of females parting with their relations and friends. Several, overcome by their feelings at leaving home, country and kindred, were deeply affected, and as they pronounced the word 'farewell' burst into tears, or swooned in the arms of their parents, brothers and sisters. The leave-taking, however, went off as well as could be expected under such circumstances, and the majority of the women appeared in high spirits.[71]

As a Mrs William Radcliff noted when she left Scotland in the early nineteenth century, 'the prospect of happiness and independence qualified every sentiment of regret, and reconciled me to the painful alternative we had chosen.'[72]

Migrant ships were usually used to transport goods, rather than people. The Puritans' *Mayflower* voyage of 1620 was mounted in a ship that was 50 years old – a slow, but reliable, wine ship known with its fellows as a 'sweet ship' owing to the frequent spillages on the way back from France.[73] This need not mean that they were necessarily totally unsuited to their task. John Crossman of Torquay used his empty cargo vessels, the *Margaret* and the *Sarah Fleming*, to convey emigrants to Quebec in the 1840s and 1850s in relative comfort.[74] The profits made on the voyage back helped to make the voyage affordable for the poorer migrants.[75] But many ships were hastily put together below decks, with captains scrambling to employ carpenters speedily to redesign their steerage hold if they could not load up with enough cargo to make a suitable profit.[76] Such an outcome was, indeed, one of the chief reasons for captains' and crews' periodic brutality towards passengers. When Robert Garnham sailed to New York on the *Northumberland* in the nineteenth century, he found that the Quebec traders carrying him saw himself and his fellow travellers as a bore and a distraction. All the captain wanted was to get to Quebec and offload the emigrants, before heading home with his hold full of profitable timber. Garnham decided to stand up to the crew after they had administered one beating, and told the captain that 'if I saw any person, never mind who he was, struck down and ill treated, I, as an English gentleman, should of course go to his assistance.'[77]

Having been kept waiting for many days, there was usually a scrabble to get into the little wooden boxes that would pass for bunks on the passage. The Reverend William Bell later remembered his passage to America on the *Rothiemurchus* in 1817: 'the crying of the children, the swearing of the sailors, and the scolding of the women who had not got the beds they wanted, produced a concert in which it was difficult to discover any harmony.'[78] Even once ensconced, the start of the voyage was hardly a pleasant experience. Seasickness was one of the first maritime realities to hit the passengers. As Rachel Hemming recalled just a few days into her voyage on the *Calcutta*: 'Some of the passengers have been dreadfully ill ... I was seasick all Saturday afternoon, which I spent in my berth.'[79] A Thomas Trotter, very early in his voyage to Australia, recorded on 26 May 1836 that 'the scenes I ever witnessed that night was the worst. Scarcely a man woman or child but was sick and ... it was impossible to git any thing for them to vomit in.'[80]

Thereafter, life on most migrant ships settled down into a rather grim but ordered regularity. By the 1870s this had taken on a fairly fixed pattern, far at least from some of the grimmer experiences recorded in the 1830s and 1840s. The day would begin at 6 o'clock, when those elected from the mess to fetch water would get up and bring it back to their part of steerage. Bedding would then be packed away as best the passengers could, before women cleaned the floors while the 'mess captains' again queued up, this time for breakfast. Much of the rest of the day's work might be spent in a ritual washing of clothes, hold and deck, though practices varied from ship to ship. On the *Adamant* in 1875 there were 3 days for washing clothes – Mondays,

Wednesdays and Fridays – while on the 2000-ton steamer *Atrato* the year before there were only 2 days when clothes might be washed on deck, though there were two washhouses where it might be done at any time. Two more days were usually set aside for cleaning steerage as well, with the bedding brought up onto deck to be 'aired'.[81]

Boredom set in quickly, especially towards the end of our period as oceanic crossings became more regular and secure. Rachel Hemming reported with deeply illuminating repetition that 'it [the voyage] is most wearisome. The noise is wearisome, the people are wearisome and life is wearisome. It is too hot to work, and I am getting quite tired of novels, and there is nothing else on board.'[82] The dullness and the tedium of oceanic crossings were two of the main observations made by passengers. John Moore, bound for Australasia on the *Dunedin* in the 1870s, found it difficult to shake off *ennui*, frequently recording 'a long and tedious day, full of the same everlasting unchanging monotony'.[83]

Diary entry after diary entry reads like a dull, repetitive list from the ship's log. 'The early part of these 24 hours a moderate breeze from the NW which gradually died away till it became calm at the close of the day' is just one such example from 1838. The migrants were left to play at those roles they imagined appropriate: explorers, natural historians or weather experts. William Wood made the rather banal note that 'the appearance of the [Atlantic] Ocean differs greatly from that of the Irish sea, the former being dark Prussian Blue whilst the latter is quite Green.'[84] Any animal or fish sighting was eagerly rushed over to, and assiduously recorded. So, for instance, Moses Melchior wrote thus in one diary entry on the way to Australia in October 1853: 'we see a lot of flying fishes, also albatrosses. The birds fly very quickly around the ship and we have caught several of them on lines baited with a piece of pork.'[85]

Sick and bored as the passengers usually were, the food on board became a constant subject of anger and discontent. William Wood found the beef on board the *Constance* 'very bad; so salt[y] that I could not possibly eat it'.[86] On board the *Rothiemurchus*, Rev. Bell thought the bread inedible: 'I have never seen anything like the latter presented to human beings.' And the soup was just as bad, 'merely stinking water in which stinking beef had been boiled, which no dog would taste unless he was starving'.[87] The entire day revolved around mealtimes and food preparation, and emigrants would react angrily to any suspicion that they were not getting their 'dues'. On the *Scottish Admiral* in 1883, suspicion arose as to the crew's provisioning, and the passengers 'managed to get a pair of scales and weighed it & found every thing that was allowed us short weight'. They complained to the Captain, who publicly berated the Third Mate for the shortfall.[88] The water was usually no better, at least until the introduction of condensers in the late nineteenth century:

the Surgeon Superintendent on Cornelius and Elizabeth Voice's voyage to Canada admitted that 'water on board of a Ship is at no time (without a filter) a very palatable beverage.' A ton of water had to make do for four adults over 9 weeks, working out at 8 gallons every 2 days for each family. Late-twentieth-century water use worked out at 220 gallons for the same family over the same time-period.[89]

Drinking, games and horseplay broke the tedium. The American poet Ralph Waldo Emerson on board the *New York* from Liverpool to New York in 1833 recorded that 'I tipple with all my heart here. May I not?'[90] William Wood, of a rather austere temperament himself, thought near the end of his journey's first month that 'almost every day the amusements become more extraordinary and ludicrous . . . knocking each other down, pulling men out of bed and other such mean sport.' The ship's 'insufficient' stock of alcohol became a problem later in the voyage.[91] Music, often chosen to remind the migrants of home, was another means of passing the time. The *Southesk* had 390 Scots on board as it sailed to Australia in 1883, and only five passengers from other countries. Several nights of Scottish music were held, and a Robert McAlpine recorded in his diary for 20 July 1883 that his wife Maggie 'sang the auld Scotch songs and she sung very well'.[92]

Sickness, reform legislation and the steam revolution

Migrants were relatively lucky by the later nineteenth century, for boredom was much worse than the sickness and disease that had so marred earlier crossings. The most common maladies on board emigrant ships in the eighteenth and early nineteenth centuries were typhus, dysentery and yellow fever: a host of dangers described at the time as pestilential, putrid, malignant, bilious, infectious or 'purple' maladies.[93] More than half of all deaths on government-assisted passages to Australia between 1848 and 1885 were listed as 'diarrhoea-related', 'fevers', measles or 'respiratory' diseases.[94] The young and old were particularly vulnerable. Out of the 200 children on board the *Pearl* in 1773, 25 died of smallpox before they could reach New York.[95] The scant medical provisions of Parliamentary legislation were little protection long into the nineteenth century. In Liverpool, for instance, two doctors would look at migrants' tongues and try to stamp as many papers as they could without paying much more attention to the one thousand or so they would see in any one day.[96] Jessie Campbell had to watch the youngest of her five children die of sickness, even in cabin class, over 3 weeks in 1840:

My dear little lamb [she wrote] lingered in the same state all night. She expired this morning [23 October]; she resigned her breath as quietly as if she were going to sleep without the slightest struggle. What would I give to be on shore, with her dear little body, the idea of committing it to the deep distresses me very much . . . .[97]

It took a long time for government intervention to have an effect on these conditions. A sequence of 13 Passenger Acts, from 1803 to 1870, gradually tightened regulations covering the conditions on board migrant ships. The first stipulated that there had to be no more than three persons for 5 tons of space. Later laws gave further powers to the Emigration Commissioners to enforce the rules, specified the provisions that had to be carried on board and laid down basic rules for the type and amount of food that had to be provided.[98] So innovative was this legislation that some historians, for instance, Oliver MacDonagh, have taken it as a prime example of 'the intrusion of the executive corps' into British life: of the increasing influence of bureaucratic intercession, the deadweight proliferation of experts, specialist information and further government involvement that followed the initial decisions to intervene almost without reference to changing ideologies at a political level.[99]

Other historians, such as Peter Dunkley, have questioned such assumptions, arguing that the Passenger Acts were inextricably linked to changing and more positive views of migration within both the Imperial and the colonial bureaucracies. But no one, least of all Dunkley, has challenged how important they eventually became in regulating the movement of peoples. The 1827 sailing season was the first since 1803 with no passenger legislation in force, the existing Passenger Acts having lapsed: typhus quickly took hold, and Canadian officials soon persuaded London of the need for renewed regulation if emigrant numbers and morale were not to collapse.[100] Appalling overcrowding and abuses continued long into the era of the Passenger Acts. But the combination of massive holds, designed for transport of cotton and timber from the USA and Canada respectively, and tightening regulation meant that space on board became less of an issue. White emigrants 'enjoyed' a passenger-per-ton ratio eight to ten times smaller than that of their black slave counterparts.[101]

More preventive measures reinforced mortality and morbidity's downward trends. Doctors at government emigration depots were not as lax as elsewhere, as one passenger at Deptford in 1850 noted: 'one man and his wife and child [were] stopped, child having the whooping cough.'[102] Ships' surgeons insisted on constant washing, scrubbing, bathing and good ventilation under colonial governors' instruction after the 1830s. Empirical knowledge was gradually shared between ships' surgeons, and the Emigration Commissioners studied and spread their techniques.[103] Colonial authorities, for instance, the Australian Agents General, who gradually assumed responsibility for recruitment from the 1860s onwards, carried this tradition forwards to the end of the century.[104] Large families of children under seven were usually not permitted to embark on the longest southern routes from the 1840s onwards. This was a wise precaution against contagion among the young, who had not had time to build up their immune systems: when this stipulation was relaxed, as during 1852 and 1853 on the passage to Australia, mortality rates rose significantly. A very rapid fall of adult mortality on convict ships bound for Australia (which by definition did not carry young children) had set in following Governor Macquarie's 1814 insistence that doctors be carried on board. This was replicated on board free emigrant ships from the 1830s, at least while the regulations were in force.[105]

Everything became a good deal less dangerous, and vastly less boring given that voyages were much shorter, once steam had replaced sail on most long-distance routes. In 1830 emigrants from Britain were advised to bring food for 6 weeks; by 1867 the average length of the passage was a little under 2 weeks.[106] This transition took a long time. The US steamship *Savannah* travelled between Britain and the USA as early as 1819, but she was under steam for only about 85 hours of the 27-day passage. Until Isambard Kingdom Brunel built his *Great Western*, and it made its record crossing of the Atlantic in 15–and-a-half days in April 1838, no shipowner was able to even contemplate a regular steam crossing.[107] Even Brunel had to work for years, until the *Great Britain*'s maiden voyage to New York in July 1845, before he perfected the screw propeller. This proved a much more stable solution under steam than paddles at ships' sides.[108] As late as 1861, only 30 per cent of New York's immigrants were arriving on steamships. It took until the mid-1870s for sail to be completely eliminated on the Atlantic. Sail was cheap, to begin with, but even when steam technology became cheaper and more adaptable, falling migrant numbers following the Irish potato famine and due to the US Civil War constrained steamship building.[109]

The ships were huge by the time the migration business reached its climacteric. The Inman Line's *City of Paris* was the world's largest ship when she was launched in 1889, weighing in at 10,650 tons, but by 1906 the new Cunarder *Mauretania* has reached a vast 37,938 tons gross. She was 790 feet long, and 88 feet in the beam: quite a contrast to the little ships that prevailed on these routes just a hundred years previously.[110] Even the average ship crossing the Atlantic from Liverpool rose from 2500 tons to over 5000 between the 1860 and the 1890s, measuring by the later period a length of 400–500 feet, and carrying between 150 and 300 first class and 1000 to 1500 steerage passengers.[111]

Such ships were much safer than the tiny vessels that so dominated the age of sail, though they could still sink, as the example of the *Titanic* showed. When the *Atlantic* ran aground near Halifax in April 1873, she broke up straightaway. Out of 862 on board, 546 lost their lives, and an Irishman named Patrick Leahy remembered how 'a large mass of something' had passed by the survivors:

> As it passed by, a moan – it must have been a shriek, but the tempest dulled the sound – seems to surge up from the mass, which extended over fifty yards of water; it was the women. The sea swept them out of steerage, and with their children, to the number of 200 or 300, they drifted thus to eternity.[112]

In general, though, the arrival of steam made migrants' passages much safer. Analysis of official reports on voyages to Australia shows that mentions of ill health fell precipitously between the 1860s and the 1890s. Such observations were present in 60 per cent of the reports from the prior age of sail; by the 1890s, only 27 per cent of the reports tackled the subject.[113]

Conflicts on board emigrant ships

Emigrant ships were deeply divided places: as Andrew Hassam has argued, each ship 'was not just a physical space marked out by decks and bulkheads, it was a social space, which aligned the passenger with a certain social class'.[114] And, one might add, with ideas of gender and sexuality – themselves related to class – as well as ties of nationality and race. Rachel Hemming, the daughter of a vicar herself, was deeply concerned with such class distinctions. 'Some of the second-class passengers are very troublesome,' she recorded on the *Calcutta*: 'the first day one of them with his wife took their seats at the captain's table, and refused to show their tickets, alleging that they were first-class passengers.' On another voyage in 1882, second class passengers tried to colonise the exclusive poop deck, and the captain 'ordered a large spar to be placed across the centre of the poop the 1st class to have the use of the stern, the 2nd class the other department'.[115] The poop deck was the driest on board, and some cabin class passengers felt 'very sorry for the people on the main deck (2nd cabin people I mean). They cannot come out in this weather owing to the water covering the deck, indeed sometimes they have to keep their door shut for fear of the water getting inside.'[116] But the '2nd cabin people' were still shut out.

There were even problems during religious ceremonies, with some steerage passengers on the *Duncan* in 1849 insulting the cabin passengers so much that the latter would no longer come to Sunday prayers.[117] The Petworth Emigration Committee that assisted Cornelius and Elizabeth Voice's emigration in 1834 was very concerned about the social milieu on board, and of what the more 'upright' passengers would think of their fellows. As one of the organisers noted, 'some of the emigrants going out on our ship are very respectable, I am therefore the more anxious to provide handsomely for them.'[118] William Wood witnessed the traditional maritime ceremony of 'crossing the line' of the Equator marred by similar divisions in 1852: 'the Gentlemen in the first Cabin have been busy drinking healths in Commemoration of Crossing "the Line". The Third Cabin gentlemen had the pleasure of hearing of the wine but not of tasting.' Even so, he found the 'Second Cabin Passengers . . . Upstarts, troubled more with Pride than Means'.[119]

Tensions between different national groups could be as acute as those between classes, or those between men and women. Even migrants speaking their own Jersey or Guernsey dialects were objects of suspicion; one nineteenth-century migrant enumerating the Welsh, 'Scotch' and Germans around him thought that 'respectable young men are very scarce on board.'[120] This phenomenon was particularly pronounced on British ships that also carried Irish emigrants, many of whom necessarily left their native country *via* Glasgow or Liverpool. Thomas Small was a Scottish shoemaker who experienced continual friction with the 343 Irish aboard the *Donald Mackey*, bound for Australia in 1863. He thought that they were 'ignorant . . . peasants': the Irish, in return, threatened to beat him up if he continued laughing and joking through their after-dinner prayers.[121] One nineteenth-century observer dismissively outlined the tension between English speakers and the Irish, who 'gabbled in [their] . . . language a number of "Paters and Aves", as quickly as the devotees could count their beads'.[122]

Crews were often contemptuous of their usually land-loving passengers, and the sentiments were then heartily returned. William Bradford's account of the *Mayflower* voyage contains a famous passage about one of the crew, a 'proud and very profane young man', who 'would always be contemning the poor people in their sickness and cursing them daily with grievous execrations'. He was one of those to die on the passage, which Bradford took as a sign of divine displeasure.[123] John Winthrop on the *Arbella* was told by the ship's captain that 'our landmen were very nasty and slovenly, and that the gun deck where they lodged was so beastly and noisome with their victuals and beastliness as would endanger the health of the ship.'[124]

Mass emigration's organisers were constantly worried about the dangers to women's virtue and person on the voyage – a fact which says just as much about their views of women as it does about the dangers of the passage by this time. Steerage was usually mixed: a Parliamentary Committee on this was told in 1851 that it was the practice out of Liverpool to 'leave the whole deck on which emigrants were berthed undivided in any way'. The 1852 Passenger Act duly tried to ban this, though it was widely ignored.[125] Colonial authorities were particularly anxious as regarded the 'dangers' to women travelling alone, as they needed Britain's womanpower, and potential wives, to keep coming. In 1866, a Board of Immigration inquiry was convened in Australia after the ship's surgeon, a Dr Hallows, was accused of carrying on illicit relationships on board the *Bayswater*. 'The scenes exhibited on board this ship', recounted one Queensland immigration official, 'were most disgraceful, and calculated to interfere seriously with inclinations and tendencies at home which would induce a flow of immigration of respectable persons into this colony'.[126]

Women's virtue was a recurring and central concern of nineteenth-century diarists and travel writers. Travelling so closely together, and with so many single men and women packed into one small space, the social mores of the time came inevitably under strain. William Wood recorded general consternation on board the *Constance* when one 'young female ... felt a man's hand placed upon her face, and instantly screamed out'.[127] Daniel Matthews, travelling to Australia in February 1870, recounted the tale of a man pulled out from one girl's quarters:

> Two or three attempts have been made to get into the Gloucester girl's cabin. The carpenter's mate informed me of this, and I casually mentioned it to Gordon adding that I thought it was an infamous shame. He said, 'what's the use of you blabbing a thing of that kind all over the ship; I can tell you something about that girl', and then he began to relate some story about her in relation with the minister in whose family she served.[128]

The danger to Victorian virtues was widely publicised, and had to be met by emigration's propagandists.[129] Maria Rye and Jane Lewin, who founded the Female Middle Class Emigration Society in 1862, deliberately set out to counter the notion that the voyage out must be full of chaos, moral confusion and sexual danger. They wrote to the *Times* describing their governesses as 'the right set of girls' and 'women of sterling worth': the correct type of women, in short, to protect the virtue of the Society's charges.[130] One 1909 issue of the promoters' *Imperial Colonist* argued that 'there is an idea that the departure of Colonists from the Old Country is generally attended with a vast amount of confusion.' But it tried to put its readers' minds at rest:

> [This] is certainly not a true picture of colonisation as conducted by any of the well-known societies now responsible for so much of the circulation of the arterial blood of the British Empire – its men, women and children. Perhaps this is especially noticeable in the work done by the Societies for the protected Emigration of women. [131]

By this time, passenger preferences and increasing competition had forced the great passenger liner companies into making more provision for women's perceived need for more care and protection. Most carried a stewardess, at least for the cabin passengers, by the 1870s; by 1911 large transatlantic liners regularly employed 16–19 stewardesses and matrons.[132] Colonisation's promoters were probably right that women migrants faced less 'danger' on the high seas than ever before. But the higher pitch of their rhetoric says much about the increased segregation on migrant ships, driven by what was perceived to be 'proper', dignified and seemly.

One way of getting round these tensions, and of avoiding the sense of 'us' and 'them' that poisoned some voyages, were regular maritime ceremonies. Prime among these was that of 'crossing the line' of the Equator, an opportunity for subversion and ordered disruption not without its own bizarre set of rules. The crew on one such voyage in the 1870s dressed up as Neptune, his followers and family, before 'kidnapping' the captain. The crew then set up a pool on the deck before dunking the baker in. He then got to watch as other passengers and crew were thrown in, before everyone got their own back by 'drowning' Neptune and his entourage in their turn.[133] But such celebrations were, by definition, out of the ordinary; they might happen once or twice on a long voyage of more than 2 months, if the destination was Australia. And the very existence of such safety valves lays bare at least some of the tensions on board.

Conclusions: migration and 'Britishness'

The main outlines of the British diaspora should now be clear. A growing population put immense pressure on resources at home, apart from a lull that lasted from perhaps the last third of the seventeenth century through to the middle of the 1700s. Many Britons felt they had to move, and they were indeed attracted by cheap land and higher wages elsewhere – in the colonies, and later in the USA and the British Empire. The English, always more numerous, dominated this great outpouring of peoples if we take the period as a whole. But they were joined by disproportionate numbers of Scots and Ulster 'Scots-Irish', especially so in the middle of the eighteenth century, when the latter groups dominated an absolute, as well as a relative, share of migrant numbers. The development of a more profitable but less labour-intensive agriculture in the first instance, and successive recessions in the latter case, drove many from the Celtic 'fringe' onto the migrant ships. In the nineteenth century, technological innovation, better communications, faster population growth and increased knowledge meant that the tide became a flood among every national group and class in the country.

The meaning of those migrations is less clear. 'Migration' was increasingly constructed as simply a movement from one part of Greater Britain to another. As Stephen Constantine has recently noted, 'historians of the

"British world" are now again emphasizing the Britishness of this Greater Britain, even in the self-governing dominions, and the lingering appeal of empire culturally as well as politically.'[134] Emigration itself is sometimes thought of as having forged some sense of Britishness out of Scots, Welsh, Ulstermen and Englishmen, as well as out of peoples of different classes and religions: imagined as one massive flood of countless streams. This is particularly influential in the US context, given Americans' mythic sense of forging one nation out of many national groups.[135] There is an inherent temptation to read travel by sea, highway that it was, as forming one of those 'networks' that gave the British world its meaning and purpose. As one scholar has put it: 'the migration of the Scots, Irish, Welsh and English combined to make the Atlantic a linchpin of the empire for three centuries.'[136] Games have made these migrations seem more 'mundane' than before, and also speculated that 'migration ... may have had a greater impact creating a *British* identity ... [since it] eroded different cultures and brought people from remote parts of Britain into contact with each other.'[137]

This chapter has revealed, on the contrary, how fundamentally divided the migrants remained, and how multifarious their experiences remained – a point Constantine himself has made, emphasising the many directions and destinations inherent in the very word 'diaspora'. Cooped up on migrant ships for long periods of time, bored (if they were lucky) and increasingly at odds with one another, they fought over access to different parts of the ship, over religious observations and with the crew. And nineteenth-century migrants and publicists remained fundamentally uneasy about female passage in and of itself, especially that of single women. Perhaps these tensions arose because the emigrants did not actually want to be forced together; because they were usually migrating for economic reasons. Though it is important to be clear that these economic motives were usually *not* rooted in the fact that the emigrants were poor rural labourers, at least for the most part, but because of the new lives and opportunities they could divine on the new frontiers of the Americas, Australasia or – less noticeably – Asia and Africa.

There undoubtedly were ideological reasons to move away and forge a New Britain of wider horizons: a sense of religious salvation, perhaps, in the early seventeenth century, or of Imperial opportunity and the operation of a social 'safety valve' by the late nineteenth century. But to concur with David Cressy's judgement on New England's Puritans, those narratives militate against a proper understanding of the chaos and contingency that this diaspora represented, changes that were 'untidy, fractured and complex rather than rational, purposeful and coherent'.[138] Emigrants confronted with Liverpool's dockside in the nineteenth century, where William Wood remembered that 'anxiously did we wait, hour after hour', would have agreed.[139]

Timeline of events

1500–50	Scottish migrations to Germany, Poland and Scandinavia
1600–50	Further large Scottish migrations to Poland and Scandinavia
1607	English settlement at Jamestown
1620	*Mayflower* sails for New England with 102 colonists on board
1630	The 'Winthrop fleet' brings 11 English ships to Salem, Massachusetts
1630s	'Busy years' of Puritan migration to New England
1718	Transportation Act regulates transatlantic convict trade
1756–63	Seven Years' War reduces transatlantic migration
1763–75	Large-scale Scottish and Ulster Protestant emigrations to North America
1771–72	'Black winter' in Scotland causes rural hardship
1772	Transatlantic trade in convicts so profitable that state bounty removed
1773–75	Government survey of migrant numbers and type
1776–83	American Revolutionary War again lowers migrant numbers
1788	'First Fleet' arrives in Botany Bay in Australia
1803	First of 13 British Passenger Act regulates conditions on ships
1819	Parliament agrees assistance scheme for migrants to South Africa
1830s	Liverpool begins to dominate trade in outwards migration
1830	New South Wales begins to offer assisted migration
1834	Cornelius and Elizabeth Voice sail to Canada on the *British Tar*
1836	South Australia proclaimed with a 'bounty' system for immigrants
1837	Agent General for Emigration appointed
1838	*Great Western* makes record crossing of the Atlantic in 15-and-a-half days
1840	Colonial Land and Emigration Commission created
1845	SS *Great Britain*'s maiden voyage to New York

1846–48	Irish potato famine accelerates mass migration from that country
1848	New South Wales remittance scheme begins
1850–1900	Great flood of migration out of Great Britain and Ireland of 9 million people
1851–53	First Australian gold rush
1852	William Wood sails to Australia on the *Constance*
1853	Final women convicts arrive in Australia on board the *Duchess of Northumberland*
1868	End of transportation to Australia
1870	Last of the 13 British Passenger Acts regulating conditions on migrant ships
1880s	Peak of migration out of Great Britain at 818,000 in one decade
1886	New South Wales remittance scheme discontinued
1906	Cunarder *Mauretania* launched

6

Warriors

The Royal Navy was the most obvious, and the most important, symbol and tool of British maritime power. New technologies, skilful crewmen and high morale granted Britain a long period of being the most important naval power in the world. From around the time of the Battle of Quiberon Bay in 1759, to the rise of German naval power in the late nineteenth and early twentieth centuries, Britain's navy unquestionably 'ruled the waves'. The period from 1815 to the 1890s is even known as the *pax Britannica* – the 'British peace' – and the power and prestige of the Royal Navy rose to its height in this period. The 'two power standard' formally adopted towards the end of that period meant that, not only could British ships defeat the next most powerful fleet, but the two largest rival navies in the world in alliance. But what explains this dominance, and this insistence on a 'blue water' strategy that could project force anywhere in the world? This chapter considers the rise of English and then British naval power to the point where it became the most important strategic force in the world. It traces the rise of naval dominance to the mid-seventeenth century, a time of ideological and economic disputation with the Dutch Republic that ended in three wars and that helped put England on the road to maritime supremacy. It then considers the long wars with France that stretched from the late seventeenth to the early nineteenth centuries, making clear that British statesmen could never entirely dispense with European allies and entanglements. On the one occasion when this was attempted, in the War of American Independence, it ended in disaster. The chapter then goes on to consider four areas in which the Royal Navy helped to shape modern Britain: the economic demands of the fleet; popular patriotism; naval service and the press gang; and naval discipline and its reform. The fleet was an absolutely central component of British history in each respect. The economic sphere will be considered first. The Royal Dockyards helped to spark the Industrial Revolution of the eighteenth century; paying for this vast maritime effort played a key role in constructing Britain's unique system of debt financing. The social implications of the Royal Navy's constant presence in national life are then considered. The fleet's reform became a focus and exemplar of what it meant to be 'British', with a unique belief in freedom and the seaborne 'band of brothers' that was explained at the time as part of Britons' island identity. But it also demonstrated the shared bonds – for critics, the tyrannical demands – of nationmaking and the relentless warfare that nurtured and protected it. Only in the late nineteenth century did policymakers and the public perceive Germany as true threat to Britain's naval dominance, in truth more imagined than real: Britain then stood on the brink of long naval wars that would bring the country's economic and diplomatic supremacy to an end.

The rise of English and British naval power

The Tudor monarchs initiated the first English build-up of naval power in the sixteenth century, though slowly, and in a piecemeal manner: only Henry VIII can be said to have been a real enthusiast. The invention of the porthole made it possible for ships to carry heavy guns at sea, and allowed Henry VIII to dream of outstripping the sea power of his continental rivals. He had inherited only five fighting ships from his parsimonious father.[1] But the younger Henry's reign saw Royal ships play an ever-larger role in the fleet, as well as the more consistent enforcement of rules as to the upkeep and availability of merchant ships to act as wartime auxiliaries and transports.[2] Elizabeth I's resistance in the face of Spanish sea power later created a powerful myth that was to motivate Englishmen and Britons for centuries to come. The defeat of the Spanish Armada in 1588, and the feats of Drake, Raleigh and Grenville, fixed 'Protestant liberty', seamanship and above all private, cheap warfare in the public mind as the real navalist promise.[3] This tradition was not, however, carried over into the early seventeenth century. The early Stuarts at first concentrated on peaceful trading and a commercial policy that seems to have lasted up until the Civil War, so much so that more suspicious Englishmen grew frustrated at the lack of a more aggressive policy towards Spain and the Dutch.[4] James I's forces concentrated their efforts on diplomatic interventions and the suppression of piracy in the Narrow Seas.[5] Charles I was forced to concentrate his efforts on piracy in the 1630s, following a series of disastrous military adventures.[6]

It was the English Republic that was to re-organise and re-equip the navy so that it became one of Europe's most formidable: within just a couple of years of the regicide in 1649, 20 ships were added to the fleet by building, and 25 more by capture. Between that year and the Restoration of 1660, £7.52 million was spent on the navy, an average of nearly £684,000 a year. In total 218 ships were added to the fleet, of which 110 were prizes. Adding in losses and sales, the Commonwealth's navy amounted to 154 ships by 1660. Charles I had been able to contribute only 30 of the 90 'navy' ships that sailed against the Ile de Rhé off La Rochelle in 1627: the rest were armed merchantmen.[7] There were several reasons for this vast expansion of state power. There was the ideological rivalry with the Dutch, in whose country many royalists had taken refuge; the trade rivalry between the two countries also mounted in these years, meaning that the restored Stuarts found plenty of reasons to fight the Netherlands long after the English Republic had passed into memory.[8] The three naval wars with the Dutch, fought in 1652–54, 1665–67 and 1672–74, helped to provide the first real proof of England's growing naval power. Huge battles of concentrated force were fought between very large fleets, of warships and converted merchantmen alike, the numbers involved in each engagements numbering up to 150 ships.[9]

By no means did English forces win a series of unchallenged victories. The First Dutch War was marred by serious reverses in the Mediterranean. In 1667, during the second war with the Netherlands, the Dutch sailed up the Medway and towed away the English flagship, the *Royal Charles*.[10] The third war against the Dutch Republic, fought in alliance with the French, saw the new and at first sight strange allies fumbling their strategic advantage and failing to properly co-ordinate their operations at Solebay (1672) and the Texel (1673). Allied Anglo-French attempts to land troops in the Republic during the latter battle were finally thwarted.[11] Charles II, nothing if not practical, opted to abandon his allies and make a separate peace.[12] But overall, the Rump Parliament's Preamble to its Articles of War against the Dutch in 1652 was a symbol of a new and more consistent maritime policy: 'it is upon the navy under the Providence of God that the safety, honour and welfare of this realm do chiefly attend.'[13] The wars with the Dutch were only broken off with reluctance. The revelation that the heir to the throne, the Duke of York, was a Catholic terrified English Protestants who were already in open opposition to war against their fellow religionists in the Netherlands; allied to French inertia at the Texel, this domestic crisis tipped the balance against war in 1673–74.

The Commonwealth and Protectorate bequeathed a powerful force to the restored monarchy of 1660. The long struggle with the monarchy, and then the Lord Protector's 'western design' or attack on Spanish interests in the Caribbean during 1654 and 1655, ensured that it was re-equipped and re-organised.[14] The fleet consisted of about 120 capital ships, of which four were first rates of between 80 and 100 guns, there was one second-rater, 15 were third rates of between 54 and 64 guns and 45 were fourth rates of about 34–54 guns.[15] They were immediately to be tested in the new Protestant monarch's Nine Years' War with the 'universal monarchy' of Louis XIV's France (1688–97). This conflict, too, was marked by some disappointments, particularly the battle off Beachy Head on 29 June 1690. England's Dutch allies blundered into the main body of the French fleet, warnings as to the size of which the Government back in London had chosen to ignore. Having left the French vanguard unchecked, the allies were soon forced to retreat in some disorder.[16] A British merchant fleet, left on its own once off the coast of Spain, was seized by the French Brest fleet in 1693: ninety-two vessels, carrying cargoes for Smyrna in Turkey worth over £1 million, were destroyed or seized. Still, the French were unable to press their advantage, fought to a draw both off Brest and in the Mediterranean. It was a pattern that would become familiar in the decades to come.[17]

War on land or war at sea?

Britain (as she stood after the Act of Union of 1707) could not win any general war with a European power without allies on land, and without at least some continental commitment. As David French has noted, the country did not emerge as Europe's leading imperial power in the mid-eighteenth century 'by disengaging from the European alliance system ... on the contrary, membership of a series of European alliances was fundamental to her ability to expand her extra-European interests'.[18] The Duke of Newcastle made just this point in 1749 when he said that 'France will outdo us at sea, when they have nothing to fear by land': if France ever felt completely comfortable on land, his reasoning went, she would probably be able to outbuild the British at sea.[19]

Naval forces had played a key role in defending Britain against French invasion during the Nine Years' War, especially off Barfleur and La Hougue in May 1692. French plans contained little room for manoeuvre if the tactical situation – assuming that their ships could get to sea and attack their enemies before the latter had a chance to concentrate. Rather than retreat once his Anglo-Dutch enemies had in fact joined up in the Channel, the French decided to fight a combined force that was numerically far superior to their own. Twelve French warships were destroyed by fireships, and three ran aground, at the climax of the action.[20] British ships furthermore allowed anti-French forces to land in Spain in 1705, during the War of the Spanish

Succession (1702–13), and the navy's capture of Minorca allowed the allies to blockade the French naval base of Toulon from 1708. But such victories could not bleed France dry: only the Duke of Marlborough's great land campaigns in Flanders, culminating in victories at Blenheim, Ramillies and Oudenarde, could do that.[21] The first two Hanoverian monarchs, George I and George II, also understood the necessity of a continental strategy, worried about protecting their rights in Hanover and finding a balance of power that would constrain France and preserve the 'liberties of Europe'. Hence the decision to work with the French, the long period of Anglo-French *détente* between 1716 and 1731 and Britain's subsequent alignment with Prussia in the 1750s.[22]

It was George III's accession in 1760, and especially the hubris of imperial victory in the Seven Years' War with France in 1763, that marked the real break with the past as regarded continental strategy. The navy's victory at Quiberon Bay off the coast of Brittany in November 1759 was one of the navy's greatest, Admiral Edward Hawke destroying six and taking one of the 21 French ships that he faced. French plans to invade Britain were wrecked, and the Royal Navy was free to campaign against French and Spanish colonies almost at will.[23] The importance of maintaining at least some military capacity on land was to some extent forgotten.[24] But it was only with the Elder Pitt, and the colonial strategy he espoused during the Seven Years' War of 1756–63 – a policy that helps explain his ejection from office in 1761 – that a thoroughgoing 'Blue Water' ideology really gained a hold on the official or public imagination. Its essentials were easy to grasp. The eighteenth-century naval theorist Thomas Lediard phrased it thus in this *Naval History of England*: 'our trade is the Mother and Nurse of our Seamen; Our Seamen the Life of our Fleet; And our Fleet the Security and Protection of our Trade ... both together are the WEALTH, STRENGTH and GLORY of GREAT BRITAIN'.[25]

Elizabethan and Cromwellian strategists had been fully aware of the importance of naval warfare; but few, then or later in the eighteenth century, ever espoused seaborne war *in place of* war on land. 'Patriot' oppositions, for instance, the High Tories in 1704, might use navalist language with which to berate 'corrupt' ministries. The Tories saw the capture of Gibraltar and Malaga as a good counterpoint to the hard-won triumph of the Whig hero Marlborough. They advocated 'blue water' strategies as an alternative to the bloody and prolonged land war in Flanders, arguing for an attack on the Mediterranean in 1707–08 and then Canada in 1711.[26] But Britain's colonial war against Spain in 1739–41, undertaken with great hopes of seizing land and treasure from the Spaniards, ended in humiliating failures at Cartagena, Cuba and Panama when British forces arrived late and were decimated by yellow fever. This undermined British public opinion's confidence in the navy for some time, and helped to bring about Robert Walpole's resignation as Prime Minister a year later. One writer in 1747 was moved to bemoan that 'there was a time when our Superiority at Sea was uncontestable . . . [but] we have but the Shadow of what we had forty Years ago.'[27] During this British naval recessional the Duc de Choiseul, France's most ambitious navalist minister of the era and the Elder Pitt's chief rival in this respect, even began to think that France might rival Britain in colonial and naval ambition: 'upon the navy depend the colonies, upon the colonies commerce, upon commerce the capacity of a state to maintain numerous armies . . . and to make possible the most glorious and most useful enterprises.'[28]

Historians have more recently emphasised sound reasons for scepticism as to the efficacy of purely 'navalist' policies. Admiral Lord Nelson's three greatest victories left the British not totally victorious, but with yet another series of dilemmas. Nelson destroyed the French fleet at Aboukir Bay off Egypt in 1798; attacked Copenhagen and took the Danish fleet out of commission in 1801; and most famously of all, cut the French line at Trafalgar and prevented the union of the French and Spanish fleets in 1805.[29] But those three victories still left the problems, respectively, of what to do about the French army in Egypt; how to undermine or destroy the Second League of Armed Neutrality; and most of all, how to challenge Napoleon on land – where he still reigned supreme – after Trafalgar. In none of these cases had the application of sea power ended the French threat.[30] Immediately after Trafalgar, on 2 December 1805, Napoleon's Grand Army routed the Russians and Austrians at Austerlitz. The Younger Pitt's Third Coalition had failed, even after Nelson's heroics, and the Prime Minister despaired. As he said: 'roll up that map [of Europe]; it will not be wanted these ten years.'[31]

One key reason for Britain's humiliating admission of defeat in 1783, at the close of the War of American Independence (1776–83), had been precisely this lack of a European partner. Britain's hasty 1763 peace with France had alienated Prussia, the island kingdom's ally during the Seven Years' War. Ministers believed that they had simply been overmatched. Lord Sandwich, at the Admiralty, claimed that 'England till this time was never engaged in a sea war with the House of Bourbon thoroughly united, their naval force unbroken . . . we have no one friend or ally to assist us.'[32] But it is worth pointing out that the anti-British alliance of American colonists with French, Spanish and (eventually) Dutch forces did not in itself guarantee Britain's defeat, for she in fact still enjoyed global naval superiority over her enemies. General Cornwallis' decision to make a stand at Yorktown in Virginia was supposed to strengthen the British position in North America by taking advantage of British naval strength and to keep open the lines of communication with New York and London. It was only Admiral Sir

Thomas Graves' failure to bring the French decisively to battle in the mouth of the Chesapeake during early September 1781 that doomed the British at Yorktown to surrender in October of that year. There was little inevitable about that defeat, at least from a naval standpoint.[33]

The real problem was with the type of ships the Admiralty could deploy, and where the Admiralty had chosen to station them, especially in the first months and years of the war. Ministers (including the Ban of Sandwich) thought during 1775 and 1776 that they could deal the revolt a swift knock-out blow, and defeat the colonists before any other power could enter the fray. This outlook not only delayed any new programme of capital ships, but the entry into service of cruisers and frigates that might have allowed the effective blockading of North America in a longer war.[34] The navy had inevitably been much diminished in the years of peace that had followed 1763: only 30 ships were available in the North American theatre at the outbreak of the colonial revolution, half of which were used to blockade the coast. As the pace of land operations quickened during 1776 and 1777, as few as 20 ships had to patrol the entire North American seaboard.[35] The temptation was to fight the Seven Years' War all over again, and focus Britain's naval efforts on blockading Europe and protecting the home islands while the army dealt with North America.[36] This would also avoid the need to stop or seize neutral ships, and perhaps fend off the day on which Europeans would intervene on the side of the colonists.[37]

All this may have been unavoidable given the risks of European defeat, especially after France's entry into the war in 1778, but for 2 years it permitted arms to flow easily to the Americans, and allowed the rebels to start building up an effective privateering effort. Perhaps 300 vessels fought privately in the American cause throughout the war alongside 57 'regular' ships. The majority of that latter fleet was loaned by the French, bought abroad, or seized from the British, and it was vital in protecting American commerce and threatening British supply lines. But almost nothing of this force existed in the first 2 years of the conflict. 'General Washington's navy' amounted to just seven ships in 1775, all operating out of Boston.[38] The British lacked neither warlike capacity, nor fighting ability, but rather a sounder strategic sense of priorities: to choke off supplies to the Americans and fight their privateers in 1776–77, and to be ready for a general war at sea, rather than a blockade campaign, should continental Europeans enter the war.[39] There were simply not enough of the smaller cruising ships that would have been required to protect Britain's Atlantic and global trade avenues, fight American and French privateers and blockade American and European ports. But that was not a *necessary* concomitant of fighting three other world powers at once; it was due to the strategic decisions made in the run up to, and the early years of, the war.[40]

Very few of Britain's far-flung operations during the Revolutionary Wars could have been mounted without the Royal Navy – a lesson decision-makers had learned from both the successes and failures of such operations during the Seven Years' War and the American War of Independence.[41] The navy supplied marines to supplement land expeditionary forces, for instance, during the attack on Fort Royal on Martinique in 1794. They provided haulage for the troops, and supplemented heavy lift capabilities even on land, for instance, during the Egyptian campaign of 1801.[42] Despite the failure of early amphibious expeditions against the French, for instance at Toulon in 1793, larger operations owed a great deal to the navy. The Peninsular Campaign in Spain could not have been mounted without the navy to land the army at Lisbon, or directly to resupply the Duke of Wellington's forces in a country where the roads were terrible or non-existent.[43] As the General himself said, 'our maritime superiority gives me the power of maintaining my army while the enemy are unable to do so.'[44]

So there were limits to what naval power could do. It could not obviate the need for a continental ally; it could not achieve decisive victory on land; and without enormous efforts, even colonial victories were uncertain, as the lesson of 1739–41 demonstrated. And yet key lines of strategic interest and interpretation remained constant throughout the seventeenth, eighteenth and nineteenth centuries. The freedom of the narrow seas, home defence, the security of trade and the ability to wage amphibious warfare were all vital to Britain's interests: the disaster at Smyrna in 1693, and the French privateering war against merchantmen, was enough to make the point without further argument.[45] Losses to American Revolutionary privateers, and the convoys that had much success in protecting them from 1776 onwards, helped to reinforce the lesson.[46] This remained the case whether policymakers were 'blue water' advocates like Pitt, or continental thinkers like Newcastle: they differed over the means to their ends, not the point of warfare itself.

The scale and scope of the naval effort

England's and then Britain's naval power could not be maintained without an extraordinary measure of warlike capacity at home. The royal dockyards were a key link in this chain, and they became more so as the demands of total warfare increased. When, as Lord Treasurer, the Marquis of Winchester came to reform naval dockyards and victualling in the 1550s, it cost the Exchequer £157,638 over 2 years: admittedly this was during wartime, but that amounted to five and a half times the ordinary budget. Part of the reason Charles I resorted to unpopular Ship Money impositions in the 1630s was the huge amounts – up to £412,000 per annum – that the French were spending on their navy. He eventually raised £800,000, though not all of it was spent on ships.[47] The King felt he could not rely on armed merchantmen, or accept the damage to trade that their large-scale use in war might involve.[48]

The scale of this military archipelago was little affected by political changes in London. The Royal Dockyards employed only just over 1000 workmen when William III came to the throne in 1688. By the early years of George I's reign, they engaged nearly 7000 men, of whom somewhat under 50 per cent were working at Portsmouth and Plymouth. By 1730, 10,000 men were employed in the docks, and by the end of the Napoleonic Wars over 17,000 men worked in them.[49] Many of these men were specialists, who would take their skills with them into the wider economy when they left the state's employ. The building of a first-rate ship might absorb 120 shipwrights, six caulkers, seven sawyers and ten labourers during its construction. Glaziers, plasterers and ironmongers would also be needed.[50] This insatiable demand for labour persisted even though government shipyards were hardly able on their own to keep up with demand, and were only one part of the entire effort alongside private yards.[51] Ships had not only to be built, but constantly maintained and refitted, especially in the second half of the seventeenth century when the wars with the Netherlands and France meant that older ships could not simply be allowed to rot.[52] At the peak of the Revolutionary and Napoleonic wars, the dockyards were required to keep in commission at sea 113 ships of the line and 596 smaller vessels; blockade duty, requiring ships to be at sea for 12 months at a time and to be re-equipped on a rotational basis, added to the strain.[53]

Administrative reforms were constantly necessary to manage this huge martial organisation. Roger Morris has recently tried to reinstate some of the force behind what A.V. Dicey once termed the 'revolution in nineteenth-century government', attributing it not to the utilitarian social reformer Jeremy Bentham, but to his brother Samuel. Samuel Bentham was appointed to the new post of Inspector General of Naval Works in 1796, and proceeded to implement a recognisably 'Benthamite' plan for the docks' total reform.[54] The load of naval stores alone was enormous, and very expensive. By 1804 – a crisis year for naval supply – a single load of American timber, made up of 50 cubic feet of great oaks that might form only one part of a ship's hull, cost more than £4. Timber suitable for more specialist parts of the ship, whether they were stern-posts or rudder-pieces, could cost more than £12 per piece. Masts might cost over £100.[55] They did not have to come as single trunks, despite the emphasis of early twentieth-century historians on the importance of North American forests in this respect. Shipwrights were experienced in the use of smaller lengths, held together with iron and rope. But these were still expensive, and had to be shipped in from Norway or the Baltic.[56] Huge numbers of these timbers were used while the fleet was still mainly built of wood. In 1692 the Royal Dockyards ordered 19 loads of ash, 705 of fir, 48 of beech, 1129 of elm and 6789 of oak.[57]

This huge naval endeavour cost a great deal, for it was a highly complex and technological effort. The amount of money that went into building a navy ship was much higher than the cash stocks invested in the new industries of the 'industrial revolution'. Ambrose Crowley's iron works cost £12,000 in fixed capital during the late seventeenth century; naval projects were huge by comparison, costing between £33,000 and £39,000 for a first-rater, and £24,000 and £27,000 to build a second-rater.[58] Timber contractors might make fortunes by supplying the dockyards. When a large programme of war construction was approved by Parliament in 1691, the Navy Board reckoned it needed 2586 masts. Four men – John Taylor, Joseph Martin, Francis Riggs and Sir Peter Rich – provided almost all of them, making huge profits in the process.[59] Though the army was just as expensive as the navy in the eighteenth century, naval spending for every fighting man was double that of a soldier in the army.[60]

A warlike and a patriotic people

Naval victories helped to create, and then to reinforce, a popular patriotism based around maritime power. There was widespread rejoicing when news arrived of Admiral Vernon's success against the Spanish at Porto Bello in March 1740. Celebrations of the victory, and the Admiral's birthday, were recorded in 54 towns in 25 counties across England and Scotland. In Stratford, Essex, an effigy of the Spanish admiral Don Blass was burned, as the onlookers gathered around and sang 'Britons strike home'.[61] Admiral Rodney's victory in the Battle of the Saintes off Dominica in April 1782 not only thwarted a Franco-Spanish invasion of Jamaica, but gave patriotic opinion at home something to celebrate at the tail end of a miserable war. When news of the victory reached London on 18 May 1782, 'there was a general illumination' in the capital; soon after, in York, 'ye City was generally illuminated, with bonfires, & fireworks'. Stamford, Reading, Abingdon, Newnham, Kirkaldy and many other towns and cities reported similar celebrations.[62] Naval dramas dominated the stage during the middle years of the Napoleonic Wars; the Sadler's Wells spectaculars of the time ended with great spectacles of model ships that played to huge audiences.[63]

This is not to say that there was no undertow of criticism, still less that there were no doubts at all as to the point or morality of military force. As Timothy Jenks has recently shown, even Nelson's pain and wounds could be used in a satirical or subversive manner: they seemed, for instance, manly and uncomplicated compared to the 'schemes' and 'corruption' of the Ministers in London. The Admiral's dissolute behaviour at Naples in the 1790s and his notorious vanity were moreover constant matters for bemused or hostile remark back at home.[64] Even so, there was a sense that British 'nationhood' was actually bolstered, even characterised, by such criticisms. This general sense of naval superiority gave the Royal Navy a sense of its own high worth, even inevitable victory – and permitted the toleration of a measure of dissent. Numerous examples may be given of this high morale. While chasing the 185-feet French battleship *Foudroyant* into Cartagena harbour in February 1756, the much smaller *Monmouth*, at 151-feet long, had to anchor for the night. Captain Arthur Gardiner's words to his men seem to have been accepted with cheers: 'she looks to be above our match; but Englishmen are not to mind that, nor will I quit her while this ship can swim.' The next day the *Foudroyant* was indeed forced to surrender, though Gardiner was killed in the action.[65]

Women were as involved in these pervasive discourses of martial pride as they were to be in the campaigns for the abolition of the slave trade: jewellery and memorabilia were once again two accepted and 'feminine' sites of that celebration. The ladies in the royal party who visited Admiral Howe's flagship with King George III in June 1794 wore small gold anchors on chains round their necks. It became fashionable a little later for upper class women to wear gold anchors round their necks with the date of the Battle of the Nile engraved on them, and lockets would often bear Nelson's name or likeness.[66] Women of more humble origins had to choose different paths to fight for Britain's naval mastery. Hannah Snell, a woman marine who served the Royal Navy in disguise between 1745 and 1750, was an extremely popular celebrity on her return partly due to her patriotic songs. A typical verse sung by her at the New Wells Theatre in Goodman's Fields will suffice to show the patriotic nature of the material. She sang of being in 'the midst of blood and slaughter, / bravely fighting for my king, / Facing death from every quarter, fame and conquest home to bring'.[67]

Snell was not alone as a women serving at sea, and in fact her celebrity rather obscured other examples. In 1759 Mary Lacy, a service-girl from Wickham in Kent, ran away from home, and managed to get into naval service on board HMS *Sandwich* at Chatam under the name of William Chandler. 'Not having before seen any larger vessels than the hoys at Sandwich haven', she remembered, 'I could not conceive it was possible for so great a ship to live at sea.'[68] She eventually became a qualified shipwright in 1770, though by this time her rheumatism was making the work ever more difficult. She applied for, and won, a naval pension in 1772: it seems as if she retired from navy service with a Mr Slade, and worked profitably as a house-builder in Deptford for the next decade. She may have died in 1795, for a Mary Slade was buried at St Nicholas, Deptford, on 6 February 1795.[69]

What these men and women were celebrating and fighting for was not only victory, but its means and techniques. Few eighteenth-century officers thought themselves well-informed about the arts or literature, but they usually thought of themselves – and were thought of – as encouraging gunnery as a modern, technical and expert art.[70] Britain's enormous overseas trade simply gave her more seamen for recruitment than the French could drawn on, though recruitment problems persisted; and the Royal Navy's ships were constantly at sea, as opposed to French fleets that were more often kept in harbour as the eighteenth century wore on. They were thus more skilled, and more experienced, than their rivals.[71] It was precisely their great accuracy that allowed them to divert from the line of battle techniques that had dominated naval warfare since the mid-seventeenth century. Traditionally dated to the Battle of the Gabbard against the Dutch in June 1653, when the English sailed in single line ahead and inflicted great damage with their broadsides, this tactic allowed great ships of the line to employ all their armaments at once. But as the eighteenth century wore on, the British increasingly aimed to get close and fight at close range.[72]

Their accuracy and confidence had both to be higher than the enemy's if they were to make a success of this technique. The French, firing at long range and trying to take down sails and masts, did not have the same confidence in their fighting and firing ability at close quarters.[73] Admiral Collingwood, one of Nelson's most trusted subalterns, was said to have trained the crew of the *Excellent* to such a pitch that they could fire an extraordinary three broadsides in 3-and-a-half minutes during the 1790s.[74] Gunnery skills were once again emphasised in the Victorian navy. During the 1830s a permanent gunnery school was established, and each ship was instructed to employ a set number of gunners and gunners' mates.[75]

This twin inheritance of confidence and skill allowed the British to undertake truly remarkable feats of arms. British tactics at the Saintes are often thought to highlight the transition to a new type of naval warfare. There Rodney took advantage of a slow and straggling French line, and the chaos of battle, to cut through the middle of their formation. Five more Royal Navy ships followed Rodney's *Formidable* through the breach, causing immense damage to the French ships as they passed through. Rodney had been lucky, as well as desperate to bring the battle to a conclusion; but he had shown that smashing into the enemy line might pay huge dividends.[76] Lord Howe had used similar tactics in 1794, on a more modest scale, at the Battle of the 'Glorious First of June' fought against the French in mid-Atlantic.[77] At the Battle of Cape St Vincent in 1797, the Spanish ships involved bore nearly twice as many guns as the largest of the British ships. Some of the Spanish ships were huge, with the vast four-decker flagship *Santissima Trinidada* mounting 130 guns. But it was here that Nelson first famously 'cut the line'. It was a much more unorthodox manoeuvre than Rodney's, as the young rear-admiral detached his ship from the British formation and attacked the Spanish line head-on and alone.[78] Nelson ran into the Spanish ships in only the relatively small 74-gun two-decker *Captain*. He then took on the huge *Santissima Trinidada* and her two consorts, 112-gun three-deckers, as well as an 80-gun two-decker. It would have been suicide had his men not been so skilful and so confident, and Nelson in any case only just escaped with his ship and his life.[79]

Discipline, punishment and reform

There is absolutely no doubt that maritime service could be extremely harsh, and unforgiving discipline was often meted out to the men. The poet and writer John Masefield, who in addition to being appointed Poet Laureate in 1930 had served as a merchant seaman, popularised this view in his 1905 book *Sea Life in Nelson's Day*. Corporal punishment usually amounted to flogging with a cat o' nine tails, a short stick on the end of which hung nine knotted cords: Masefield called this 'the most cruel and ineffectual punishment ever inflicted'.[80] There remains a good deal to be said for Masefield's appalled impressionism, given the frequency and the apparent pettiness of many whippings: even Captain Cook, thought of in his own time and since as a model of restraint and reform, had recourse to flogging for the men's simple refusal to drink spruce beer for their own health.[81]

Floggings might indeed be brutal. There was *supposed* to be a limit of twelve to the number of lashes that might be administered. In practice, a crew member guilty of several crimes committed at the same time might receive several rounds of twelve in succession.[82] A dozen lashes might well not break the skin of the offender, and the average seaman took pride at not crying out during that 'regulation' punishment. But the binding of his hands and feet and the impassive looks on the faces of the officers as they watched the punishment being carried out were symbolic of the man's helplessness. The men 'below decks' often thought this worse than the physical pain inflicted.[83] It was this destruction of his British 'liberty' that a seaman might complain of. William Richardson, whose *Mariner of England* was an account of his service in the late eighteenth-century Royal Navy, made this as clear as he could:

> People may talk of negro slavery and the whip, but let them look nearer home, and see a poor sailor arrived from a long voyage ... when a press gang seizes him like a felon ... if he complains he is likely to be seized up and flogged with a cat, much more severe than the negro driver's whip, and if he deserts he is flogged round the fleet nearly to death. Surely they had better shoot a man at once: it would be greater lenity![84]

During Richardson's time, men might even be 'flogged through the fleet' for the most serious crimes. Though very unusual, the cruelty makes some of Masefield's points for him. Seamen receiving this sentence would be placed in a whaleboat and hauled from ship to ship: each time they were brought on board a new vessel, they would be whipped again. This, inevitably, usually ended in the death of the man involved.[85] Overall, as Isaac Land has recently reminded us, 'long-standing debates' about the severity, meaning and frequency of punishment should not 'distract us from the simple fact that common seamen were subjected to beatings, while officers were not'.[86]

It was the Rump Parliament which passed the first 'Laws and Ordinances Martial' for conduct on board ship in April 1649, following these up with another Act in 1652. Before this the Laws of Oléron, promulgated by Richard I in the C12th, or those 'normal' laws enforced by the High Court of Admiralty, had sufficed.[87] The 1649 regulations stipulated the death penalty in 7 of the 20 clauses they contained, and the political emergency of these years made these rules harsher than they might otherwise have been. The need to defend Parliament from counter-insurgency was, indeed, one of the main reasons for the legal innovation. Article 4, for instance, dealt with attempts to stir up revolt, and article 12 with carrying away a warship from the service of the state. [88] From 1663 onwards, the Duke of York's 'General Instructions . . . to Commanders', a set of 40 regulations supplemented by additional rules for onboard discipline, were in force.[89] These were but little changed until the inception of the new *Articles of War* in 1749, which even then regularised and carried over many of the 1649 and 1663 regulations. Homicide, robbery, desertion and sedition were to be particularly severely treated, though even here some discretion was left to commanders on active operations. Unlike in an onshore court, for instance, the death penalty was not compulsory for robbery.[90]

Naval punishments were, moreover, not always what they might appear to the modern eye. Their ferocity and their long history did not mean that brutal force and power governed all the relationships that were found on board a fighting ship: the word 'discipline' itself, for instance, was rarely used.[91] A sailor might get a dozen lashes for what would be defined in the twentieth century as a petty crime, but on land, these same offences would often have been punished by life in prison or transportation.[92] It was also better to be beaten immediately than wait for what might be a capital judgement before the courts back home. Men punished for deserting from William Bligh's *Bounty* in 1788 rather made this point when they took 'this earliest opportunity of returning our thanks for your [Bligh's] goodness in delivering us from a trial by Court-Martial'.[93] The severity of punishments handed out in the navy also showed some tendency to decline, irregularly but constantly, over time. Between the Seven Years' War and the American Revolutionary

War, the number of capital convictions, convictions involving the lash as a punishment and the lashes actually handed out per sentence all fell.[94]

There were several reasons for this, and all of them were rooted in the nature of service at sea. Many of the men had been press-ganged, but many volunteers were also taken on, even though Admirals and Captains often complained about their quality. This was in order to stop ships relying on pressed men who might desert at the first available opportunity.[95] The Parliamentary Opposition, too, often questioned pressing during the American War of Independence – though it was more often resisted at a plebeian rather than an elite level. The right to press seafarers was thought to be an integral part of the Royal Prerogative, though its legal basis always remained rather dubious. Even seamen themselves were in fact more likely to quibble over the details and conduct of impressments, rather than the principles on which they were based. 'Turnover', during which men would be seized from ships before they could even set foot on land, was a particularly unpopular practice.[96]

The demands of the navy after 1815, for a smaller but more professional and more disciplined force, meant that the press gang was never employed again – though it would undoubtedly have been used in the event of a general war with France.[97] Though the idea is still mentioned in Admiralty papers as late as 1882, the most ardent advocates of national defence had long turned their mind to the creation of a voluntary reserve. However, though there was a rather disappointing experiment with a naval militia in the form of the Royal Naval Coast Volunteers between 1853 and 1873, the creation of a modern and more professional Royal Fleet Reserve would have to wait until 1900. Moreover, the reservists did not start to take part in regular fleet manoeuvres until 1906.[98]

Promotion, whether from the ranks or that of a young 'gentlemen', depended on ties of honour and regard, rather than brute force. This was the case for officers as well as men, and was a powerful incentive to play by widely accepted rules. Only in the early nineteenth century did the Admiralty, rather than individual captains who might feel the pressure of local or family ties particularly acutely, begin choosing the majority of those taken onto ships as recruits.[99] Sea officers usually had to secure certificates of good conduct from captains, dockyard officials or flag officers if they were to progress further up the chain of command. Though this often led to faction, and usually reinforced the sense of social superiority and inferiority that pervaded the fleet, it also meant that the officer corps possessed a powerful sense of unity and mutual respect. They were, moreover, a tight-knit group: Admiral Sir Thomas Allin, controller of the navy in the late seventeenth century, was followed into the service by his three Ashby nephews, an Ashby great-nephew, an Utber brother-in-law, two Utber nephews and several more distant relatives from the Mighells and Leake families.[100] 'Maritime' counties and cities were naturally overrepresented: Devon (and particularly Plymouth) men were particularly noticeable among both officers and men in the wars of 1792–1815.[101] Officers with a particularly sense of local or regional connection, for instance, the Cornishman Admiral Boscawen, might draw on local connections to recruit unskilled labourers for their ships. Many of Boscawen's men were Cornish, and the sense of shared endeavour was notable when he was killed in action in 1780: one of his lieutenants wrote to Sandwich that 'the ship's company have lost a father.'[102]

By the early nineteenth century, a time when punishment became somewhat less severe and many captains tried to get through voyages without meting out any beatings, the men might even come to admire their leaders.[103] This was, indeed, part of Nelson's appeal to the wider nation. As one of the *Victory* seamen put it after Trafalgar: 'I can't do it! To lose him now! I can't think of parting with Nelson.'[104] Captains of the time became increasingly keen to stress that they did not have to resort to capital punishment. As one officer noted, 'it is his [the captain's] duty to see himself that the poor seaman be not wrong'd of his due, or the service carried on by *noise, stripes,* or *blows*.'[105] A series of Parliamentary and public campaigns were aimed at reducing the severity of sentences and punishment. Captains lost some of their freedom in this respect when the Admiralty insisted on full statistical returns for every single punishment between 1862 and 1867. It was a relatively effective attack on 'abuses': the official responsible was discharged in 1867, with congratulations for a job well done, and the Admiralty's legal branch took over the job. A range of evidence suggested that punishments had been regularised, and discipline improved. The use of corporal punishment was also gradually restricted before being finally suspended in 1879, though lashes might theoretically still be administered for mutiny or gross personal violence to an officer until the end of the Second World War.[106]

Rough-and-ready codes and on-the-spot judgements were more useful than laws while actually at sea. Much distaste was, for instance, expressed over the 1749 stipulation of the death penalty for striking an officer. Immediate beatings were often meted out instead. In 1758 the captain of the *Royal Sovereign* contented himself with summary punishment for an Alexander Grant, who had attacked a petty officer while on duty.[107] Breaking these rules might carry grave consequences for relations on board ship. Lieutenant Ralph Dundas, the 'severe' first lieutenant of HMS *Coventry*, gained a 2 days' head start on the men when they were paid off in 1763. That did not stop them catching him and administering a severe beating for his dictatorial practices.[108] The officers who were singled out by the Spithead mutineers of 1797 were those who had broken these *ad hoc* 'rules' and principles.[109]

The naval race with Germany, 1890–1914

For the best part of a century, from Waterloo in 1815 to the 1890s, Britons comforted themselves with the idea that they really did 'rule the waves'. But this sense of effortless superiority relied on the absence of rivals. France, Spain and the Netherlands were exhausted by endless warfare; Germany and Italy hardly existed, except as geographical conventions; the USA had been humbled in 1812, and was tearing itself apart by the 1860s. Russia had no oceanic warm water port, and few financial reserves. In general the British were able to make do with a very small force indeed, going by the standards of the long wars with France. All the pressure was for retrenchment and low taxes. The navy's relative failure in the War of 1812 with the USA had not helped it to become more popular, and Ministers had the utmost difficulty in getting their Naval Estimates as early in the peace as March 1816. The general view of Members of Parliament was well summated in the conclusions of the 1818 Select Committee of Inquiry on Finance. The Government should bear in mind, it argued, 'that not ships and stores, and military arrangements, are alone necessary for the ... glory of the country in the event of war; but that finances recruited during peace ... are at least of equal importance'.[110]

The lack of naval rivals was particularly notable at moments of international tension, or even in time of war. The Russians, during the British and French assault on the Crimean peninsula between 1853 and 1856, did nothing to prevent the Royal Navy's operations in the Black Sea.[111] The British soon matched the French *Gloire*, clad in iron around a wooden hull, with the entirely iron-built HMS *Warrior*, launched in 1861. The British ship was faster, more heavily armed, and had a greater range than the French.[112] Most of the diplomatic crises of the 1860s and 1870s did not allow Britain to utilise naval power to any great extent. Neither the Austro-Prussian (1866) nor Franco-Prussian (1870–71) Wars, Russia's growing influence in the Balkans, nor the 'War in Sight' scare of 1875 leant themselves geographically or militarily to 'blue water' intervention. Britain had to be content to stay on the military sidelines, exerting her enormous political influence, but realistically unable to threaten naval action.[113]

This relatively benevolent situation was brought to a close by the ambitions of the German Empire, founded in 1871 following military victory over France, and especially by the accession of Wilhelm II as its Emperor in 1890. British policymakers had been suffering a sense of foreboding and anxiety as to their maritime security for some years, influenced by the great American naval thinker Alfred Mahan's *Influence of Sea Power upon History* (1890). Mahan argued, in similar vein to many 'blue water' thinkers, that naval power – and especially the clash of great navies – was the key to the international balance. He had his detractors and opponents. Other imperial thinkers, such as Halford Mackinder, believed that the twentieth century would be dominated by the great continental powers, Russia and the USA, who could open up the resources of their vast hinterlands using electricity and railways.[114] But Mahan's influence in naval circles was unmistakable. As France and Russia began to rearm in the 1880s, journalists such as W.T. Stead pressed for more British naval building. A 'two power standard' was formally laid down in the Naval Defence Act of 1889. Castlereagh as Foreign Secretary had informally settled on such a policy in 1817, to guard against any potential Franco-Russian combination.[115] Now it was codified in statute. Britain's fleets were always to be more numerous than the next two powers' forces put together, an exceedingly expensive pledge at £21.5 million spread over 5 years.[116]

The new German challenge was to seem much more threatening than the French or Russian in the years to come. The Kaiser liked to declare that 'Germany's future is on the water.' But until his appointment of Alfred Tirpitz as Navy Minister in March 1897, Tirpitz having already served for some years as the High Command's Chief of Staff, Wilhelm had little means of delivering that vision. The vision of a German High Seas Fleet was held back by what the Emperor rightly perceived as the timidity of his civilian Ministers, Parliamentary obstruction and the Reich's fragile tax base. But the appointment of Tirpitz, at a time when Britain's apparently selfish ambitions in Southern Africa and the notorious 'Jameson Raid' on Boer land were fresh in the memory, helped to force through two new Naval Laws in 1898–99. This allowed the German government to build battleships without reference to an annual vote of funds in the Reichstag: and the High Seas Fleet that Tirpitz envisioned would eventually amount to 38 battleships in four battle squadrons.[117] This would constitute a formidable and determined rival, its forces concentrated in the North Sea: the Germans were gambling that the British would never dare go to war with them in such circumstances.

British sea power was, by contrast, scattered across the world's oceans, and outside European waters there was what Arthur Marder once termed an 'odd assortment of ships', 'able neither to fight nor to run away', and referred to at the time as 'bug traps'.[118] It was this situation that the First Lord of the Admiralty, Admiral Sir John 'Jackie' Fisher, resolved to bring to an end by concentrating his forces in British home waters. The inception of steam and iron fleets from the 1860s had long implied this shift in any case. A 'bolt from the blue' against the British Isles became possible under steam, and the navy's ironclads became gradually and relatively more prominent in the home fleet. By 1868 there were five British ironclads in the Mediterranean, but ten in the home fleet.[119] Fisher's re-organisation was not, therefore, a retreat. Fisher envisaged the creation of powerful 'flying squadrons', based at strategic points around the Empire, and capable of rapid command and control via the new telegraph and cable network. Gladstone had sensed this possibility as long ago as the 1860s.[120] Fisher, indeed, insisted on war plans that were congruent with his view that commercial warfare and attacks on merchant shipping would be a vital battleground in any general war with Germany.[121]

Fisher's emphasis on communications, rapid response and worldwide communications allowed him to compromise over his initial design of a cruiser fleet to protect seaborne trade. Building more powerful capital ships based in home waters was permissible, in this worldview, if they could be moved around the world as different challenges arose. It was this that triggered the building of a whole new generation of battleships, beginning with the immense HMS *Dreadnought* in 1906. Only later, with Winston Churchill at the Admiralty, advised by Admiral Prince Louis of Battenberg and Sir John Jellicoe, did these battleships really constitute a battle fleet with the fixed intent of fighting in the North Sea.[122] On the eve of war the Germans were planning eventually to have 25 battleships ready for the North Sea, and the British were projecting that 33 of their own capital ships would be needed to meet that challenge. They used the 1904 *entente cordiale* with France, for instance, to withdraw most of their ships from the Mediterranean, leaving the French to guard that flank. The two-power standard was by now obsolete; in 1912 the First Lord of the Admiralty, Winston Churchill announced a new 60 per cent 'margin' over Germany in the North Sea to ensure Britain's security on that frontier.[123]

Britain's politicians, Liberal or not, were determined to prevent Germany gaining a strategic advantage over the Royal Navy in European waters. The Foreign Secretary, Sir Edward Grey, made this clear to the House of Commons in 1909: 'our Navy is to us what their Army is to them...if the German Navy were superior to ours...maintaining the Army which they do, for us it would be a question of defeat. Our independence, our very existence, would be at stake.' Churchill made the same point during a 1912 speech in Glasgow: 'the German Navy is to them...in the nature of a luxury. Our naval power involves British existence. It is existence to us; it is expansion to them.'[124] A series of Fleet Reviews in 1897, 1902, 1909 and 1911, each larger and more spectacular than the last, theatrically but unmistakably made the point that Britain would not allow naval supremacy to be wrested from her grasp.[125]

Britain's position was in fact a good deal more secure than it looked. Although Germany had *plans* to expand the High Seas Fleet, the actual military dispensation by 1914 is highly revealing. Britain could put out 29 large naval vessels, displacing 2.2 million tons; Germany could manage 17 ships at just over 1 million tons. This is, indeed, the reason why the British could reject German overtures for a 'naval building holiday' in 1912, in return for which London would at least have had to promise neutrality in the event of France and Russia attacking Germany. Liberal Ministers knew that they were so far in the lead that they did not have to stop building. They did not have to alienate France and Russia, who threatened their imperial frontiers, in order to relieve the military budget.[126]

The moment of maximum danger had come in 1909, when Ministers discovered that German manufacturers could outpace their own in building heavy gun mountings, and therefore build *Dreadnought*-class ships more quickly.[127] By 1914 that moment had passed. Britain's leaders were now armed with the income tax contained within the 'People's Budget' of 1909, passed partly in order to keep up with German competition. Their revenue was more buoyant and more flexible, and their debts lower, than a German state that had to rely on indirect taxes and duties for its income.[128] 'We want eight and we won't wait': the populist navalist slogan of 1908, which called for more Dreadnoughts, was eventually met.[129] By the time of the First World War, the German General Staff had concluded that they could not win a general naval war against Britain. Even if a single great victory was won in the North Sea, Britain's general maritime predominance meant that she could not be finally defeated in this manner.[130] Even so, the wars against Germany that opened in 1914 – initially, at least, motivated by the desire to constrain German naval ambitions – were to help destroy Britain's naval hegemony forever.

Conclusions: the Royal Navy and the 'nation'

Britain's emphasis on maintaining a large navy helps us to understand both her system of maritime trade routes and revolutionary changes within her domestic economy, as well as more specialist issues of strategy and tactics. War, trade and finance went together in Britain's rise to maritime pre-eminence, and they have to be treated together. In what may be seen as an updating and reinterpretation of pre-Second World War historiography, David Ormrod has recently demonstrated the importance of England's victories over the Netherlands between the 1650s and 1670s. His emphasis on *state* competition in explaining economic growth – the destruction of Britain's Dutch rival – has been a welcome addition to the historiography.[131] The scale and scope of the naval dockyards, which had a huge effect on the national economy, and the financial revolution of the seventeenth and eighteenth centuries, were two key elements in Britain's rise to economic dominance; the technology they provided to the Royal Navy helped her politicians defend that hegemony.

The ideological and philosophical implications were perhaps more diffuse, but they were even more pervasive. Naval power and the Royal Navy became inextricably bound up with the idea of what it meant to be British. The poet

Henry Newbolt argued in the 1920s that the sea was a Briton's 'boundary', and 'safeguard', as well as being 'the only highroad of his food supply'.[132] One popular book, *The Naval Side of British History*, published in 1924, summed up this vision when it concluded that '[naval wars] have played so vast a part in British history that to ignore them is to set up a false perspective, against which plain facts and upright figures appear no better than distorted images.'[133] As late as 1965, G.S. Graham could still conclude that 'war at sea is still far from being the most important part of a nation's history; but it has had a considerable determining influence on Britain's development and its prosecution has provided a test of national quality.'[134] The whole idea of the British Empire was in some respects a maritime one.

More modern historians have usually concurred with these judgements. The sheer scale of the maritime military effort had implications for 'nationhood' itself. As Stephen Conway has noted, 'the experience of serving in the regular armed forces or even the militia may well have furthered a sense of Britishness for men from all parts of the British Isles.'[135] This was partly due to the enormous significance of the Royal Navy in British national life – not just military, but social, legal, political, financial and imaginative. As J.D. Davies has noted of the English in the late seventeenth century:

> The king's navy was not some alien force, out of sight and out of mind on distant seas. It was an immediate and noticeable presence, at once the largest spending department of the state, the largest industrial concern in the country, a floating community that could be as large as many a town or county community, and in the eyes of most Englishmen ... the only effective and desirable defence of the nation.[136]

The ideological connotations might be even more far-reaching. By 1700 at the latest, and as Raphael Samuel has concluded, British national identity was bound up with concepts of 'liberty, both religious and constitutional ... hegemony over the sea ... [Britain's] equal standing with the best of Greece and Rome; and its imperial destiny'.[137] Historians of the late nineteenth century divine a 'maritime nationalism', or 'island mentality' in its people. As the Conservative Prime Minister Lord Salisbury once said, 'we are fish.'[138]

The Royal Navy might in this respect become a prism through which the making of 'Britishness' as a whole can be seen more clearly. Margarette Lincoln has shown how the Royal Navy became one of the central tropes of 'Britishness'. It became 'a national symbol', indeed, that was so powerful that it 'could be adapted to both government and opposition views', partly because it was an ever-shifting 'agent of state policy aimed to protect national freedoms and consequently the very "public sphere" in which it featured so largely'.[139] The emphasis on national freedom, indeed, has become a constant theme of historians. David Armitage has shown just why and how seventeenth–century thinkers believed that 'an empire of the seas would not be prey to the overextension and military dictatorship which had hastened the collapse of the Roman Empire, nor would it bring the tyranny, depopulation and impoverishment which had hastened the decline of Spain.' As William Petty put it, 'such as Desire Empire & Liberty, says Aristotle, let Them Encourage the Art of Ship-building'.[140] The British thought that they had done just that – a confidence that the twentieth century would test to the limit.

Timeline of events

1509	Henry VIII accedes to the English throne: more aggressive naval policy adopted
1588	Defeat of the Spanish Armada by English ships in the Channel
1627	English naval expedition against the Ile de Rhé off La Rochelle
1634	Charles I imposes 'Ship Money' in peacetime
1649	English Republic: appointment of Naval Commissioners
April 1649	'Laws and Ordinances Marshal' passed by Rump Parliament
1652–54	First Dutch War
1654–55	Cromwell's 'western design': English expedition to the Caribbean, seizure of Jamaica
1663	Duke of York's 'General Instructions . . . to Commanders' issued
1665–67	Second Dutch War
June 1667	Dutch force their way into the Thames and Medway; seize the flagship *Royal Charles*
1660–79	Samuel Pepys' administration as Clerk of the Navy Board and Secretary to the Admiralty
1672–74	Third Dutch War
May 1672	Inconclusive Battle of Solebay off the Suffolk coast
August 1673	Battle of the Texel: Dutch fleet under De Ruyter frustrates Anglo-French invasion
1684–88	Pepys' second administration as King's Secretary for the Admiralty
1688–97	Nine Years' or 'King William's' War with France

May 1692	Allied Anglo-Dutch fleets frustrate French invasion plans off Barfleur and La Hougue
June 1693	French Brest fleet seizes British merchant convoy bound for Smyrna in Turkey
1701–14	War of the Spanish Succession
1705	Royal Navy secures and covers Allied landings in Catalonia
1707	Act of Union between England and Scotland
1708	Capture of Minorca and Port Mahon neutralises Toulon as a French base
October 1711	Preliminaries of Peace signed with France in London
1713–31	Treaty of Utrecht; period of *détente* with France
1739–41	'War of Jenkins' Ear' against Spain
March 1740	Battle of Porto Bello, Admiral Vernon victorious over Spanish fleet
1756–63	Seven Years' War with France and Spain
1756	Marine Society founded
1757–62	Coalition between Newcastle and Pitt advances global maritime strategy
1759	Mary Lacy joins HMS *Sandwich* at Chatam
November 1759	Battle of Quiberon Bay: Admiral Hawke wins decisive victory over French fleet
1760	Accession of George III
1776–83	War of American Independence
1778	France joins War of American Independence against Britain
1779	Spain joins the war against Britain
1780	The Netherlands join the war against Britain
October 1781	Battle of the Chesapeake. Royal Navy fails to secure sea-lanes to Yorktown
April 1782	Battle of the Saintes. Admiral Rodney victorious over French fleet
1793–1802	Revolutionary Wars between France and Britain
June 1794	Battle of the 'Glorious First of June'. Admiral Lord Howe defeats French fleet

1796	Samuel Bentham appointed to new post of Inspector General of Naval Works
February 1797	Battle of Cape St Vincent: Admiral Jervis defeats Spanish fleet
April–May 1797	Spithead and Nore naval mutinies in the fleet
August 1798	Battle of Aboukir Bay in Egypt: Admiral Nelson defeats French forces
April 1801	First Battle of Copenhagen: navy forces Danes out of the League of Armed Neutrality
1802–03	Brief 'Peace of Amiens' between France and Britain
1803–15	'Napoleonic' Wars between France and Britain
October 1805	Battle of Trafalgar: Admiral Nelson defeats combined French and Spanish fleets
December 1805	Battle of Austerlitz: Napoleon defeats Austrian and Russian armies
June 1815	Battle of Waterloo: End of Revolutionary and Napoleonic Wars
1853	Royal Naval Coast Volunteers founded
1853–56	Crimean War fought by Britain and France in alliance against Russia
1861	HMS *Warrior* launched
1862–67	Admiralty statistical returns on summary punishments
1879	Corporal punishment suspended in Royal Navy
1889	Britain passes Naval Defence Act
1890	Alfred Mahan publishes *The Influence of Sea Power upon History* (1890)
1897	Alfred Tirpitz appointed German Navy Minister
1898–99	German Naval Laws hugely expand German High Seas Fleet
1900	Royal Fleet Reserve founded
1904	*Entente cordiale* with France
1904	Admiral Sir John 'Jackie' Fisher becomes First Sea Lord (and serves as such until 1910)
1906	Launching of HMS *Dreadnought*

1908	Naval rearmament crisis: 'we want eight and we won't wait'
1909	People's Budget raises money for four new dreadnoughts, and four more later
1911	Winston Churchill becomes First Lord of the Admiralty
1912	Churchill announces '60 per cent' margin of safety over German High Seas Fleet
August 1914	Outbreak of the First World War; Britain at war with Germany

Part II
The Ebbing Tide

7

Victories?

Histories of Britain's war effort in the twentieth century have often been dominated by a 'declinist' outlook – painting each defeat or retreat as part of an overarching and in some ways inevitable decline, by which Britain was replaced by the USA as the world's foremost military and maritime power. The historical narrative has also remained dominated by images of trench warfare during the First World War, and Fighter Command's defence of the UK itself during the summer of 1940. Such approaches often underestimate the vital role, and the victories, of the Royal Navy during the prolonged struggles of 1914–18 and 1939–45. Without Britain's preponderance of naval might over her enemies, the country would not have been able to feed itself, re-equip its industries or move its armies. At key moments of national crisis below the oceans' surface, when German submarines threatened to end the British war effort – in the spring of 1917, and during 1941–43 – British naval forces were able to forestall and deflect the threat. Her ability to threaten surface naval forces with decisive defeat was also a crucial reason why Britain was not effectively blockaded during the First World War, and it helps explain why Britain was able to continue with her war effort at all when she fought on alone against Nazi Germany in 1940–41. Without the vast number of British battleships collected together in the Grand Fleet during the First World War, the German High Seas Fleet might have isolated Britain altogether, perhaps without the need for the unrestricted U-boat campaigns that eventually caused the USA to enter the war. If German battleships and cruisers had been able to operate unmolested against British forces as they were evacuated from French beaches in May and June 1940, the result would have been catastrophic. The British Expeditionary Force, the core of the professional army, would certainly not have survived – and the invasion or surrender of Britain would have been likely. The liberation of France that began with D-Day on 6 June 1944 would have been a disastrous failure without naval protection from submarines and the guns of huge battleships that helped to prevent counter-attack from the shore. Far from being a weak and declining military power, Britain had remained in the forefront of naval building throughout the inter-war years, and indeed her maritime forces still outweighed those of any single rival in 1939. The danger came when she had to fight three naval powers at one and the same time, particularly in late 1941 and early 1942, before the USA could come decisively to her aid. The combination of Nazi Germany, Fascist Italy and Imperial Japan did for some months threaten to overwhelm her, though even in this period she was able to hold her own in home and European waters against Germany and Italy. The USA did indeed become the world's foremost naval power by 1945, and usurped the place Britain had enjoyed before 1914; but the British navy played a central and continuing role throughout the intervening struggle.

The First World War: surface campaigns

The war with Germany that opened on 3 August 1914 began as a worldwide conflict, partly because the new oil-fired ships upon which the Royal Navy now depended could sail much further and faster than their coal ancestors of the previous generation.[1] But it was also a renewed struggle between a whale and an elephant, reminiscent of France and Britain's inability to force a final conclusion to their eighteenth-century wars. Britain and her allies soon overran almost all of Germany's overseas territories: the German and Austrian navies were bottled up in the Baltic and the Adriatic, leaving only those cruisers that were beyond home waters at the outbreak of war to conduct what commerce raiding they could. These would be quickly neutralised, as we shall see.[2] But police actions of this type could hardly win the war. Even Winston Churchill, serving as First Lord of the Admiralty, soon began to fear that 'England, without an army ... with only her Navy and her money, counted for little.'[3]

Britain's naval commanders had read their Mahan. They expected a new Trafalgar, a decisive battle that would decide the outcome of the war. But the experience of the war itself elevated maritime historian Julian Corbett's ideas above the Mahan school of thought. Corbett emphasised the role of combined operations, and of keeping open one's lines of communication – both notable features of the First World War. Mahan's emphasis on the battle fleet turned out to be anachronistic.[4] There was little chance that the German High Seas Fleet would steam out to open battle in the North Sea, given that they would almost certainly be defeated. There was similarly almost no possibility of any large-scale German military action against the UK mainland, given Britain's lead in battleship numbers and the inherent difficulties of any such operation. Only the much-debated 'bolt from the blue' could threaten to wipe out Britain's naval lead, and this was highly unlikely. The Royal Navy was on exercises in July 1914, and ordered not to disperse once the implications of Austria's conflict with Serbia sank in. The Grand Fleet was already at its base at Scapa Flow when that Balkan crisis became a world war.[5]

Attempts actually to break the deadlock turned into disasters. The most famous of these were Allied operations against Germany's ally, Turkey, in spring 1915: first in naval attacks at the Dardanelles, and then through landings at Gallipoli. The Dardanelles connect the Aegean with the Sea of Marmara and the approaches to Constantinople, modern-day Istanbul. The naval attack which opened on 19 February 1915, and the armed landings that followed, represented an attempt to force Turkey out of the war and to open up the supply routes to Russia through the Black Sea. Churchill conceived this plan in January, prompted by Russian pleas for help. Despite the misgivings even of other early enthusiasts for some action against Turkey, including Fisher, Churchill used his considerable persuasive powers to argue for a 'navy-only' operation that would destroy Turkish defences and sail on to Constantinople.[6] Unfortunately, as both Nelson and Mahan had argued in the past, any battle between capital ships and forts would be a very uneven one. Only direct hits on the Turkish guns proved adequate to silence them; and the low trajectory of naval guns made that very difficult indeed. It took until 18 March to disable most of the big guns and progress into the straits. But even then the sinking of one French and two British battleships by undetected mines necessitated an Allied retreat, and a victory for the German-trained Turkish forces ashore.[7]

This embarrassing failure caused enormous political upheavals in Britain. Fisher had become more and more hostile to the project during January and February, due to the perceived delays, indecision and lack of commitment of his army colleagues. By the time landings actually took place, on 25 April, the Turks had been given plenty of time to prepare their positions: and the results in terms of army losses were appalling. The battleships *Triumph* and *Majestic* were also lost, as well as the older battleship HMS *Goliath*.[8] By late May Fisher was exhausted, emotional at the losses the navy was taking, and furious that his colleagues would not order the prized battleship *Queen Elizabeth* back home from the Straits. Now Fisher's patience completely snapped, and he resigned over the weekend of 15–16 May. Though he had retracted such threats on a number of previous occasions, this time he did not come back. Fisher had, indeed, intended to resign at the War Council of 28 January that finally fixed on the adventure, only to be talked out of it.[9] Though he expected to be recalled, he sealed his fate with a letter to Herbert Henry Asquith as Prime Minister asking to be put in sole and unchallenged charge of the war at sea. The First Sea Lord had hugely overreached himself, and the Prime Minister was all too happy to accept his final resignation.[10]

The political crisis also saw the end – for now – of Churchill's political career, since Asquith now formed a coalition government with the Conservatives. Unionist distaste for the First Lord, and Liberals' appalled reaction to the Dardanelles adventure, saw Churchill replaced by a previous Conservative Prime Minister, Arthur Balfour.[11] The British went on pouring forces into the breach – five more divisions landed in August – but the terrain, the Turks' tenacity, and their own tactical mistakes, cost them dearly. There were 120,000 British Empire casualties in the campaign, including 27,500 Australians: two of every nine Imperial troops sent to the theatre.[12] Allied forces were evacuated during December and early January, leaving behind only Churchill's claim that a more rapid, decisive and determined campaign might at least have forced the Central Powers to negotiate.[13] That in fact may have been wishful thinking, since the Ottoman forces on the ground had most of their ammunition left, and most of their mines were intact and protected by their heavy guns. Forcing the Straits would have required a much larger force than the Allies in fact ever assembled in that theatre. The potential 'breakthrough' may always have been an illusion.[14]

The Dardanelles campaign having failed, the stalemate persisted. The one chance the British got to break out of this, and the nearest the two main opposing fleets came to their new Trafalgar, came off Jutland on 31 May and 1 June 1916. Admiral Reinhard Scheer, in command of the German fleet since January 1916, planned to lure the British battle cruisers out with his own cruiser fleet before delivering them a crushing defeat, evening the odds for a future decisive battle between the main forces. Characteristically, the navy's codebreaking Room 40 had already detected Scheer's plan, and the movement of the High Seas Fleet itself. But the news handed on to Admiral David Beatty, in command of the cruiser force, and Admiral John Jellicoe, in overall command of the Grand Fleet and its battleships, was incomplete. They knew that Admiral Hipper's cruiser squadron had left harbour, but crucially not that the entire German battle fleet was in the North Sea. Beatty's ships were thus on their own, looking for the German cruiser force, when they stumbled on them just after 2 o'clock in the afternoon of 31 May. They found, not just the cruisers that they expected, but the entire German High Seas Fleet. The odds were now heavily stacked against Beatty. His flagship, *Lion*, took a great deal of damage as the German battleships opened up; the battle cruisers *Indefatigable* and *Queen Mary* blew up under fire. Beatty was obliged to break off and 'run to the north' under this attack, looking for Jellicoe and the main force of British ships. But it took hours for Jellicoe to find out what was happening to his south, and it was not until he could actually see Beatty in the *Lion* just after 6 o'clock that it became clear what was happening. He then deployed his entire force of 27 battleships.[15]

This rapidly turned the battle in the Royal Navy's favour, and it was now the Germans' turn to come under withering fire. The battle cruisers *Lützow* and *Derfflinger*, in particular, were hit again and again. Scheer, appalled at the prospect of total defeat, ordered a 'battle turn-around', in which each ship began to turn as soon as the one astern to her was seen to move round. British numbers were overwhelming, and this retreat was clearly the most rational course of action: though it did not stop Scheer turning quickly around once more and inexplicably moving right back into the Grand Fleet's way. Realising his mistake, he raised a smokescreen, launched a rather poorly aimed torpedo attack and fled again to the south-west at about 7.35 p.m. Night was now only 40 minutes away, and confusion among the British fleet meant that the High Seas Fleet was free for now.[16]

Scheer was able to make his escape under cover of darkness: Jellicoe declined to order a night action. The British commander decided that his preponderance of force might be risked in the inevitable chaos, especially given that German forces were known to be better trained and equipped for night fighting.[17] But this decision meant that British forces were wary of revealing their position, and were ordered to maintain radio silence; the Germans might therefore slip through them and make for their home ports. When Hipper in his new flagship *Moltke* ran into their starboard column, only a series of small and confused ship-to-ship actions took place. Scheer then tested Jellicoe's rearguard, finding it weak enough to slip through. The Germans suffered only damage to the battleship *Nassau*, renewed damage and fatal flooding to the *Lützow*, and the sinking of the pre-Dreadnought *Pommern* as well as three light cruisers.[18] The British intelligence advantage represented by Room 40 had been squandered. Admiralty codebreakers knew that Scheer had requested air reconnaissance cover over Horns Reef at daybreak, where he would find a way through the North Sea's minefields. But this information was never passed to the Grand Fleet. Jellicoe thought instead that he was dealing with destroyer attacks on his screen, testing him out for the next day. By the time he realised his mistake, Scheer was away and heading home.[19]

The Germans High Seas Fleet, despite its operational mistakes during Jutland, had escaped. British naval experts cast around for a reason for this inexplicable failure, and Fisher's precious battle cruisers came under immediate suspicion. The loss of the *Queen Mary*, in particular, prompted Beatty's famous observation that 'there seems to be something wrong with our bloody ships today!' A third such ship, *Invincible*, in the Third Battle Cruiser Squadron, was also destroyed. All three – a good cross-section of the pre-war battle cruiser classes, having been commissioned in 1908, 1911 and 1913 – blew up after enormous internal explosions that saw them disappear in just seconds.[20] None of them had been under particularly heavy fire. It seems likely from recent research that these ships, having been ordered to carry more shells and fire as quickly as they could, were carrying large amounts of cordite, possibly in open crates, in their gun turrets. This probably explains the explosions that followed the impact of enemy shells. So Fisher's design may be vindicated; but in practice the battle cruiser lost its allure because its speed was thought to have reduced its armoured protection.[21] Their gunnery was also not as accurate as it might have been. Fisher had been convinced by subordinates that the naval writer Arthur Pollen's proposed analogue firing system was not necessary.[22]

Jellicoe had in fact become a victim of the same stalemate that had brought Scheer out to face him in the first place. He knew that Britain could lose the war if the Grand Fleet were defeated at Jutland; the consequences would be grave, but not nearly so disastrous, if the High Seas Fleet were to get away. So caution remained his watchword throughout the battle, to the Royal Navy's relative disadvantage. The German High Seas Fleet sank 111,980 tons of shipping from the British fleet and killed 6945 Royal Navy personnel; Britain's much vaunted Grand Fleet sank only 62,233 tons of German ships, and inflicted casualties of 2921.[23] The British public, expecting a famous victory in the event of a large-scale clash between the two fleets, was bitterly disappointed. The *Express* summed up the general mood when it bemoaned 'Heavy and Unaccountable British Losses', and when on 5 June HMS *Hampshire* hit a mine off the Orkneys Islands and took the Secretary of State for War Lord Kitchener down with it, the despair was compounded.[24]

A long debate would follow, initiated and sustained by Beatty in a long-running campaign designed to burnish his own reputation, about whether Jellicoe had failed to press an easily grasped advantage.[25] If the British had managed to cut off Scheer's escape, either late in the day on 31 May or later during the night, the German High Seas Fleet might – but only *might* – have paid much more dearly for its commander's rather poor performance.[26] There was at least still some point in Germany continuing the struggle, a fact which would have seemed much more uncertain had the entire force been sent to the bottom. Scheer himself claimed a victory. But overall, it is hard to disagree with the *New York Times*' famous judgement: 'the German Fleet has assaulted its jailor, but it is still in jail.'[27] German conclusions were even gloomier. Scheer himself concluded, in his final report on Jutland, that 'even the successful outcome of a Fleet action in this war will not force England to make peace.'[28] Avoiding being annihilated was not much of a triumph.

The main German force would come out of harbour only three more times during the war, in August and October 1916, and then for a last sortie in April 1918. When ordered into a final desperate offensive in October 1918, the crews mutinied: there was to be no catastrophic last effort. Germany's armistice with the Allies involved surrendering her fleet, a final defeat for the 'risk strategy' of challenging and constraining British power. Between 22 and 27 November 1918, 70 Germany ships – almost the entire High Seas Fleet – steamed into Scapa Flow and confinement.[29] It was one of the most resounding victories, and humiliations, in military history – all the more so for the German fleet having never been defeated in battle. The Royal Navy stood unchallenged as the most powerful maritime force the world had ever known.

The First World War: submarine threat (I)

The greatest threat to Britain's maritime efforts in the First World War did not come, as expected, from battlefleet actions. The threat was much more insidious, and amounted to an attempt to starve her into submission by cutting off her trade. Britain's free trade economy meant that she had relied on food imports since the early nineteenth century: from the late 1870s onwards, a majority of the population depended on cheap wheat from abroad to feed their families.[30] The British agricultural sector was relatively small by 1914, meaning that land could be pressed fairly rapidly into use to feed the population; state control was extended over as much as 85 per cent of domestic production by the end of the war. Local rationing was brought in during autumn 1917, and extended nationally in 1918. So the British were able to reduce their need for foreign bread and meat.[31] But 7 million tons of food were still carried from North America to the UK during the First World War.[32] Cutting off this supply would threaten Britain's continued participation in the war.

The Germans were not certain how to employ submarines, the main force they were to use against British trade, in this novel strategic environment: during the first 6 months of the war these craft accounted for only 7 per cent of the 273,000 tons of British shipping lost. Allied politicians were little moved in the face of such a campaign: in 1915 Churchill argued that the U-boats were unlikely to play a major role in the war. This, indeed, was the accepted wisdom of the conflict's first year. When Admiral Sir Percy Scott predicted in 1914 that submarines would do enormous damage to Britain's trade, the *Manchester Guardian* dismissed his views as 'imaginative . . . fancy picture making'.[33] But the Admiralty, its ships menaced by U-boats in the

North Sea, knew better. Beatty was furious at his superiors' inaction, and eventually ran a competition with a cash prize to garner suggestions on what to do about the submarine threat. Many of the suggestions were totally unusable, but some did interest the Admiralty. One submission, signed only by 'Endeavour', proposed using merchant ships disguised as neutrals carrying hidden guns: as soon as the Germans attacked, they would throw off their disguise and fight back. These 'Q-ships', as they became known, were first used against the U-boats late in 1914, though they only sank a few vessels: after the spring of 1917 they managed to destroy only six, for the loss of 27 Q-ships in return.[34]

By February 1915, Germany was ready to mount an unrestricted campaign of submarine warfare, sinking all merchant vessels in British and Atlantic waters on sight and without warning. The British 'starvation blockade' of Germany was cited publicly as the reason for the new policy, but the economic damage that could be done was enormous. By May, they had sunk 115 merchant ships for the loss of only five boats.[35] But at this point the drawbacks of this unrestricted warfare became clear. On 7 May the liner *Lusitania* was sunk, with the loss of 1198 lives, including 128 Americans. Although the US Government knew that the ship had been carrying arms for the British, public and political anger against Germany was fierce. The German Ambassador, for one, was convinced that war would be the result if the *Lusitania* disaster did not at least mitigate the U-boats' behaviour.[36]

But even the loss of the *Lusitania* did not quite bring this first period of unrestricted warfare to an end. This in fact only followed U-24's sinking of the British liner *Arabic* on 19 August, with the loss of 30 lives – including three more Americans. This time the complaints from Washington were so loud that in late August the Germans did abandon unrestricted U-boat warfare against liners. In September the entire campaign was suspended.[37] This announcement meant that British trade was safe, for now at least. The British merchant marine at the end of September 1915 was only 4 per cent smaller than before the war.[38]

Germany's return to unrestricted submarine warfare early in 1917 amounted to a last frantic attempt to destroy the Allied economies. As von Trotha, the Chief of the German Naval Staff, wrote in December 1916: 'if we can break England's back the war will at once be decided in our favour... England's mainstay is her shipping.'[39] The harsh winter of 1916–17 made Germany's position seem desperate; the diplomatic hopes of the Chancellor, Bethmann Hollwegg, seemed to be fading; political pressure was building up for more decisive measures. Submarine building also meant that Germany could mount a much bigger campaign, with twice the number of U-boats on station as against 1915. On 1 February 1917 the waters around the British Isles were declared a prohibited area, and shipping in that area was likely to be sunk without warning.[40] By the end of April 869,000 tons of Allied shipping and 155 ships had been sunk, 101 without warning. The odds of a British merchant ship surviving the voyage from Gibraltar to a UK port during the month of April were only one in four. British losses amounted to 545,282 tons of that Allied total, while neutral losses rose to a further 189,373 tons. So over a million tons of shipping was sunk in 1 month by all enemy action, 90 per cent of which was due to U-boats.[41] This campaign was critical in bringing the USA into the war.

Neutral shipping refused to move and huddled in British harbours, and traffic overall was only a quarter of what it had been a year earlier. The U-boat campaign was far outstripping the shipbuilding rate of the Allies and neutrals put together, and in just 3 months reduced the world's shipping total by 2 million tons: of those losses, 1.25 million tons were British. April turned out to be the worst month for losses, during which 154 U-boats could be massed by Germany: but that would be small comfort, for the last week of the month saw an attrition rate of 50 per cent.[42] U-boat losses were very small, and the craft themselves were usually able to evade enemy ships: they were for the most part of much more advanced design than during 1914–15, though only about 70 were able to take to the sea at any one time.[43] Neither was much respite expected. Britain's new American allies could do little in the short term to help her, and in fact U-boats' increased freedom off the US eastern seaboard increased the rate of loss.[44]

The crisis nearly brought Britain to its knees. The Government estimated that she was receiving only 60–70 per cent of the supplies she needed to continue the war, even in her straitened wartime circumstances.[45] Her oil reserves, critical for keeping the Royal Navy at sea, were severely depleted, and limitations had to be placed on the movements of the Grand Fleet between June and November 1917.[46] The multi-national seafaring community which kept Britain fed was taking enormous risks, and huge losses. When the *Cabotia* was sunk 120 miles west of Ireland in October 1916, her 74-man crew included Greeks, Italians, Portuguese, Americans, Danes and Norwegians. Even the category 'British' at this time was perhaps 20 per cent Indian: another 10 per cent was drawn from other Crown Colonies and Protectorates.[47] The U-boat campaign killed 14,287 sailors on 2479 British ships alone.[48]

In retrospect, as many historians have noted, the overall solution was staring the Admiralty in the face: convoys, with merchant ships travelling in groups escorted by warships. Britain's troop transports had been escorted since the start of the war, and precisely none of them had been sunk by U-boats.[49] The Dutch, and latterly the French, coal trade – as well as Scandinavian shipping in the North Sea – had also been effectively protected in this manner. Junior officers, for instance, those in the blockading cruiser squadrons, began to press for a wider experiment in convoying. Beatty himself took up this cause at the start of 1917.[50] Admiralty objections to the system had always run thus: firstly, convoys would divert Royal Navy ships from offensive hunter-killer operations. Next, staff work up until 1917 counted all British ships leaving port in the UK as ocean-going traffic, and concluded that there were simply not the destroyers to screen their passage. This ignored the fact that many of those ships were coastwise traders, and would not need deep-sea protection.[51] Officials also objected that slowing down faster vessels would lead to even higher losses; and finally, that large-scale convoys would be easier to find.[52]

Eventually, the sheer scale of the losses, agitation from within the Admiralty from officers such as Commander Reginald Henderson and political pressure from David Lloyd George as Prime Minister broke down such resistance.[53] The first trial convoy left Gibraltar on the evening of 10 May, consisting of 16 merchantmen escorted by two Q-Ships. It reached Plymouth on 20 May without being subjected to any submarine attacks at all.[54] The system was soon extended throughout Britain's trade routes. Convoys directed from the Admiralty's Convoy Room began to operate on all the major sea-lanes near Britain: from Sierra Leone; from Gibraltar; from Halifax in Novia Scotia; from New York City; and finally from the Hampton Roads off Virginia for South American traffic.[55]

Submarine attacks and sinkings immediately dropped. British ships sunk in the last quarter of 1917, at 702,779 tons, were only just after half of the total in the second quarter.[56] The success of convoying can be attributed to a number of factors. The exertions of Room 40 were critical, for single ships could not realistically be radioed all the time with U-boats' positions; but Royal Navy escorts, shepherding a large number of civilians, certainly could be. Convoys were *not* easier to find than stragglers; the ocean was so vast, and the area occupied even by a number of ships so small, that the risk of discovery was only increased by a tiny amount. Lastly, U-boats might surface to attack a convoy near a warship, or in a poor position to fire on a cluster of ships. They would then have to manoeuvre, perhaps underwater and therefore slowly, to launch their attack. All of this severely limited their effectiveness, and helps to explain the eventual outcome of the struggle.[57] But Britain had come perilously close to defeat by Imperial Germany's U-boats, and only the very late and contested introduction of convoys had saved her.

The Second World War: surface campaigns

It could hardly have been imagined, as the German High Seas Fleet sailed into Scapa Flow, that British power would be challenged for many generations. But the rise of the fascist dictatorships in Europe, and of Japanese imperial power in the East, in fact brought about another general war within a generation. The first decisive task for the Royal Navy was in fact to salvage what it could from defeat through the evacuation of Europe following the collapse of French and British land forces in May and June. The 'miracle' of Dunkirk between 26 May and 4 June was later to become famous as a victory for 'little boats' in the face of organised tyranny and defeat. J.B. Priestley lionised them at the time in his radio broadcasts as 'the little pleasure steamers'. As he said, 'we've known them and laughed at them, those fussy little steamers, all our lives.' Now Priestly termed their bravery 'very English' (though he claimed he meant 'British'): the ultimate symbol of British improvisation and ingenuity.[58] Eventually the navy commandeered 588 of these small boats, many of them very small leisure craft from the Thames and the Thames Estuary.[59]

But the operation was in fact organised, protected and conducted by the professional navy. Even a majority of the men were taken off in Royal Navy ships; and very few would have returned without destroyer cover against U-boats and surface E-boats. The operation saw every possible destroyer despatched to evacuate the British Expeditionary Force. A cruiser, 56 destroyers, 38 minesweepers and 6 corvettes were involved in that single operation, despite the fact that the Royal Navy was still engaged in trying to prevent the German conquest of Norway.[60] Forty Royal Navy ships were lost at Dunkirk, including nine destroyers.[61] During 'Dynamo' and its southern and western successor 'Aerial', 558,032 fighting men were rescued, including 368,491 British soldiers. At Dunkirk itself, 308,000 men had come off in British ships and 29,238 in other Allied vessels.[62]

France having sued for peace, the constant sense of retreat turned into one of resolve should a German army attempt to cross the Channel and invade the UK. Four destroyer flotillas, numbering 36 ships, lay in wait for them initially, along with a host of smaller craft. This force was to grow to 67, and six cruisers, in the coming weeks, as compared with Germany's ten. The risk of Royal Navy interception was simply too great for invasion in these circumstances to be considered as a realistic option, and even if the balance of forces had been more favourable, German forces were in no position to mount a complex three-pronged assault so soon after the conquest of Western Europe.[63] Wargames held at the British Staff College in 1974, and involving some of the original participants as umpires, suggested that even if the Germans had landed some forces, their supplies and reinforcements would have been cut off in the Channel once the Royal Navy sailed southwards. They would have been forced into a humiliating surrender.[64] The German General Jodl put it a little more colourfully: as he said, as long as the Royal Navy was in existence, an invasion would send his 'troops into a mincing machine'.[65]

Not every Royal Navy operation in the war's first 2 years was a retreat or a defeat. There was, for instance, a good deal of success against German surface raiders, and small-scale engagements continued to raise morale. The Battle of the River Plate on 13 December 1939 is a good case in point. This saw the German cruiser *Graf Spee* forced into the neutral port of Montevideo by the smaller *Exeter* and the light cruisers *Ajax* and *Achilles* under the command of Commodore Henry Harwood. Though the Royal Navy ships could not pierce the *Graf Spee*'s heavy armour, their 8- and 6-inch guns did significant damage to the ship's command and communication systems in enormously brave close passes. *Graf Spee*'s captain, Hans Langsdorff, then made the fateful decision to take her into Montevideo for repairs. On 17 December, rather than sail out to a losing battle, Langsdorff had the ship scuttled, and 3 days later he committed suicide.[66] A signal had been given that, for all the Third Reich's expenditure on surface craft such as the *Graf Spee*, German surface raiding was not going to be tolerated. Such attacks claimed only 15 ships in the first 4 months of the war.[67]

Dunkirk and the Battle of Britain, and the suppression of surface raiding, allowed Britain to fight on. Maritime supremacy had saved Britain from capitulation; but the Royal Navy itself was to endure a number of disasters on its own account during 1941. The great German battleship *Bismarck* broke out into the open Atlantic, along with the heavy cruiser *Prinz Eugen*, intending to menace Allied supply lines. At 50,000 tons, *Bismarck* would have been able to wipe out any convoy in her way. As she attempted to pass through the Denmark Strait, in the early hours of 24 May, she was engaged by the pride of the Royal Navy – the battleship *Hood* – as well as the brand-new *Prince of Wales*. *Hood* managed to fire on the *Prinz Eugen* before that ship's 8-inch shells hit her boat deck, causing the 4-inch ammunition to burn out of control. But as she tried to close the range with the German ships and even the odds, *Hood* was then hit by a salvo from the *Bismarck* itself, which caused a huge explosion near the mainmast. Ted Briggs, one of only three men to survive as the ship went down in moments, recalled the scene: 'the ship which had been a haven for me for the last two years was suddenly hostile. After the initial jarring she listed slowly . . . to starboard . . . [before a] sudden, horrifying cant to port. On and on she rolled, until she reached an angle of forty-five degrees.' She then sank in just 3 minutes, leaving Briggs and two others to be picked up by the destroyer *Electra*. But 1415 other men had lost their lives.[68]

Bismarck did not long outlast the *Hood*. Only 2 days later, during the night of 26–27 May, aircraft from the carrier *Ark Royal* found her and crippled the great ship's ability to manoeuvre as she steamed towards Brest. The next day the inter-war battleship *Rodney*, and the new *King George V.*, moved in for the kill. By just after 10 in the morning *Bismarck* was a burning hulk, and the destroyer *Dorsetshire* put six torpedoes in her to make sure.[69] Yet another German attempt at a surface raiding campaign was over. But the loss of the *Hood* was an enormous shock back in Britain. The 24th of May was Empire Day: *Hood*, through 'goodwill visits' and her 1923–24 'Empire Cruise', was synonymous with the pride and the might of the Imperial Navy. Now she had lasted only a few minutes in battle. *The Times* called her loss 'the heaviest blow the navy has received in the war'.[70]

Italy also entered the war against France and Britain in June 1940, critically endangering Britain's position in the Mediterranean.[71] The British were in this respect lucky that Hitler had failed to secure an alliance with Franco's Spain as well. Franco's fascist regime offered to enter the war, and seize Gibraltar, in June 1940. This would have made Mediterranean naval campaigns, and Britain's economic links to India and the Pacific, almost untenable. British ships would have had to fight their way into that sea before they could even begin operations. But Hitler overplayed his hand, and demanded German bases in Morocco and the Canary Islands, concessions that Spain was not prepared to grant.[72] Even so, Italy was a formidable enemy, and stood ready to do enormous damage to Britain's communications and supply lines throughout the Mediterranean. She had only two capital ships to Britain's two in this theatre at the start of the war. But the addition of four more brought her total to six by November 1940, including the two new large 15-inch battleships *Littorio* and *Vittorio Veneto*. Admiral Sir Andrew Cunningham, British commander in the Mediterranean, decided on a preemptive strike on the enemy fleet at Taranto, mounted from aircraft carriers. Carried out on the night of 11 November from the carrier *Illustrious*, this succeeded in crippling three of the Italian battleships, including the *Littorio*.[73]

The Germans became heavily involved in the Mediterranean theatre during 1941. German Stuka dive-bombers disabled *Illustrious* and sank the cruiser *Southampton* in January of that year.[74] In May Crete had to be evacuated after a German airborne invasion in the days following 20 May. Roughly half the garrison, or 16,000 men, were taken off. But the ferocious German air assaults continued, and 4 days after the attack began the Royal Navy had to stop operations in daylight due to their ceaseless attacks. By 27 May the evacuation decision had been taken, and destroyers and cruisers had to steam close to the Cretan beaches and embark the men before turning for home under bombardment. The cruisers coming into Heraklion on the north of the island had to pass within 40 miles of enemy air force bases on Scarpanto. Cunningham lost two light cruisers, an anti-aircraft cruiser and six destroyers. Three further battleships, five cruisers, another anti-aircraft cruiser and seven more destroyers were damaged, some of them beyond local repair. *Orion*, the flagship at Heraklion, had to be towed back to Alexandria. It was another terrible blow to the Mediterranean fleet.[75]

The Mediterranean situation became even worse by the start of 1942. Admiral Cunningham had no aircraft carrier to call on, while the Italians and Germans could fly from a range of bases on land. German U-boats had been ordered to the Mediterranean along with the Luftwaffe, and U–81 had sunk the carrier *Ark Royal* on 13 November 1941.[76] Worse, by the end of February, Field-Marshal Rommel's Afrika Corps had overrun the Cyrenaican airfields in Libya from which Royal Air Force (RAF) fighters had been able to protect Malta and Allied shipping in the middle of the Mediterranean.[77] This made resupplying Malta extremely hazardous, and following failed attempts to reach the island from the west, a convoy from Alexandria had to be attempted. Rear-Admiral Philip Vian, in command of the escort, very nearly managed to shepherd his convoy through to Malta. During the Second Battle of Sirte on 22 March 1942, the British force, spearheaded by only four light cruisers, was able to drive off the two Italian 8-inch gun cruisers *Gorizia* and *Trento*, as well as the heavily armed battle-ship *Littorio*. It was a tremendously impressive feat of arms, though many of the British officers were unimpressed by their opponents given that the Italians turned away in the face of a smokescreen and torpedo attack.[78] But the engagement had so delayed Vian's force that the precious cargo ships under his protection were caught by the Luftwaffe in broad daylight the following day, rather than arriving at Malta's capital, Valletta, in the dark. The *Breconshire* and the *Clan Campbell* were disabled and sunk within just a few miles of Malta, and only 5000 tons of the 26,000 tons carried by the convoy got through to the island.[79]

The island's position, and indeed the whole British presence in the Mediterranean, was extremely precarious. March and April 1941 brought massive air raids on Malta, which nearly broke the island's resistance. The dockyard was virtually destroyed; all surface ships had to be withdrawn.[80] The hot summer months would see Malta forced to surrender, if no new convoys got through. More Spitfires were flown in, and they began to turn the tide in the air battle. But clearly the navy would once more have to take the brunt of carrying heavy supplies. Operation 'Harpoon', mounted from the west in June, brought in only two of the six ships that had started from Gibraltar, while relentless German and Italian air attack forced Vian's Operation 'Vigorous', from Alexandria, to turn back.[81] Given the relative failure of 'Harpoon' and 'Vigorous', a much more powerful force was assembled to execute the final and decisive relief of the island. 'Operation Pedestal', which sailed out of Gibraltar on 10 August 1942, finally involved three fleet-carriers, flying a total of 72 aircraft, two battleships, six cruisers, one anti-aircraft cruiser, 24 destroyers and two fleet oilers with a corvette escort.[82]

Even this formidable escort only just managed to bring any of the merchantmen safe into Valetta. Continuous air attacks, particularly heavy during

13 August while the convoy passed between Sicily and Axis-held North Africa, took enormous tolls. Nine out of the fourteen civilian ships were sunk by over a hundred German and Italian torpedo- and dive-bombers, as well as E- and U-boats. Italian cruisers that might have intervened were withdrawn, the Germans having refused them air cover – an omission that helps to explain 'Pedestal's' strategic success.[83] The Royal Navy still lost the older fleet carrier *Eagle*, two cruisers and a destroyer.[84] But 'Pedestal' had at least secured Malta's survival. Royal Navy submarines and RAF aircraft had already been gathering once more at the island, and the critical arrival of the oil tanker *Ohio* meant that they could continue their campaign against Axis shipping. *Ohio* limped into the Grand Harbour 2 days after most of the rest of the ships, crippled by bombs; but the oil in her hold was the most critical part of 'Pedestal's' achievement.[85]

Correlli Barnett has described Malta as the Verdun of maritime warfare, sucking in men and materiel far out of proportion to its significance. There can indeed be little doubt that Malta did exercise an influence that its threat to the Axis powers did not deserve. Efforts to resupply the island during 1942 cost the Royal Navy dear. But there were sound strategic reasons for relieving the island, quite apart from the propaganda disaster and damage to morale had it fallen to the Axis powers.[86] Arguments to the contrary run the risk of circularity. Malta was not standing in the way of Axis supplies in 1941–42, for it was besieged; that does not mean that a well-supplied and secure garrison could make no difference in the decisive campaigns. When submarine and surface forces could operate under adequate air cover, Rommel's forces in North Africa were substantially affected. In November 1941, more than two-thirds of the Afrika Corps' supplies failed to arrive due to Allied pressure from Malta's 'Force K', the small light cruisers *Aurora* and *Penelope* joined by two destroyers.[87] In the lead-up to the critical second battle of El Alamein in October–November 1942, the figure was one-third, and the convoys that did arrive had to take a huge detour via the Corinth Canal and Crete.[88]

As the Allied cause began to look brighter in 1942–43, with the expulsion of German forces from North Africa and Russian advances in the East, planning commenced for the liberation of continental Europe. This would necessarily involve a vast amphibious operation, which eventually resulted in D-Day – the invasion of Normandy – on 6 June 1944. The naval part of this 'Operation Overlord' was codenamed 'Neptune', and it opened at 5.30 in the morning with a naval bombardment along a 50-mile front: the largest in history, up to that point. Naval gunnery was an essential part of the operation's success; where the Allies met with stiffer resistance, for instance, on the Americans' Omaha sector of the coastline, it was barely adequate.[89] But along the British 'Sword' landing area, HMS *Warspite*, HMS *Ramillies* and the gun monitor *Roberts* silenced the powerful German batteries at Villerville, Benevrville and Houlgate, which would otherwise have threatened the landing beaches. And in the area designated 'Juno', the cruisers *Ajax*, *Argonaut*, *Emerald* and *Orion* also kept up an extremely effective support operation.[90] One veteran later remembered the bombardment: 'the battleship HMS *Warspite* was lying off, maybe 3 or 4 miles, and as she was firing her broadsides, the flames from the big 15 inch guns were rolling over the sea . . . it was quite an awesome sight.'[91]

On D-Day, 2468 Allied landing vessels were under Royal Navy control: only 346 of them were American. Out of the 23 cruisers covering the landings close in to shore, 17 were also from the Royal Navy: nine battleships, 104 destroyers and 71 corvettes were also in action. In addition, 4000 landing craft had been prepared to take the troops onto the beaches.[92] The effort was on a truly enormous scale. In just 12 days, 21 divisions were landed and just as huge numbers of transports were used, large numbers of escorts would also be required. A total of 629,000 troops, 95,000 vehicles and 218,000 tons of supplies were landed in Normandy. The strategic breakthrough was assisted by the technical feat of building two floating or 'Mulberry' harbours complete with piers and pier heads. Each was bigger than Dover harbour itself.[93] Though it would be nearly another year before Nazi Germany was defeated, these amphibious landings were probably the largest, as well as the riskiest, step along that road.

In contrast, the Americans conducted most of the Allied effort in the Pacific, winning tactical and then decisive victories at the Battle of the Coral Sea in May 1942, and at Midway in June 1942. The British were forced back on Colombo in Ceylon (modern Sri Lanka), where a very mixed force was commanded by Admiral Sir James Somerville. Somerville's five battleships amounted to four old and slow 'R' class First World War ships, and one (*Warspite*) that dated from before that war, though she had been extensively modified. He had three carriers, *Indomitable*, *Formidable* and *Hermes*, but the last had been laid down as early as 1919. They could mount only 90 aircraft between them. They were certainly no match at all for the combined Japanese force under Admiral Nagumo that had raided Pearl Harbor in December 1941, and which contained five aircraft carriers and four modern battleships.[94]

Only with the imminent end of the war in Europe could the Royal Navy afford to make an offensive effort in the Far East. The British Pacific Fleet – four carriers, two battleships, five cruisers and escorts – arrived in March 1945 and started to operate under the command of Admiral Nimitz, Commander in Chief of the US Pacific Fleet. Here they joined the operations already in progress against Okinawa, to the south-west of the Japanese mainland. However, given the British forces' small size and relative inexperience – three fleet carriers as against the Americans' 34 in the entire theatre – they were asked to operate on their own in attacking Japanese supply lines during May.[95] They acquitted themselves extremely well, and the very heavy armament of British carriers' flight decks made them more resilient than their US counterparts against kamikaze attack from the air. But the crews, and the ships themselves, were often exhausted: the effort was draining some of their last reserves. Following re-equipment in Australia, British forces at last took their place as an integral part of the American Third Fleet only in early July. They then took part in the widespread bombing of Japan's cities leading up to the dropping of the atomic bombs on Hiroshima and Nagasaki on 6–9 August and the subsequent Japanese surrender.[96]

The Second World War: submarine threat (II)

The British had been caught off guard by submarine warfare during the First World War; this time, there could be no such misconceptions. Not only was the experience of 1917 fresh in British memories, but U-boats also struck deep within Britain's own naval defences very early in the war. On the night of 13–14 October 1939, U-47 under the command of Lieutenant Günter Prien slipped into Scapa Flow and sank the battleship HMS *Royal Oak*. The ship went down in just 13 minutes, taking 833 officers and men with it. Only the fact that most of the rest of the fleet was at Loch Ewe prevented wider carnage.[97] The Admiralty put its faith in sonar, in the form of its Asdic detection equipment mounted on ships, and in the convoy system that had turned the tide in 1917. There were two problems with this. The first was that Asdic, as participants in the battle later recalled, gave a good idea of 'plan', and where on the horizontal battlefield a U-boat may be: but depth-charge armaments meant that a hunter had to pass over its location to attack. Depth – much less susceptible to detection via Asdic – thus became a critical and uncertain factor. The U-boat could meanwhile take evasive manoeuvres.[98]

The second problem was the sheer volume of traffic the Royal Navy had to protect, and its inadequate destroyer forces for conducting convoy operations. The Second World War faced the British with a challenge potentially even more serious than the underwater threat that had nearly defeated them in 1917. For following the fall of France the Germans now controlled the whole of the North Sea and Atlantic coastline, from the north of Norway to the south of France: U-boats could issue from any point between Brest and Trondheim, evading any British attempt to stop them by distant blockade in the North Sea. The period between July and October 1940 – between the fall of France and the onset of winter – therefore became known among U-boat commanders as the first 'happy time'. In this period individual U-boat aces were able to roam the Atlantic and sink Allied shipping seemingly at will. In August Hitler declared the British Isles blockaded, and in that same month U-boats sank 56 ships of 267,618 tons. They went on to increase those totals to 295,335 tons in September and 352,407 tons in October. The U-boats' commander, Karl Dönitz, was himself a veteran of the First World War submarine campaign. His 'observation service', or 'B-Dienst' for short, had copied the success of Britain's Room 40 in the First World War, and cracked a series of Admiralty codes that allowed Dönitz to direct U-boats towards merchant shipping.[99]

Convoys were extremely stretched. Even in February, before the fall of France, ships spent an average of 23 days at sea covering trade between Scotland, Iceland and Greenland. It was an enormously gruelling regimen, and the winter weather especially took its toll on the crews.[100] There were simply not enough deep-sea escorts available to cover Britain's overseas trade. Short-range destroyers and corvettes intended for coastal work were forced to cover for this absence, and by September 1940 the UK had to turn to the Americans for the loan of 50 destroyers. In return, the British had to offer 99-year leases on eight British possessions in the Caribbean and in the western Atlantic.[101] It was a heavy price to pay for some very old ships, which required extensive refits. Only nine were in service before the end of the year 1940, and only 30 during 1941.[102] The US destroyers were aged, highly unstable and lightly armed; none were fitted with Asdic when they arrived. Eric Harlow, who joined one of them in October 1940, remembered how the ship's guns would regularly seize up in action. But they filled a gap at a critical point in the campaign.[103]

By spring 1941 Dönitz could deploy 100 U-boats, most of them from the new and most effective Type VIIC, linked directly to his command centre by radio.[104] His campaign was extremely effective, as he assembled hunting 'wolf packs' to replace the 'aces' of the previous year. Between March and May 1941 the Allies lost a total of 1.7 million tons of shipping to enemy action and natural causes: 818,000 tons of the losses came from U-boat action. Imports, including desperately needed machinery and equipment from the USA, ran at about three-quarters of planners' estimates if Britain was to maintain her economic effort; oil stocks ran alarmingly low.[105] On 6 March Prime Minister Churchill felt moved to issue his famous Battle of the Atlantic Directive, setting out his aims and goals and creating a special 'Battle of the Atlantic Committee' with himself in the chair.[106]

A number of British innovations and strategic changes helped turn the tide of this first U-boat campaign during 1941. The first was a tightening of links between the navy and the RAF. In February 1941 Coastal Command was placed under the operational control of the Admiralty, and a new joint command headquarters was established in Liverpool. Control of Icelandic air and sea bases, secured from the time Britain occupied that country in May 1940, allowed air escorts to fly from that country, and Royal Navy escorts to refuel there. The arrival in service of the long-range Catalina in spring 1941 meant that the British and Canadians could cover shipping up to 700 miles out of British ports, and 500 miles east from Newfoundland on the other side of the Atlantic.[107] As in 1914–18, U-boats had to stay on the surface if they were to maintain good speed, large operational ranges and attacking efficiency. That left them vulnerable to air attack until they adopted the underwater schnorkel towards the end of 1943.[108] The Canadians were also beginning to increase their contribution to the transatlantic effort as their destroyer forces grew rapidly.[109]

German successes dropped away precipitously in the late summer of 1941. In August of that year only 83,000 tons of shipping was sunk, barely a third of the level at which successful U-boat attacks were running in the autumn.[110] The major part of this success was not, however, due to the existence of Churchill's committee. The Prime Minister had envisaged arming merchant vessels with fighter aircraft, increasing the number of ships running independently and not in convoy, cutting turnaround times in British ports and increasing the rate of shipbuilding. Only the last two objectives in that list proved practicable or sensible, and that last item was achieved only with American help.[111]

There was another, and much more secret, reason behind this British success. By June 1941, following the capture of German naval codes, British codebreakers at Bletchley Park in Buckinghamshire could read most of Dönitz's orders within 48 hours. The U-boats' commander himself described the consequences: 'time and again there occurred between one convoy battle and another a long hiatus during which the U-boats swept the seas fruitlessly in a vain attempt to find the enemy.'[112] The German navy used the Enigma encoding machine to send orders, employing a machine that encoded messages through a cipher consisting of a series of rotors. The Poles had procured a prototype of Enigma in the early 1930s, and one such machine was smuggled out to the UK via France in 1939.[113] British codebreakers had been able to use this machine, new computer technology and their own ingenuity to break the German codes. This was nothing like the 'magic ingredient' or 'magic bullet' that some writers hailed when the secret of 'Ultra' was revealed in the mid-1970s. The decrypts had to be read as well as deciphered, and this led to inevitable delays.[114] But there is little doubt that, along with many other factors, Ultra played a key role in winning the war in the Atlantic – as experience would prove during 1942.

That year was marked by a renewed wave of U-boat sinkings, opening up a second stage in the Battle of the Atlantic that ran right through the summer of 1942 and into the spring of 1943, only interrupted by the inevitable bad weather of the intervening winter. North Atlantic sinkings rose from the trough of late summer 1941 to 534,064 tons by March 1942, and fluctuated around that level until the end of November.[115] One of the reasons for this renewed danger was the fact that Enigma ceased to be the fertile source of intelligence it had been during 1941. At the beginning of February 1942 the Germans added a fourth rotor to the Enigma cipher. This left Bletchley Park half blind for much of the remaining year, and periods of clear 'vision' alternated with weeks when they were almost completely in the dark. Only in December 1942 did the codebreakers begin to read Ultra signals with any rapid certainty again. HMS *Petard* seized U-559's code books in the eastern Mediterranean in October 1942, which provided Bletchley Park with a crucial insight into the new ciphers. Together with other information still transmitted in the 'Hydra' codes, Bletchley Park once more secured a mastery over the Germans' codes.[116]

B-Dienst's knowledge of the Admiralty's 'convoy cipher', massed 'wolf pack' tactics on fixed patrol lines and the sheer numbers of U-boats Dönitz was able to deploy still caused enormous losses. Dönitz was appointed head of the entire German navy in January 1943, which allowed resources to be diverted to this theatre rather than the futile search for advantage in surface campaigns. He could now direct 240 U-boats in total, 98 of them new or refitted. Enormous and long-running massed battles dominated the campaign early in 1943. Almost all the 34 ships lost in February 1943 went down in two convoys attacked by 'wolf packs' that intelligence had failed to detect. Convoy SC118, comprising 63 merchantmen, endured 13 sinkings when it was attacked by no less than 21 U-boats across 1000 miles of ocean. Convoy SC121 lost 13 ships, in a battle during which no U-boats were destroyed at all.[117]

The worst thing about this crisis was that the majority of ships sunk were now supposed to be protected. Of the 627,000 tons sunk by U-boats in March 1943, 68 per cent were in convoys. There now seemed no easy answer to these head-on tactics, at least pending further developments in the secret war of codes that helped shape the entire campaign. Admiralty codes were changed early in 1943, when Allied commanders became suspicious about the level of German knowledge as to shipping movements: this hugely reduced B-Dienst's efficiency.[118] Only at that point, as American ships poured into the Atlantic using codes the Germans never cracked, did Dönitz's ability to 'see' his enemies decline rapidly.[119] However, though the numbers of British and Allied ships being sunk at this was extremely worrying, later historiographical interpretations labelling this the 'crisis' of the war in the Atlantic can be exaggerated. The huge and long-running battles in the North Atlantic may have had a psychological impact out of proportion to their quantitative significance: four different months in 1942 had seen more ships lost to enemy action overall.[120] The British and Americans were building ships faster than the Germans could destroy them at this point, and with the single exception of November 1942 had been doing so every month since July 1942. By the time SC121 was attacked, they had added over 2 million tons of gross shipping to their totals since the previous summer.[121] Britons had again proved adept at reducing their import needs, for instance, by turning over more land to food production: a pre-war total of 60 million tons per annum had already been cut to 26 million tons.[122]

American shipyards' output was huge compared to the inevitably cramped British effort, which operated on a much smaller scale. British output in 1942 amounted to 1.3 million gross tons, whereas the American launched 7 million tons.[123] These figures help explain why the situation by 1943 was never quite as precarious as it had briefly been in the spring of 1917. Britain lost relatively more shipping in the Second World War – 62 per cent of the tonnage afloat in 1939, as against 41 per cent of the 1914 total in the earlier war. And more than twice the numbers of sailors died in the Second World War than in the First.[124] But the global *Allied* position by this time was far less liable to lead to surrender, since American and Canadian shipyards were producing Liberty, Fort and Park ships so quickly.[125] Though the numbers of ships lost in convoys mounted to new heights early in 1943, and this troubled the Admiralty in particular, Dönitz had in fact moved too slowly to make a decisive impact.

Escort carriers were another key element in the defeat of this last and final German attempt to win the war in the Atlantic. HMS *Audacity*, the first of these new escorts to demonstrate just how critical air power was, was commissioned for this role in September 1941. She was converted from a German prize, the merchant ship *Hannover*, and displaced a mere 5527 tons. But she was fast, managing up to 15 knots, and could deny Luftwaffe Kondors their role as reconnaissance aircraft directing U-boat attacks. Her major success was in warding off an attack on convoy HG7 in December 1941, though *Audacity* herself was sunk by enemy action that same month. It made a huge difference when newly designed ships sailed out to conduct these specialist operations themselves. USS *Bogue*, taking up her station off Greenland in February 1943, prevented Convoy SC123 taking any losses at all during the climax of the battle.[126]

Air cover as a whole was one of the reasons why this second German campaign eventually faded away. Several operational and technological breakthroughs coincided in 1942–43 to allow the RAF to become much more effective in actually destroying U-boats. Aerial depth-charges began widespread deployment late in 1941. Air cover out of the UK, Canada and Iceland was steadily increased until the 'air gap' south of Greenland, between cover provided from the UK and Canada, was gradually closed by American and RAF Liberators, though they remained in very short supply until spring 1943.[127] More importantly, many Allied aircraft were now equipped with radar capable of detecting U-boats. Radar had first been used by British destroyers in November 1940, and had become widespread across the fleet in 1941, though its aerial use only became general in both British and American air forces during 1942.[128] By November of that year the British were reporting more radar contacts than either visual or asdic contacts.[129] 'Leigh lights' also allowed them to scan the ocean in the dark, forcing U-boats under at night and causing them to surface during the day, when they might also be bombed.[130] The 'hedgehog', a mortar that could fire forwards from its shipborne position and thus reduce U-boats' room for manoeuvre, helped in combination with radar to make up for Asdic's deficiencies in the early days of the war.[131]

The Allies may have been taking enormous losses during the period March to May 1943, but U-boat losses were also mounting. In a combined attack on three convoys from 20 April onwards, the U-boats sank only four merchantmen for the loss of three of their own number. The new U-boat crews, often quickly trained in batches in their French bases, began to plead any number of reasons as to why they should not attack, or why they should break off from their operations. These cracks in U-boat morale steadily widened, and U-boats had to be cajoled to stay on station – promptings which the British intercepted with a rising sense of relief. Seven U-boats, and 300 submariners, were lost in their attack on convoy ONS5 in early May 1943, a totally unacceptable rate of exchange given that they had only destroyed 12 Allied ships in a 3-day assault: Dönitz lost 41 U-boats during that month, at a rate of one boat for every 10,000 tons of Allied shipping sunk. The ratio in parts of 1941 and 1942 had been one to 100,000, and the large-scale U-boat campaign in the Atlantic was called off in the light of that declining success rate.[132] This second attempt to throttle Britain's trade had failed.

Conclusions: the meaning of 'victory'

British naval power in the first half of the twentieth century presents us with something of a conundrum. On the one hand, Britain's enormous losses – and equally stupendous war debts – meant that she was only a minor participant in the Pacific War by 1945.[133] American power had outstripped her in every respect. The UK was now the world's biggest debtor, and the USA its most powerful creditor. A £3.75 billion loan made in 1945, and subsequent large injections of Marshall Aid under the Americans' European reconstruction programme, demonstrated this state of dependence.[134] Admiral Bruce Fraser, commander of Britain's Pacific Fleet, did indeed stand next to General Douglas MacArthur and Admiral Nimitz as they took the Japanese surrender in Tokyo Bay on 2 September 1945. But there was no doubt who had won this war. The surrender ceremony symbolically took place aboard the USS *Missouri*.[135] Critical damage had also been done to Britain's shipping industry, as British ships were destroyed, shipyards diverted to building for the Royal Navy and neutrals allowed to take over previously British routes. The UK owned 39.3 per cent of the world's fleet in 1914, which fell to 32.8 per cent in 1921, 26.1 per cent in 1939 and only 22.4 per cent in 1948.[136] The USA was supplying 38 per cent of even her military ships by 1945.[137]

Correlli Barnett is in this respect quite justified in arguing that 'British power...quietly vanished amid the stupendous events of the Second World War.' And it is appropriate that he uses a naval image to demonstrate that truth: Barnett imagines 'a ship-of-the-line going down unperceived in the smoke and confusion of battle'.[138] But the implied sense that this was *inevitable*, and that this had been brought about long-held 'dreams', 'illusions', even 'hallucinations', is at the very least open to question.[139] It contains inevitabilist and 'declinist' preconceptions that, in retrospect, fail to grasp the situation as it appeared at the time; and it gives insufficient weight to tactical and political choices that might have issued in quite different results.[140]

Barnett has always been quick to put the most pessimistic gloss possible on critical, and sometimes misleading, documents in the National Archives.[141] In this particular field, he has consistently argued that inter-war defence policy was neglected, and indeed misguided by pacifists and disarmers. Barnett has singled out the Washington Naval Conference of 1921–22, which established a British: American: Japanese naval tonnage ratio of 5:5: 3, for special opprobrium.[142] In this respect, he posits an implicitly militarist 'Bismarckian' counterfactual that assumes a healthier economy between the wars, and a far greater ability to fight back in 1939–45 than in fact developed.[143] The raw numbers tell a rather different story to Barnett's 'declinism'. Not only did the Royal Navy avoid some of the deepest cuts that the RAF and the Army had to endure, but between 1918 and 1939 the British outbuilt all other Powers, in every class of warship.[144]

In 1941, the Royal Navy would have had 18 battleships in commission had it not been for the loss of *Royal Oak*, *Hood* and *Barham*: to some extent, its 'inadequacy' was a consequence of 2 years of war, not of inter-war neglect. And even then, Britain's global battleship force stood at 15, to Japan's 11: only the disastrous loss of HMS *Prince of Wales* and *Repulse* off the coast of British Malaya on 10 December 1941 brought their numbers closer together.[145] All of the Royal Navy's 15 battleships in commission during 1939 had been expensively refitted or remodelled in the 1930s. Five of them – *Barham*, *Malaya*, *Royal Oak*, *Renown* and *Repulse* – had gone through refits costing between £1 and £1.5 million. Three more – *Elizabeth*, *Warspite* and

Valiant – were rebuilt on top of earlier refits. By the end of 1941 the three main Pacific powers – the USA, Japan and Great Britain – were actually at rough parity in terms of their total numbers of large ships with long-range guns. Even in terms of aircraft carriers, where the service has been severely criticised, it possessed six aircraft carriers in 1935, while Japan and the USA had both built four. In 1939 the Royal Navy had seven carriers and the other two Powers six each. By the end of 1941, had it not been for the loss in action of *Courageous*, *Glorious* and *Ark Royal*, Britain would have had 11 carriers to the Japanese eight.[146] Britain's naval building between the wars would probably have been sufficient to win a war against any two of her adversaries in 1941–44, namely, Germany, Italy and Japan. What threatened her very survival was their alliance against her, which only began to look at all possible in the late 1930s, when her rearmament effort was accelerated for just this reason.[147]

In the end, though naval power was hardly sufficient to actually win either war, without it both Britain and the Allies would have lost – particularly in 1917, 1940 and again during the Battle of the Atlantic in 1942. 'Declinist' critiques risk losing sight of that one overriding fact. Destroyer-led convoys and the deterrent effect of the battleship fleet saved Britain from blockade and starvation in 1917. The navy played, if anything, a greater role in 1939–45. Without the Royal Navy the British Army would never have escaped from France, and it could never have been launched, with its allies, back onto the continental mainland in 1944. The Royal Navy kept open Britain's supply lines, at enormous human cost. In the First World War, 33,361 Royal Navy officers and men were killed; over 50,000 naval personnel lost their lives in the Second World War as 1525 warships of all types were sunk.[148] But as the great British economist John Maynard Keynes put it, 'we saved ourselves, and we helped save the world.'[149]

Timeline of events

23 August 1911	Committee of Imperial Defence decides on continental strategy against Germany
3 August 1914	British declaration of war on Germany
November 1914	First use of 'Q-Ships' against U-boats
9 November 1914	*Emden* sunk at the Battle of Cocos
8 December 1914	Battle of the Falkland Islands
28 January 1915	War Council decides to attack Turkey at the Dardanelles
1915	Progressively more extensive food rationing begins in Germany

19 February 1915	Allied naval attack on the Dardanelles
March 1915	First German U-boats sail into Mediterranean
11 March 1915	British Order in Council announces all German trade will be blockaded
18 March 1915	Allied naval retreat in battle for the Dardanelles
25 April 1915	Allied land forces attack Gallipoli
7 May 1915	Sinking of the *Lusitania*
15 May 1915	Resignation of Fisher as First Sea Lord
18 September 1915	Germany announces suspension of first unrestricted submarine warfare campaign
December 1915	Allied evacuation begins at Gallipoli and the Dardanelles
31 May–1 June 1916	Battle of Jutland
December 1916	Anti-Submarine Division formed within the Admiralty
1 February 1917	Unrestricted submarine warfare resumed by Germany
6 April 1917	US declaration of war against Germany
10 May 1917	First British merchant convoy leaves Gibraltar bound for the UK
June 1917	Limitations on Grand Fleet movements due to lack of oil
29 October 1918	Mutiny in the German High Seas Fleet when it is ordered out against the British
11 November 1918	Armistice between Britain and Germany
21 November 1918	German High Seas Fleet begins to arrive at Scapa Flow to be interned
February 1922	Washington Naval Treaty limits UK, US and Japanese ships to a 5: 5: 3 ratio
3 September 1939	Britain declares war on Germany
13–14 October 1939	HMS *Royal Oak* sunk by a U-boat in Scapa Flow
13 December 1939	Battle of the River Plate
17 December 1939	*Graf Spee* scuttled by her crew off Montevideo
26 May 1940	Beginning of 'Operation Dynamo' evacuation at Dunkirk
4 June 1940	End of 'Operation Dynamo' evacuation

10 June 1940	Italy declares war on Britain and France
17 June 1940	Sinking of RMS *Lancastria* off St Nazaire
July–October 1940	First 'happy time' in Atlantic for German U-boat commanders
August 1940	Hitler announces British Isles 'blockaded'
2 September 1940	UK–US 'bases for destroyers' deal
17 September 1940	Hitler cancels 'Operation Sealion' – the invasion of Britain – for that year
11 November 1940	Royal Navy airborne raid on Italian naval base at Taranto
February 1941	Coastal Command placed under the operational control of the Admiralty
6 March 1941	Churchill's 'Battle of the Atlantic' directive
20 May 1941	German invasion of Crete
24 May 1941	HMS *Hood* sunk by the *Bismarck*
27 May 1941	*Bismarck* sunk by Royal Navy forces
28–31 May 1941	Royal Navy evacuates Commonwealth army forces from Crete
June 1941	'Ultra' codebreakers achieve near real-time mastery of German codes
September 1941	Escort carrier HMS *Audacity* enters action
13 November 1941	Aircraft carrier HMS *Ark Royal* sunk by U-81 in Western Mediterranean
7 December 1941	Japanese attack on Pearl Harbor brings the USA into the war
10 December 1941	Sinking of *Prince of Wales* and *Repulse* off Malaya
15 December 1941	Fall of Penang to Japanese forces
21 December 1941	Sinking of HMS *Audacity* under U-boat attack
February 1942	Germans introduce fourth rotor on Enigma which prevents decoding
15 February 1942	Fall of Singapore to the Japanese
22 March 1942	Second Battle of Sirte
4–8 May 1942	Battle of the Coral Sea prevents Japanese landings in New Guinea
4–7 June 1942	Battle of Midway between US and Japanese fleets
12–16 June 1942	'Operation Harpoon' brings only limited supplies from Gibraltar to Malta

12–15 June 1942	'Operation Vigorous' fails to reach Malta from Alexandria
10–15 August 1942	'Operation Pedestal' brings oil and other supplies into Malta
3 October–5 November 1942	Second Battle of El Alamein. Decisive defeat of Rommel's Afrika Corps
30 October 1942	HMS *Petard* seizes U-559's code books in the Mediterranean
December 1942	Bletchley Park codebreakers regain good access to encoded messages
January 1943	Change of Admiralty codes reduces efficiency of B-Dienst codebreakers
February 1943	Specialist escort carrier USS *Bogue* enters action in the Atlantic
4–8 February 1943	Running battles around Convoy SC118 as it is attacked by U-boats
6–10 March 1943	U-boat attacks against Convoy SC121 in North Atlantic
6 June 1944	'D-Day': Allied invasion of Normandy
March 1945	New British Pacific Fleet arrives in that ocean
May 1945	British Pacific Fleet engaged against Japanese supply lines at Battle for Okinawa
8 May 1945	'VE-Day' marks Germany's unconditional surrender
6 August 1945	Atomic bomb dropped on Hiroshima
9 August 1945	Second atomic bomb dropped on Nagasaki
15 August 1945	Japan announces that it will accept Allied terms
2 September 1945	Formal Japanese surrender on board USS *Missouri*: end of the Second World War

8

Immigrants

By the twentieth century the British had been pouring out into the world for 300 years. They had peopled an entire Empire in successive waves culminating in the great emigration of the Edwardian period. They took and brought with them their language, habits, customs and ideas. But in the twentieth century the Empire itself began to 'come home'. Hundreds of thousands of Imperial and Commonwealth citizens came to Britain itself, especially during the 1950s and 1960s, fundamentally altering the United Kingdom itself. 'British' culture – food, music, cinema and even the language itself – changed given the impact of these new immigrants. Those changes were slow in coming, and the indigenous population often resented and resisted them: racism, preconceptions and ingrained prejudices were all very common throughout the second half of the late twentieth century, though they abated somewhat as time went on. The new immigrants themselves had usually come by sea, at least initially. That meant that many of their experiences paralleled that of emigrants' lives in the eighteenth to the early twentieth centuries. Crowded bunks, slow and indirect journeys and seasickness were all just as prevalent as they had been in the previous great movements of Britons across the oceans. The sense of hope, optimism and lives 'opening up' was also similar, and often expressed in the idea of the 'freedom of the seas' – again, drawing on very similar words and concepts to the English, Welsh and Scots as they sailed away from Britain in earlier decades. But the jet revolution of the 1950s and early 1960s made travelling by air faster, cheaper and safer than the passage by ship. By the 1970s it was exceedingly rare for immigrants to arrive by sea: flying was ubiquitous, as the example of the Ugandan Asians' expulsion from East Africa showed in 1972. One of the key experiences of 'Britishness' had withered, presaging a wider collapse of maritime society and the shipborne economy. The emigration from the British Isles continued – indeed, it experienced something of a renaissance both in the years just after the Second World War and in the first years of the twenty-first century. Commonwealth governments initially encouraged this diaspora, often paying for it themselves to buttress politicians' ideas of a healthy and stable 'race'. But this movement, too, gradually but fundamentally changed its nature. Emigrants' preference for the 'Old' – and mostly white – Dominions gave way to a much more complex picture. Subsidies were withdrawn, by both Britain and Commonwealth states. Europe became the destination of choice for more and more Britons leaving the country; a 'near abroad' developed, shaped once more by the airliner. Spain and France, in particular, played host to archipelagos of British settlement that were constantly in flux, as individuals moved, perhaps to retire, came back to visit their 'home' country and then travelled back again. Emigration had helped to make Britain what it was. Now the continued movement of peoples once again remade Britain into a much more complex nation – though one less bound to the sea.

The contours and scale of Commonwealth immigration

The West Indian migrants who arrived at Tilbury on the converted troop carrier *Empire Windrush* on 22 June 1948 were in fact to become a symbol of vast changes in Britain's racial, social and cultural character – a transformation that would change the country forever. The (for the most part) Jamaicans on board were small in number. They were often ex-servicemen, and the number of immigrants in total was in fact to remain until the mid-1950s. But what they symbolised has come to seem far more significant than their quantitative importance.[1] As the Jamaican poet Louise Bennett put it in 1966, the Empire was coming home and 'colonizin England in reverse'.[2] The *Empire Windrush* was not even the first ship to make the post-war trip, for the *Ormonde* had brought 108 immigrants on the same route in 1947.[3] But she became a symbol, both because she was met by newsreel cameras and because her arrival caused the first widespread tremors of concern about immigration among both elites and the people at large. Britain was suffering, economically, under the weight of her post-war debts, her exhausted industries and her need for social reconstruction. Without Marshall Aid from the USA, Britain would have been totally bankrupt and may have been forced to implement a siege economy and widespread conscription and direction of labour.[4]

The migrants' desire for jobs was the first and most obvious reason why the men and women on board the *Windrush* have come to seem so symbolic. Post-war labour shortages encouraged migration from all over the Empire, and Britain was indeed desperate for more workers to boost her export drive. Still, at a time of national economic uncertainty, the complaint that immigrants were 'taking our jobs' was widely heard.[5] The National Union of Mineworkers and the National Union of Agricultural Workers were particularly vocal in complaining about the use of immigrant labour in the late 1940s.[6] These fears seem far from objective reality. West Indian migration was, in fact, very strongly *inversely* correlated with unemployment in the UK. When unemployment fell, in the early 1960s for instance, Caribbean immigration surged; when joblessness increased in Britain, as it did in the late 1950s and early 1970s, the numbers of newcomers fell back.[7] The same point held, though less strongly, for South Asian immigrants.[8] Indians and Pakistanis also came to work, for instance, in the textile areas of the North and North West of England and the light industries of west London.[9] In this case, rather than 'take' from an imaginary fixed stock of jobs, migrants were often ready to work hard before their imagined return home. Social investigators found that, even by the 1970s, most Pakistani workers in British factories thought they would return home after a period of sending money back to their families.[10]

Many Indians and Pakistanis had made as many sacrifices for the Empire as had many of the men and women on board the *Windrush*. During the Second World War, 700,000 had served in the Indian Army, sustaining 180,000 casualties, of whom 24,000 were killed. There was also a specifically maritime element to this sense of shared endeavour and entitlement: this second element in the narrative of post-war immigration and wartime service, namely, the shared ties created by maritime service, is perhaps a rather less familiar one. In the Merchant Navy, where of course a large proportion of the crew had always been provided by Indians as well as men from the Caribbean, the sub-continental contribution was even larger. Most 'Lascars' – the word is probably derived from the Persian 'Lashkar', denoting a military camp or army – had been Muslims during the eighteenth and nineteenth centuries: Sylhet, in what is now Bangladesh, was a particularly rich source of labour.[11] Poor, rural and flooded in the rainy season, British Bengal was the single greatest source of India's imperial seafarers.[12]

That dependence on Muslim Bengal gradually faded in the twentieth century, as Hindu religious objections to seafaring and leaving India began to fade, and non-manual jobs began to open up for Indians.[13] This greater level of participation served to boost Indians' overall service in imperial shipping: 26 per cent of the labour force on British merchant ships was Indian in 1938. They were recruited on a highly segregated basis. Sylhettis tended to work in the engine room, while Hindus and Christians worked on deck or with passengers and cargo.[14] An estimated 6600 Indians (from a contingent of perhaps 59,000 at its peak) lost their lives in the subsequent conflict, while 1022 were wounded and 1217 were taken as prisoners of war. During the First World War, 3427 had been killed, and 1200 taken prisoner.[15] Many 'imperial' and colonial peoples from around the Empire and Commonwealth served in the Merchant and Royal Navies. During the Second World War, 2000 Maltese sailors served in the Royal Navy, and probably well over another thousand in the Merchant Navy. From that tiny country, 409 men lost their lives: in all, probably a third of all Second World War casualties in both services came from outside the UK.[16]

Despite such sacrifices from across the sub-continent's religious and ethnic divides, Indian seamen's terms of employment – the so-called lascar articles which governed their treatment – prevented their discharge at any port outside British India. That meant that they had to desert if they wanted to work in Britain while under contract, and surprisingly few crewmen (perhaps 400 a year) were actually prepared to do so. Most of the Indians coming to Britain during the Second World War were seamen waiting to go home, or who had slipped through the authorities' attempt to deport them back to India at the end of their seafaring contract.[17] About 300 Sylhetti men lived in East London in the early years of peace, and they proved to be a spearhead of newcomers who were to be 200,000 strong (35,000 in East London) by the time of the first Commonwealth Immigrants Act in 1962.[18]

Britain's position as a net exporter of people was transformed by this influx. The balance between people leaving and entering the UK, so skewed towards emigrants in the Edwardian period, changed completely. Between 1901 and 1921, 174,000 more people left Britain than entered it; between 1921 and 1951, the figure was 45,000; but between 1951 and 1971, the number stood at just 2000. During the 1970s and 1980s, 16,000 more people actually entered Britain than left it.[19] The arrival of the *Windrush* has come to seem so important because it heralded enormous changes in the racial composition of Britain's population. The Irish, as they had always done, continued to form the largest single group of incomers: during the second half of the twentieth century, more than a million Irish people, from both North and South, moved to Britain.[20] Moreover, 120,000 Poles and large numbers of other Europeans came or remained, frightened of returning to an Eastern Europe dominated by Stalin, as is indeed evidenced by the presence of the Poles on the *Windrush* itself.[21] But after the Second World War black Caribbean, African and Asian faces also became a familiar sight in many parts of the UK, especially in large metropolitan areas.[22] More than half the newcomers originated in the Caribbean in the 1950s, their numbers peaking in 1955 (at 27,000) and during 1961 and 1962 (at over 100,000).

Many borrowed money from friends and family to afford the trip, though as time went on more West Indian governments subsidised their passage.[23] Between 1955 and 1968, 200,000 Indians, 146,000 Pakistanis and 324,000 West Indians entered the UK.[24]

The British government eventually brought the relatively liberal 1948 immigration regime to an end during the 1960s. Clement Attlee's Labour Cabinet had first considered doing so in 1950 and 1951.[25] The Conservatives then debated the idea in 1955 before deciding that the damage to Commonwealth and colonial relations – and the risk of losing centrist voters to Labour – would be too great.[26] But in 1962 Harold Macmillan's Conservative government did move to pass the first Commonwealth Immigrants Act, which controlled the entry of all Commonwealth migrants except those born in Britain, those holding passports issued by Britain or those included on the passport of those who had already entered the country under the previous regime. Work permits would be issued to those immigrants who were 'needed'. To the fury of most Caribbean and South Asian observers, this continued to allow uncontrolled immigration from the 'Old' Dominions – Canada, New Zealand and Australia – as most 'British' subjects in those countries could claim British origin or descent.[27] To add insult to injury, these new restrictions were joined by Part II of the Act, which codified the courts' powers to recommend deportations. This appears to have been an official attempt to mollify the highly visible anti-immigrant lobby: though in the event, these powers were most often used against Irish citizens suspected of being Irish Republican Army (IRA) sympathisers.[28] The Labour Party opposed the initial Act, but once back in power from October 1964 tightened voucher rules, eliminating so-called non-priority cases. The Labour government also passed a second Commonwealth Immigration Act in 1968. This subjected all British passport holders who had not been born in Britain, or did not have parents or grandparents born in the country, to controls. The most noteworthy effect of this was to nullify 200,000 passports issued to East African Asians by British High Commissions in that region.[29]

Black and Asian immigrants continued to come even after the passage of the 1962 and 1968 Acts, both on voucher work schemes – although those numbers soon declined, and in any case only amounted to 78,000 in the years between the two Commonwealth Immigration Acts – and as relatives of the original migrants.[30] Primary immigration continued as the dependents and relatives of men who had moved to Britain before 1962 came to join them.[31] Numbers did fall. In 1967, the year before the second Act, 'New' Commonwealth immigration to the UK stood at 61,000; by the early 1980s, it was only 28,000.[32] But this was still enough, over time, to gradually change the ethnic composition of the country. By 1991 there were, perhaps, between 5 and 5-and-a-half million people of Caribbean birth or immediate descent living in Britain; 1.5 million from Asian backgrounds; and just over 200,000 people from Africa.[33] The influx was accompanied by a slow and steady, though small, movement in the other direction. It has been estimated that perhaps 86,000 West Indians returned to their 'home' region in the period 1966–88 – a figure that yields a possible total of just under 4000 returnees a year.[34]

Immigrant voyage narratives

The actual journey to Britain has been less well-treated than the consequences of mass immigration. Mike and Trevor Phillips, of Guyanese descent themselves, have written how they have 'imagined the scene [of arrival] many times'. But there are few actual studies centring on black and Asian journey experiences as a whole.[35] Robert Foulke's 2002 book *The Sea Voyage Narrative* mentions only one relevant author: Derek Walcott, the St Lucian dramatist, poet and winner of the Nobel Prize for Literature, who has lived for most of his professional life in the USA.[36] Walcott's long 1990 poem *Omeros* and his earlier 1965 collection *The Castaway* are both steeped in the lore and the feel of the sea.[37] The dream journey of Achille, one of *Omeros'* main protagonists, captures that character's maritime flight to the Africa of his ancestors. The voyage becomes an expedition into that continent's past and its enslavement. Dreaming he was submerged, Achille imagined that 'the parchment overhead / of crinkling water recorded three centuries / of the submerged archipelago, in its swell'.[38]

The challenge is to look into broader immigrant encounters, beyond poetry and literature, and to divine something of the mass experience of movement that so marked out the second half of the twentieth century. Many less well-known immigrants were explicit about the link between Britain and the sea. Donald Hinds, a Jamaican of Indian ancestry who came to Britain in 1955, felt affronted by the fact that he was not seen as a citizen of a maritime empire:

> If British 'Oceanic achievement' began in the second half of the eighteenth century with the conquest and the settling of the three favourite white Dominions ... then it means that Britain's rise to world leadership in the seventeenth, eighteenth and early nineteenth centuries is being dismissed too easily, and sea dogs and buccaneers such as Hawkins, Drake, Raleigh and Morgan and more honest sailors such as Benbow, Hood, Rodney and Nelson, all of whose careers flourished in the West Indies, are being swept aside. Had Nelson not received the wrong information while in Barbados, he could have caught up with Villeneuve at Martinique, and Britain might have been saved in the West Indies and not at Trafalgar. All this is part of Caribbean history as it is part of Britain's. Australia and New Zealand are too young to know anything of it. This ... is what is meant

by our Englishness. With England we have a common history going further back than any other of her ... former colonies.[39]

Hinds' views also demonstrate the extent to which Caribbean migrants of the 1950s thought of Britain as their home, and indeed many of them had already proved loyal to the Empire during their military service in the Second World War. The London *Evening Standard* in fact ran its first article on the *Empire Windrush* under the title: 'WELCOME HOME'.[40]

There were and are as many immigrant stories about the voyages to Britain as there were individual migrants, but several themes stand out whether or not unusual or more regular journeys are singled out for attention. The first is the chaos and confusion of the harbourside at the start of the journey. 'Devon', a Jamaican interviewed by Hinds for his 1966 book *Journey to an Illusion*, thought that moving 'was more in the line of something I had to do', but he still found 'Number One Pier [at Kingston Harbour] ... a seething mass of humanity. At least seven of my relations had turned out to see me off, and if an average of three had turned out to see other migrants off that would give a fair idea of what the scene looked like from the deck of the ship.'[41] The Jamaican-British author Ferdinand Dennis remembers his own voyage from Kingston Harbour to Southampton: 'Surrounded by my two brothers, sister and mother, I had no reason to shed tears, but tears are seldom caused by reason .... My memories ... are of four children huddled around their mother. A cold, sharp wind tore through my thin cotton clothes and flesh, penetrating, it seemed, into the marrow of my bones.'[42]

Most migrants remembered, secondly, the indirect and sometimes interminable nature of their voyages. The majority of the West Indians came to Europe via Italy during the 1950s, where over half the ships carrying them were registered. As the Barbadian Ann Bovell has recalled of her 1960 voyage:

I leave Barbados the last week of May in 1960, and I got to England the twelfth of June. I figured it'd be two weeks on the sea. I went by boat of the name *Serrienta*. To tell the truth, I had a very lonely voyage ... when I leave here I was scared. I feared that I would get sick and that, if I died on the sea, they would throw me body overboard. My mother told me that I no be sick. She did tell the truth because, when the boat came into the harbour at Bridgetown to carry us to England, a doctor came aboard and sprayed [germicide] all about, and so I not get sick on the sea. The boat take us to Genoa, and then we take the train and boat and train again to England.

Another Barbadian, Roy Campbell, remembers the *Serrienta* with rather more colour, and certainly as more comfortable than the spartan *Windrush*: 'the food was good, and at night you could go down to the cinema and watch a movie or to the lounge . . . and they had a nice little bar where you could have a drink. The ship had an Italian band, but they mostly played samba music so that both the Italians and the West Indians could dance to it.'[43]

A sense of daring adventure, of picaresque and romantic voyages conducted in defiance of life, is a third trope of these narratives. 'Devon' had to guard against this sense of unreality: 'after a week's sea voyage, it dawned on me that emigration was not merely a romance. Names, places and faces would soon be blurred by events. I had to learn to make friends.'[44] The Jamaican Wallace Collins was driven to migrate himself by the death of his father, and his family's poverty given the lack of jobs in his homeland. Collins' memoirs of the migrant experience are at their liveliest during his voyage narrative. Tricked on board a ship out of Port Antonio with promises of a job, he spent his first night at sea in the hold, 'huddled in a pool of water' and listening to 'huge waves being chopped down on the ship's bow . . . while my body went through the motions of a bronco rider in a rodeo'. He was then discovered as a 'common stowaway' and 'criminal', but was then at least asked by the ship's Purser to act as an intermediary and spokesman for the other six illegal travellers on board. None of this prevented the Purser condemning Collins to the immigration authorities in London as 'the scum of Jamaica'. He was forced to work for the shipping company for 3 weeks, 'paying my debt to that society that I lived in for twenty-two years, five thousand miles away . . . paying for its rock-like deficiency, and its greedy overlords'.[45]

These ships were often extremely crowded, a fact that made them seem more oppressive as they grew successively in size. The scale of the migration from the mid-1950s onwards made it more profitable for shipowners to provide much bigger vessels. In 1953 no ship carried more than 300 migrants; by 1960, many carried more than a thousand.[46] 'Devon' travelled with 1100 other Jamaicans on the SS *Auriga* in 1955, and for his £85 one-way fare had to share a cabin with another five passengers. Friends elsewhere on the ship had to live in cabins of 24, conditions which put some of the migrants in mind of 'the horrors of the Middle Passage'. The last part of the journey – arrival at the dockside – could often come as a shock. 'Devon's' arrival in Plymouth felt exactly like this: 'from the deck could be seen knots of white people staring back at us. I had hardly ever seen more than twelve white people together . . . I had always been a member of the majority race.'[47]

The continuing importance of British emigration

The mass immigration of the 1950s and 1960s did not mean that Britons had themselves ceased to move. On the contrary, although the First World War temporarily blocked the possibility of emigration, Britons continued to pour out into the world. In the 1920s, a natural population increase of 2.7 million was scaled back by 667,000 under the impact of mass emigration. Just over a million people left in the years between 1922 and 1931, at which point the Depression put paid to further mass movement.[48] They went, increasingly, to the Empire, attracted for the most part by lands where the majority of people spoke English, and – as we shall see – there were financial inducements that made the idea seem even more enticing. In 1900–04 the number of emigrants moving to 'foreign' locations had outstripped those travelling to Britain's dominions overseas; by the 1920s, 1930s and late 1940s, the Imperial voyagers outnumbered those sailing to 'foreign' lands between three and five to one.[49]

Scottish migration, in particular, remained very high, and outstripped every other country in Europe in the 1920s. It only tailed off after the economic crisis of 1929–31, and the outflow continued – albeit at a lower level – even during most of the Depression. Only in one year (1932–33) did Scotland experience any net gain in population from migration. During the 1920s, over 400,000 Scots left the country, 70,000 of them to live or settle overseas. The single greatest number of them moved to Canada.[50] In the 1930s, this fell to just 33,595, under a fifth of the country's population growth, only about a third of whom sailed to Imperial or foreign destinations.[51] Even so, this fall was not as precipitous as elsewhere in the UK. Scots had a long tradition of emigrating, as we have seen. And the low wages that had hitherto made Scottish manufacturing so competitive, combined with the economic disaster of the Depression, made the need to move even greater than in England and Wales.[52]

The post-Second World War period was also one of sustained emigration. Emigrant numbers expanded to nearly 600,000 in 1946–49 alone, and three quarters of a million Britons left their country for overseas destinations between 1946 and 1950. Official reports began to express concern at the drain of 'the young, the virile, [and] the adventurous'. This outflow more than matched the inflow from outside: in the first 9 months of 1947, 43,000 people arrived in Britain, but 88,000 left.[53] But the total peaked at 1.33 million people moving overseas during the 1950s, and many more in the 1960s. By this time the single most important destination was Australia, and nearly half a million moved in just the 2 years 1967 and 1968. Even these enormous movements were actually less than during the Edwardian period at the beginning of the century.[54] The British economy was growing; demographic pressures and the increase in population were easing and slowing. The new surge was very real, but it was not to return to its Edwardian peak.[55]

Even so, and at least until the 1990s, wages were still much higher in most of the 'old' Commonwealth countries and in the USA than they were at home.[56] Propaganda, especially Australian publicity, made the point about what migrants could achieve very explicitly: 'Australia – Land of the Better

Chance', published in 1926, spoke of 'infinite opportunity' in this 'rich and generous young country'. The Australian authorities published a monthly paper, *Overseas Settler*, to make much the same case.[57] Here was the most explicit parallel with the nineteenth-century publicity that had previously encouraged so many to travel overseas: the attraction of a freer, cleaner and more virtuous country, open to merit and competition, remained. Emigrants could still take advantage of the well-established seaways that linked the British Empire together. For self-financing passengers, and these always remained the majority of emigrants even during the years of assisted travel, P&O in the late 1920s operated nine different vessels to Australia via Cape Town.[58]

But the continued outflow also relied on official encouragement and subsidies. An official Overseas Settlement Committee was established in April 1919, which eventually assisted 86,027 emigrants with their passages to Britain's Dominions. An Empire Settlement Act was then passed by the British Parliament in 1922, which set aside £3 million to assist emigrants' costs. Colonial governments, too, spent vast sums on settlement schemes: Australia paid out £7 million between 1925 and 1932. New Zealand's Assisted Passage Scheme of 1922 lowered the cheapest third-class fare for adult migrants from £36 to £18. The price fell again, due to lower shipping costs, to just £11 in 1926.[59] In 1925 Canada's federal government provided land for British settlers under their '3,000 Families Scheme', and provided the White Star, Cunard and Canadian Pacific steamship companies with a C$15 subsidy for each Briton carried to the country. At their peak, in 1928, these and other schemes helped pay for nearly 30,000 Britons to travel to Canada.[60] Overall, between 1923 and 1929, one-third of Britain emigrants to Canada, and two-thirds to Australia, received assistance.[61]

The Empire Settlement Act was renewed on a number of occasions, latterly as the Commonwealth Settlement Act, before finally lapsing in 1972. By 1936 over 400,000 people had taken advantage of this scheme to move to new countries.[62] Many more were to take advantage of such schemes after the Second World War, and the cost to the British taxpayer mounted. From £52,000 in 1947–48, the cost of the Settlement Acts rose to £1.4 million in 1951–52, before the Government cut spending back to £150,000. By the time of the Acts' final abolition, just over a million people had taken advantage of them to emigrate to Australia alone.[63] Related schemes were provided by individual Dominions. The Australian Free and Assisted Passage Agreements were funded jointly, from March 1947, by both British and Australian governments. Ex-servicemen and women were given free passages, while civilians had to pay £10 – the so-called ten pound poms – and children between 14 and 18 cost £5. The New Zealand government paid the whole cost of its own resettlement scheme, also announced in 1947. West Indians and other 'imperial' peoples were not eligible: Arthur Calwell, Australia's Minister of Immigration at the time, had unofficially laid down a 'White Australia' policy that would last into the early 1970s.[64] In 1957 Australia launched a 'Bring Out A Briton' publicity campaign, the first migrants arriving on board the Orient Line's *Oronsay* in June 1957. Though the campaign did little to boost numbers in total, the personal welcome given to one ship by Athol Townley, by now another pro-British Immigration Minister, was very revealing: 'Australia is a British Country. The great majority of native-born Australians are the descendents of British stock.'[65]

Children and young people, being relocated without their parents, were one noticeable part of this continuing flood. The Empire Settlement Act specifically encouraged child migration for children in care, which Westminster paternalists thought was a more attractive 'solution' than leaving these children in state institutions. Here the authorities were only continuing a long-established system, whereby the churches, voluntary organisations and charities separated 'problem' children from their surviving families, regardless of other solutions that may have been pursued. Between 1900 and 1914, 31,210 children had been relocated to Canada, and perhaps 80,000 children overall in the period from Canadian federation in 1867 to the schemes' curtailment during the U-boat crisis of 1917.[66] A few more followed in the 1920s, to bring the Canadian total to 90,000. At the peak of this effort, over 50 organisations were involved, including the Church of England Waifs and Strays Society and the Methodist organisation National Children's Homes.[67]

Some of these schemes survived into the period following the Second World War, though they operated on a much smaller scale. Between 1947 and 1967 – when these systems were terminated – childcare charities such as Dr Barnardo's and the Salvation Army sent about 3200 boys and girls to the 40 or so childcare institutions to which they were linked in Australia.[68] Between the 1860s and 1967, about 150,000 children may have been sent abroad unaccompanied, a fact that came to seem inexplicable in a more liberal and humanitarian era. Even in the post-war period, birth certificates often had the parents' names removed if they could not 'cope' with their children; brothers and sisters were split up; abuse was widespread. One child migrant to Australia remembers being separated from his siblings at the dockside: 'where it hit me particularly was when they dragged the brothers and sisters from one another, I can still hear the screams today.' As the Chief Executive of Barnardo's put it in 1998: 'it was barbaric; it was dreadful. We look back on it in our organisation with shock and horror'.[69] The use of such methods attests to the power of the 'unofficial state' that buttressed the power of local councils and government, but also of the lure of 'imperial' social and economic policies.

Even given the economic, social and ideological attractiveness of Commonwealth destinations, the trend towards emigration to the Empire, which had begun before the First World War, was no smooth or linear process. Migration to Canada – as to other destinations – fell precipitously in the late 1920s and during the 1930s, and even the Empire Settlement Act could not reverse the situation. Despite the attractive subsidies, many of the working class migrants did not wish to work in farming, where Canada most desperately needed an influx of workers. The newcomers also met with hostility, not only from Canadian populists who objected to taking the 'dregs' of the mother country's industrial workers, but also from authorities who were willing and indeed eager to deport them if they proved 'failures' in the job market.[70] A new Conservative government in Canada moved quickly to cut off that country's unilateral aid to settlers in 1930.[71]

The British may have moved in less impressive numbers than they had in the early years of the twentieth century. But it was often the young, the mobile and the highly skilled who now moved, prompting widespread scares about a 'brain drain' in the 1960s.[72] Nearly a fifth of male Aberdeen University graduates in the period 1860–1960 eventually found jobs, and settled down, outside the UK.[73] But the transoceanic option was about to recede quite quickly, and even the limited renaissance of emigration experienced during the 1950s and 1960s would fade. The white Dominions and the USA became less attractive sites for British emigration in the 1970s and 1980s, as they raised barriers to entries through such mechanisms as points schemes for migrant workers. The English language, Caucasian race and 'shared culture' of the British no longer seemed so relevant in a highly competitive, multipolar and unsentimental world. Canada abolished preferential treatment for immigrants from the UK, France and the USA in 1962; the USA tightened visa controls on British entrants in 1968; Australia launched a points system regardless of the country of the immigrants' origin in 1979; and New Zealand finally abolished easier entry for Europeans in 1987.[74]

Conditions on British emigrant voyages

Conditions on emigrant ships were much better in the twentieth than in the nineteenth centuries. For one thing, the voyage was much shorter. When the SS *Metagama* took 800 men and women from the Scottish island of Lewis, it was scheduled to take 8 days; only bad weather delayed its entry into St John's harbour until the eleventh day out of Stornoway.[75] It usually took only 5–6 weeks to travel even to Australia by the 1920s and 1930s.[76] After the Second World War, it might take only 3 weeks to make it to Fremantle, the port of Perth in Western Australia – though moving on to Sydney or Melbourne might take another couple of weeks.[77] These short journey times, over such long distances, would have been seen as miraculous in William Wood's time. British migrants were also looked after with much more rigorous care than they had been before, even if the attention of the authorities on board ship often seemed stifling. Colonial and Dominion agents played a key role in enticing migrants to move, on a much more widespread and organised footing even than in the nineteenth century. Britain's Ministry of Labour officers were usually provided, for instance, with immigration pamphlets and forms, as well as occupational booklets focusing on the need for skills that were abundant in each of Britain's regions.[78]

From 1923 almost every ship had its own Welfare Officer, a policy promoted by the Young Men's Christian Association (YMCA) in the face of opposition from the shipping companies and Australian officials, who thought this policy too accommodating.[79] In the late 1940s and 1950s, emigrants to New Zealand were issued with 'Notes for Passengers', which detailed likely expenses on board. By the 1960s, that country's Migration Office in London issued 'General Notes for the Information of Passengers', which included advice on packing, expenses and finding a job on arrival. New Zealand's Information or Liaison officers travelled with the ships, providing talks, advice and even libraries of information, as well as organising sports, entertainment and, in some cases, school lessons. In the early years of New Zealand's organised immigration drive, Ministry of Labour officials met the ships on arrival to shepherd the new arrivals to their jobs.[80]

One Australian welfare officer remembered the scene in the 1950s: 'all the food was fresh every day. The bread was baked daily and if you were served stew one day you wouldn't ever get it the next – that all went overboard.' Food was important to breaking up the monotony of life on board: the separate sittings often brought migrants together who would become friends for life. In any case, the food was often better than that back in Britain, where rationing continued until 1954.[81] Even so, the level of comfort during the voyage depended on the vessel being employed for that task. Twentieth-century migrants found, for the most part, that conditions – even in third class – did live up to the extensive propaganda mounted by shipping companies such as the White Star Line. Annabella Sinclair, who migrated from Orkney to Australia in 1929 on board the *Baradine*, noted that they were 'conducted to our cabin . . . which is a nice four berth place one bunk for each of the boys one for Duncan and one for myself and baby'.[82]

The majority of assisted migrants to Australia took passage on P&O ships, on which block bookings had been made by the Australian government. On these ships, the 'ten pound migrants' had access to the same facilities as the non-assisted tourists on board; most of the crew were British or Australian; and most of the food was familiar to them. Other migrants, for instance, those travelling on the *Fairsea* and *Fairsky*, were less lucky. These ships were converted carrier escorts, and they were therefore much smaller than the P&O vessels. There were no other passengers on board, only the assisted migrants; and the crew, as well as the food, were Italian. Not surprisingly, these voyages were much less fondly remembered by the migrants who had to travel on *Fairsea* or *Fairsky*.[83] Migrants travelling on ships chartered by the New Zealand government in the 1940s and 1950s experienced just the same distance from their 'commercial' fellows. The *Atlantis*, which together with the *Captain Cook* and the *Captain Hobson* brought the majority of New Zealand immigrants from Britain just after the Second World War, was described by one migrant as 'spartan': '[we] were in an 8-berth cabin, with bunks spaced very close together.' The eight-berth cabins were the most numerous on the *Atlantis*, showing how relatively parsimonious government-organised emigration could be; though after these three ships were retired in the late 1950s, all of New Zealand's arrivals came by commercial service.[84]

Seasickness was one reality that was still unavoidable in many cases. One man remembers that he 'soon joined in the "mal de mer" chorus. One of the cabin members was ex-merchant navy and he kept us and another three sufferers supplied with bread rolls from the dining room three times a day . . . the outer decks were one long line of tensed up sufferers taking it in turn to stagger to the rail and make their forlorn offerings to the grey Atlantic.'[85] A 32-year-old Scot, Mary Gibson, travelled on the *Remuera* to New Zealand in 1938. She remembered a similar feeling, at least to start with: 'I missed Lunch on Sunday feeling sick. Went to lie on my back with whiskey & was ready for tea at 4 and never felt bad since.' Once she had got over the initial nausea she felt much better, along with most of the passengers.[86]

Religious tensions on board had faded almost entirely by the post-Second World War era. The Australian government, indeed, organised one Catholic priest, one Presbyterian minster and one Anglican pastor on each ship which carried more than 950 people.[87] But class conflict, or at least a feeling of class consciousness, had not entirely disappeared, even by the 1950s. Commercial ships were still divided into first and tourist class, often visibly and physically so even up on deck. A one-class ship, such as the *Northern Star* on its passages to New Zealand, could also contain just as much division and snobbery as its divided sister ships. One immigrant who sailed on the *Northern Star* remembers that 'I must admit among the passengers who were sailing around the world, many noses were looked down when the owners of those noses realised that someone sat at the table next to them were on government assisted passages.'[88] Mary Gibson recorded that, on Empire Day, 'some of the first class are glad to mix with us. They are bored stiff as there is very few first class'. The constant tension between 'mixing', and keeping separate, was a negotiated borderline that nineteenth-century migrants would have recognised.[89]

Racial and national conflicts also remained near the surface, especially when it came to reflecting on the country the emigrants were leaving. Immigration into Britain was, rather ironically, often recorded as one of the main reasons to leave. An anti-immigration campaigner in Smethwick before the famous by-election had already argued that 'emigration figures are rising. Of those I have spoken to all have told me that their reason for leaving their homeland is that that they could no longer live in a multi-racial community'.[90] The Conservative politician Enoch Powell used his 1968 tirade against immigration to report one of his constituent's words: 'If I had the money to go, I wouldn't stay in this country'.[91] The broad-caster Robyn Williams made several journeys by sea between Britain and Australia in the 1960s and 1970s, and on one particular 1964 voyage he memorably summed up the mix of Anglo-Australian dislike of one another, and overt racism: 'the other immigrants were little Englanders, "one step ahead", as they put it of all the "fuzzy-wuzzies" – who'd taken over . . . They appeared to be in training for the Whingeing Pom Olympics. And the forced repatriation of nig-nogs'.[92]

This unappealing frankness was perhaps little surprise, for the feeling of being cut off, and of having some license to behave and speak as one liked, was similar to the 'liminality' of the twentieth-century seaside resort back in Britain. Storms and the endless seascape created a sense almost of a nuclear community, separated from the rest of the world. Even boredom contributed to the sense of self-containment. Ivy Skrowronski, a Bournemouth woman with a Polish refugee husband, has recalled her 1959 voyage to Australia with these words:

> One never reads what happens to migrants during the journey to their new country. Temporarily homeless, plunged into a no-man's land between countries, it is a very strange feeling indeed. One door has closed behind them, another remains unopened, but the prospect of three weeks on an ocean liner . . . is enough to tuck their worries away for a while.[93]

Calm weather in particular could bring about a state of reverie, as one Irish-woman remembered: 'I looked out and saw nothing but water and it was, even though kind of scary, you thought oh, I'd just love to see land or a house or something, because I had never seen that mass of water'.[94] Visiting exotic ports such as Bermuda, Panama or Aden helped reinforce this feeling of confined togetherness and shared experiences in more positive ways. One migrant to Australia wrote thus of her friend in the 1950s: 'there were lots of young people on board and she had a very good time. In fact we all did. It was a glorious holiday. We went to Gibraltar, Naples, through the Suez Canal'.[95]

Youthful high spirits, and the need to pass many dull hours at sea, combined to allow much more leeway in social behaviour than it had done in the nineteenth century. One ship, the SS *Ballarat*, became caught up in a seaman's strike at Cape Town in 1925. Officers were beguiled by a lady dressed as a nun; many of the crew took sweethearts, as did men on shore. The captain refused to step in, asking the welfare officer: 'surely you don't believe . . . that modern women are faithful to their husbands?'[96] Janet Francis, who travelled to Australia at the age of 18 in 1956, fell in love with one of the waiters on board her ship, the *Otranto*, and met him in Adelaide as the ship began its long journey back to Britain. 'As soon as the ship got back to Tilbury', she remembers with some humour, 'he sent me a "dear John" so that was the end of that romance'.[97] Many ships' watch officers turned down the lights on deck at night to allow for 'romancing' among couples separated in their cabins. Older, often married migrants might flirt with others in a way they would not countenance on dry land. One 70-year-old grandmother attracted an admirer on the voyage out to Australia who she ignored when arriving at Melbourne. 'That was her bit of fun on the ship,' commented her daughter later.[98]

The triumph of air travel

A new age of supersonic jet travel would make these ships redundant. The British Comet made its first flight in July 1949, and Boeing's 367–80 in July 1954. BOAC and Pan-American started the first Atlantic jet services within 3 weeks of one another in 1958. Jet services started to Australasia, with Qantas, in October 1959.[99] In 1951, 2.6 million people entered the UK through its seaports, and only 865,000 via its airports. By 1959 those two figures were 3.8 million and 2.7 million; by 1970, 5.9 million and 10.8 million; and by the late 1970s twice as many people were entering the UK by air than by sea. The decisive year in which incoming air travel had first outstripped arrivals by ship was 1962.[100]

Scheduled liners were able to keep up with competition from airlines in the pre-jet period, relying on a mix of government subsidies, opulence and a certain fashionable cachet to compete with their newer rivals. Cunard's *Queen Mary*, launched in 1934, was refitted in 1946–47 to resume her Atlantic sailings; the company's *Queen Elizabeth*, launched in 1938, made her first commercial voyage in 1946.[101] Cunard ran adverts starring models such as Roger Moore, just about to take a cocktail in a portrait-lined music room, while the Duchess of York sent ahead to demand different colour schemes for her suite – though there was only a tiny amount of room for steerage passengers, both in their rooms and up on deck.[102]

About a million people travelled the transatlantic route in 1957, the peak year for travel by ship in that ocean: the previous decade had been North Atlantic passenger shipping's most profitable era ever. Air travel did not easily or quickly kill off the passage by sea, particularly on the Australian and New Zealand routes. Air services to those countries were initially slow, and might take about a week, as compared to 5 weeks on a ship. When Margaret Foden flew to Australia and New Zealand in 1960, the journey took 8 days, with stops at Damascus, Karachi, Singapore, Darwin and Brisbane before arriving in Auckland.[103] The end of the Second World War in fact opened a new era of luxury and speed in liner design. The *United States*, for instance, was completed in 1952: capable of nearly 40 knots, she was easily able to outstrip the previous British record for crossing the Atlantic. British firms bought the *Southern Cross* (1955), the *Oriana* (1960) and the *Canberra* (also 1960) for the Australasian routes that would soon witness their obsolescence.[104]

But air travel did take the other half of the market, even in the climacteric year of 1957. And the next year, 1958, not only saw the launch of jets capable of tackling the Atlantic on a routine basis. That year also witnessed the introduction of an economy-class service on the air routes in the North Atlantic: it was the first in which more people crossed the Atlantic by air than by sea. At $450, these were certainly competitive with the $350 that the liners might charge. By the mid-1960s, the result seemed inevitable: the age of sea travel, and of emigration by ship, was over. Magazines had for some years been running articles with titles such as 'Cunard-on-Sea', comparing the empty tourist classes on the ships with Britain's declining seaside.[105] In 1966 Cunard even sold the *Queen Mary* and *Queen Elizabeth*, those symbols of what had once been its most profitable route: the ships made their final Cunard sailings in 1967 and 1968.[106] The first became a hotel in California; the second eventually caught fire and sank in Hong Kong Harbour. P&O's *Oriana* and *Canberra* stopped making the scheduled run to Australia after the closure of the Suez Canal during the 1967 Arab–Israeli War.[107] The extraordinary *Queen Elizabeth 2* was fully equipped on its 1969 launch with libraries, discos, bars, restaurants and promenades: but her production had to be subsidised by the Government, and by the 1970s she made regular Atlantic runs only in the summer months. Her future lay in the lucrative cruising trade.[108]

Jet aircraft made intra-'imperial' travel easier. In 1964, 5000 of Canada's migrants came from Australia, rather than from Britain itself.[109] And by the end of that decade, especially following Qantas' purchase of Boeing 707s and its much faster direct flights from the mid-1960s, almost all journeys to Australasia were made on jets.[110] The last assisted child migrants to Australia arrived in that country during 1967 by air, rather than from the sea lanes. The 'stock' of children at home who could be relocated in the

Commonwealth had dried up, as local authorities now believed that children were much better kept by adoptive or foster families in the UK.[111] The very last shipload of 'ten pound poms' arrived on the *Australis* in 1977: there were to be no more long voyages to the Antipodes.[112] The airliner, not the ship, then became a symbol of 'home' itself. John Williams, living rather unhappily in Queensland during the 1960s, remembers seeing 'the vapour trail and shiny body of a jet, obviously a passenger Boeing 707. Then, as I realised that the aircraft was probably on its way to England ... the now familiar lurch of the stomach hit me, and my eyes filled full of tears.'[113]

Even poorer migrants from less economically developed countries could now afford to fly to Britain. In 1960, 22,000 West Indians had taken a ship to Britain, whereas 29,000 had flown; by the mid-1970s, only about a thousand came by ship, but 130,000 people came by air. Not all of these people were migrants, of course, especially as the holiday trade to the Caribbean took off in the 1970s; but the tiny number of people coming by ship at all shows that almost nobody now undertook the long and arduous journey by sea. Out of 50,000 travellers from South Asia, 22,000 came by sea in 1960; by the late 1960s the statistic was too small to record in official publications.[114] Louise Bennett's 1966 poem, 'Colonisation in Reverse', imagines both 'by de ship load, [and] by de plane load, / Jamaica is Englan bound'.[115] Charter flights from the West Indies were common by the early 1960s.[116]

When Idi Amin expelled Uganda's Asian citizens from that country in 1972, very few left by ship. Only those heading for India by boat travelled to Mombasa to try to find passage to their forebears' country. Those coming to Britain left by air, whether directly or from Nairobi in Kenya.[117] By the autumn, as the crisis came to a head, 28,000 were airlifted out of Entebbe airport.[118] Amin agreed to let the immigrants leave on East African Airlines, and two British carriers, paying their own way at a cost of 2000 Ugandan shillings each. It was only due to this concerted effort in the air that allowed Amin's 8 November deadline for all British Asians to leave Uganda to be met.[119]

Conclusions: immigrants, emigrants and 'Britishness'

In 2000 the Runnymede Trust, a charity established in 1968 to build bridges between Britain's new immigrant communities and policymakers, published *The Future of Multi-Ethnic Britain*. Chaired by the political philosopher Lord Parekh, himself born in India, the Commission recommended a fundamentally new concept of British history as a first stage in building a 'successful community of communities'. In place of the view 'that the sea round Britain aptly symbolises its independence and isolation from the rest of the world', it had become clear that Britain's place in the maritime world actually made it more, not less, subject to the movement of peoples.[120] Interchanges, engagements and constant globalisations were always more noticeable than any constant, unchanging visions of the national past could ever provide for – as this book has consistently shown. Where once the British had sailed out into the world searching for cheap land, higher wages and new opportunities, now the Empire 'came home' – and Britons continued to move out – on faster and more efficient ships than William Wood could ever have imagined.

The new migrants brought with them some uncomfortable truths about Britain and its maritime empire. In 1994 David Dabydeen, born in Guyana but educated in Britain, re-imagined Turner's famous anti-slavery painting *Slavers Throwing Overboard the Dead and Dying*, casting Turner himself as the captain who dumped slaves at sea for the insurance money rather than trying to sell sick men and women. Dabydeen implicates all the British in the crimes of slavery, lest they forget the Empire they were trying to efface in the aftermath of decolonisation. As Dabydeen's slave narrator cries out: 'the sea has mocked and beggared me for centuries, / Except for scrolls in different letterings / Which, before they dissolve, I decipher as best I can. These, and the babbling / Of dying sailors, are my means to languages / And the wisdom of other tribes'.[121]

On the other side of the equation, emigration did slow down in the post-war world, especially as a proportion of the population, but it remained an enormously important experience for huge numbers of Britons. By the turn of the twentieth and twenty-first centuries, 5 per cent of the British-born population lived abroad: one million in Australia, 600,000 in Canada, 210,000 in New Zealand and 680,000 in the USA.[122] Both immigration and emigration remained at the heart of the British experience in the early twenty-first century. The numbers moving abroad, indeed, actually accelerated rapidly in the years following the millennium: in the years 2004–06 they were the highest they had been since the late 1970s. There was also evidence of a renewed interest in long-distance migration to the 'Old' Commonwealth. Emigration to Australia and New Zealand picked up rapidly in the first 5 years of the new century as 2000 Britons a month moved to that country.[123]

But emigration's nature had fundamentally changed. Improved communications and transport technology meant that nothing was permanent as the shipborne journey had made it seem. Migration had now become a much more complex set of journeys, almost always made by air, very quickly, and paradoxically on shorter routes than nineteenth-century migrants had taken.

By the 1990s and early 2000s, the Spanish coasts and rural France were proving much more attractive than Commonwealth destinations. From the early 1980s onwards, there was only one year in which the European Union was not by far the greatest recipient of British newcomers, who often lived in highly concentrated communities in traditional holiday resorts such as Malaga or the Canary Islands.[124]

This gave rise to a very complex British diaspora in the 'near abroad', constantly coming home, visiting or being visited by British people constantly taking cheap flights to see relatives 'in the sun'. Few of the emigrants actually desired to come home permanently, perhaps assisted in their new home by those very permanent links they could maintain with their country of origin: of a stock of perhaps 6 million living abroad, 91,000, or about 1.5 per cent, were in fact doing so early in the 2000s. This figure is even lower, as a proportion of original migrants, than the number of West Indian 'returnees' from the 1950s onwards.[125] Those who had travelled a long way were less likely to return, due to the long air journey and the expense. Perhaps a quarter to a third of post-Second World War emigrants to Australia returned, which is actually a lower figure than the estimated 40 per cent before 1914. Better communications links – the trans-continental telephone – for instance – probably made it feel easier to stay.[126]

Much of the scale and scope of the two-way movement of peoples – and some of its consequences – are clear. Historians have been much more reticent on the actual personal experience of travelling, and the hopes and fears of immigrants and emigrants themselves while they remained in transit. Angela McCarthy has noted just this gap in her work on Scottish and Irish migrants in the twentieth century.[127] There are a number of reasons for this failure to analyse relatively contemporary voyage narratives. Britain's twentieth-century immigrants were often looking for jobs, and had such a profound effect on their new home that the social and economic transformations they wrought seemed more important. Emigrants were supposed to assimilate within the 'imperial' societies to which they usually travelled; and they tended to settle for good, paradoxically aided by faster travel and better communications. Increasingly nationalist outlooks within Britain's celtic nations saw out-migration as an undesirable drain on their manpower and cultures. These changes meant that it became easier to overlook these movements, even within the new 'transnational' and border-crossing contexts within which historians work.[128] Be that as it may, the stories of British immigrants and emigrants demonstrated how maritime Britain was in many ways a world society as well a world power. The triumph of the jet aircraft, however, was a harbinger of the collapse of that maritime system: a process which we will now consider.

Timeline of events

1919	Establishment of official Overseas Settlement Committee in Britain
1922	Passing of first Empire Settlement Act
1922	New Zealand begins funding assisted passages to that country
1925	Canada and Australia begin subsiding British immigrants
1930	Canada discontinues subsidies to British immigrants
1931	Onset of Great Depression halts mass British emigration until late 1940s
1944	Hurricane hits Jamaica, devastating its economy
1947	SS *Ormonde* brings 108 West Indian immigrants to Britain
March 1947	Australia relaunches Assisted and Free Passage schemes
24 May 1948	SS *Empire Windrush* leaves Kingston in Jamaica
23 June 1948	SS *Empire Windrush* arrives at Tilbury
August 1948	Liverpool race riots aimed at 'foreign' seamen
September 1948	Arrival of SS *Orbita* in Britain
July 1949	Maiden flight of British Comet jet aircraft
1950	V.S. Naipaul sails from New York to Southampton
August 1951	Hurricane Charlie causes Jamaica's worst natural disaster of the twentieth century
1953	Baynes Street Riot in North London
July 1954	Maiden flight of the Boeing 367–80
1957	Peak year for gross passenger figures on North Atlantic ships
1957	Australia's 'Bring Out A Briton' campaign
1958	First year in which more people cross the Atlantic by air than sea
1958	First economy-class flights across the Atlantic
August 1958	Race riots in Nottingham and Notting Hill
October 1959	First Qantas jet services from the UK to Australasia
1961	Census: 63 per cent of Caribbean immigrants live more than one and a half people to a room

1962	Canada abolishes preferential treatment for British, US and French citizens
1962	First Commonwealth Immigrants Act
October 1964	Conservatives hold Smethwick in West Midlands after racially charged campaign
1965	Immigration White Paper tightens rules on work permits
1966	Cunard sells *Queen Mary* and *Queen Elizabeth* liners
1967	End of 'voluntary' resettlement of orphan and adoptive children
1968	Second Commonwealth Immigrants Act
April 1968	Enoch Powell's 'Rivers of Blood' speech at Birmingham
May 1969	First commercial voyage of *QE2* luxury liner
1972	Idi Amin expels East African Asians from Uganda; many flee to Britain
1972	Commonwealth Settlement Acts allowed to lapse
1979	Australia introduces points quota system for immigrants
1987	New Zealand ends system of preferential immigration treatment for Europeans

9

Collapse

Much that was 'British' in the mid–twentieth century was still identified with the sea. Shipbuilding and shipping were the industrial image
of Britain's seafaring past and future. Seaside holidays constituted the
popular image of how Britons spent their leisure time. Fishing was
a large and vibrant industry, and 'fish and chips' the nation's signature dish. The Royal Navy had won two conclusive victories over
the German fleet. But this interlocking system would collapse very
quickly after 1945. The crisis in shipbuilding and shipping was the
most prolonged, since the entire free trade system upon which they
had relied up to 1914 was destroyed by the First World War. Tariffs
rose, trade contracted and the world economic crisis of the Depression caused demand for ships to stagnate or fall. After the Second
World War, the inherent conservatism and failure to re-equip that characterised this industry became more evident with the rise of more
'modern' competitors such as Sweden and Japan: Britain's share of
the shipbuilding market contracted rapidly after the recession that
affected the industry in the late 1950s. In shipping, 'flagging out',
the practice whereby developed world companies employed ships flying flags of convenience to avoid high taxes and labour costs, caused
the British rapidly to lose market share in that industry as well. Even
though absolute numbers of British ships held up well throughout
most of the post-Second World War era, the recession of the early
1980s, and the withdrawal of government aid, helped to devastate
Britain's carrying and cargo business in that decade. At the same
time, the British seaside holiday failed to adapt to new competition
from sunnier and more exotic destinations, first in the Mediterranean
and then worldwide. Seaside resorts were caught in a spiral of economic decline, attracting ever-ageing populations and creating many

seasonal, low-paid jobs that failed to maintain economic growth in these towns. By the 1980s housing, accommodation and amenities in Britain's resorts were at a very low ebb. The British fishing industry was, if anything, in an even worse state. The first signs of overfishing had appeared as long ago as the Edwardian period, and the new science of fisheries management began to reveal just how ubiquitous the practice had become even in the inter-war years. But massive trawling and industrialised fishing methods after 1945 then caused many fish stocks around the British Isles to go into near-terminal decline by the 1990s, a process that was made worse by the incompetence and waste associated with Europe's Common Fisheries Policy. Some well-managed coastal stocks held up; deep-sea fishing for meatier white fish such as cod did not, and indeed this iconic fish was in critical danger by the end of the century. Along with these industries' decline, the Royal Navy shrank in size and reach in the late twentieth century, losing most of its global capacity in a series of cost-cutting packages that reduced its ability to respond quickly to crises around the world. Taken together, these multiple calamities constituted the greatest threat to Britain's seaborne interests since the struggles with France in the eighteenth century: it no longer seemed fanciful to speak of the 'collapse' of maritime Britain.

British shipbuilding and shipping in decline

The entire structure of British maritime capitalism as it had developed by 1914 slowly broke up as the twentieth century progressed. This system was enduring profound agonies as early as the inter-war years: even in 1914, Britain's shipbuilding industry was hardly a picture of technological advance, with newer yards in Germany able to use new flow production techniques, machinery and electricity to better effect.[1] Clyde shipbuilders including even the biggest, John Brown & Co., made relatively little investment in equipment as against their continental rivals: the company reported having only £200,000 of machinery in 1910.[2] Labour relations were often poor, with waves of strikes and lockouts in 1890–91 and 1911: the Shipping Federation even owned three vessels, the *Lady Jocelyn*, the *Paris* and the *Ella*, for the purposes of moving non-union labour between ports and breaking strikes.[3]

Britain could, on the other hand, at least rely on commercial contacts, and a plentiful, cheap supply of skilled labour, as well as on past experience. The heavy concentration of shipyards in certain regions – the North East of England and the Clyde in Scotland in particular – meant that there was a critical mass of workers with specialised skills that employers could always draw on. Though German shipbuilders invested in new machinery, this was expensive and could not always be kept in continuous operation. Their costs suffered accordingly.[4] It is true that Britain's share of the world market fell from 80 per cent to 60 per cent between the 1860s and 1914; but this had much to do with the protective tariff barriers placed around German, and to a lesser extent Dutch and French, shipbuilders. There seemed little chance of Britain being surpassed in shipbuilding for many decades to come.[5] The labour force in shipbuilding rose, rather than falling, as ever larger and more sophisticated ships were launched. The industry employed 75,000 workers in 1870, but 200,000 on the eve of the First World War.[6]

All those advantages were to count for nothing in the increasingly competitive world ushered in by the First World War. By virtue of her war debts and economic exhaustion, Britain lost her place as arbiter between commodity producers and manufactures: she could no longer buy and sell from and to both. But the USA, hiding behind a tariff wall, enjoying reparations payments from the war's losers, and from 1929 mired in a depression of her own, would nor or could not yet play this role either. A brief but inflationary post-war boom, followed by a painful retrenchment, for the first time brought the future of shipbuilding in Britain into question. The First World War marks a clear break or discontinuity in production and productivity. Part of the reason is probably the closure of the free-market world economy that Britain had come to dominate; part, too, lies in the waste of skilled labour and experience that the war itself represented.[7] In March 1925, the shipowners Furness Withy ordered five new ships for its Prince Line from German builders in Hamburg. It was a rude shock at the time, but it foreshadowed the future relative decline of the industry. Subsequent large orders, and industry inquiries, demonstrated beyond doubt that better quality work was available, more cheaply, from foreign builders.[8]

The world commercial and payments systems eventually froze entirely, with world trade falling by two-thirds in the crisis of 1929–31. Commodity prices collapsed; tariff barriers were raised ever higher; the markets for manufactured goods contracted.[9] The effects of all this on Britain's merchant fleet were catastrophic. The huge expansion of worldwide shipbuilding capacity which followed the war, stimulated by congested ports and slow turnaround times during the frantic boom of 1919–21, caused the building of a great glut of ships that would carry the world's trade in the more straitened circumstances of the later 1920s and 1930s. British shipbuilders, who had quickly built up their capacity to a potential 4 million tons a year in 1919–21, found themselves with less than 1 million tons of annual orders on their books. And where they had once dominated their industry, they now seemed to be slipping behind. While the world merchant fleet continued gradually to expand in the inter-war years, Britain's tonnage remained stagnant at 18 million tons.

Shipbuilders' long-standing ties to local companies now mattered less and less, and they struggled to find new markets. Britain's retreat from its long-held commitment to free trade, and the protectionist Import Duties Act of 1932, also hurt the industry. Its imports of semi-manufactures and machinery were heavily taxed, with the duty on steel imports rising to 33? per cent, and the effect of these duties overall was to reduce turnover by 6 per cent.[10] The crisis also soured industrial relations, further entrenching traditional methods of working and the 'demarcation' lines between the different types of work each category of tradesmen was allowed to do; there was no longer the money to smooth over the problems of managing a large, but highly skilled, workforce. Most employers spent the 1920s trying to force down wages in the industry, rather than innovate or change working practices overall.[11] But relative production costs still rose, accelerated by the pressures of rearmament in the late 1930s.[12] Shipbuilding's contribution to manufacturing output very nearly halved between 1907 and 1935.[13]

Shipowners were no better off, as they were forced successively to cut their prices and profits, with freight rates falling by up to three quarters. Whole fleets were sold, and tonnage laid off increased from 630,000 tons in 1929 to 3.6 million tons in 1932. Liner companies only survived by amalgamating into the 'big five' – P&O, Royal Mail, Cunard, Ellerman and Furness-Withy – and even the huge Royal Mail group collapsed in 1931.[14] But even as ships were scrapped and Britain's share of the world carrying trade declined, shipowners continued the traditions of their industry and were reluctant to seek external finance for re-equipment. Even when P&O did bring in the banks and outside investors under Lord Kylsant's leadership, power was still concentrated in a remarkably narrow range of cross-shareholdings that gave Kylsant almost total control over the group. Its collapse was even more spectacular once the Treasury and his investors discovered the true (and weak) state of the group's finances.[15]

Britain's role as a world trading centre was disintegrating, victim to the increasing power of large multinational manufacturing and commodity firms. Producers increasingly chose to select, price and package goods for themselves, and ship them direct, rather than sell them to wholesaling middlemen who would organise sales for them. The financial worth of Britain's entrepôt trade fell from £110 million in 1913 to only £62 million by 1938, even at current prices.[16] Workers were laid off in great numbers: in 1923, 44 per cent of men on relief in West Ham were dockers. Dockworkers' earnings in the 1930s were 15–25 per cent lower than in other manual trades. They might often have been higher per day, but the uncertainties inherent in daily hiring, underemployment and irregular earnings meant that, overall, dockers were some of the worst treated workers in the country. This helped further to poison industrial relations, a problem that would continue well into the post-war era and beyond.[17]

The late 1940s and 1950s in some respects gave both shipbuilders and shipowners a respite. World trade boomed in this period, and although Britain's share of the world trade fell relative to the total, there was more than enough work to go round. Total world ship launchings trebled between 1958 and 1973.[18] By the end of the 1950s, some 275,000 were employed in ship-building, repairing and marine engineering combined.[19] But while British launchings were holding their own in terms of gross tonnage, the country was losing vast swathes of the expanding world market for new ships. She was overtaken by Japan in 1956, and then by Germany and Sweden by 1966. Investment figures showed that the period of relatively buoyant orders that followed the Second World War had not been used to best advantage. While German and Swedish yards went in for massive re-equipment, British yards invested only £4 million out of their £120 million annual turnover in the 3 years 1951–54.[20]

The very rapid growth of shipping tonnage flying competitor flags, in Japan, Germany and Scandinavia in particular, helped shipbuilders in those countries outstrip British investment. High and buoyant demand encouraged them to adopt new practices and equipment that would not have paid off to the same extent in Britain, even during the post-Second World War boom.[21] But there were specifically British reasons, too, for the fall in that country's share of the world market, for the post-war breathing space had not been used to best effect. British yards were slow to adopt the practice of welding steel plates together, rather than riveting them: this technique was widely and erroneously believed to be unsafe after a number of accidents in the USA.[22] British yards were in general smaller than their competitors, building fewer ships per company, and subject to the constraints of small-scale sites in which components and parts of new ships constantly had to be moved and manipulated by new teams of workers.[23] A wealth of private and public reports continued to draw attention to deep flaws within the industry, documents which caused deep concern within the higher reaches of the British government, but upon which Ministers and officials found it hard to base specific policies. A Department of Scientific and Industrial Research Paper from 1960, for instance, found productivity stagnating, production control primitive and research and development efforts severely lacking.[24]

Each 'side' of this industry – both owners and trade unions – acutely remembered the pain, and what they perceived to be the lessons, of the 1930s. Over-building and unemployment were perceived to be the main dangers, to be avoided at all costs. In this situation, any market uncertainty or slowdown rapidly slowed down modernisation efforts, and a defensive attitude gained hold that stalled large-scale change while orders were still high. Shipbuilders and shipowners, indeed, complained more than most about the 'stop-go' culture of the time, during which governments would boost demand to avoid recession, but then raise interest rates and taxes as inflation rose and the international value of sterling came under pressure.[25] The official Geddes Report into the industry, published in 1966, acutely dissected two of the main problems associated with this defensive conservatism. Firstly, the industry was 'used to wide and unpredicted fluctuations in demand', and had therefore 'developed short-term attitudes towards markets, men and money'. Secondly, 'within the industry management and the unions have failed in their attempts to negotiate constructively.'[26]

Managers and men engaged in a peculiar sort of cold war, during which workers would often refuse to adopt new techniques, and their 'bosses' would then fatalistically accept their conservatism. Sheet metal workers and joiners both went out on strike at Cammell Laird in 1955 when management could not decide which group of workers was to drill the holes for aluminium sheeting. The Trades Union Congress (TUC) had to step in at Stephen's yard in Linthouse in 1957 when boilermakers and shipwrights clashed over how to change the ubiquitous 'rule book' when working practices were modernised.[27] One manager has recalled that 'there were occasions when machines were bought and the men would not use them and they were laid in cold storage. I remember some welding machines, and it was two years before they were allowed to use them.' On the other side of the equation, workers only achieved security from casual, indeed often daily, contracts in 1965, and the attitudes of management could be dismissive. The dissolution of casual labour practices and higher incentives for productivity had come far too late to save the industry from the industrial stand-off that had developed. One Clydeside shop steward singled out 'better job security, sick pay, pensions [and] better working conditions' as vital if employers were to 'have won the co-operation of the workers'.[28]

The Geddes Report recommended that firms be brought together, so that the civil industry could cluster around 'at least four big and compact shipbuilding groups'. This would allow more industrial concentration, better marketing and increased research and development: in short, the creation of bigger and more competitive champions in the global marketplace.[29] Shipbuilding did, overall, become more concentrated. The share of the five biggest firms in the industry was 62 per cent in 1957, but had reached 74 per cent in 1969 — a sign that Geddes' recommendations were, at the very least, pushing with the grain of industrial developments that would have occurred in any case.[30] The multiplicity of yards that Geddes had studied in the mid-1960s appeared much more streamlined within 3 years of his report. Scott Lithgow on the Lower Clyde, Upper Clyde Shipbuilders further up the river, Swan Hunter on the Tyne and Tees, Austin and Pickersgill on the

Wear, Cammell Laird on the Mersey, Vickers at Barrow, Vosper Thorney-croft at Southampton and Harland and Wolff in Northern Ireland constituted the vast bulk of both civil and military shipbuilding.[31]

But Geddes' recommendations may in some ways have made the situation worse, for they helped set off a wave of mergers and takeovers that – beyond mere scale – seemed to lack any analytical rationale. One internal memorandum at Vickers captured the confusion: 'there is a great deal of jockeying for position going on and no-one [is] seeing clearly what they are aiming to achieve. The danger in this position is that a number of new groupings may appear which do not make the best use of the capacity and the talent which now exists'.[32] The effects of this 'jockeying' could be long-lasting. The Scott and Lithgow yards did indeed merge in 1967, but it was many years before they looked anything like a combined company in their new guise. Neither the management team nor the owners, both from long-established shipbuilding dynasties, had any intention of losing their independence. The two planning departments were not merged until 1981, and the new division continued to have a poor image. It was also short of staff and overburdened by work.[33]

Governments in the end got tired of providing more and more money without the benefits of control over how it was spent, and Labour came back to power in 1974 committed to state ownership for the entire sector. But the merged and nationalised company set up in 1977 was haunted by the same problems of divided management, local agreements and small-scale planning that had plagued the private industry. It not only took Labour 3 years to bring the yards into public ownership, it took another 2 years to unite and rationalise the production and marketing departments of British Shipbuilders.[34] The so-called Blackpool Agreements of 1979, in retrospect the last chance for centralised productivity bargaining and a more flexible working culture imposed from above, suffered from just this localism. Decentralised productivity agreements, bonuses and other deals undermined the whole system.[35] Meanwhile, British Shipbuilders continued to lose money, which amounted after government help to about £150 million in 1977/78 and £50 million in 1978/79. Orders had been relatively buoyant in the mid-1970s, but declined thereafter in the general downturn after the first OPEC oil shock of 1973. The industry seemed as far from breaking even as ever.[36]

The end of Britain's mass shipbuilding industry in the early to mid-1980s came at exactly the same time as the rest of Britain's traditional heavy manufacturing base was collapsing. Between 1977 and 1988, by which time most of the group had been sold off, £2 billion was spent supporting the nationalised company when South Korean yards could do the same work, more quickly, for less than the price of the raw materials alone in Britain.[37] By 1984, British shipbuilders was clearly no longer in any state to compete in the market for large-scale ships. On the brink of the very last round of 'rational-isation', employment in the industry had declined from its late-1950s highs to just 48,000, of whom only 12,500 were building new merchant ships.[38]

The Government proceeded to announce, later that year, that its corporate plans for new contracts had been reduced by 50 per cent. Scott Lithgow was privatised; Cammell Laird was redesignated as a warship builder; and a series of other yards was closed. In 1986 only North East Shipbuilders (a combi-nation of Austin and Pickersgill and Sunderland Shipbuilders), Govan and Ferguson on the Clyde, Appledore in Devon and Clark Kincaid's engine works at Greenock remained. In 1988–89 NESL was closed, and the rest sold off.[39] Cammell Laird ceased to build even Royal Navy ships in 1993, and concentrated on small-scale repair and conversion work.[40] Volume mer-chant shipbuilding in the UK remained with Harland and Wolff in Northern Ireland, sustained by the Government's need to support employment during the long conflict in that province.[41]

The shipping industry underwent a similarly painful decline in the post-war era. The UK-registered fleet initially expanded, as did shipbuilding, with registered tonnage expanding from 17 million to 20.6 million gross tons between 1939 and 1968. But the world fleet rose from 60 million to 180 million gross tons in the same period, meaning that the British share of the market had fallen from 28 per cent to 11 per cent. This was partly due to the disruption of the two World Wars and the Depression, to some extent caused by Britain's relatively slow-growing trade in the post-Second World era, and also owed something to competition from air travel in the 1950s and 1960s.[42] It was also due to the growth of so-called flags of convenience, which shipowners used to avoid high taxes and wages in the developed world. Panama was the traditional home of such shipping in the inter-war period, though the Liberian fleet grew very quickly in the 1950s.[43] Latterly Cyprus, Singapore, the Bahamas and even the Isle of Man became important countries for so-called flagging out, mainly by Greek and German shipowners.[44]

British shipping did undergo something of a renaissance in the late 1960s. A new generation of managers was coming to the fore who did not share the stifling memories of the 1930s, and the climacteric of the 'long boom' of 1950–73 was boosting world trade. And perhaps even more importantly, home shipbuilding loans were guaranteed by the Government under the 1967 Shipbuilding Credit Scheme. The British civilian fleet continued to grow in terms of absolute numbers: it amounted to 22.4 million gross tons in mid-1969, and 27.7 million gross tons in June 1972.[45] It was only in the 1970s that the really precipitous fall in Britain's share of the world merchant fleet, as opposed to all shipping, began: by 1984, Britons owned only 9 per cent of world tonnage. The story was similar even in the world tanker fleet, in which field Britain as the home of two of the world's biggest oil companies had enjoyed some success.[46] In 1968, nearly 12 per cent of the world tanker fleet was British-owned; by 1985 that had fallen to just under 5 per cent.[47]

It should once more be noted that this was a declining share of a generally very fast-growing market. The decisive decline in the actual and absolute capacity of Britain's merchant navy was actually a fact of the 1980s. In 1982, 22.5 million gross tons was under British control, but by 1988 that had fallen to just over 8 million. There were 30,000 officers and over 20,000 ratings in the British merchant fleet in 1980: there were less than 10,000 of either by 1997.[48] The world recession of the early 1980s squeezed profits, and wage costs were now even higher on British ships in comparison to 'flagged out' vessels than during the 1960s and 1970s. The Conservative government of the time looked favourably on a practice that helped to control the maritime trade unions, and in 1984 withdrew depreciation allowances and other tax incentives for British shipowners to register in Britain itself.[49] Owners had by then fulfiled their obligations under the 1960s assistance schemes, which required that the ships built with the money stayed 'British' for a number of years. The number and size of the ships flying the Red Ensign thus fell very quickly.[50] Britain had passed from a position of unparalleled strength in shipbuilding and shipping to total eclipse in less than a century.

The travails of coastal tourism

Peter Hennessy has evoked the post-Second World War seaside through the means of *Holiday*, a 1956 'short' (of 17 minutes) made by British Transport Films. Men in jackets and open-necked shirts, and women in summer dresses, get off the trains at Blackpool to an enthusiastic voice-over: 'sun and breeze bring a first reviving whiff and promise of the world of *Holiday*. Office and kitchen, school and factory and mill have escaped to the seaside of Lancashire.' The film is a picture of a Britain for which many would soon become nostalgic. All ages holidayed together; dressed alike; paddled on the beach; and were happy with the 'all in' boarding houses into which they were packed.[51] The popular Ward Lock Guides were astonished by the resort's vitality in the mid-1950s:

> Blackpool romps through the superlatives . . . the happy faces and ready friendships of the holiday multitude are a fine 'mixture as before' . . . The catholicity of the town is one of its chief attractions. It is one of the most cosmopolitan towns in the world, and every taste is provided for.[52]

In their golden age, roughly from the 1930s to the 1950s, seaside resorts became a central part of every Briton's experience of the 'new leisure' – the novel and exciting world provided for by paid holidays, increased social and geographical mobility, and rising wages. Holidays with pay had been provided by legislation in 1938, and although they had only just started to take effect by 1939, 80 per cent of workers were entitled to them by the coming of peace in 1945. Boom conditions prevailed in the immediate post-war years, with record numbers arriving by coach, and 625,000 travelling even to the relatively out-of-the-way Isle of Man.[53] Blackpool could claim 7 million visitors a year by the late-1930s, and could accommodate half a million in a single night. Southend in Essex had 5½ million visitors, Hastings 3 million and Bournemouth and Southport a million each. The 1940 report of the Royal Commission on the Distribution of the Industrial Population portrayed mass seaside tourism as one of Britain's most dynamic industries.[54]

But these resorts now entered a period of relative, and then absolute, decline: a process Richard Butler identified as long ago as 1980 as the 'tourism area life cycle'.[55] First, a period of stagnation saw environmental problems accumulate without being properly addressed, while visitor numbers remained high. In this respect the industry resembles British ship-building, which also stood still during the 1950s. Then a period of relative decline saw the loss of markets to newer and perhaps more exotic locations.[56] Chief among a new set of rivals were cheap package holidays to the Mediterranean, especially Spain, which could more or less guarantee sunshine in the summer months. Horizon Holidays was founded in 1950, and took its first charter passengers by air to Corsica that same year, though there were only 500 of them. By 1970 Britons were making 7 million overseas visits, a figure which reached over 17 million by 1989.[57] The new destinations promised not only the traditional freedom from the cares of the workplace, but whole new cultures that could merge with and to some extent transform their own. As one 1963 visitor to Ibiza put it, 'I was a really faddy eater, but on holiday I tried everything. Fish that was not battered and had a head and tail on was a real shock'.[58]

In this situation matters of 'taste', broadly defined, became much more important than previously. Holidays became more a matter of choice, and of social positioning, than the communal experiences that had marked the previous era.[59] In this new 'permanent present' of gratification, the images reflected and projected by the holiday became almost as important as the realities of the break itself: an argument popularised by John Urry among others.[60] Up-market 'consumerist' experiences had, to be sure, always been near the heart of British resorts' appeal, and local authorities spent a great deal of money upgrading the inter-war infrastructure. Blackpool had been one of the first resorts to take advantage of the Housing and Town Planning Act of 1919, which gave councils extensive powers to remodel the urban environment. The landscape architect T.H. Mawson was employed to lay out the 256 acres of Stanley Park in an area that had previously been wasteland.[61] Seven miles of promenade were built at Blackpool between the wars, complete with sunken gardens and other amenities, at a cost of over £1.5 million. An open air bath, a park costing over £250,000, an indoor sea water bath and improvements to the Winter Gardens all kept up the resort's 'tone'.[62] British seaside resorts spent an estimated £3–4 million on 'improvements' even during the Depression.[63]

The creation of more impressionistic fantasies might also have worked in the post-war era. But British resort authorities did not always grasp the need to uphold their special nature and 'sense of place'. The number of small guest houses fell by half in the 1950s and 1960s, and the number of grand seaside hotels by a similar amount in the 1970s. A less salubrious impression of multi-occupancy housing and tired, abandoned hotels was often created.[64] When striking and individual municipal attractions closed in the 1960s and 1970s, their replacements could often have been anywhere in the country. When Rhyl's Victoria Pier and Pavilion Theatre closed, they were replaced with the simulated tropical heat and wave machine of the Sun Centre, and a Children's Village that contained a variety of 'novelty' retail units. Other attractions, for instance, Alton Towers in Staffordshire, could compete most effectively if this was supposed to be the basis of a new and more homogenised seaside break.[65]

Britons did not immediately stop going to their own seaside resorts. Indeed, domestic tourism continued to rise in the 1960s and 1970s, even as foreign competition quadrupled. But in the later 1970s and in the 1980s the number of 'major' holidays of more than a few nights did drop away in the home market. These fell from 27 to 20 million between 1975 and 1985, while those taken overseas leapt from 12 to 22 million to overtake the British holiday. Even so, many resorts were able to adapt to the market for shorter, perhaps weekend, breaks, as well as catering for the conference and incentives market. These were all extremely lucrative. Although holiday tourism nights fell from 76 to 72 million nights overall between 1977 and 1981, the amount spent nearly doubled, from £365 million to £635 million.[66] Short breaks grew at over 20 per cent a year in the 1980s, a growth that accelerated in the 1990s.[67] As we shall see in Chapter 11, these destinations were certainly not locked into an inevitable spiral of decline.

But resorts faced wider economic and social challenges that went beyond their problems with international tourism: crises that were both cause and effect of changes to their general 'air' and appearance. By the 1990s average unemployment levels in resorts were higher than the national average, and average wages were much lower. This was, in part, the inevitable consequences of reliance on seasonal, underpaid and low-skilled service jobs. Resort towns attracted migrants in significant numbers: between 1971 and

2001, 360,000 people of working age moved to Britain's seaside towns. But they tended to be relatively old, the majority of them being over 35, and rather more likely than the background population to be registered permanently sick or to be retired. This influx outstripped the jobs that could be created, for instance, in seaside shops and restaurants.[68] By the early 2000s the Index of Local Deprivation, an overall measure of various economic and social indicators, ranked eight coastal districts among the worst 20 deteriorating areas in the UK. Although the image of poverty has remained that of 'inner-city' deprivation, coastal towns and especially resorts have not been far behind. Breaking the figures down into local authority wards, 62 out of 87 seaside towns in England covered in one study come in the top 25 per cent of the most deprived wards in that country.[69]

In 2006 England's unemployment rate was 5.1 per cent; for seaside towns the rate was 5.6 per cent. The percentage of the English population on Incapacity Benefit was 7.4 per cent; in coastal areas, the figure was 9.3 per cent. Some traditional resorts were performing particularly badly. Great Yarmouth had an unemployment rate of 10.1 per cent and an Incapacity Benefit claimant count at 11.2 per cent.[70] The House of Commons Communities and Local Government Committee reported on the situation in 2007. Large boarding houses, the committee found, had often been subdivided into low-cost social housing that concentrated the poor into specific districts at the same time as the demand for retirement properties was pushing house purchase out of the reach of young and middle income families. Physical isolation, poor public transport links and the rehousing of vulnerable adults and children in these areas made these problems even worse.[71]

The importance of 'image' was borne in on British seaside resorts by the new environmental movement. Few officials or holidaymakers joined environmental groups in the 1960s, and an 'out of sight, out of mind' mentality suited both officials and seaside businesses. But the appointment of a standing Royal Commission on Environmental Pollution in 1969 began to change attitudes.[72] Sir Eric Ashby, a botanist and Master of Clare College, Cambridge, was the Royal Commission's first chair, and he was keenly interested in coastal pollution.[73] Ashby presciently observed that 'as other social needs are satisfied, the abatement of pollution rises in the hierarchy of social values,' and the Royal Commission's third report was devoted entirely to coastal pollution. But at the same time, and despite increased government action on this issue, enormous damage was done to the public image of Britain's coasts. By the time Britain came to implement the European Economic Community's (EEC) 1975–76 Bathing Water Directives, only 27 beaches were found to comply with the European Commission's declared standards of cleanliness. Britain, with the Community's longest coastline, had the fewest number of 'clean' beaches among the EEC's nations with coastlines. The national and local press, led by *The Times* and BBC2's *Brass Tacks*, made great play with these figures.[74] In 1993 the European Court declared that Blackpool had unacceptable levels of coliform bacteria in its bathing water.[75]

Holiday had celebrated a bright, shining optimism; late twentieth cen-tury films set at the British seaside were much more downbeat affairs. Films such as 1998's *I Want You*, directed by Michael Winterbottom and starring Rachel Weisz, painted the seaside as what one critic has termed 'a limbo zone devoid of opportunities, where the failure of hopes and desires closely correlates to the landscape. The liminal remains, but as an ironic touchstone, so that the travel of tourism becomes the stagnation of stasis.' The film seems to go nowhere, like the denizens of the resort in which it is set: it starts and finishes with a voiceover narration played over a body being dumped at sea.[76] When in the mid-1990s the journalist Nick Danziger returned to the same Blackpool in which *Holiday* was filmed, he also found the seaside had become much less salubrious than it had seemed to British Transport Films. 'It seems few if any people would want to swim in the sea,' he wrote: 'its tobacco-coloured water is given a daily dose of sodium hypochloride, a chemical found in household bleach', in order to make the water 'safe' for bathing.[77] The importance of resorts' image, of particular and original 'attractions', and of real or perceived environmental cleanliness, were all too plain from Danziger's account. Their decline, absence or abuse had helped to throw the very future of the British seaside holiday into doubt.

Overfishing and the crisis of the marine environment

Fishermen and their families were once among the quintessential heroes of Britishness. 'The inshore fisherman should be perpetuated at all costs', the Ministry of Reconstruction announced in 1919, 'for he comes nearer than any other type of man to embodying those qualities of grit and self-reliance which we all agree to be the greatest of national assets'. State neglect of his interests would 'weaken the race'.[78] More than 30 years later, the regional Festival of Britain guidebook to East Anglia imagined that region's people as an 'eternal landing party', always close to the 'neighbourhood of the sea'. The brochure came complete with a full-page colour picture of 'one of the Scottish lassies for whom Yarmouth is the terminus of a yearly migration'.[79] There could be little doubt that the fisheries were a key part of both official and popular 'Britishness' itself.

Statistics detailing fishing's decline ever since are, however, irrefutable. In 1938 there were nearly 48,000 part- or full-time fishermen in the UK; in 1994, nearly 21,000; but by 2004, only about 11,600. The number of boats has fallen from 9174 as recently as 1995 to just 6341 in 2005.[80] Numbers of full-time fishermen have fallen even more rapidly than the overall total.[81] The peak year for British fishing in terms of landings was 1973: thereafter, though there have been peaks and troughs, the numbers of fish brought to shore have steadily declined. In 1997 they were 653,000 tons, down from over a million tons in the early 1970s.[82]

Any number of examples could be given of what this has meant for particular catches. Herring landings halved in the 1950s, from around 200,000 tons a year to under 100,000. The catches off Lowestoft and Yarmouth that had brought the Scots south to prepare them for sale all but collapsed. The autumn Downs stock failed in 1955, and very few seasonal drifters made the trip thereafter. The Festival of Britain's 'Scottish lassies' were gone within a generation, and the North Sea had to be closed to herring fishing during 1977 and 1978.[83] Herring numbers did then recover, to the extent whereby fishing could once more be allowed in the North Sea. When stocks came under threat again in the early 1990s, drastic action was taken to cut the allowable catch by half, a policy which caused herring numbers to rise once more, albeit slowly. The herring story demonstrated what could be done, with the requisite political will.[84]

There had been many warnings as to the eventual outcome of overfishing, so obvious in the falling catches of the 1980s and 1990s. The ubiquity of the new trawlers in the 1850s and 1860s set off a wave of protest that obliged the Government to appoint a Royal Commission on these complaints in 1863.[85] This Royal Commission, however, eventually decided that there was no evidence of falling fish stocks, and that all limits on fishing should be lifted – a conclusion in which the biologist Thomas Henry Huxley proved decisive.[86] Expert evidence to the Dalhousie Royal Commission of 1883–85 concluded, on the contrary, that 'there has been a falling off of the takes of flat fish,' in inshore waters.[87] Even so, this second Royal Commission decided that there was no evidence of damage to the food chain, and no conclusive proof of damage to immature fish – despite a mass of evidence to the contrary presented at its hearings.[88]

But evidence of overfishing continued to mount. Whatever Huxley thought, a Practical Fishermen's Congress held in 1883 expressed similarly grave concerns about the fall in the numbers of flat fish, and the increasing numbers of immature specimens in the catch. In 1892 the Scottish Fisheries Board felt moved to close the waters around the Moray Firth to fishing.[89] The Cornish pilchard shoals simply stopped coming to Britain's shores in the early 1900s, causing the majority of the St Ives fleet that had historically caught them for export to disappear.[90] The newly industrialised fishing of the late nineteenth century was already creating its own crises, and the characteristic anxieties that went with a dawning sense that the sea was not, after all, inexhaustible.

The decades from the 1930s to the 1950s witnessed a growing sense of the oceanic environment's fragility. The American writer Rachel Carson in particular wrote for a wider public, summoning up a romantic, organic vision of the world's oceans as a complex, beautiful and above all interconnected whole that determined the fates of land- as well as sea-dwellers.[91] British scientists were to add rigorous evidence on overfishing to the sense of wonder caused by Carson's pioneering work. The inter-war Development Commission headed by E.S. Russell contained a number of scientists who effectively founded the modern science of fisheries research. Russell was in no doubt by the 1940s that white fish such as cod were being grossly overfished.[92] Michael Graham in particular mounted the first consistent studies of cod numbers in British waters, and provided indeed a new 'Great Law of Fishing': that 'fisheries that are unlimited become unprofitable'. He even produced a famous graphic, which showed that fishing 90 per cent of any cohort would reduce its yield to nothing in just 4 years. Taking out 30 per cent, on the other hand, would allow the catch to continue when the fish had become mature.[93]

Two young men Graham recruited just after the Second World War – Ray Beverton and Sidney Holt – went even further. By reconceptualising 'sustainable' fish stocks and basing them on quantitative studies of yield per recruit to the population, they carried Graham's work into new realms. He had suspected that consistent overfishing could deplete future recruitment to the stock as well as the stocks of fish that spawned every year; Beverton and Holt proved it.[94] But not everyone heeded these warnings, and in fact the post-war era was a period of relative popular and official complacency in the countries around the Atlantic and the North Sea. In 1961, Hawthorne Daniel and Francis Minot published *The Inexhaustible Sea*, described on the jacket as 'the exciting story of the sea and its endless resources'.[95] Even Beverton and Holt had been looking confidently for ways to maximize yield and profits, rather than new techniques for conservation. The idea that fish stocks might actually run out was still an alien one.[96]

This situation was undoubtedly made worse by Britain's entry into the EEC in 1973. The six countries that made up the EEC before Britain, Denmark and the Republic of Ireland joined in that year had agreed a 'Common Fisheries Policy' in June 1970, just one day before enlargement negotiations began. This was a deliberate strategy, to settle a shared fisheries 'pool' as part of the EEC's *acquis*, or achievements, before the new countries joined. The newcomers would thus have to accede to the arrangements, or stay out.[97] The British were desperate to enter the Community, and deep sea fishing businesses were keen to share the North Sea with Norwegian fishermen as common and open waters.[98] But when Norway decided to remain outside the EEC, partly due to this very issue, Britain suffered disproportionately. Her deep-water fishermen, who had always fished within what in

1977 became in international law a 200-mile-wide protected zone off the shore of Norway, suffered a major blow from which they would struggle to recover.[99]

The European Commission has always put forward conservation measures in the hope rather than the expectation that politicians will agree them in full. The so-called Hague Compromise of 1977, which settled the Community's own 200-mile fishing limit from its communal borders, was a case in point. The Commission aspired to reach a conservation strategy that year, but allowed for member states to take their own action in the interim. In fact, Total Allowable Catches (TACs) for each fish stock and overall quotas were not settled until January 1983.[100] The bartering system within the Council of Ministers lends itself to this constant dilution of conservation measures: if Spain manages to resist cuts, Denmark will then insist on similar concessions, and so on. In consequence, the TAC for each species' breeding stock – the main element within most 'fisheries management' schemes – is consistently far too high within European Union (EU) waters. Inside Iceland's 200-mile limit the TAC is 25 per cent of the stock; in EU waters, 60 per cent.[101] European scientists live in fear of what they call 'the dreaded phone-call': the hectoring call from a politician to ask them whether they might or could massage down their figures for fishing limits.[102]

The Common Fisheries Policy (CFP) also generates 'by-catch', a perennial problem in industrial trawling which involves pitching unwanted fish over the side, but one made much worse in a regime that forbids or strictly limits the landing of certain stocks.[103] The United Nations Food and Agriculture Administration estimates that perhaps a third of what is caught worldwide, some 27 million tons, goes over the side every year.[104] The situation may be even worse in EU waters, because it is illegal to land these species some quotas have been met. In 2007 the British Government prosecuted 17 Newlyn fishermen – the so-called Newlyn 17 – for defying by-catch rules. Drew Davies was one of them, and he claimed that on one trip he had to dump 1000 cod overboard.[105] Questionnaires on 'black fish' – those landed outside the rules, beyond quotas – show that only 20 per cent of British fishermen even try to claim that they land no illegal fish.[106] Lord Selborne, chairman of a House of Lords select committee, has stated that he thinks that 40 per cent of cod landed comes onto land illegally.[107]

Even official reports note that, in the words of the Prime Minister's Strategy Unit, 'the current...management system does not have the trust of the UK fishing industry.' Policy is made a long way from the quayside, in incomprehensible bargains at European level; fishermen have little trust in scientists they believe know little about the reality on the spot.[108] This black or grey economy, of course, makes estimating remaining stocks, and setting 'manageable' populations, that much harder. By 2009 the European

Commission itself was making clear that this situation could not continue. Radical de-centralisation of the policy, with its detailed targets and implementation left to local authorities and the industry itself, was at the centre of the Commission's reform agenda.[109]

The crisis does not extend to every type of fish. Herring stocks, as we have already noted, have recovered; mackerel, too, are doing well. The pelagic fishing industry which takes fish from near the surface, and more than half of which was based in Scotland by the end of the twentieth century, remained profitable – testament to what can be done with proper fisheries management such as the closure of the herring fisheries in the 1970s.[110] In all about 13 per cent of the stocks in EU waters to which the British have access are in danger, though another 23 per cent are listed as 'at risk'. 'Demersal' or deep sea fish such as cod and haddock are the most notable examples. Still, even the Prime Minister's Strategy Unit, which was asked to look into this question after yet another 'compromise' brokered in Brussels during 2002, has recommended that trawling for white fish be much more strictly controlled. The Unit recommended in 2004 that 13 per cent of the white fish fleet be laid up, and a further 30 per cent prevented from fishing until stocks have recovered.[111]

Even tighter fishing limits within the existing regime do not seem to meet the case. Academics are virtually unanimous in calling for the creation of completely protected wildlife reserves at sea: they have been championed in a number of official reports, including the 2004 report of the Royal Commission on Environmental Pollution.[112] In the words of Callum Roberts, Professor of Marine Conservation at the University of York, marine reserves 'have to be placed centre stage as a fundamental underpinning for everything we do in the oceans'.[113] Marine reserves might allow the seabed to recover, as well as giving the entire food chain a breathing space, rather than just 'preserving' one fish or another because of the crises of the moment; reserves would limit by-catch as well.[114]

The creation of Marine Conservation Zones became policy under Labour during 2005–06, though the March 2007 White Paper in which this was announced was very light on detail as to what this might mean for the fishing industry, exactly how many zones there would be and where they would be established.[115] Consultation on a draft Bill was still continuing at the time of writing. Strict enforcement of the new marine reserves seems vital to the health of the marine ecosystem. Without such measures, advertisers may soon be forced to rename some of the seas' less attractive-sounding fish for supermarket consumption: spur-dog, scaldfish, lumpfish, weever and the like. The white demersal fish that Britons have been used to will be all but extinct in British and EU waters: the pernicious but familiar practice of destroying the stocks of whole new species will then begin all over again.[116]

Decline of the Royal Navy

The transition to peace after 1945 inevitably involved enormous cuts to the navy. It essentially returned to its pre-war strength, with defence plans during 1946 and 1947 accepting that it would be the smallest of the three services. The navy had 135,000 active personnel at the outbreak of war in 1939; now those numbers would return to about 144,000, about 11 per cent of whom were conscripted. By the end of 1947 the Royal Navy was tiny by previous standards. The Home Fleet was based on a single cruiser and two large destroyers: Mediterranean strength was down to one operational light carrier, and the Pacific Fleet had temporarily lost its carrier and was reduced to three operational cruisers and four destroyers.[117] In fact, the Royal Navy would shrink further throughout the post-war period. It possessed 12 aircraft carriers in 1950, and only two in 1980. Its destroyer numbers fell from 280 to 64; conventional non-nuclear submarines from 66 to 28; and mining and coastal craft from 66 to 52.[118]

This was, however, no straightforward or processional retreat, any more than the wars of 1914–45 witnessed the complete eclipse of British naval power. The 'Yangtze Incident' of April to July 1949, in which the British frigate *Amethyst* fought its way out of China under attack from the People's Liberation Army, made a tremendous impression on public opinion back in the UK.[119] The inception of the Cold War in the late 1940s, and then the Korean War that broke out in 1950, finally brought the period of severe post-war retrenchment in naval spending to an end. The naval estimates rose by £90 million between 1948 and 1950, while spending on the army shrank by £6 million. The proportion of dockyard orders placed by the Royal Navy rose to 11 per cent from a mere 2 per cent.[120] Between 1952 and 1960, 26 frigates in four different classes were laid down in response to the Korean emergency and the consequent realisation that the Cold War might easily become 'hot'.[121] Even more emphasis was placed on submarines in these early years of rearmament, since the former were thought to be the one really effective counter-measure that might protect civilian and military vessels from a Russian submarine offensive. The submarine fleet in service or refit was 45 strong in 1947, and was still at about that level in 1955: an increase of almost a quarter on 1945 numbers, with flotillas in the Mediterranean and off Australia as well as in home waters. It was pared down to around 30 boats by the time of the first British-built nuclear submarine's commissioning in 1963, though by now all of these were of modern post-war construction.[122]

There was, even so, a new emphasis on slimming down Britain's conventional forces, including a navy that could only be expected to play a subsidiary role in any 'broken backed' post-nuclear warfare.[123] Eventually a new and more focused role as part of the North Atlantic Treaty Organization (NATO) deterrent, or alternatively as supplying what aid could be managed after a nuclear exchange, had to be constructed. Other developments encouraged this general reappraisal. The Suez crisis of 1956, in which Anglo-French forces attempted to wrest back control of the canal that the Egyptian leader Colonel Nasser had nationalised, was a case in point. The Royal Navy successfully landed the bulk of British forces and helped to suppress Egyptian resistance both in the air and on land. Three Royal Navy aircraft carriers – *Bulwark*, *Eagle* and *Albion* – and two light carriers – HMS *Theseus* and HMS *Ocean* – provided air cover for the operation.[124] It was not, all the same, a particularly well-executed operation. The relevant Royal Marine forces were not immediately available, and the invasion fleet had to be brought together from disparate and far-flung units, a process that took months. The period between July, when Nasser nationalised the canal, and 6 November, the date of the seaborne landing, allowed international opinion time to build up against the invasion. Economic pressure, mainly from the USA, then forced the British and French to retreat.[125] It was a signal lesson in the new realities of a superpower world that did not include either the UK or France. This changed the strategic situation so profoundly, and along with the nuclear threat made massive naval engagements so unlikely, that new ideas were clearly required.

The Government's 1957 White Paper heralded far-reaching changes. Duncan Sandys, the Minister of Defence, was determined that Britain's armed forces reflect her straitened economic circumstances.[126] His relations with the Chiefs of Staff reached boiling point when Sandys' intention to slash conventional forces and rely more explicitly on the nuclear deterrent became clear. The plans radically reduced the size of the Royal Navy: Sandys aimed to reduce manpower from 121,000 to 75,000 over time, and the remaining elements of the Reserve Fleet would for the most part be scrapped.[127] Smaller guided missile destroyers would replace the navy's long-hoped-for large missile cruisers; the nine frigates then in service were to be run down to three; and the last battleship, HMS *Vanguard*, was finally scrapped in 1960. It was the end of an era for the surface fleet, but one from which it would emerge modernised and better able to conduct limited conventional operations such as those at Suez. As the First Sea Lord Mountbatten said, he had got the Navy 'a reasonable deal – better than the Army and RAF'.[128] He had used his personal friendship with Sandys to resist attacks on the navy's carriers, which would continue as the core of anti-submarine operations and convoy warfare in the NATO North Atlantic theatre.[129]

The surface fleet's importance was still to some extent eclipsed by Britain's adoption of a maritime nuclear deterrent in the 1960s. The Royal Navy became the preferred weapon of choice for Prime Ministers considering war with the Communist *bloc*, not because it could protect convoys during 'broken backed' warfare, but because it might deter a Soviet nuclear attack, or indeed deter the Russians from pressing their advantage in a limited conventional war. Britain's nuclear deterrent had from the mid-1950s been carried by the V-Bomber force of the RAF, a role they would maintain until the late 1960s.[130] But replacing them with Blue Streak, the planned British missile system that would allow the RAF to carry on deploying nuclear weapons, proved too expensive and technically difficult. From at least the late 1950s onwards, senior naval figures such as the First Lord of the Admiralty, Lord Selkirk, as well as Mountbatten, began to see the American Polaris system as a way of maintaining the Navy's relevance in the new nuclear age.[131]

Traditionalism, the sheer cost of the programme and a certain moral revulsion at carrying nuclear weapons did mean that the navy was rather divided and uncertain about the new submarine-based deterrent.[132] Nevertheless, the failure of the American Skybolt programme, and the cancellation of Blue Streak, left the British with little alternative but to ask the reluctant Americans to sell them Polaris. President Kennedy gave his approval at the Nassau summit in the Bahamas during December 1962.[133] Four Polaris submarines would eventually be ordered: *Resolution*, the first of them, was commissioned in October 1967, and by June 1968 she was on operational patrol.[134]

The adoption of Polaris was not meant to signal the end of the surface fleet, and the Conservatives indeed decided during 1963 that the older carrier *Ark Royal* would be replaced by a new model, the CVA-01. The carrier HMS *Victorious* would also be phased out in 1971, leaving CVA-01, *Hermes* and *Eagle* to carry the navy's airborne threat. But the decision to 'go nuclear' had profound consequences for the navy's building programme. Along with a Treasury-inspired decision to employ competitive tendering for shipbuilding orders from 1960, the smaller number of orders caused a number of specialist warship shipyards to close. Only three such firms were left, outside the Royal Dockyards, by the end of the 1960s.[135] Nor was CVA-01 actually ever built. On coming to power in October 1964 Labour was committed to making savings, particularly on the military side of government expenditure. The new government set a £2 billion cap on defence spending, which would make paying for the carrier much more difficult.[136] The Government was also considering whether to buy the American F111, a long-range fighter-bomber that might stand in for carrier aircraft in a crisis. Influential voices, including the powerful Paymaster General George Wigg and the Foreign Office, argued that enormous savings were possible if the F111 replaced the new carrier.[137]

Denis Healey, Labour's Defence Secretary between 1964 and 1970, was similarly ruthless in his strategic judgement. Given the need for regular refits to these new carriers, and the lack of trained personnel to man them, only one could ever have been maintained east of the Suez Canal in any case. Given that this would have been their prime role, at a cost of £170 million a year, Healey decided that they could not be afforded. One of the carriers rotated on station would still have been *Hermes*, with only 8 strike aircraft and 12 fighters: hardly a good investment for the amount of money involved. The Navy could justify such a commitment only in the unlikely event of a prolonged naval battle in the Straits of Sumatra, during which any enemy would be equipped with Russian MIGs. Other commitments could be met by land-based RAF aircraft.[138]

Britain was hoping to withdraw many of its standing forces from East of Suez once it had brought its 'Confrontation' with Indonesia over Malaysian Borneo to an end. Future operations were much more likely to be amphibious 'police operations', such as all three forces' deployment to Kuwait in 1961 in an operation that successfully deterred Iraq from an invasion of that country.[139] CVA-01 would have been irrelevant during that deployment; the much smaller 'commando carrier' HMS *Bulwark* played the initially critical role of landing Royal Marines to protect Kuwait.[140] The relevant Cabinet Committee had little difficulty in deciding, during January 1966, that 'there were no acceptable means of continuing a carrier programme within a defence budget of £2,000 million.' They were helped in their decision by the sheer complexity of the project. The project leader in the Admiralty's Ship Department declared the day that CVA-01 was aborted 'the happiest... of my life'. The carrier had been bedevilled by design changes, cost overruns and skilled manpower shortages from the start.[141] Last minute navy representations before the matter came before full Cabinet won only the concession that four carriers would continue into the 1970s. *Victorious* would still eventually be decommissioned, but *Ark Royal* would be refitted so that it could serve until the mid-1970s. CVA-01 was indeed cancelled, and with it went any long-term hope that the Royal Navy might maintain a large-scale and global air strike capability.[142]

The subsequent Defence Review White Paper of February 1966 announced that there would be no major interventionist operations without allies, there would be no military assistance offered without a 'red carpet' of welcome and no interventions would be countenanced without land-based air cover. It was a massive retreat from the navy's historic role, though Ministers maintained that they were not abrogating a role East of Suez – a rather disingenuous claim that caused the Navy Minister, Christopher Mayhew, to resign.[143] Even that commitment was scaled down in July 1967, when a new *Supplementary Statement on Defence Policy* announced withdrawal from Singapore and Malaysia in the mid-1970s. Further cuts following upon the pound's November 1967 devaluation meant that this date was brought forward to 1971, and an explicit signal was sent that Britain's 'East of Suez' defence policy was all but over. The Cabinet's growing enthusiasm for entering the EEC, and the threat that speculators would force another devaluation of sterling if public expenditure was not visibly reduced, necessitated some overt symbol of retrenchment.[144] *Victorious* had already been an immediate casualty of the devaluation, as she was decommissioned straightaway rather than serving until the 1970s.[145]

The navy's Future Working Party tried to start more or less from the beginning, and reassess British naval commitments in the light of the probable end of its carrier capability. It was this period, rather than the post-war retrenchment or the post-Suez cuts carried out under Sandys, that marked the real change in Britain's maritime defence posture. Smaller commando carriers, equipped with helicopters rather than fixed-wing fighters or bombers, would have to bridge the gap; Vertical Take Off and Landing (VTOL) aircraft would have to be launched from smaller-than-expected platforms. But overall, the Working Party reacted with some despair to the cancellation of CVA-01, concluding that there was simply no way that the navy's commitments could be met without a large carrier.[146] By the late 1960s British strategic thinking had undergone a decisive shift. No more would the Royal Navy attempt to be the world's policeman, or even the chief lieutenant to the real maritime power, the USA. Instead, she would concentrate on her contribution to NATO operations in the Atlantic and the Mediterranean, and perhaps on amphibious operations in those theatres, along with NATO's northern flank in Norway.[147]

Certain lines of continuity with previous era remained. A medium-sized surface force of frigates in fact remained stationed at Singapore, along with Australian and New Zealand forces, until 1974.[148] There was no clean and obvious break with the 'imperial' past, but, rather, a gradual diminution of the ability to commit 'heavy' conventional forces, quickly, wherever they might be required. Military bases remained in places as far afield as Ascension Island and the Falklands in the South Atlantic, Hong Kong (until 1997), Gibraltar, Malta, Cyprus and the British Indian Ocean Territory.[149] *Hermes* and *Ark Royal* were eventually kept as carriers, the former after a period as a commando carrier for amphibious warfare and the latter after an expensive refit. *Hermes* concentrated on anti-submarine warfare under the NATO umbrella, along with her new partner *Invincible*, while *Ark Royal* was pensioned off in the late 1970s, to be replaced by a newer and smaller namesake.[150] The procurement of Sea Harrier vertical take-off aircraft, capable of taking off and landing on very small carriers, was announced by the Labour Government in May 1975. This would allow Britain to deploy seaborne air forces around the world in the future. But, for now, the force was part of the general NATO commitment to Western Europe, and the carrier force and its aircraft were smaller and lighter, and carried much less firepower, than CVA-01 would have done.[151]

On taking power in 1979, Mrs Thatcher's new government adopted a sceptical view towards all public expenditure, even that on the military might that helped her wage the Cold War. Her administration therefore took a series of further steps towards ending the Royal Navy's global reach. John Nott, her Defence Secretary, mounted a new and even more aggressive defence review. The consequences, announced in 1981, would make even the navy's narrower commitments as they stood in the 1970s almost impossible to meet. The Atlantic fleet would concentrate on submarines, backed up by RAF shore-based aircraft, to fight off any Soviet attack in that theatre. The active fleet of frigates and destroyers would be reduced from 59 to 50, and the two assault ships, *Fearless* and *Intrepid*, would be decommissioned. Perhaps most controversially of all, the new carrier *Invincible* would be sold, and *Hermes* scrapped, leaving the Royal Navy with only two such ships: the light carriers *Illustrious* and its sister, the new *Ark Royal*.[152] The Argentine invasion of the Falkland Islands in the South Atlantic was to change all these plans, ironically since the Defence Review had at least helped to encourage the view in Buenos Aeries that the British could not, or perhaps would not, defend the islands.[153] But for now the situation was clearer than ever: Britain no longer aspired to be a global naval power, and was content to make a middling and regional contribution to collective defence.

Conclusions: why 'collapse'?

The Festival of Britain did not just sit, entirely static, on its South Bank site in London: nor were its regional guides, such as the East Anglian example, the Festival's only engagement with 'the regions'. There was also a 'festival ship', *Campania*, that sailed round Britain's coastline to carry the stories of 'the land of Britain', 'discovery' and 'the people at home' to the country's port cities.[154] *Campania* had her own story to tell, for she had served the Admiralty as an escort carrier in the Second World War: but in 1951 her crew were happy to take her festival displays to Southampton, Dundee, Newcastle, Hull, Plymouth, Bristol, Cardiff, Belfast, Birkenhead and Glasgow. Thousands flocked to see the ship and its exhibition.[155] The display's evocation of a 'seafaring people' who would starve without their seaborne trade was fairly conventional. But its convenor, C. Hamilton Ellis, had a vision of the future as well as of the past and present:

> The British tradition has been continuous. We are proud enough of our great
> days of sail; but . . . in the passing of the flag from sail to steam we built on our

inheritance. So, while we may look back at past achievement, it is only for a glance over the shoulder while our hands and minds still make the pace in the design, construction and operation of ships for every purpose that the modern world requires.[156]

Ellis' vision would speedily collapse in the years to come. Mass-volume ship-building was gone by the early 1980s; Britain's role as a world carrier and shipowner collapsed at the same time. The seaside holiday and Britain's fisheries were undergoing a prolonged crisis which seemed to go on forever. The Royal Navy was no longer able to fight more than one limited war at a time: its greatest striking power, the Polaris nuclear deterrent, could hardly be employed except in the uttermost need. There was a sense that something indefinable was passing, a feeling of lost identity that many writers noted. 'The peoples of Britain ... should take much more notice of the seas around them', Ian Friel has argued, 'of the people who work on them and of what happens there'.[157] More specifically, the American Mark Kurlansky wrote in 2008 that 'if this island loses its fisheries, it will have lost its cultural heritage. Without commercial fishing, Britain will no longer be the same place and the British will no longer be the same people'.[158]

Some of this 'collapse' may have been unavoidable, whatever mix of policies had been adopted. Although quicker modernisation and better labour relations would have ensured that Britain's shipbuilders went on being competitive into the 1970s, even such an advance would probably not have guaranteed the civilian industry's long-term survival. Sweden, so admired at the time, also succumbed to Asian competition.[159] High-technology rationalisation was no answer to the simple economics of 'catch-up and convergence': the tendency for manufacturing jobs to pass to nations that could simply copy and adapt previously 'European' or 'Western' methods, at lower cost and with fewer labour problems.[160] By the early twenty-first century, virtually all industrial-scale shipbuilding was conducted in East Asia. South Korea had 40 per cent of the market, with China and Japan having a quarter each.[161] It is also difficult to see how Britain's overburdened defence economy could have sustained a truly world role for the Royal Navy. The country's balance of payments was perpetually in deficit, mainly due to British defence spending overseas. Higher defence spending might have made her constant 'stop-go' crises even worse.[162] But much more could and probably should have been done to save Britain's coastal resorts, and conserve her fish stocks: and the continuing relevance and vibrancy of some elements of Britain's maritime identity demonstrate some of the neglected room for manoeuvre. To this continuing role – this 'afterglow' – we now turn.

Timeline of events

1863–65	First Sea Fisheries Royal Commission
1883–85	Lord Dalhousie's Royal Commission on Sea-Fisheries
1892	Scottish Fisheries Board closes waters around the Moray Firth to fishing
1919	Housing and Town Planning Act gives councils powers to improve environment
1919–21	Brief, inflationary post-First World War economic and trade boom
March 1925	Furness Withy orders five new ships from German builders in Hamburg
1929–31	Onset of Great Depression: world trade shrinks by two-thirds
1932	Import Duties Act establishes protection of British Imperial markets
1935	Herring Industry Board set up
1938	Legislation introduces statutory holidays with pay
1940	Report of the Royal Commission on the Distribution of the Industrial Population
April–July 1949	'Yangtze Incident' with HMS *Amethyst* trapped on that river
1950	Start of Korean War
1950	Horizon Holidays takes its first package tourists to Corsica
1951	Festival Ship *Campania* tours Britain's coastline
1951	First publication of Rachel Carson's *The Sea Around Us*
1955	Autumn Downs stock of herring fails
1956	Amphibious landings off aircraft and assault carriers as part of Suez expedition
1956	British Transport Films makes 17-minute 'short', *Holiday*
1956	Japan overtakes the UK in terms of shipping tonnage launched
1957	Defence White Paper radically pares down Britain's conventional military forces

1960	Last Royal Navy battleship, HMS *Vanguard*, scrapped
1961	'Operation Vantage' mounted to deter Iraq from invading Kuwait
December 1962	Nassau Summit in the Bahamas between President Kennedy and Prime Minister Macmillan
1963	First British nuclear submarine – HMS *Dreadnought* – launched
1966	Geddes Report into shipbuilding recommends widespread amalgamations
February 1966	Defence White Paper announces cancellation of CVA-01 aircraft carrier
1967	Shipbuilding Industry Act provides £5 million to encourage shipbuilding mergers
1967	Scott and Lithgow yards in Glasgow announce they are to merge
July 1967	Announcement of withdrawal from Singapore and Malaysia in the mid-1970s
January 1968	Withdrawal from Singapore and Malaysia brought forward to 1971
1969	Appointment of a standing Royal Commission on Environmental Pollution
1973	The UK enters the European Economic Community (EEC)
1973	Peak year for fish landings in UK waters
1975–76	First European Bathing Directives issued
1977	200-mile national 'economic zones' offshore become international law
1977–78	North Sea temporarily closed as a herring fishery
1981	Nott Defence Review published
1982	Exclusive 'economic zones' take effect
1983	British Shipbuilders Act establishes legislative framework for privatisation
1983	EEC's Total Allowance Catches (TACs) settled
1984	Thatcher government withdraws tax incentives for British-registered shipowners
1988	Govan Shipbuilders privatised and sold to Kvaerner
1993	European Court finds Blackpool sea water contains high levels of bacteria

1998	Michael Winterbottom's *I Want You* released in cinemas
2002	European Council of Ministers waters down planned TAC reductions on cod
2007	House of Commons Committee publishes report on *Coastal Towns*
2007	'Newlyn 17' prosecuted for defying by-catch rules
2007	Government White Paper on Marine Bill published

10

Afterglow

In 1982 the British Royal Navy went to war to re-assert British sovereignty over the Falkland Islands, a tiny British territory off the coast of South America. The conflict was to usher in a new age for the navy, in which it was to be seen as more relevant to Britain's defence needs. Although its numerical decline was to continue, the speed and depth of that process were slowed during the 1990s by the obvious continued need for amphibious forces. 'Small wars' – the increased number of far-flung conventional conflicts to which Britain's service personnel were committed – also became important in the 1990s and the early years of the new millennium. Taken together, these two facts prevented the continued run-down of the navy. Instead, it was re-equipped for a newly internationalist role in peacekeeping and enforcement, though it was still capable of large-scale commitments against Iraq in 1991 and 2003. The confirmation of two new aircraft carrier orders in 2008 demonstrates that the Royal Navy can no longer be thought of as in even relative 'decline'. Rather, its role and scale have necessarily shifted since the mid-twentieth century. This chapter argues, more broadly, that the general impression of disengagement from the sea, and the collapse of traditional maritime industries, has been exaggerated. 'Flagging out' caused a successive decline in British shipping tonnage since the 1960s, but this trend was reversed in the early twenty-first century by a new and much simpler tax system that was much more attractive to owners than the old regime. The 1980s witnessed perhaps the greatest economic windfall Britain had ever experienced, in the shape of North Sea oil; and the ocean promised to be the source of a new energy revolution early in the twenty-first century, given governments' and businesses' interest in offshore wind turbines. Britain's ports were

211

handling more traffic than ever, in a highly competitive international environment. Coastal tourism was beginning to recover, helped by more realistic and more comprehensive renewal schemes that brought together local companies, councils and government regeneration agencies. Cleaner beaches, free of sewage and industrial pollution following long public campaigns and a great deal of European pressure, assisted this revival. Many seaside towns were still in great economic distress, but this seems to have had less to do with the 'decline' of tourism, and more with chronic underdevelopment and social problems that they often shared with inner cities far from the sea. There was certainly no general withdrawal from the ocean, a misleading impression that can be created by focusing too closely on shipbuilding and fishing, both industries that were extremely unlikely ever to recover from their prolonged slumps. Lastly, the chapter considers the British maritime imagination – the books, poems, films and plays that portrayed and re-imagined the sea in the years after 1945. Here, too, vibrant continued interest, engagement and excitement were evident. In general, although the UK was never likely to lead the world in any marine industry, or indeed in maritime warfare, the country seemed likely to remain a major oceanic presence.

The Falklands conflict and the rejuvenation of British sea power

The origins of the Falklands conflict went back as far as the sixteenth century. Argentina argues that the islands were first sighted by the Italian explorer Amerigo Vespucci, or Esteban Gomez, a Portuguese who sailed with Magellan in 1520. Britain, in return, has claimed that Captain John Davies discovered the Falklands in 1592. Britain and Spain launched rival claims in 1766, before Britain withdrew its own settlers in 1774 – though without accepting the Spanish claim of sovereignty, or the rights that Argentina claimed to inherit on its independence in 1816. On the outbreak of hostilities between Argentina and the USA in 1832, the British seized their opportunity to send warships and raise their flag again. The last Argentine military forces left the Falklands in January 1833. The dispute over the islands was at the start a rather arcane one; during the nineteenth century, the UK often did not even bother to respond to occasional Argentine protests on the matter. But the latter began to take up the matter inside the United Nations from 1964, and tension began to mount over the territory's future.[1]

The military junta that took power in Buenos Aires during 1976 was, by 1982, clinging to power in the midst of economic crisis and political stalemate. Years of brutal oppression, 'disappearances' and murder had done little to solve Argentina's problems with chronic inflation, while unemployment and business failures were accelerating. The junta's leaders decided on a bold but risky gamble: the seizure of the Falklands.[2] As we have already seen, the Nott defence review of 1981 had encouraged the idea, inside Argentina's military junta, that Britain would not defend the Falklands. Parliament was told that the ageing ice patrol ship HMS *Endurance* would not be replaced at the end of June 1981; MPs, the Foreign Office and the Falklands Islands Council all protested at the time, to no avail. Newspapers in Buenos Aires announced that Britain had 'abandoned' the islands.[3]

The Prime Minister, Margaret Thatcher, and her advisers had already decided on a military response even before Argentine forces landed on the islands. It was a political necessity, without which the Government may well fall; and it met the case for the administration to be able to announce some sort of response immediately. During a hastily assembled meeting in the Prime Minister's House of Commons room during the evening of 31 March, the Chief of the Naval Staff Admiral Sir Henry Leach made the Navy's case. He knew that he was drawing on forces that his own Secretary of State had already decided to scrap: he relished the opportunity to prove Nott wrong, and argued that a Task Force could and should be sent to the South Atlantic. 'It was exclusively a navy matter,' he declared, before returning to his own staff and announcing: 'the task force is to be made ready and sailed.'[4]

The navy had begun to take action as soon as reliable intelligence began filtering in of Argentine intentions over the weekend of 27–28 March. The nuclear-powered submarine HMS *Spartan* sailed from Gibraltar, followed by her fellow submarines *Splendid* the day before the Argentine invasion, and *Conqueror* 3 days later. It was clear immediately to Leach and his colleagues that an enormous force would be needed, including aircraft carriers, a powerful escort and an amphibious assault force. The Argentine navy included strong surface forces, and over 200 aircraft, 8000 miles from UK home bases. To sail out against them without all the resources the Royal Navy could muster would be negligent, at best.[5] The aircraft carriers *Hermes* and *Invincible* left Portsmouth with *Fearless*; Britain's advanced destroyers – *Glasgow*, *Sheffield* and *Coventry* – as well as frigates joined up from NATO exercises off Gibraltar. Many men from 3 Commando Brigade were initially ferried by the 45,000-ton cruise liner *Canberra*, which was requisitioned by government order to carry 2200 men. It was STUFT – one of the Ships Taken Up From Trade – as the ironic acronym of the time had it.[6]

Britain's Task Force actually possessed remarkably little room for manoeuvre, for the ships available were barely adequate. *Hermes* and *Invincible* were due to be scrapped and sold, respectively; *Intrepid* and *Fearless* were listed for the scrapyard as well, though their retention was being considered.[7] Even with the ships available, service chiefs were not optimistic about their ability to mount a blockade of the islands, despite the fact that this option was still envisaged as 'live' by some captains as they steamed southwards. This therefore had to be what the commander of 3 Commando Brigade called 'a one-shot operation': an amphibious assault without clear strategic alternatives or contingency plans. Official policy had languished since Nicholas Ridley, at that time a junior minister in the Foreign Office, had attempted to launch negotiations over sovereignty in the winter of 1980–81: there was simply no Prime Ministerial, Cabinet and Parliamentary support for such a departure. An official review of military preparedness had merely noted the 'formidable' difficulties of an operation to retake the islands. In this situation, no one could assume the success of any such operation.[8]

The Royal Navy's first task was to eliminate the threat from the Argentine surface fleet. On 7 April the British announced a Maritime Exclusion Zone around the Falklands, to take effect on 12 April: all Argentine shipping within that area would be liable to attack without further warning. This was the moment Admiral John Sandy Woodward began to accept that he was really going to lead the task force into a shooting war. As *Hermes* approached the Exclusion Zone on 1 May, the British forces' situation was challenging, at best: they were faced to the landward by the Argentine carrier *Veintecinco de Mayo*, and away to the south-west of the Falklands, by the cruiser *General Belgrano* and her escorts. The *Belgrano* was an old ship, US-built in the 1930s; 'on her own, not that big a threat', as Woodward accepted. But her two destroyers, with their own ship-to-ship Exocets, might be able to threaten the task force while the Argentine carrier closed in from the other direction. Woodward decided to 'take out one claw of the pincer'.[9]

Belgrano was outside the Exclusion Zone; she was probably heading away from it. Later in the morning, Woodward was fairly clear that the Argentine carrier had flinched from a direct attack on the task force. Even so, there remained another motive for attacking the cruiser, this time a more basic one. The *Belgrano* could easily tack back towards the task force, and indeed Woodward believed that she was already doing so. Vice Admiral Sir Terence Lewin, the Chief of the Defence Staff, met with Mrs Thatcher and asked for a change to the rules of engagement, specifically so Woodward could order the nuclear-powered submarine *Conqueror* to attack. He did not believe the fact that *Belgrano* was outside the Exclusion Zone was remotely relevant: as he said later, 'here was an opportunity to knock off a major unit of the Argentine fleet.'[10] As one British officer said, 'you have got to start something like this by showing that you're bloody good and you're determined to win.' On the afternoon of 2 May – and following a request for orders from the

Cabinet back in London – *Conqueror* fired three torpedoes at the *General Belgrano*. Two of them found their mark; the ship quickly began to list, and then sank. As a result, 368 Argentine sailors lost their lives, many of them trapped in the ship's stern.[11] But Lewin and Woodward had their symbolic victory: the Argentine surface fleet was not to venture out again.[12]

In the end, British marines and paratroopers were able to fight their way across East Falkland, supported by further landings at Fitzroy and Bluff Cove on that island's southern flank. British forces secured the islands' capital, Stanley, on 14 June.[13] Britain's naval forces had to some extent been lucky. The initial Argentine plan had been to attack in late May, at which time the South Atlantic winter would have made an immediate response almost impossible. Only the signs of a robust British response panicked them into acting earlier than they had intended.[14] Argentine air attacks on 21–22 May had focussed on Royal Navy ships on picket duty, which were for the most part able to defend themselves; *Canberra* sat in the middle of San Carlos Bay all day without being attacked. Many Argentine bombs which hit their targets failed to explode, due to technical problems with the fuses. Argentina's one operational submarine, with another in port for repairs, stayed away; the country only had five of the air-launched Exocet missiles that proved so deadly, and a major diplomatic and intelligence effort was mounted to prevent her acquiring more.[15] But British losses were still grievous. The frigates HMS *Ardent* and *Antelope* were sunk supporting the initial landings on May 21 and May 23, respectively.[16] On 8 June the landing ship *Sir Galahad* was bombed at Bluff Cove: 48 men lost their lives as the ship burned. Most shocking of all, the Type 42 Destroyer HMS *Sheffield* was fatally wounded by an Exocet air-to-sea missile on 4 May, before sinking 6 days later.[17]

Much of the conflict was perceived and understood in terms that most naval thinkers from the past 400 years would have understood. On the morning the carrier group left Portsmouth, *The Times* ran a huge leader titled 'We are all Falklanders now.' 'We are an island race,' it argued: 'and the focus of attack is one of our islands, inhabited by our islanders.'[18] Mrs Thatcher herself had opened the emergency debate on Argentina's invasion with the words 'the people of the Falkland Islands, like the people of the United Kingdom, are an island race.' Enoch Powell evoked the Battle of the Falkland Islands in 1914; other MPs compared the coming military action to the navy's Norway campaign of 1940.[19] The *Daily Express* made sure it mixed almost every naval metaphor it could think of, from Drake to Trafalgar, with its headline: 'Our Armada Prepares in the Shadow of Nelson's Victory.' The *Sun*, in particular, kept up a stream of jingoistic headlines reminiscent of nineteenth-century popular imperialism throughout the campaign.[20] Even opponents of the war couched their protests in terms of Britain's previous maritime campaigns. Les Gibbard, the *Daily Mirror*'s cartoonist, echoed Zec's famous 1942 drawing of a seaman clinging to wreckage trying to bring petrol to Britain. Underneath, the post-*Sheffield* caption ran: 'The price of sovereignty has been increased – OFFICIAL.'[21]

The journalist Hugh O'Shaughnessy remembers speaking on the telephone to a contact in Argentina, conscious that two intelligence services were probably listening in: 'in the middle of it, breaking their cover, two hearty English voices broke in ... and voiced, in the purest and strongest barrack-room demotic, the same sort of views about people who spoke Spanish as the Elizabethan seafarers would have done in the time of Drake and Hawkins.'[22] If the message had to be hammered home, Ian McDonald – who briefly found fame as the official spokesman of the Ministry of Defence – closed the Emergency Press Centre on the conflict with Prospero's final speech from *The Tempest* (1610–11), the Shakespeare play most closely associated with the sea.[23]

The Falklands had uncovered some surprisingly resilient popular perceptions and memories of naval power; it may have played some role in preserving the Royal Navy against further cuts beyond those already planned. Nott announced in the 1982 Defence Estimates and a White Paper of the same year that he would continue to run down the numbers of destroyers and frigates to 50. Losses would be made up, and *Endurance* retained; but the fleet would still have to shrink.[24] There was to be no large-scale reconsideration of the fleet's role until the end of the Cold War in 1989–91. There were subtle shifts in priorities, all the same. The two amphibious assault ships would now definitely be kept on. Most of all, aircraft carriers, under immense threat in 1982, would clearly have to be treated with more care than they had been in Nott's first review. Key civil servants within the Ministry of Defence accepted three carriers, of the *Invincible* class's power at least, as the UK's necessary standard in the late 1980s. *Invincible* itself had been fitting out as the Falklands War was fought, though it provided cover for the islands while a new runway was being built at Stanley: the war made all plans to sell her obsolete.[25]

An ever-more complicated, and even seemingly chaotic, international scene then allowed the navy to resist many of the defence cuts that followed the collapse of the Soviet Union in 1991. Two government White Papers – *Options for Change* in 1991 and *Frontline First* in 1994, followed by the Strategic Defence Review of 1998 – carved out a new role for the navy. It gradually came to be seen as means of projecting power quickly, with great precision and at long distance, to defend Britain's interests or regional stability. The presence of the 'Armilla Patrol' in the Gulf between 1980 and 1988, usually made up of a destroyer and a frigate, or two frigates, and with the task of ensuring safe passage for British merchant ships, had already showed what might be achieved in the way of projecting force at minimal cost.[26]

There was a feeling of returning to the navy's past role intervening in 'small wars' – though these conflicts were also be managed in the light of new technological and strategic realities. Official strategy, as expounded in *The Fundamentals of British Maritime Doctrine*, published in 1995, now stressed the sophisticated range of powers the navy could bring to bear alongside political and diplomatic efforts, and the need to understand the joint context of air force and army operations.[27] The new amphibious platforms to replace *Fearless* and *Intrepid*, ordered in 1996 and entering service in 2001 and 2003, were deliberately named *Albion* and *Bulwark*, to reflect continuity with the old commando carriers of 1940s vintage.[28]

This renewed interest in limited conventional wars was tested much more quickly than most strategists had believed possible. When President Saddam Hussein of Iraq ordered an invasion of Kuwait in 1990, US and Allied forces responded to expel Iraqi forces from that country early the following year. This campaign required some quick reactions on the part of Britain's armed forces. The Royal Navy's effort was in some respects improvised, just as the Falklands had been. The authorities in London refused to let the ageing *Ark Royal* sail into the Gulf without expensive modifications that the Government refused to countenance. The Commodore in charge had to make do with using the frigate HMS *London* as his flagship, with his entire staff crowded into the ship's sonar room. And given that there was no seaborne assault on Kuwait – contrary to the feint the allies managed to mount – it might be thought that the navy played a subordinate role in this conflict. Nevertheless, the frigates HMS *Brazen* and *London* herself, and the two destroyers HMS *Cardiff* and *Gloucester*, later joined by two more frigates and two additional destroyers (*Exeter* and *Manchester*), did provide immensely important services in the conflict. They helped to maintain the fiction of a marine assault on the coast, causing Iraq's forces to be spread out away from the actual land-based attack; and they covered vital resupply efforts through the Persian Gulf itself. Submarine and diesel-electric boats put Special Boat Service and other special services ashore as well.[29]

It was a much smaller effort than Suez, or Britain's defence of Kuwait in 1961, or even the Falklands; though as part of a multi-national coalition, it hardly needed to be bigger. Overall, 11 destroyers and frigates, two diesel-electric submarines, four minesweepers with two support ships and three patrol craft, often deployed very close to Iraq, was a large commitment that did not need to be bigger given the six US aircraft carrier groups involved in the operation.[30] The struggle also witnessed the first deployment of women in an active naval combat role in the Royal Navy. Women had been serving with the WRNS, the Women's Royal Navy Service or 'Wrens', since the First World War, though the service had been disbanded while peacetime lashed between the two wars.[31] In September 1990 the decision was finally taken to allow women to serve on board ship: by April 1991, 148 women were serving on warships or auxiliaries and 62 had served in the Gulf on board HMS *Invincible, Brilliant, Juno* and *Battleaxe*.[32] The captain of HMS *Brilliant*, Toby Elliot, described the work of these heirs to Hannah Snell as adding 'a lot to the fighting efficiency of the ship ... [they were] absolutely first class'. The WRNS was abolished, and women absorbed into the 'regular' Royal Navy, in 1993.[33]

This preparedness for limited war dovetailed, under the New Labour government that took power in 1997, with the 'doctrine of the international community'. The new government gradually took the stance that human rights and Western-style democracy had to be defended proactively, wherever threats to them emerged.[34] Prime Minister Tony Blair's 'liberal internationalism' was to utilise the navy most notably in Kosovo in 1999, and then later in Sierra Leone in West Africa. The submarine *Splendid* fired its first Tomahawk cruise missiles in anger against Serb targets in Kosovo during NATO's attempt to prevent Serb atrocities in that province. *Invincible* once again provided air support, as in the Falklands. The new 22,000-ton helicopter carrier HMS *Ocean* (commissioned in 1998), along with *Fearless*, prepared for a marine assault, though this became surplus to requirements once Serb forces left the disputed province.[35]

Britain's role was even more central in Sierra Leone. A brief ceasefire in that country's long civil war brought Ahmad Tejan Kabbah, a former UN official, to power in relatively free and fair elections during 1996: but he was deposed in a coup in May 1997. Kabbah was returned to power by Nigerian forces acting under UN auspices in March 1998, but this peace process broke down for the last time late in April 2000.[36] The rebel Revolutionary United Front refused to comply with the disarmament process, aborted negotiations and seized 500 Kenyan and Zambian peacekeepers. The RUF's leader, Foday Sankoh, apparently believed that he could use brutal intimidation to seize the country's diamond mines. Only the arrival of 700 British paratroopers as part of an Amphibious Ready Group, deployed over 3500 miles in 7 days, prevented the legitimate government's morale from collapsing: seven Royal Navy warships, including *Illustrious* and the frigates *Argyll* and *Chatham*, anchored close offshore. It was the largest Royal Navy deployment since the Falklands, and helped to ensure both the defeat of the RUF and the resumption of political talks.[37]

The Royal Navy reached its nadir in the months leading up to the Falklands conflict; by the early twenty-first century it was an unquestioned part of Britain's re-equipped, but also overstretched, armed forces. It was not that the conflict had immediately changed the economic realities that had caused the Thatcher government to announce cuts to the surface fleet: little of that intent was in fact altered, as we have seen. But the continuing relevance and importance of naval warfare had indeed been demonstrated. Wars in Afghanistan, and again in the Gulf in the hugely controversial attack on Iraq during 2003, again involved the navy as a key part of a new British strategy involved in the so-called war on terror that followed the terrorist attacks in the USA on 11 September 2001. The submarines *Trafalgar* and *Triumph* fired cruise missiles at targets within Afghanistan in late 2001.[38] Royal Marine Commandoes attacked the Al Faw Peninsula in southern Iraq on the first day of the renewed war against Saddam Hussein in 2003, striking from the same HMS *Ocean* that had prepared for an amphibious assault in the Balkans campaign. By so doing they 'kicked down the door' to southern Iraq.[39] But they also showed that the Navy continued to be one of the most flexible and powerful implements that the British state still possessed. It is a trend that will probably continue: two huge new aircraft carriers, though delayed by a spending review late in 2008, are due to come into service during 2016 and 2018. They will be able to deploy 150 combat aircraft between them.[40]

North Sea oil, the sea and the British economy

Nor had Britain's maritime economy been entirely extinguished. North Sea oil and gas, Britain's ports and increasingly wind power ensured the sea's continuing relevance in economic policy. The shipping industry also showed signs of life in the early twenty-first century; John Prescott, who served as Deputy Prime Minister between 1997 and 2007, had himself been a steward for Cunard in his first career, and appointed a Shipping Working Group after Labour's return to office.[41] That group asked the Government to think about ways in which the tax system could be used to reduce the attractiveness of 'flagging out' and reverse the long-standing decline of Britain's merchant fleet.[42]

The result, following a Treasury review, was a 'tonnage tax'. Instead of being liable to Corporation Tax on actual profits, and a complex raft of subsidies and exemptions, shipping companies would pay Corporation Tax based on the tonnage of their ships. This would be a much simpler system, and allow small- and medium-sized shipowners to plan and raise capital on a much clearer and more stable basis.[43] The resulting tax, introduced in 2000, must be accounted a success. Between 2000 and 2007 the UK merchant fleet began to grow again, for the first time in generations, from 1050 to 1518 vessels, and from under 5000 to nearly 13,000 gross tons. This was only a return to the levels British shipping had stood at in the early 1980s, before the withdrawal of capital allowances; but it was the first sign since the early 1970s of any growth at all in the industry.[44]

Offshore oil and gas had been even more important during the previous three decades, at one point even turning Britain into an oil-exporting nation with a vested interest in keeping the price of energy high, in stark contrast to the oil-hungry USA.[45] Exxon and Shell, working together under a joint company agreement they had settled as far back as 1933, discovered the first natural gas off the coast of the Netherlands in 1959; British Petroleum (BP) found more gas off the coast of the UK in 1965. But the oil companies had to wait until 1969–71 for their first great breakthroughs. The American independent company Phillips discovered oil in Norwegian waters in 1969. In 1970 BP uncovered the Forties field north of Aberdeen, and Shell and Exxon drilled successfully in the so-called Brent field off the Shetlands the following year.[46]

These discoveries were, in time, to have profound consequences for the British economy. Aberdeen, for one thing, became an unlikely boom town. By 1976 its population of 185,000 was buttressed by 5000 oilmen, mostly from the USA. Wages and property prices were pushed up, and unemployment down.[47] The American writer Al Alvarez visited the city in the mid-1980s, and found the city's 'shops far better stocked than they used to be – the Marks & Spencer is one of the best outside London – and crowded with customers with money to spend'.[48] Even so, in general oil was a mixed blessing. It certainly added to GDP, by as much as 7 per cent in the mid-1980s before oil prices fell away again, and helped to ensure general economic growth at a time of great crisis for the international economy.[49] But by boosting sterling at a time of very high interest rates in the early 1980s, it may also have helped to make British exports uncompetitive and assisted in the widespread destruction of traditional manufacturing jobs.[50]

In 1975 the UK had been almost entirely dependent on imported energy. The discovery of oil in the North Sea, together with the steep rises in the price of that commodity experienced due to the Arab–Israeli War of 1973 and the Iranian Islamic Revolution in 1979, changed that picture entirely. Before the first price shock, a barrel of oil cost £3 (in 1980 prices) to import, and would have cost about £5 to extract from the North Sea. But the quadrupling of world oil prices meant that it was now cheaper to drill at home than import from abroad – as well as increasing pressure from Labour's left wingers for full-scale nationalisation of the industry, a call that was successfully stifled by the party's leadership while in government between 1974 and 1979.[51] UK oil production soon rose from almost nothing in the middle of 1975 to 10 million tonnes a year in mid-1977.[52] First production came from the Auk field at the end of 1975, and then from the much larger Brent field off Shetland in 1976.[53] By 1985, the year of the first peak of British production, Britain produced 4.5 per cent of world oil output, a figure that stood at 7 per cent if the Communist bloc were excluded.[54] Offshore oil rigs were producing 953 million barrels a year, more than more traditional oil states such as Iran.[55]

A huge and technologically advanced industry soon emerged to bring oil and gas to the surface. Drilling might cost £26,000 a day, even in 1975 prices, making up about 90 per cent of the cost in bringing the oil to market. Huge fixed installations had to be ordered that would stand up to winds of 130 miles per hour: they cost perhaps £400–500 million for a medium-sized field of two or three platforms.[56] Even the huge semi-submersible rigs that looked for oil in the first place might cost £3.5–10 million. But the majority of the equipment was to begin with supplied by Norway, Japan and Texas: of the 119 rigs on order for this market in the mid-1970s, only three were being built in Britain. Brent Spar, a huge floating storage tank for the Brent field anchored to the seabed by huge chains set into 1000-ton concrete blocks, was built in the Netherlands and Norway.[57] And although BP and Shell controlled more than a third of the fields between them, the Americans controlled more.[58]

Some familiar technical failings, especially in product design, were again in evidence. The delay in developing an integrated planning office at the merged shipbuilders Scott Lithgow, for instance, helps to explain that company's failure to break into the market for offshore drilling ships and platforms to work in the North Sea. *Ben Ocean Lancer*, its first drilling ship, came in £10 million over budget, and the firm was also responsible for the disastrous *Ocean Alliance* rig, which lost the company £200 million.[59] Even so, British firms were extremely competitive in a number of markets. Offshore Support Vessels, essential if platforms were to be kept resupplied and accounting for more than half of all offshore service vessels, were one such area. Though UK shipowners were slow to act in the early days of the oil rush, by 1974 British flagged vessels were the single largest group in the North Sea. Out of 256 such vessels, the British owned 59, the Americans 53 and the Norwegians 44. Many of these ships, for instance, those operated by Seaforth of Glasgow, were also British-built. They were still the largest single group in the North Sea at the time of the oil price crash of the mid-1980s, though the 1990s would see many of these companies sold to US or Norwegian competitors.[60]

Following the second and almost certainly final peak of production in 1999, the amount of oil coming out of the North Sea fell gradually away: it had dropped by 40 per cent by 2008. New fields were further out at sea, with the oil deeper and available only at higher pressures: it cost increasingly prohibitive amounts to reach. The UK is scheduled to become a net importer of crude oil once more by 2010, and the oilfields will probably run dry altogether in the 2020s.[61] Attempts to impose windfall taxes on the industry – a 10 per cent and then a 20 per cent surcharge were levied on the industry on top of normal corporate taxes in 2002 and 2005 – have brought in much less revenue than the Treasury hoped. The Government eventually wrote off two-thirds of the £2 billion they had hoped to raise in the latter operation, a good example of how North Sea oil's rundown might affect the national accounts.[62]

New technologies have helped to prolong this most important of British maritime industries. In 1980 it was foreseen that production might peak at about 2.6 or 2.7 million barrels a day.[63] But output remained above that level, at 3.1 million barrels a day, even into 2007.[64] The Buzzard field, which came on stream in January of that year, was the largest discovery for 10 years, though others given the go-ahead in 2008 were much smaller. Even so, official estimates of reserves still stood at 25 billion barrels – about the same as in the late 1970s.[65] Furthermore, the Government argued that 380,000 jobs still remained dependent on the North Sea extraction industries taken as a whole. The UK was still the European Union's largest producer of oil and gas.[66]

Despite the likely decline in North Sea oil, power seemed likely to continue flowing from the sea. By the early 2000s, the UK was already Europe's second most important producer of electricity from offshore wind turbines, after Denmark. Given her long coastline, and in particular Scotland's position in the fierce North Atlantic, simple geography made this one of the most promising sources of carbon-neutral power.[67] Government-commissioned studies, published early in 2009, revealed that there might be room for between 5000 and 7000 turbines to be sited around Britain's coasts. This would form much the greatest part of the Government's aim to have 25 GW of electric power coming from renewable offshore sources by 2020 – a vast increase from the 2 GW being produced from those turbines in 2007.[68] If this programme is successful, power from the sea will provide about half of the 15 per cent of Britain's energy that the Government hopes to see produced in a sustainable manner by 2020. The seaborne wind programme alone is an enormous undertaking, comparable with the oil rush of the 1970s and 1980s: 10,000 km^2 will be covered by fields of turbines.[69] Already 'Phrase one' has gone ahead at 15 sites from Tunes Plateau off Northern Island to the Kentish Flats in the Thames Estuary. The much bigger 'Phase two' projects began to gain planning consent during 2007 and 2008. This included the huge London Array, 12 miles off the Kent and Essex coasts, and containing over 300 turbines over a hundred metres in height.[70]

There was, overall, a remarkable amount of continuity in the offshore economy. As the government White Paper on shipping had it in 1998, 'despite a widespread view to the contrary, the UK is still a central player in the world's maritime activity'. Her shipping industry was the country's fourth or fifth largest service-sector exporter; 95 per cent of her trade by weight arrived or left by ship (the figure was 77 per cent in terms of the value of those goods); and if the ships flying the British flag or managed in the UK were added together, she accounted for 6 per cent of the world's shipping tonnage.[71]

These facts, combined with the rapid growth in world trade in the 1990s and 2000s that led up to the world financial and economic crisis beginning in 2007, helped to ensure that Britain's ports remained a vital part of the national economy as a whole. This was not achieved without much pain on the part of dockside communities, for instance, during the 3-week national strike in 1989 that unsuccessfully attempted to stop Mrs Thatcher's government dismantling national conditions of employment and bargaining. But as the great majority of Britain's ports passed back into private hands after their 1970s nationalisation – the exception being Sullom Voe in the Shetlands, still run by those islands' council – they were at least able to compete with other European container terminals on equal terms. Felixstowe, for instance, handled nearly half of Britain's deep-sea container traffic in the mid-1990s, and was the fourth largest container port in Europe. Bristol, too, revived under a new private-sector management.[72] Bulk British shipbuilding may have passed into memory, and the fishing fleet may have shrunk to become only a shadow of its former self; but by the early twenty-first century shipping itself was advancing, not retreating, while Britain's oil rigs, wind farms and offshore turbines all made the sea just as relevant as ever to the nation's economic life.

Resurrection of the British seaside?

'The seaside has been written off more times than the English novel, and just as often has been reinvented': the words are from a newspaper article published in 2006. Though the journalist in question went on to give familiar figures for the 'decline' of seaside visitor numbers, his first insight might have been more profound, for by the early twenty-first century there were indeed signs of life in British coastal resorts. For one thing, actual tourist number proved remarkably resilient. During 2005 domestic tourists took 25.5 million seaside holidays in the UK, spending around £4.7 billion. They also took a further 270 million day trips, spending another £3.1 billion.[73] The numbers of British coastal tourists had indeed fallen, from perhaps 32 million to 22 million trips lasting more than one day every year: but they had hardly been extinguished.[74] When the *Guardian's* John Ezard visited Skegness in 1999, he noted the remaining interest in the town's beach despite the opening of a new all-weather Butlin's camp. The town had lost 3200 serviced rooms between 1950 and 1998, but it had gained more than 15,000 caravans in those same years. As he concluded: 'the bucket-and-spade holiday is by no means totally dead'.[75]

No narrative of *overall* or *general* decline does any justice to the local factors that have made many coastal resorts a resounding and continuing success.[76] Few resorts are just like others, a point that most locals made to the American travel writer Paul Theroux on his journey round Britain's coast in the early 1980s. 'Every British bulge is different and every mile has its own mood,' he wrote then: 'I said Blackpool and people said, "Naturally!" I said Worthing and they said, "Of all places"! The character was fixed, and though few coastal places matched their reputation each one was unique.'[77] Decline caused by poor resort image, or a lack of accessibility, might therefore be reversed just down the coast. Isolated Llandudno on the North Wales coast has thrived compared to Rhyl nearby, since the latter was exposed for many years to the 'lowest common denominator' tourism markets of Manchester and Liverpool. Bournemouth has thrived, while Weymouth, just a few miles away, has not.[78] In short, the local and specific has come to seem increasingly important despite, and perhaps even because of, the global marketplace for holidays.[79] High-end attractions such as Southport Pleasureland's Traumatizer, 'the "tallest and fastest" suspended looping [roller] coaster in Britain', could still bring in vast numbers of tourists: in Pleasureland's case, 2.1 million during 1997 alone.[80]

Such regeneration could have striking effects, if it chimed in with local traditions. As English Heritage put it in 2003, 'new high quality buildings and open spaces that make the most of their seaside context' were vital to recapture the way in which 'seaside architecture, design and engineering, never afraid of being and idiosyncratic, continued to dazzle right up to . . . the Second World War.' Renovation of the modernist De La Warr Pavilion at Bexhill-on-Sea and the creation of a new Bournemouth Square complete with mosaics and camera obscura were two of the organisation's examples.[81] Writers touring through Britain usually seized on just these quirky reminders of different pasts. David St John Thomas, for instance, recommended that no one miss a 70 feet-high and five-bedroom folly on the coast at Thorpeness in Suffolk: 'the famous House in the Clouds, in reality a disguised watertower [in] . . . mock-Tudor' style.[82] Individual and private projects, such as Simon Conder's stunning 'Polymer House' based on a fisherman's cottage at Dungeness, and completed in 2003, helped to make just this point: seaside living needed a revolution in quality.[83]

Peter Williams' photographs of the English coast, gathered over more than a decade and published by English Heritage in 2005, are a good example of the 'quirky' in action. Pub signs, ruined concrete gun emplacements, martial statues on seaside buildings, painted mines and replica Viking longboats fill his pages in full colour. The book begins with the characteristic claim: 'the regeneration of the seaside proceeds apace'.[84] Rather than focus on one-dimensional decline, it is important to note that the picture was fragmenting, along with most other consumer markets. Niche clienteles were becoming more important, for instance, the gay market in Blackpool and Brighton: 'as camp as Blackpool illuminations' was a phrase passing into popular use at the end of the twentieth century.[85] Visitor numbers could and did recover wherever the bland and everyday was replaced by the local, the different and even perhaps the strange or outlandish. As the Association of District Councils put it as early as 1993, 'there is ... a danger in seaside resorts all promoting the same sort of facilities. Each one needs to develop something unique. Visitors ... will not be interested in a duplication of the leisure facilities available to them in their own home towns and cities'.[86]

During the 1990s the idea of a 'sense of place' replaced the idea of futile competition with mass tourism in the sun. New and more 'joined-up' groups of interested parties such as district councils, Tourist Boards, English Heritage and the Civic Trust worked together on novel strategies to the seaside environment. In Weston-Super-Mare, for instance, the town's Tourism Development Action Programme opened up the seafront to the surrounding streets, insisted on 'strong' shop frontages rather than mass-market signage, rationalised parking and insisted on the creation of café forecourts where before there had only been a confused set of roads and barriers.[87] In 2007 the Blackpool Taskforce, which brought government agencies together with the council and local business, listed £937 million in existing programmes, and £2.4 billion of new plans, aimed at regeneration. The Taskforce's comprehensive package included transport improvements, a new seafront and the relocation of public buildings so that they became more accessible on new sites in the town centre.[88]

Other countervailing trends were also in evidence. Older people retired to the coast in ever-greater numbers in the 1990s and 2000s. By 1971, 35 resorts with populations over 15,000 had populations that were more than 20 per cent above pensionable age. Just over 44 per cent of Bexhill's population was made up of pensioners, 38.8 per cent of Worthing's and 36.4 per cent of Clacton's.[89] They brought with them a preference for better and more expensive housing: in resorts such as Salcombe, Sidmouth and Exmouth, house prices rose even quicker than the national average. Some fashionable towns, for instance, the surfing resort of Newquay in Cornwall, continued to experience fast-rising property prices even during the incipient recession of 2008.[90] Although younger people therefore experienced hardship in buying their first home, this also meant that the housing stock began to change in character. Larger houses have been sub-divided for high-quality flats and sheltered housing, or renovated and repaired. Such sub-division and rebuilding was certainly not just a matter of poorer residents or state benefit claimants moving into these areas.[91]

The emergence of new social movements centred on alternative lifestyles, new sports and concern for the environment concentrated and deepened the emphasis on cleaning up Britain's coastline.[92] Greenpeace, for instance, became famous for their seaborne publicity feats on board the *Rainbow Warrior*, the first of which vessels was refurbished in 1978 to campaign against nuclear testing and whaling. The group's 1995 campaign against the dumping of the Brent Spa at sea was eventually successful.[93] Surfers Against Sewage, another good example of such movements, was founded in Cornwall in 1990 following surfers' mounting concern about raw sewage being pumped out on a popular surfing beach near St Agnes. Post-war surfing had in any case taken on many of the irreverent and 'anti-establishment' attitudes of youth sub-culture, and the revolt against corporate pollution could be seen as another example of that attitude in action.[94] The group's membership grew quickly, and peaked at 12,500 in 1994, though it had fallen back somewhat to 7700 by 2004. They were joined by even larger groups such as the Marine Conservation Society, which itself grew out of divers' increasing concern for water quality around Britain. These campaigners' publicity materials, membership drives and press coverage were all highly effective, not only focusing on the need to meet EU standards first laid down in the Bathing Water Directive in 1975–76, but to reform them so they were much stricter.[95]

This change in sensibilities, and in policy, would of necessity take a long time. In 1994, 71 of about 500 English beaches failed to meet the Marine Conservation Society's water quality standards; around a hundred did not come up to EU specifications.[96] But progress was certainly being made. In 1973, ten stronger and more powerful regional water authorities replaced the unwieldy River Boards that had been created in the 1940s. The 1974 Control of Pollution Act extended controls over industrial discharges to cover most tidal and coastal waters. The creation of a standing North Sea Ministerial Conference in 1984 increased pressure on the UK government radically to reduce pollution, and in 1990 agreement was reached on an end to all untreated sewage dumping by 1998.[97] Only 44 per cent of British beaches lived up to EU standards in 1986, but 89 per cent did so by 1998. The number of 'Blue Flag' awards also increased. This prestigious award is granted by the Foundation for Environmental Education on the basis of standards 20 times more onerous than those of the Bathing Water Directive: Surfers Against Sewage have campaigned for its adoption as the accepted measure of water quality. Seventeen British resorts were able to win a Blue Flag in 1994, a number that had increased to 57 by 1999 and 77 by 2007. Sensing the link between cleanliness and the 'sense of place' that might help ensure resort success, local authorities began to promote the awards won by their beaches, and compete with others nearby on that basis.[98]

Even monuments to dereliction might not be all that they seemed. Brighton's West Pier closed at the end of the 1975 summer season, and despite being protected as a Grade 1 historic monument, was allowed to fall into skeletal ruin. Then, in 2002, its old Concert Hall partially collapsed before two arson attacks in 2003–04 finished the pier's destruction. The *Daily Telegraph* called the affair 'a parable for everything that's wrong with Britain'. And it would indeed be easy to see this as an encapsulation of the subsidence of the British coastal tourist industry – were it not for the presence of the rival Palace Pier just a few hundred yards away. In 2004, this attracted 3.5 million visits, and was Britain's most successful pier, high in the lists of free attractions valued by tourists. Brighton's transformation into a newly fashionable locale was best represented, not by the sad state of the West Pier, but by the rejuvenation of its rival.[99] That partial redefinition is confusing, mixing in many elements, but that also to some extent quintessentially represents the seaside town's new role. When the travel writer Paul Gogarty visited early in the new millennium, he found just that: 'party town. Shopping town. Foody town. Bursting-at-the-seams town. Fallen-down-pier town. Brighton is where England is simultaneously most English, most continental and, increasingly, fledgling Californian'.[100]

British resorts faced enormous challenges in the twenty-first century. Their share of the UK tourism market was indeed declining, from 75 per cent in 1968 to 44 per cent in 1999.[101] It is important to note that extreme deprivation remained in many traditional resorts: there were signs that in Blackpool, for instance, the trend was worsening. Parts of inner Blackpool were in 2007 among the 5 per cent most deprived areas in the country, and over 20 per cent of the working age population had no qualifications, as against a national average of 14 per cent.[102] Other towns may contain less acute poverty, but still struggle to attract high-quality and highly rewarded jobs. Hastings in East Sussex has managed to attract or create far fewer jobs in finance and IT, and far more in the public sector, than the region taken as a whole. Wages are well below that of the surrounding areas, and unemployment much higher – all of which the council and local businessmen put down to the town's very poor transport links to London when compared to Brighton, its much more successful rival.[103]

Even so, these towns still remained easily the most important single destination for holidaying Britons: and this was a rapidly expanding industry, meaning that a smaller share of the spoils could still mean absolute expansion. Seaside visitor numbers during the early 2000s were gradually increasing at about 4 per cent a year, rather than falling.[104] And the very fact that coastal areas have very different problems demonstrates how far their struggles are caused by factors far removed from British tourism's secular 'decline'. Blackpool was clearly struggling with the implications of a fast-changing leisure market; Hastings had the very different handicap of slow and unreliable road and rail links. As a House of Commons inquiry concluded in 2007, there can be no 'one size fits all' approach to understanding these towns' difficulties.[105] The cheap holidays in the sun that were supposed to destroy the British tourist industry have, at the same time, come to seem anything but glamorous. Time Out's guide to the British seaside put it like this in 2008: 'now that the masses are flying to Thailand, it almost seems passé. But making an epic journey to a wild and wonderful Scottish beach – now that's exotic . . . [the British seaside] takes you to places that you never knew existed or can't get to on easyJet'.[106]

A greater sense of place; an influx of relatively well-off incomers; cleaner beaches; and the downmarket image of many 'foreign' holidays and the journeys involved; all have helped the British seaside holiday to survive and begin to recover. As the most recent and most comprehensive economic study of English seaside resorts has concluded, 'there has actually been strong employment growth in seaside towns . . . [this] indicates that the assumption that the rise of the foreign holiday has led to severe economic decline in British seaside towns is well wide of the mark.' Furthermore, 'the common assumption that the British seaside tourist business is in terminal decline is profoundly wrong'. There was in fact a growth in employment in these towns of 320,000, or more than 20 per cent, much faster than the national average. And these towns could boast 45 per cent more jobs in hotels and restaurants in 2001 than they could in 1981, employment growth that was second only to the fast-growing banking and insurance sector.[107] These resorts probably were written off too soon.

Representations of the sea since the Second World War

Picturing, writing about and representing the sea have deep roots in Britain, and such visions go very far back into the country's history. Hagiographic versions of the story of Saint Brendan, the Irishman who traditionally sailed to America, may have been circulating at the Anglo-Norman court in the early twelfth century.[108] Middle English versions of the Quest for the Holy Grail and the fourteenth-century magical romance *Sir Eglamour* are both full of the image of the rudderless boat, representations of threat and survival that represented guilt and pollution, or political hazards, or the 'dangers' associated with women. Richard Hakluyt's massive *Principal Navigations . . . of the English Nation* (1598–1600) tried to construct a particularly English patriotism by collecting stories demonstrating the fighting spirit of maritime adventurers such as Martin Frobisher.[109] The traveller Edward Terry thought of the propitious tides and winds on his 1616–19 voyage to India as part of the divine providence that oversaw England's trade with the East.[110]

This tradition encompasses not only voyages and triumphs but the danger and cupidity of the ocean. All the characters in Shakespeare's *The Tempest* are set adrift: Prospero and his daughter on 'a rotten carcass of a butt', and the duke and his daughter on a much larger and more seaworthy ship. But it is only after their shipwreck that they begin to recover their true selves.[111] In John Milton's *Lycidas* (1637), written to commemorate and mourn his friend Edward King's loss in a shipwreck, the sea – that 'remorseless deep', and 'perilous flood' – became a metaphor for the Fall itself: deadly and holy, necessary both to feel loss and attain salvation.[112] Dampier's *New Voyage Around the World* opened an age of ethnographic and cartographic writing that would be exemplified and satirised by Defoe, among others.[113]

These traditions would survive the great upheavals of the mid-twentieth century. The writer and poet W.H. Auden was deeply affected by a journey to Iceland in 1936, where the violence of a whale's beachside dismemberment sickened him.[114] The sea would thereafter become something of an indifferent witness of life in his work, as in *Dover*, Auden's 1937 poem about that town where 'the eyes of departing migrants are fixed on the sea, / Conjuring destinies out of impersonal water'. This was hardly an evocation of excitement or adventure, but rather of foreboding normality in the face of possible war: 'Vows, tears, emotional farewell gestures, / Are common . . . unremarkable actions / Like ploughing or a tipsy son'. In *Musée des Beaux Arts*, written in Brussels in 1938, he summoned up the fate of Icarus in Peter Breughel's 1558 painting on the same theme. This was, in short, to be ignored as he drowned: in Auden's words, 'while someone else is eating or opening a window or just walking dully along'.[115]

Auden's long 1944 poem, *The Mirror and the Sea*, imagined extended monologues by the characters in *The Tempest*. Alonso, with whom Auden seems to have had a special affinity, imagines the sea as a place of sensual, lustful and chaotic loss, a place where his son, Ferdinand, might fall from the strenuous life 'as in his left ear the siren sings / Meltingly of water and a night / Where all flesh had peace'.[116] It was a deliberately frightening evocation of the sea, intentionally reminiscent of the storm with which *The Tempest* opens and clear that the ocean might destroy as well as save. Auden went on to trace out the use of the seas as metaphor in the whole Romantic canon, both as 'free places' and as 'lonely places of alienation' in which the traveller must 'from time to time . . . be visited by desperate longings for home and company'.[117]

The way in which the sea can strip away certainties, and remove inhibitions, is central to Vita Sackville-West's *No Signposts in the Sea* (1961), itself based on Sackville-West's love of worldwide cruises. The main character, Edmund Carr, in the end fruitlessly, romantically pursues Laura, another passenger. He finds it difficult to understand life itself without the 'signposts' of his past on land: 'I am at sea in more ways than one', he confides to his diary.[118] The main character in Iris Murdoch's 1978 Booker Prize winner, *The Sea, The Sea*, also finds it impossible to escape his past: though the actor Charles Arrowby retires to the sea to escape theatrical life, he finds it harder and harder to swim there, and is literally faced by himself as an imagined monster of the deep – predictably, in some ways, nature punishes him, for he has defined the sea only as he can observe, enjoy and even subdue it. 'My sportive sea', he calls it – but it was still an ocean where 'the pebbles hurt my feet and . . . the beach shelves and the waves and the waves kept tumbling the pebbles down against me'. And this is even before he thinks he spies the monster he has metaphorically brought with him: 'an enormous creature . . . [with] a long thickening body . . . [and] a ridgy spiny back [which] followed the elongated neck'.[119]

This sense of dread also provides the backdrop to Ian McEwan's *On Chesil Beach* (2007), dealing with the painful inability of two newlyweds – Edward and Florence – to understand each other, or to consummate their marriage. Here the 'sound of waves breaking' is 'like a distant shattering of glasses': Edward ultimately sees his wife leave him, as he watches her 'hurry along the shore, the sound of her difficult progress lost to the breaking of small waves, until she was a blurred, receding point'.[120] In all these books and poems, the sea offers the promise of release and freedom, given its literal and metaphorical lack of waymarkers: but the characters' own natures and imperfections pull them back. The sea gains its power and threat as a theatre of frustration.

The sea was not, even so, always represented as threatening danger – as its dual nature in Auden's vision of Dover in fact implied. Both C.S. Forrester and Patrick O'Brian drew on the works of Captain Frederick Marryat, the nineteenth-century sailor and author whose most famous works included *Peter Simple* (1834) and *Mr Midshipman Easy* (1836). Marryat took Lord Cochrane, the naval captain and adventurer who became a popular hero and assisted in the Chilean revolution of the 1820s, as his model; and Cochrane in his turn became one of the inspirations behind O'Brian's Jack Aubrey. Forrester and O'Brian's novels, in which the sea is a place for great exploits and quests rather than of simple danger, belong very much to the times in which they were written. Forrester's Horatio Hornblower, appearing in novels written between the 1930s and 1960s, finds it difficult to express his feelings: women are hard to relate to, and his relationships with his friends, particularly his closest companion William Bush, are relatively under-written. Aubrey, who first appeared in 1970s, has in contrast an – eventually – happy marriage, and is as warm and engaged as Hornblower is withdrawn. But the work of both novelists is still characterised by a picaresque maritime search for glory and honour, something they owe in part to Marryat.[121] And both shared a reverence for a sea that could change in moments, in front of Hornblower, from 'the bluest the Mediterranean could show' to 'the clearest emerald green'.[122] Aubrey looks at the ocean in O'Brian's *Master and Commander* 'with loving relish . . . the brilliant sea, darker blue than the sky, and the white wake across it kept drawing his eyes to the stern-window'. His first ship, too, 'sent such a jet of happiness through his heart that he almost skipped where he stood'.[123]

Film, that most popular of mid-century mediums, drew on maritime experiences and naval heroism to understand and encapsulate social change itself. *In Which We Serve* (1942), written and co-directed by Noel Coward in a thinly fictionalised account of his friend Louis Mountbatten's loss of HMS *Kelly*, was a celebration of cross-class comradeship and devotion. Here, the ship came to resemble the nation itself, pulling together in times of struggle: one critic has dubbed the film 'pathologically conservative'.[124] Later, in the even less socially democratic 1950s, the tone of Ealing Studios' wartime epics shifted slightly, and began to celebrate officers' and leaders' endeavour. *The Cruel Sea* (1953), *The Battle of the River Plate* (1957) and *Sink the Bismarck!* (1960) all bear the hallmarks of this approach.[125] The main character in *The Cruel Sea*, Commander George Ericson, was played by Jack Hawkins, an image of forceful but sympathetic command.[126] His bond with his crew, particularly Lockhart played by Donald Sinden, is deliberately intense: it excludes women, for instance, who are defined in terms of their relationship with the men.[127]

Even so, these naval war films – *The Cruel Sea* in particular, dramatising as it does the struggle between Royal Navy convoys and U-boats in the Atlantic – remain a story of men's fight against the maritime elements. It was the pressure, as well as social change and enemy shipping, that bonds these characters together. Technology, especially the radar room, is a key theatre of that struggle, in which 'the only villain is the sea, the cruel sea.'[128] Officers did get an increasing share of the characters' time on screen in the 1950s, for instance, in the submarine epic *Above Us the Waves* in 1955. Commander Fraser, played by John Mills, that paragon of upright British manliness, is undoubtedly the central character. But the grave nature of the mission – disabling the German battleship *Tirpitz* as it hides in a Norwegian fjord – militates against any simplistic portrait of British heroism. The submarine crews are well-drawn, with families at home and careers to go back to. The downbeat ending, as the men are taken into captivity past the crippled *Tirpitz*, amounts to a subdued warning about the realities of naval warfare.[129]

The life of Derek Jarman, a gay polymath who was not only a film director but an artist and writer as well, sums up some of these themes. He loved the sea's beauty, but he also understood the haunting nature of its pull on the imagination. After 1987, and in the years leading up to his death from

HIV-AIDS in 1994, Jarman lived next to the English Channel, at Dungeness in Kent. There, on the huge shingle beach that makes up the headland, he created an extraordinary garden around a small fisherman's cottage. Gogarty has described it as a 'shipwrecked coastal garden... [where] a tide line of beachcombed *objet trouvés* has been arranged with an artist's eye amid poppies, marigolds, dog roses, cornflowers and beds of gorse and sage'.[130] Here Jarman, drawing on a suitably nautical concept, felt able to 'anchor' himself in a new and secluded paradise. Indeed, he recalled that the word itself derived from the Persian word for 'walled garden'.[131] It was a place where purple rugosa, artichokes, peas, lavender, peonies, marigolds, irises and poppies surrounded metal and wood sculptures to build up a 'magic of surprise' on the shingle.[132] But the plants and ornaments were still next to the sea, to some extent threatened and thus defined by the shifting and uncertain grey-green landscape beyond. Jarman admitted that his garden recalled a parents' monument to a daughter lost in a swimming accident that he had seen in Azerbaijan, and it seems clear that he envisioned the eerie space as a commemoration of himself as well as a celebration and a retreat.[133] Jarman himself felt that the 'smell of the Ness is gorse', but even that could be 'overwhelmed by the sea'.[134]

Jarman had been playing with images of the sea as early as his poetry collection *A Finger in the Fishes Mouth* (1972), in which he had juxtaposed the ancient Greek sailing myths with the mock-heroism of Victorian travel. His vision of Queen Elizabeth I in *Albion* (1978), and his version of *The Tempest* (1979), saw the filmmaker identify himself with John Dee and Prospero, both prophets of the sea's transformative power: in the latter film, the storm at the beginning becomes part of Prospero himself.[135] In *Albion*, Elizabeth I is transported forward to the present, to see England's sad decline: a state of affairs that causes her, and perhaps the audience, to long for a transcendent youth in which they did not yet foresee that the country was going to end up in the apparent chaos of the late 1970s. To some extent, England in *Albion* resembles a lost or neglected garden – like that at Dungeness. But Elizabeth also yearns for 'the road of the surf on the shingles... what joy there is in the embrace of water and earth... The sea remindeth me of youth'.[136] Jarman had been exploring the themes of his end – and the intersection between the ocean and the land – for some time.

The British never quite forgot their maritime past, or ignored its present. It left traces everywhere, from Auden to McEwan, from war films to the celebration of round-the-world racing, from travel writing to Jarman's garden. It was evident, too, in the music of the composer, Benjamin Britten – in the tragic seascapes of his operas *Peter Grimes* (1945) and *Billy Budd* (1951). Both operas were bound up with Britten's search for the islanders' national identity that owed little to continental music.[137] It was a quest which he shared with past composers such as Elgar and Vaughan Williams, alongside his many other debts to them.[138] And it was an idea that poets, authors, filmmakers and sailors themselves all felt alongside him.

Conclusions: memory and relevance

Britain's imperial adventure in the Falklands became a good example of the more adaptable, more technologically advanced and, above all, more flexible Royal Navy of the years to come – and also of the continuing relevance of the sea in British history. Some industries, shipbuilding in particular, did seem to be gone for good. Fishing remained in crisis. Many coastal areas were economically depressed. But this was certainly not the whole picture. The British shipping industry as a whole was growing, not shrinking, in the early years of the new millennium; UK ports had experienced an unprecedented boom, and nearly all of the country's bulk imports and exports continued to pass through them. In the shape of North Sea oil, and now offshore wind farms, the UK is reaping an enormous harvest of energy from the oceans. A cleaner, greener, more considered coastal tourism had also emerged, better equipped to compete with foreign destinations and resorts that were losing some of their allure.

Above all, perhaps, the sea kept its hold on the national imagination. Images from *The Tempest*, especially that of Prospero, come up again and again in this connection. Auden and Jarman, even the relatively humble but momentarily famous press officer Ian McDonald, constantly referred to the play. At a basic level, the sea which surrounds Shakespeare's characters clearly retained its strange fascination. This would come as no surprise to many late twentieth-century critics, since a number of them felt that in *The Tempest*, Shakespeare was making play with, and reference to, the first great age of exploration, discovery and global commerce.[139] Nor does *The Tempest*'s influence stop at indigenous Britons' self-image. We have already seen how Walcott used the sea as an image and a tool of a new English language. Other post-colonial writers have looked to Caliban, not to Prospero, as their hero: to the 'wild man' of the island, not the colonising new arrivals. The Barbadian-born George Lamming's essays, for instance, transformed Shakespeare's words to focus to the power and resistance of indigenous peoples as well as the magic of the Europeans. Prospero's 'gift' of language and reason became, in this framework, an ambiguous prison.[140] Many citizens of the Empire, and then the Commonwealth, saw themselves on Shakespeare's storm-struck island – but in ways that could not have been imagined in 1945.

The sea's cultural ubiquity was just as evident in a more straightforward manner on television, the portal through which most Britons saw the outside world at the end of the twentieth century. *The Blue Planet*, BBC Natural

History's enormously ambitious series of 2001, explored the depths in vivid, colourful detail never seen before on television. The series made very clear that the existence of the oceans is the reason why Earth is habitable at all: the seas, the accompanying book related, are 'essential to life on land. Without it much of the world would be barren ... [and] water's super-efficiency as a solvent makes it the basis for all forms of life.'[141] The huge success of *Coast*, a BBC documentary series following the coastline and exploring its physical character and history, similarly meant that the surrounding ocean was rarely out of the public eye. The official book of the series makes this clearer than ever. 'As islanders we are drawn to the edge,' Nicholas Crane, the series' first leader presenter, argued there: 'it is where we sense most strongly the essence of our floating landmass'.[142] As Brian Lavery has put it, 'the British will remain a maritime people, not just because of the facts of geography or economics, but because of deeply ingrained attitudes'.[143] The sun may have set on Britain's worldwide oceanic presence, but an afterglow remains.

Timeline of events

1936	W.H. Auden travels to Iceland
1937–38	Auden writes poems *Dover* and *Musée des Beaux Arts*
1937	First of C.S. Forester's 'Hornblower' novels published
1942	*In Which We Serve* released
1944	Auden writes *The Mirror and the Sea*
1945	Benjamin Britten's opera *Peter Grimes* first performed
1951	Benjamin Britten's opera *Billy Budd* first performed
1953	*The Cruel Sea* released
1955	*Above Us The Waves* released
1957	*The Battle of the River Plate* released
1959	First North Sea gas discovered off coast of Netherlands
1960	*Sink the Bismarck!* released
1961	Vita Sackville-West publishes *No Signposts in the Sea*
1965	First North Sea gas discovered in UK waters
1969	Oil discovered in Norwegian waters
1970	Patrick O'Brian's *Master and Commander* is published
1970	Forties oil field revealed off Aberdeen
1973	First oil shock caused by Arab–Israeli war
1974	Control of Pollution Act

1978	Irish Murdoch's *The Sea, The Sea* published
1978	Derek Jarman's *Albion* released
1978	Launch of first Greenpeace *Rainbow Warrior*
1979	Derek Jarman's version of *The Tempest* released
1979	Second oil shock caused by Iranian Islamic Revolution
1980	Armilla Patrol of Royal Navy ships begins patrolling in Persian Gulf
1981	Defence Review announces withdrawal of *Endurance* from South Atlantic
27–28 March 1982	HMS *Spartan* sails from Gibraltar for South Atlantic
31 March 1982	Prime Minister Thatcher decides a Falklands 'Task Force' is possible
7 April 1982	British Government announces Maritime Exclusion Zone around Falklands
12 April 1982	Maritime Exclusion Zone around Falklands takes effect
2 May 1982	Argentine cruiser *General Belgrano* sunk by HMS *Conqueror*
4 May 1982	HMS *Sheffield* destroyed by air-launched Exocet missile
21 May 1982	HMS *Ardent* sunk
22 May 1982	First British troops put ashore at San Carlos on East Falkland
23 May 1982	HMS *Antelope* sunk
14 June 1982	Stanley recaptured by British forces: Argentine forces surrender
1987	Derek Jarman buys his cottage at Dungeness
1990	Surfers Against Sewage founded
August 1990	Iraqi forces invade Kuwait
January–February 1991	'Operation Desert Storm' removes Iraqi forces from Kuwait
1991	*Options for Change* Defence White Paper
1993	WRNS abolished and women absorbed into the 'regular' Navy
1994	*Frontline First* Defence White Paper
1994	Death of Derek Jarman

1995	*Fundamentals of British Maritime Doctrine* published
1995	Successful public campaign against dumping of Brent Spa at sea
1998	Untreated sewage dumping ceases in British coastal waters
1998	Amphibious Assault Ship HMS *Ocean* commissioned
1999	Peak of British North Sea oil production
March–June 1999	NATO intervention against Serb forces in Kosovo
2000	Introduction of tonnage tax for British shipping
May 2000	British military intervention in Sierra Leone helps defeat rebel RUF
2001	Landing Platform Dock HMS *Albion* enters service
11 September 2001	Terrorist attacks on World Trade Centre and Pentagon in USA
October– November 2001	Coalition armed attack on Afghanistan and fall of Kabul
2003	Amphibious Assault Ship HMS *Bulwark* enters service
20 March 2003	Royal Navy joins attack on Al Faw Peninsula at the start of new Gulf War
2007	Ian McEwan's *On Chesil Beach* published
2010	Year in which UK will probably become an oil importer
2016–18	Probable service date of new *Queen Elizabeth* class aircraft carriers

11

Conclusion: A Star to Steer By?

Britons' trade, piracy, slavery and slaving, their migrations, technological breakthroughs and their writing home, were all fundamental to the rise of Britain's transoceanic Empire and to the British peoples' sense of themselves. The collapse of many of her maritime and coastal industries were yet one more symbol and cause of the post-industrial Britain that was forged late in the twentieth century. To that extent, these narratives are a necessary antidote to the narratives of land and air forged in a twentieth century dominated by the twin myths of the Flanders trenches of the First World War and the 'finest hour' of the RAF in the summer of 1940. 'Blue' and 'grey' stories of the ocean now seem more likely to take their proper place alongside these images, given the passing of time and its provision of increased detachment. Historians are now beginning to reassemble the maritime world that Britons once thought of as peculiarly theirs. One reason for this is the environmental crisis which faces the world's oceans, increasingly a matter of public discussion and concern in the early twenty-first century. But there are many other sources of likely historiographical innovation in the next decade or so, all driven by the social and academic changes that are transforming contemporary Britain. These are, firstly, histories of gender and sexuality; secondly, non-white British and imperial peoples' experiences at sea; and thirdly, histories of international trading networks. Fourthly, the recent re-discovery of naval warfare and its role in shaping economic, social and political identities is likely to continue, while shifting definitions of 'Britishness' and its varying relationships with the sea, especially during the nineteenth and early twentieth centuries, will undoubtedly remain a fifth and final standing issue of historiographical concern. All of these themes make clear just how much historians are sensitive to developments in the globalising world around them, and how much they might offer to the effort to understand those processes. No single history will emerge, but many: historians of other nations' oceanic engagement, demonstrated, for instance, by Frank Broeze's study of *Australians and the Sea*, have shown the potential of such an approach. In so doing, they have set the standard for a new type of work. It will have to be capable of understanding change over the long term; remain inter-disciplinary; able to bring together these disparate research agendas; and retain an ability to trace out the role of geography in human history without settling on a new form of determinism that settles on just that one factor as explaining everything. It is a formidable enough undertaking: but it is a vital task if Britain's past place in either past or contemporary worlds is to be fully understood.

Remembering Britain's maritime past

Taken as a whole, the twentieth century seemed almost designed to forge a new history of the land: a myth of woods and green fields, rather than the grey-green nation that previous generation of Britons might have better understood.[1] The 'thick associations' and shared sacrifice of those who witnessed the mud and horror of trench warfare between 1914 and 1918 began this reorientation of national story-telling.[2] The Poppy Appeal that has run every November since 1921 has enshrined the land fighting in Flanders as a national institution.[3] There were undoubtedly shows of feeling over naval deaths – the Navy League, for instance, laid wreaths at the foot of Nelson's Column on Trafalgar Day in 1916.[4] But the overwhelming losses experienced by the Army, the vast memorialisation of their sacrifice in and at Commonwealth War Grave cemeteries and monuments and, even more poignantly and acutely, the personal narratives of poets such as Siegfried Sassoon or Wilfred Owen became markers of national identity that seemed even more important than the lurking sense of the sea embodied either in the brute patriotism of 'Rule Britannia' or in Matthew Arnold's melancholic 1867 poem 'Dover Beach'.[5]

The myth of the 'Spitfire Summer' of 1940 has furthermore become *the* manner in which British people define themselves in relation to the past – a time of uncomplicated resistance to Nazism, high martial endeavour in the face of apparently overwhelming odds and for the RAF a chance to redeem themselves with the public after the debacle in France.[6] This time it was the skies and the green lands of Kent beneath that became the prime sites of collective memory. The sight of Hurricanes and Spitfires engaging the Luftwaffe has become an abiding image of Britishness itself. The air combat over South East England, and in particular over London on the night of 15 September, has come to seem decisive. The book of the BBC TV series *Finest Hour* – itself evocatively named – is conclusive that it was that night's combat that turned the tide: '15 September decisively ended Hitler's belief that Britain could be deprived of her air force and forced to come to terms. There would be no air superiority, no peace deal and no invasion'.[7] Churchill's wartime rhetoric of 1940 has been the subject of much well-deserved hagiography. Kevin Jefferys has placed this in his list of Britain's *Finest and Darkest Hours* as 'the single most impressive act of political leadership in the twentieth century'.[8]

Historians of Britain and the ocean must travel back beyond the histories of the trenches, and of the 'Finest Hour': to Dunkirk, even in that same year, to Priestley's 'Little Steamers' and the apotheosis of the Edwardian seaside.[9] And they have to press on from there: to the lasting influence of Jutland, Trafalgar, Quiberon Bay, Barfleur, La Hougue and, ultimately, the defeat of the Spanish Armada in 1588. This will uncover and emphasise the countless trading, slaving, fishing, piratical and migratory voyages made by millions of Britons. But such an emphasis will also capture the reality of today's Britain and its multifarious economic, social, economic and military challenges. Many historians are already working at just this interface of past lives and present crises. Recent histories of gender and seafaring have focused on definitions of 'masculinity', whether straight or gay.[10] The treatment of gender in terms of men and women's relationships with one another has progressed from treatments of 'under-interpreted ... eulogistic, de-problematised voyage accounts' to appreciations of men and women's relation to the maritime world in terms of work, travel, empire and home life.[11] Black and Asian seafarers are, secondly, being paid much more attention than formerly, both in the shape of full-length biographies and as workers within the maritime economy, both on board ship and at the dockside.[12]

A third field of historiographical innovation has been the quantification of the 'lumpy' and multi-dimensional nature of economic space. International trade has been one of our pre-eminent themes in this book; but its advance was difficult, halting and inconsistent. Many different types of ship, of extremely varied speeds, could co-exist on the same route by charging different rates for goods and passengers, meaning that freight and food prices did not converge as quickly as some enthusiasts for free trade have posited.[13] Fourth and last, and perhaps appropriately in an era when British amphibious forces have attracted much more attention than the public probably paid them in the 1970s and early 1980s, the nature of seaborne force and power is being re-examined. Rodger has noted that 'professional historians have been increasingly ready to accept the pressure of war in history': 'the quantity and quality of naval history published in the past quarter-century has hugely increased.'[14] Rodger's own recent histories of the Royal Navy – eventually to stand as the definitive three-volume account – are of course essential here.[15] Other historians have also been redefining how naval history might fit into national narratives, and Jan Glete's recent writings are important in understanding that process. As he has asked, 'how have historians explained the interconnections between warfare at sea and the transformation of European societies and states in this period? With few exceptions, scholarly historians have avoided the question'. This seems to be changing now, though Glete himself has pointed out that this has been most marked in terms of military historians in general, rather than naval historians in particular.[16]

Without these fundamental maritime concepts – alongside many others, to be sure – Britons' sense of themselves by the nineteenth and early twentieth centuries simply does not make sense. The manner in which contemporaries told their national stories would lack a key element if the ocean was left out, for traces of these interlocking obsessions with the sea were everywhere in late Victorian and Edwardian Britain. The civil servant, yachtsman and spy writer Erskine Childers is a good example. His 1903 novel *The Riddle of the Sands* was a huge best-seller upon its publication in 1903, and in it the most immediately admirable of his protagonists, Davies, declares, 'we're a maritime nation – we've grown by the sea and live by it; if we lose command of it we starve. We're unique in that way, just as our huge empire, only linked by the sea, is unique'. The growing 'danger' of Imperial Germany's maritime adventurism was uppermost in the author's mind. Although Childers later went on to be a strong advocate of Irish Home Rule and then independence, at that point in time he found the bracing, strong and manly common sense Davies represented to be emblematic of the British Empire's role in preserving order and civilisation.[17]

Joseph Conrad was not interested in British imperialism as any sort of moral force; he had himself been born to Polish nobles in what was then the Russian Empire. His second language was French, not English, and his collaborator Ford Maddox Ford thought that he actively disliked 'the English mind'.[18] But he still felt the lure of the sea, and employed it in his books in English, just as powerfully as his more patriotically minded fellow authors. Conrad spent 20 years in his youth working in the merchant marine, first for France, and then for Britain. He achieved the rank of master in 1886, and his service acquainted him with the dangers of real seafaring, rather than just the romantic image beloved of many of his contemporaries. He satirised 'the sea-life of light literature', so divorced from reality, in the imaginative feats of the main protagonist in *Lord Jim* (1899–1900).[19] His semi-memoir of these times, *The Mirror of the Sea* (1906), is by turns wistful and romantic, but still never forgets the menace, danger and 'dread' of the sea.[20]

But Conrad had still seen shipboard life free men from their pasts: it was 'a great doctor for sore hears and sore heads, too ... which I have seen soothe ... the most turbulent of spirits'. Sailing was 'a higher point, a subtle and unmistakable touch of love and pride beyond mere skill; almost an inspiration which gives to all work that finish which is almost art – which *is* art', 'based upon a broad, solid sincerity'.[21] It was all the modern age was not – honest, involving and revealing. Conrad's works invested the sea and its ships with an importance, a majesty and a significance that would have seemed natural to his contemporaries. 'The sea and the sky were welded together without a joint,' his 1899 work *Heart of Darkness* begins: 'the air was dark above Gravesend, and farther back still seemed condensed into a mournful gloom, brooding motionless over the biggest, and the greatest, town on earth'. No reader could miss the sense of foreboding, but nor could they fail to understand the sea's importance, either for Conrad, or for London, or for the Empire he so distrusted.[22]

In the art world, too, there was a deeply entrenched idea that the ocean was critical in the making of Britishness. As we have already seen, Turner's painting of the slave ship *Zong*, depicting slaves being pitched overboard, was seen at the time as celebrating the quintessential liberal Britishness of the early nineteenth century – possibly in contradistinction to some of the painter's own views. But the phenomenon of imaginative nation-making on canvas stretches much further back – and further forward. Many of the original members of Britain's naval painting school were ironically immigrants, for instance, the Dutch father and son William van der Veldes, who fled the invading French in 1662–63. But the long wars with France, and voyages of explorations such as Captain Cook's, created a huge commissioning market that would celebrate those achievements. Marine artists such as William Hodges, who sailed with Cook on the *Resolution* between 1772 and 1775, painted a heroic landscape of discovery and endeavour much to the taste of both the Admiralty and the public.[23]

By the time the Fine Art Society held its 'Sea Exhibition' in 1881, it showed 123 paintings and drawings mainly depicting man's activities on the coast. The *Art Journal*'s critic drew a particularly national and patriotic conclusion from these men and women's work on the edges of the sea:

> It was a happy thought ... to bring together a collection of pictures and drawings of the sea by British artists. Such works must ever have a peculiar charm for Englishmen; they wake a thousand happy memories. They touch the key-note of the old Viking spirit and impulse, which is in the blood of most of us, and is emphatically a part of our birthright.[24]

The point was never clearer: before 1914, no Briton – even if they were so different as Childers and Conrad – would have thought of the national character or past without imagining it against a grey-green background.[25]

A star to steer by?

On 6 May 1994, official celebrations were held to mark the opening of the Channel Tunnel between Dover and Sangatte: this was a lavish affair, involving both the Queen and the President of the French Republic, and it raised enormous hopes in some quarters. *Le Figaro* hoped that the event might change Anglo-French relations for good: that it would 'abolish, psychologically, all the divorces and quarrels through the centuries'.[26] And indeed the existence of the fixed link did fundamentally alter some of the building blocks on which the idea of a 'maritime nation' had been built. Britain was no longer an island, but was connected by land – for good or ill – to the rest of Europe. Planners began to consider the transport infrastructure, economic potential and fate of the 'region' between London and Paris; the Republic of Ireland, meanwhile, now came to think of itself as the EU's only island member-state.[27]

This stirred some long-held fears that went as far back as Napoleon's time, since in 1802 the French Emperor had been presented with such a scheme by the mining engineer Albert Mathieu. It was a prospect that terrified the British, as a series of prints depicting a surprising French invasion under the Channel demonstrated. The idea was periodically revived, for instance, in the 1870s – in that case, meeting fierce opposition from the War Office.[28] Another tunnel project collapsed in 1882, following a further outcry from public opinion and the War Office.[29] The French geographer Paul Vidal de la Bache understood these anxieties well, writing in 1889 that Britain possessed an innate 'repugnance to any breach of its maritime frontier'.[30] As an alternative to the extremely hazardous ferrying of an entire army across the Channel – the Admiralty estimated this would take six tides, or 3 days – a tunnel could hardly be bettered.[31]

But the situation in 1994 was totally different. For one thing, no conventional political or military enemies seemed to threaten Britain's shores at all. And the tunnel's passenger services were nowhere near as successful as its promoters had hoped: in 2003 they were 40 per cent below the projections that had been made for them in 1994. Its operators, Eurotunnel, suffered accordingly.[32] The Channel Tunnel – combined with cheap airfares – did take a large proportion of this business away from the ports. It carried nearly 14.9 million passengers in 1997, and 17.8 million by 2007. But Britons were still more likely to travel to the continent by ship: 32.1 million of them travelled by short sea ferry route to mainland Europe in 1997, and 20.4 million even in 2007: a more than 50 per cent decrease in traffic, but still a number greater than those using the Channel Tunnel. Increasing numbers of short trips, including weekends away and 'booze cruises' to the continent where alcohol was cheaper, boosted sea travel more than it helped the tunnel.[33]

These lines of continuity should remind us once more just how deeply entrenched the very idea of the sea has remained among the British. As Admiral Sir Alan West, First Sea Lord between 2002 and 2006, has put it: 'when you scrape away at the average British person, there is blue water there'.[34] But we remain in severe need of histories that do for Britain what Frank Broeze, for instance, did for Australia: show just how much it had 'a distinct tang of the sea about it', and the extent to which the 'sea [was] central to the colonists' consciousness'.[35] Nor are there many historians who have shown how myths of nationhood can be challenged and remade via oceanic history, as Benjamin Labaree and his collaborators have done in the USA: in this case, the idea of the independent farmer as model citizen has been shown to be no more important to early America than its mariners bringing trade and people to its shores.[36] There are indeed few works like that of David Kirby and Merja-Liisa Hinkkanen, who have attempted to understand 'the sea experiences of generations of maritime people around the Baltic and North Seas'.[37] Elsewhere the 'scholarly turn to the ocean' is fragmented, disparate and divided as between social, military, economic and cultural historians.[38]

Our subjects here might begin to provide a history of Britishness that pays tribute to just this relatively neglected factor in the development of national identities. The impressions of the individuals and even the themes appearing within these pages cannot provide a synoptic or 'holistic approach to the sea', but they can and do demonstrate the manifold experiences and reinventions of the British in the maritime world.[39] Understanding maritime businesses, crimes, slavery, exile and confinement, Britons' invasions, inventions, defeats, journeys, protests and service can thus help construct a new way of looking at British history in the world. They can provide us with a star to steer by.

Notes

1 Histories

1. Cf. D. Eltis, 'The Volume and Structure of the Transatlantic Slave Trade: A Reassessment', *William and Mary Quarterly* 58 (2001), pp. 17–46.
2. C. Matson, 'The Atlantic Economy in an Era of Revolutions: An Introduction', *William and Mary Quarterly* 62 (2005), pp. 358–9.
3. P.A. Coclanis, 'Atlantic World or Atlantic/World?', *William and Mary Quarterly* 63 (2006), pp. 726–7.
4. K. Wigen, 'Oceans of History', *American Historical Review* 111 (2006), p. 717; A. Games, 'Atlantic History: Definitions, Challenges and Opportunities', *American Historical Review* 111 (2006), p. 741; P. Horden and N. Purcell, 'The Mediterranean and "the New Thalassology"', *American Historical Review* 111 (2006), pp. 722–3.
5. *History in Focus* 9 (2005), http://www.history.ac.uk/ihr/Focus/Sea/articles.html, accessed 2 October 2007.
6. B. Bailyn, 'Introduction', in D. Armitage and M. Braddick (eds.), *The British Atlantic World, 1500–1800* (Basingstoke, 2002), p. xv.
7. See Cannadine's own comments at, for example, D. Cannadine, 'Introduction', in D. Cannadine (ed.), *Empire, the Sea and Global History: Britain's Maritime World, c.1763–c.1840* (Basingstoke, 2007), p. 2.
8. A.G. Hopkins, 'Globalization – An Agenda for Historians', in Hopkins (ed.), *Globalization in World History* (2002), p. 1.
9. M. Ogborn, *Global Lives: Britain and the World, 1550–1800* (Cambridge, 2008), p. 3.
10. A. Prakash and J.A. Hart, 'Globalization and Governance', in Prakash and Hart (eds.), *Globalization and Governance* (1999), pp. 9–10; on the effects, see G.E. Chortareas and T. Pelagidis, 'Trade Flows: A Facet of Regionalisation or Globalisation?', *Cambridge Journal of Economics* 28 (2004), pp. 253–71.
11. J. Stiglitz, *Making Globalization Work* (2006), pp. 270–2; for a historical perspective, see P. Aghion and J.G. Williamson, *Growth, Inequality and Globalization: Theory, History and Policy* (Cambridge, 1998), esp. pp. 105–31.
12. The phrase 'weightless world' was coined by D. Coyle, *The Weightless World* (Oxford, 1999 pbk. edn.), pp. 1–5 (see her comments on politics on pp. 14–17); the Heertz citation is from N. Heertz, *The Silent Takeover: Global Capitalism and the Death of Democracy* (2001), p. 3.
13. D. Harvey, *Spaces of Capital: Towards a Critical Geography* (2001), pp. 27–37.
14. Analysed by L. Sklair, *Globalization: Capitalism and Its Alternatives* (Oxford, 2002), pp. 277–96, put polemically by N. Klein, *No Logo* (rev. edn., 2001), pp. 439–46 and critiqued by P. Legrain, *Open World: The Truth About Globalisation* (2002), esp. pp. 320–34.
15. On tourism, cf. classically J. Urry, *The Tourist Gaze: Leisure and Travel in Contemporary Societies* (1990), and J. Craik, 'The Culture of Tourism', in C. Rojek

and J. Urry (eds.), *Touring Cultures: Transformations of Travel and Theory* (1997), pp. 113–36.

16. For a much more in-depth discussion of these issues, see G. O'Hara, ' "The Sea Is Swinging into View": Modern British Maritime History in a Globalised World', *English Historical Review* 124 (2009), pp. 1109–34.

17. For example, K. Morgan, *Bristol and the Atlantic Trade in the Eighteenth Century* (Cambridge, 1993), pp. 80–5; D.O. Flynn and A. Giràldez, 'Cycles of Silver: Global Economic Unity Through the Mid-Eighteenth Century', *Journal of World History* 13 (2002), pp. 391–427.

18. See B. Bailyn, *Atlantic History: Concept and Contours* (Cambridge, Mass., 2005); see B. Klein and G. Mackenthune, 'The Sea Is History', in Klein and Mackenthune (eds.), *Sea Changes: Historicizing the Ocean* (New York, 2004), esp. pp. 2, 5.

19. M. Rediker, *Between the Devil and the Deep Blue Sea: Merchant Seamen, Pirates, and the Anglo-American Maritime World 1700–1750* (Cambridge, 1987); and P. Linebaugh and M. Rediker, *The Many-Headed Hydra: Sailors, Slaves, Commoners, and the Hidden History of the Revolutionary Atlantic* (2000). This work is itself deeply indebted to J. Lemisch, 'Jack Tar in the Streets: Merchant Seamen in the Politics of Revolutionary America', *William and Mary Quarterly* 25 (1968), pp. 371–407. See recently on 'runaways' and 'renegades', E.J. Christopher, *Slave Ship Sailors and Their Captive Cargoes* (Cambridge, 2006).

20. The best-known work in this field is J.K. Walton, *The British Seaside: Holidays and Resorts in the Twentieth Century* (Manchester, 2000).

21. R. Ellis, *The Empty Ocean* (Washington DC, 2003), p. 300.

22. R.A. Myers and B. Worm, 'Rapid Worldwide Depletion of Predatory Fish Communities', *Nature* 423 (2003), pp. 280–3.

23. B. Worm, H.K. Lotze and R.A. Myers, 'Predator Diversity Hotspots in the Blue Ocean', *Proceedings of the National Academy of Science of the United States* 100 (2003), pp. 9884–8.

24. J.C. Kunich, *Killing Our Oceans: Dealing with the Mass Extinction of Maritime Life* (2006), pp. 3, 5–7.

25. 'Leader: A Sea of Troubles', *The Economist*, 3 January 2009.

26. Hillary Clinton's Senate Confirmation Hearing, Council on Foreign Relations Transcript, 13 January 2009, http://www.cfr.org/publication/18225/transcript_of_hillary_clintons_confirmation_hearing.html, accessed 28 March 2009.

27. Department for Environment, Food and Rural Affairs, *Making Space for Water: Developing a New Government Strategy for Flood and Coastal Erosion Risk Management in England* (2004), pp. 29, 36.

28. DEFRA, *Making Space for Water: Taking Forward a New Government Strategy for Flood and Coastal Erosion Risk in England* (2005), pp. 33–5.

29. N. Morris, 'Stark Warning on Britain's Shrinking Coast', *The Independent*, 18 August 2008.

30. J. Donald Hughes, *An Environmental History of the World: Humankind's Changing Role in the Community of Life* (2002), pp. 180, 199, 212, 218; the fundamental differences between the twentieth century and the preceding epochs are stressed in J. McNeill, *Something New Under the Sun: An Environmental History of the Twentieth Century* (Harmondsworth, 2000), pp. 137–47.

31. L. Robin, 'Ecology: A Science of Empire?', in T. Griffiths and L. Robin (eds.), *Ecology and Empire: Environmental History of Settler Societies* (Edinburgh, 1997),

pp. 63–75; see A.W. Crosby, *Ecological Imperialism: The Biological Expansion of Europe, 900–1900* (Cambridge, 1986), esp. chapter 7, pp. 145–70.

32. M.K. Søndergaard, 'The Rise and Fall of the North European Mackerel Fisheries in the Nineteenth Century', *International Journal of Maritime History* 20 (2008), pp. 115–32.

33. See in general A. Iriye, 'Environmental History and International History', *Diplomatic History* 32 (2008), p. 645, and for a specific example G.T. Jóhannesson, 'How "Cod War" Came: The Origins of the Anglo-Icelandic Fisheries Dispute, 1958–61', *Historical Research* 77 (2004), pp. 543–74. I am grateful to Professor Kathleen Burk on this point.

34. F. Braudel, *The Mediterranean and the Mediterranean World in the Age of Philip II* (Eng. trans., 1972 edn.), Vol. I, pp. 103–67.

35. H.A. Innis, *The Fur Trade in Canada: An Introduction to Canadian Economic History* (Toronto, 1956 rev. edn.), esp. pp. 385–92; H.A. Innis, *The Cod Fisheries: The History of an International Economy* (Toronto, 1954 rev. edn.), pp. 492–500.

36. R.H. Grove, *Green Imperialism: Colonial Expansion, Tropical Island Edens and the Origins of Environmentalism, 1600–1868* (Cambridge, 1996), pp. 311–16.

37. R. Drayton, *Nature's Government: Science, Imperial Britain, and the 'Improvement' of the World* (2000), pp. 94–124.

38. N.A.M. Rodger, 'Recent Books on the Royal Navy of the Eighteenth Century', *Journal of Military History* 63 (1999), p. 684.

39. R. Davis, 'Maritime History: Progress and Problems', in S. Marriner (ed.), *Business and Businessmen: Studies in Business, Economic and Accounting History* (Liverpool, 1978), p. 169.

40. For this context, see M. Hughes-Warrington, 'World and Global History', *Historical Journal* 51 (2008), pp. 754–5, 759.

41. Land, 'Tidal Waves: The New Coastal History', *Journal of Social History* 40 (2007), p. 740.

42. P. Rainbird, *The Archaeology of Micronesia* (Cambridge, 2004), pp. 70–8; C. Broodbank, *An Island Archaeology of the Early Cyclades* (Cambridge, 2000), pp. 35, 69–106.

43. Though Rainbird has criticised Broodbank's approach as still confined too much to the islands themselves, rather than 'communities of mariners': P. Rainbird, *The Archaeology of Islands* (Cambridge, 2007), pp. 43–5.

44. W. Jeffrey Bolster, 'Putting the Ocean in Atlantic History: Maritime Communities and Marine Ecology in the Northwest Atlantic, 1500–1800', *American Historical Review* 113 (2008), pp. 28–9; *idem.*, 'Opportunities in Marine Environmental History', *Environmental History* 11 (2006), pp. 567–9.

45. S. McGrail, 'The Sea and Archaeology', *Historical Research* 76 (2003), pp. 2, 5.

46. L. Colley, *Britons: Forging the Nation 1707–1837* (1992); L. Colley, *Captives: Britain, Empire and the World 1600–1850* (2002).

47. See e.g. R. Morriss, *Naval Power and British Culture, 1760–1850: Public Trust and Government Ideology* (Aldershot, 2004); M. Lincoln, *Representing the Royal Navy: British Sea Power, 1750–1815* (Aldershot, 2002).

48. K. Lunn and A. Day, 'Britain as Island: National Identity and the Sea', in H. Brocklehurst and R. Phillips (eds.), *History, Nationhood and the Question of Britain* (Basingstoke, 2004), esp. pp. 127–9.

49. T. Jenks, *Naval Engagements: Patriotism, Cultural Politics, and the Royal Navy, 1793–1815* (Oxford, 2006); J. Rüger, *The Great Naval Game: Britain and Germany in the Age of Empire* (Cambridge, 2007).

50. C. Harvie, *A Floating Commonwealth: Politics, Culture, and Technology on Britain's Atlantic Coast, 1860–1930* (Oxford, 2008).
51. R. Colls, *Identity of England* (Oxford, 2002), p. 239.
52. R. Samuel, *Patriotism: The Making and Unmaking of British National Identity* (1989), Vol. I, pp. 49–51.
53. P. Ward, *Britishness since 1870* (2004), pp. 55–7; R. Weight, *Patriots: National Identity in Britain 1940–2000* (pbk. edn., 2002), p. 66.

2 Merchants

1. R. Davis, *English Overseas Trade, 1500–1700* (1973), p. 13.
2. H.R. Fox Bourne, *English Merchants: Memoirs in Illustration of the Progress of British Commerce* (1886), p. 76.
3. C. Ernest Fayle, *A Short History of the World's Shipping Industry* (1933), p. 142.
4. C. Wilson, *England's Apprenticeship, 1603–1763* (2nd edn., 1984), p. 52.
5. R. Davis, 'English Foreign Trade, 1700–1774', *Economic History Review* 15 (1962), p. 291.
6. R. Davis, *The Rise of the English Shipping Industry in the Seventeenth and Eighteenth Centuries* (1962), pp. 11–21.
7. Fayle, *Shipping Industry*, p. 190.
8. K.R. Andrews, *Ships, Money and Politics: Seafaring and Naval Enterprise in the Reign of Charles I* (Cambridge, 1991), pp. 26–9.
9. V. Barbour, 'Dutch and English Merchant Shipping in the Seventeenth Century', in E.M. Carus-Wilson (ed.), *Essays in Economic History, Vol. I* (1954), pp. 229–31, 248–9.
10. S. Schama, *The Embarrassment of Riches: An Interpretation of Dutch Culture in the Golden Age* (1987), p. 297.
11. N. Steensgaard, 'European Shipping to Asia, 1497–1700', *Scandinavian Economic History Review* 18 (1970), table 3, p. 9.
12. M. Bogucka, 'Scots in Gdansk (Danzig) in the Seventeenth Century', in A.I. Macinnes, T. Riis and F. Pedersen (eds.), *Ships, Guns and Bibles in the North Sea and Baltic States, c.1350–1700* (East Linton, 2000), pp. 39–46.
13. L.A. Harper, *The English Navigation Laws: A Seventeenth Century Experiment in Social Engineering* (New York, 1939), p. 10.
14. R. Brenner, 'The Social Basis of English Commercial Expansion, 1550–1650', *Journal of Economic History* 32 (1972), p. 369.
15. J. Sutton, *Lords of the East: The East India Company and Its Ships* (1981), pp. 11–13.
16. Harper, *Navigation Laws*, pp. 38, 53–7.
17. N. Zahedieh, 'Economy', in D. Armitage and M.J. Braddick (eds.), *The British Atlantic World 1500–1800* (Basingstoke, 2002), p. 53.
18. Wilson, *England's Apprenticeship*, p. 40; R. Davis, *English Merchant Shipping and Anglo-Dutch Rivalry in the Seventeenth Century* (1975), p. 1.
19. J.V. Beckett, *Coal and Tobacco: The Lowthers and the Economic Development of West Cumberland, 1660–1760* (1981), pp. 102–3.
20. V. Collingridge, *Captain Cook* (2000), pp. 33–5.
21. Davis, *Merchant Shipping*, pp. 16–17.
22. Ogborn, *Global Lives*, pp. 112, 134.
23. E. Jones, 'The *Matthew* of Bristol and the Financiers of John Cabot's 1497 Voyage to North America', *English Historical Review* 121 (2006), pp. 778–95.

24. J. Price, 'The Imperial Economy 1700–1776', in P.J. Marshall (ed.), *The Oxford History of the British Empire, Vol. II: The Eighteenth Century* (Oxford, 1998), pp. 87–8.

25. B. Little, *The City and County of Bristol: A Study of Atlantic Civilisation* (1954), pp. 165, 255.

26. F.E. Hyde, *Liverpool and the Mersey: An Economic History of a Port, 1700–1970* (1971), p. 14.

27. Gately, *La Diva Nicotina: The Story of How Tobacco Seduced the World* (2001), p. 102.

28. T.M. Devine, 'Scotland', in R. Floud and P.A. Johnson (eds.), *The Cambridge Economic History of Modern Britain* (Cambridge, 2004 edn.), Vol. II, pp. 394, 402.

29. L.E. Cochran, *Scottish Trade with Ireland in the Eighteenth Century* (Edinburgh, 1985), p. 59.

30. H. Hamilton, *An Economic History of Scotland in the Eighteenth Century* (Oxford, 1963), p. 282.

31. M. Berg, *Luxury and Pleasure in Eighteenth Century England* (Oxford, 2005), p. 21.

32. S.W. Mintz, *Sweetness and Power: The Place of Sugar in Modern History* (Harmondsworth, 1985), pp. 36–9.

33. Zahedieh, 'Economy', p. 56.

34. J.J. McCusker, *Essays in the Economic History of the Atlantic World* (1997), table 14.2, p. 323; table 14.4, p. 327.

35. J.R. Ward, 'The British West Indies in the Age of Abolition, 1748–1815', in Marshall (ed.), *British Empire*, p. 421.

36. Gately, *La Diva Nicotina*, p. 45.

37. Price, 'Imperial Economy', p. 85.

38. Hyde, *Liverpool*, p. 26.

39. J.F. Shepherd and G.M. Walton, *Shipping, Maritime Trade and the Economic Development of Colonial North America* (Cambridge, 1972), p. 39.

40. A. Slaven, *The Development of the West of Scotland 1750–1960* (1975), p. 28.

41. D.A. Farnie, 'The Commercial Empire of the Atlantic, 1607–1783', *Economic History Review* 15 (1962), p. 209.

42. V.T. Harlow, *The Founding of the Second British Empire, 1763–93, Vol. I: Discovery and Revolution* (1954), p. 479.

43. Hyde, *Liverpool*, p. 39.

44. J.M. Price, 'What Did Merchants Do? Reflections on British Overseas Trade, 1660–1790', *Journal of Economic History* 49 (1989), p. 270.

45. Fayle, *Shipping Industry*, p. 195.

46. Wilson, *England's Apprenticeship*, p. 43.

47. F. Vigier, *Change and Apathy: Liverpool and Manchester during the Industrial Revolution* (Cambridge, Mass., 1970), p. 21. On canals more generally, see P. Hudson, *Regions and Industries: A Perspective on the Industrial Revolution in Britain* (Cambridge, 1989), pp. 15–17.

48. On the role of canals in this process, see M. Berg and P. Hudson, 'Rehabilitating the Industrial Revolution', *Economic History Review* 45 (1992), esp. p. 39.

49. P. Corfield, *The Impact of English Towns, 1700–1800* (Oxford, 1982), p. 45.

50. P. Earle, *Sailors: English Merchant Seamen 1650–1775* (1998), p. 35.

51. P. Earle, *The Making of the English Middle Class: Business, Society and Family Life in London, 1660–1730* (1989), p. 43.

52. Cited in W.E. Minchinton, 'Bristol – Metropolis of the West in the Eighteenth Century', in P. Clark (ed.), *The Early Modern Town* (1976), p. 298.
53. Hyde, *Liverpool*, p. 18.
54. Cochran, *Scottish Trade with Ireland*, pp. 146–8.
55. B. Lemire, *Fashion's Favourite: The Cotton Trade and the Consumer in Britain, 1660–1800* (Oxford, 1991), p. 116.
56. Little, *Bristol*, p. 161.
57. Langford, *Polite and Commercial People*, pp. 166–7.
58. Sutton, *Lords of the East*, p. 14.
59. *ibid.*, pp. 29–30, 43.
60. Fayle, *Shipping Industry*, p. 217; K.N. Chaudhuri, 'The English East India Company's Shipping c. 1660–1760', in J.R. Bruijn and F.S. Gaastra (eds.), *Ships, Sailors and Spices: East India Companies and their Shipping in the Sixteenth, Seventeenth and Eighteenth Centuries* (The Hague, 1987), appendix, pp. 75–80.
61. Wilson, *England's Apprenticeship*, p. 170.
62. Harper, *English Navigation Laws*, p. 14.
63. J. Thirsk and J.P. Cooper (eds.), *Seventeenth Century Economic Documents* (Oxford, 1972), p. 431.
64. Davis, *Merchant Shipping*, p. 1.
65. M. Kurlansky, *Salt: A World History* (2003), p. 216.
66. M. Kurlansky, *Cod: A Biography of the Fish That Changed the World* (1999), pp. 67–70.
67. G. Jackson, *The British Whaling Trade* (1978), pp. 70–3, 86.
68. Corfield, *English Towns*, p. 41.
69. Hyde, *Liverpool*, pp. 27–8.
70. Lloyd, *British Seaman*, table 2, p. 260.
71. B. Greenhill and M. Nix, 'North Devon Shipping, Trade and Ports, 1786–1939', in M. Duffy et al. (eds.), *The New Maritime History of Devon, Vol. II: From the Late Eighteenth Century to the Present Day* (1994), pp. 52–3.
72. Chaudhuri, *Ships, Sailors and Spices*, pp. 60–2.
73. N. Williams, *Contraband Cargoes: Seven Centuries of Smuggling* (1959), pp. 98–9.
74. T.M. Devine, *Scotland's Empire 1600–1815* (Harmondsworth, 2004), pp. 88–93.
75. J. Pollock, *William Wilberforce* (1977), pp. 3–4.
76. G. Jackson, *Hull in the Eighteenth Century: A Study in Economic and Social History* (Oxford, 1972), pp. 96–9, 102.
77. S-E. Astrom, *From Cloth to Iron: The Anglo-Baltic trade in the Late Seventeenth Century* (Helsingfors, 1963–65), Vol. I, pp. 158–69.
78. Sutton, *Lords of the East*, p. 36.
79. *ibid.*, p. 17.
80. Wilson, *England's Apprenticeship*, p. 167.
81. Fayle, *Shipping Industry*, p. 209.
82. Beckett, *Coal and Tobacco*, p. 18.
83. J. Smail, 'Credit, Risk and Honour in Eighteenth Century Commerce', *Journal of British Studies* 44 (2005), p. 447.
84. P. Mathias, 'Risk, Credit and Kinship in Early Modern Enterprise', in J.I. McCusker and K. Morgan (eds.), *The Early Modern Atlantic Economy* (Cambridge, 2000), pp. 23, 25.
85. K. Morgan, 'Business Networks in the British Export Trade to North America, 1750–1800', in J.J. McCusker and K. Morgan (eds.), *The Early Modern Atlantic Economy* (Cambridge, 2000), pp. 36–64, pp. 41–2.

86. Jackson, *Hull*, p. 121.
87. *ibid.*, pp. 107–8.
88. Langford, *Polite and Commercial People*, p. 175.
89. On the fading influence of the Eastland Company, see R.W.K. Hinton, *The Eastland Trade and the Common Weal in the Seventeenth Century* (Cambridge, 1959), pp. 138–61.
90. Sutton, *Lords of the East*, p. 14.
91. E.J. Evans, *The Forging of the Modern State: Early Industrial Britain 1783–1870* (1983), pp. 31–2.
92. J.B. Williams, *British Commercial Policy and Trade Expansion 1750–1850* (Oxford, 1972), pp. 449–51.
93. N. Gash, *Sir Robert Peel: The Life of Sir Robert Peel after 1830* (1986 pbk. edn.), p. 604.
94. A. Briggs, *The Age of Improvement 1783–1867* (2nd edn., 2000), p. 270.
95. A.W. Kirkaldy, *British Shipping: Its History, Organisation and Significance* (1919), p. 27.
96. S. Schonhardt-Bailey, *From the Corn Laws to Free Trade: Interests, Ideas and Institutions in Historical Perspective* (2006), pp. 96–106.
97. F. Trentmann, *Free Trade Nation: Commerce, Consumption and Civil Society in Modern Britain* (Oxford, 2008), e.g. pp. 353–4, 100, 33.
98. A.H. Imlah, *Economic Elements in the Pax Britannica* (New York, 1958), table 4, pp. 70–5.
99. Hyde, *Liverpool*, pp. 98–9.
100. G. Jackson and C. Munn, 'Trade, Commerce and Finance', in W. Hamish Fraser and I. Maver (eds.), *Glasgow, Vol. II: 1830 to 1912* (Manchester, 1996), pp. 54, 60.
101. R. Robinson, *Trawling: The Rise and Fall of the British Trawl Fishery* (Exeter, 1996), pp. 23–4, 44.
102. J.R. Coull, *The Sea Fisheries of Scotland* (Edinburgh, 1996), pp. 203–4.
103. R. Girling, *Sea Change: Britain's Coastal Catastrophe* (2008 pbk. edn.), pp. 115–16.
104. R. Perren, 'The Nineteenth-Century Economy', in W. Hamish and C.H. Lee (eds.), *Aberdeen 1800–2000: A New History* (East Lothian, 2000), pp. 87–8. I am grateful to Professor John Stewart for this reference.
105. C. Roberts, *The Unnatural History of the Sea: The Past and the Future of Man and Fishing* (2007), p. 142.
106. Robinson, *Trawling*, p. 29.
107. J. Burnett and P. Burnett, *Plenty and Want: A Social History of Food in England from 1815 to the Present Day* (rev. ed., 1979), p. 13.
108. Girling, *Sea Change*, p. 120.
109. J.K. Walton, *Fish and Chips and the British Working Class, 1870–1940* (1992), pp. 23–8.
110. J.S. Gardiner, 'Geography of British Fisheries', *Geographical Journal* 45 (1915), p. 472; see L.R. Jones, 'The British Fisheries', *Economic Geography* 2 (1926), p. 72, for post-war figures.
111. B.D. Osborne, I. Quinn and D. Robertson, *Glasgow's River* (Glasgow, 1996), pp. 16–26.
112. Slaven, *West of Scotland*, pp. 125–34.
113. T.M. Devine, *The Scottish Nation 1750–2000* (Harmondsworth, 2000), pp. 250–58.

114. P. Banbury, *Shipbuilders of the Thames and Medway* (Newton Abbot, 1971), p. 63.
115. S. Pollard, 'The Decline of Shipbuilding on the Thames', *Economic History Review*, 2nd ser., 3 (1950–51), pp. 72–89.
116. Kirkaldy, *British Shipping*, pp. 25–30.
117. Imlah, *Economic Elements*, p. 173.
118. Kirkaldy, *British Shipping*, appendix XVII, pp. 632–33.
119. A.E. Musson, *The Growth of British Industry* (1981 pbk. edn.), pp. 196–99.
120. N. Crafts, *British Economic Growth During the Industrial Revolution* (Oxford, 1985), table 4.4, p. 86; table 6.6, p. 131.
121. P. Emmer, 'In Search of a System: The Atlantic Economy 1500–1800', in H. Pietschmann (ed.), *Atlantic History: A History of the Atlantic System 1580–1830* (Gottingen, 2002), p. 170.
122. D. Armitage, *The Ideological Origins of the British Empire* (Cambridge, 2000), pp. 146–7.
123. Price, 'Imperial Economy', p. 79.

3   Renegades

1. See the account in R.C. Ritchie, *Captain Kidd and the War Against the Pirates* (Cambridge, Mass., 1986).
2. J.E. Thomson, *Mercenaries, Pirates, and Sovereigns: State Building and Extra-Territorial Violence in Early Modern Europe* (Princeton, NJ, 1996), pp. 22–3.
3. H. Turley, *Rum, Sodomy and the Lash: Piracy, Sexuality and Masculine Identity* (1999), p. 58.
4. K.R. Andrews, *Elizabethan Privateering: English Privateering During the Spanish War* (Cambridge, 1964), p. 25.
5. E. Mancke, 'Early Modern Expansion and the Politicization of Oceanic Space', *Geographical Review* 89 (1999), p. 226.
6. L. Benton, 'Legal Spaces of Empire: Piracy and the Origins of Ocean Regionalism', *Comparative Studies in Society and History* 47 (2005), p. 705; on Morgan's attack see J. Exquemeling, *The Buccaneers of America* (1898 edn.), pp. 143–9, and most recently S. Talty, *Empire of Blue Water: Henry Morgan and the Pirates Who Ruled the Caribbean Waves* (2007), pp. 209–52.
7. D. Cordingly, *Life Among the Pirates: The Romance and the Reality* (2000 edn.), p. 27.
8. M. Pearson and D. Buisseret, 'A Pirate at Port Royal in 1679', *Mariner's Mirror* 57 (1971), p. 304.
9. C. Bridenbaugh and R. Bridenbaugh, *No Peace Beyond the Line: The English in the Caribbean, 1624–1690* (1972), pp. 176–7.
10. B. Fuchs, 'Faithless Empires: Pirates, Renegadoes and the English Nation', *English Literary History* 67 (2000), p. 46.
11. D.J. Starkey, *British Privateering Enterprise in the Eighteenth Century* (1990), table 13, p. 165, and table 20, pp. 200–1.
12. E.A. Poe, *The Collected Short Stories of Edgar Allan Poe* (1999 edn.), p. 126.
13. R.L. Stevenson, *Treasure Island* (Oxford, 1998 edn.), pp. 44–5, 54, 105, 182.
14. Cordingly, *Pirates*, p. 15.
15. Stevenson, *Treasure Island*, p. 76.
16. *ibid.*, p. 191.
17. Turley, *Rum, Sodomy and the Lash*, pp. 73–4.

18. M. Rediker, *Villains of all Nations: Atlantic Pirates in the Golden Age* (2004), pp. 83–4.
19. Cordingly, *Pirates*, pp. 19–20.
20. J.M. Barrie, *Peter Pan* (Harmondsworth, 1995 edn.), pp. 38, 51.
21. *ibid.*, pp. 55, 94–6, 126–7, 146, 159.
22. J. Sugden, *Nelson: A Dream of Glory* (2005), p. 3.
23. C.I. Hamilton, 'Naval Hagiography and the Victorian Hero', *Historical Journal* 23 (1980), pp. 382–4.
24. C. Lloyd, *English Corsairs on the Barbary Coast* (1981), p. 49.
25. C. Lloyd, 'Captain John Ward: Pirate', *History Today* 29 (1979), pp. 751–4.
26. For which see Colley, *Captives*, chapter 2, pp. 43–72.
27. D.D. Hebb, *Piracy and the English Government, 1616–1642* (Aldershot, 1994), 248–57; R. Unger (ed.), *Conway's History of the Ship: Cogs Caravels and Galleons, The Sailing Ship 1000–1650* (1994), p. 113.
28. M. Todd, 'A Captive's Story: Puritans, Pirates and the Drama of Reconciliation', *Seventeenth Century* 12 (1997), p. 41.
29. Fuchs, 'Faithless Empires', p. 52.
30. C.H. Firth, *Naval Songs and Ballads* (1908), p. 27.
31. S. Clissold, 'Christian Renegades and Barbary Corsairs', *History Today* 26 (1976), p. 513.
32. M. Teorey, 'Pirates and State-Sponsored Terrorism in Eighteenth Century England', *Perspectives on Evil and Human Wickedness* 1 (2003), p. 54; see Ogborn, *Global Lives*, pp. 174–6.
33. A. Neill, 'Buccaneer Ethnography: Nature, Culture and Nation in the Journals of William Dampier', *Eighteenth-Century Studies* 33 (2000), pp. 166–8, 171–2.
34. D.J. Starkey, *British Privateering Enterprise in the Eighteenth Century* (1990), p. 61.
35. P.R. Galvin, *Patterns of Pillage: A Geography of Caribbean-Based Piracy in Spanish America, 1536–1718* (New York, 1999), pp. 26–7, 44.
36. Andrews, *Elizabethan Privateering*, p. 10.
37. *ibid.*, tables 1–2, pp. 32–3, and tables 5–6, pp. 125–6.
38. Anderson, 'Rebellion', pp. 619–23.
39. N. Zahedieh, 'Morgan, Sir Henry (c.1635–1688)', *Oxford Dictionary of National Biography*, http://www.oxforddnb.com/view/article/19224?docPos=2, accessed 6 January 2010.
40. N. Zahedieh, 'Trade, Plunder and Economic Development in Early English Jamaica, 1655–1689', *Economic History Review* 39 (1986), pp. 213–21.
41. Teorey, 'Pirates and State-Sponsored Terrorism', p. 57.
42. L. Gragg, 'The Port Royal Earthquake of 1692', *History Today* 50 (2000), p. 30.
43. J.C. Appleby, 'A Nursery of Pirates: The English Pirate Community in Ireland in the Early 17th Century', *International Journal of Maritime History* 2 (1990), pp. 21–5.
44. J.S. Bromley, *Corsairs and Navies 1660–1760* (1987), pp. 144–5.
45. C. Jowitt, 'Piracy and Politics in Heywood and Rowley's *Fortune by Land and Sea*', *Renaissance Studies* 16 (2002), pp. 222–3.
46. D. Defoe, *Captain Singleton* (1963 edn.), pp. 30–1.
47. *ibid.*, pp. 195–203, 312.
48. J. Peck, *Maritime Fiction: Sailors and the Sea in British and American Novels, 1719–1917* (Basingstoke, 2001), pp. 20–2.
49. Defoe, *Captain Singleton*, p. 335.

50. D. Defoe, *Robinson Crusoe* (Harmondsworth, 1994 edn.), pp. 23–4.
51. Appleby, 'Nursery of Pirates', p. 20.
52. Earle, *Pirate Wars*, p. 159.
53. M.C. Campbell, 'St George's Cay: Genesis of the British Settlement of Belize', *Journal of Caribbean History* 37 (2003), pp. 182–4.
54. G.M. Joseph, 'John Coxon and the Role of Buccaneering in the Settlement of Yucatan Colonial Frontier', *Terrae Incognitae* 12 (1980), p. 78.
55. C. Johnson, *A General History of the Pyrates* (New York, 1999 edn.), p. 194.
56. Johnson, *Pyrates*, p. 205.
57. Johnson, *Pyrates*, p. 244.
58. Rediker, *Deep Blue Sea*, pp. 255–6.
59. Smith, 'Early British America', p. 30.
60. Firth, *Ballads*, pp. 167–8.
61. Earle, *Pirate Wars*, pp. 160–1.
62. W. Rogers, *A Cruising Voyage Round the World* (1970 edn.), p. 127.
63. Rogers, *Cruising Voyage*, pp. 136, 214.
64. W.R. Meyer, 'English Privateering in the War of the Spanish Succession, 1702–1713', *Mariners' Mirror* 69 (1983), p. 441.
65. Galvin, *Patterns of Pillage*, p. 72.
66. Scammell, 'Maritime Economy', p. 653.
67. Earle, *Pirate Wars*, p. 135.
68. Rediker, *Villains of All Nations*, p. 127.
69. *ibid.*, p. 27.
70. *ibid.*, p. 32.
71. Cordingly, *Pirates*, p. 231.
72. Earle, *Pirate Wars*, p. 199.
73. Johnson, *Pyrates*, pp. 211–12.
74. Rediker, *Deep Blue Sea*, pp. 33–4.
75. J.H. Baer, ' "Captain John Avery" and the Anatomy of a Mutiny', *Eighteenth-Century Life* 18 (1994), p. 15.
76. Defoe, *Singleton*, p. 207.
77. Rediker, *Villains of All Nations*, p. 86.
78. J.S. Bromley, 'Outlaws at Sea', in F. Krantz (ed.), *History from Below: Studies in Popular Protest and Popular Ideology* (1985), pp. 296–8.
79. Rogers, *Cruising Voyage*, pp. 213–14.
80. M. Rediker, ' "Under the Banner of King Death": The Social World of Anglo-American Pirates, 1716 to 1726', *William and Mary Quarterly* 38 (1981), p. 212.
81. Johnson, *Pyrates*, p. 216.
82. C.M. Senior, *A Nation of Pirates* (Exeter, 1976), p. 37.
83. Thomson, *Mercenaries, Pirates, and Sovereigns*, p. 48.
84. C.R. Pennell, 'Brought to Book: Reading About Pirates', in C.R. Pennell (ed.), *Bandits at Sea: A Pirates Reader* (New York, 2001), p. 9.
85. Earle, *Pirate Wars*, p. 172.
86. Cordingly, *Pirates*, p. 127.
87. Johnson, *Pyrates*, p. 236.
88. A. Smith, *The Atrocities of the Pirates* (1997 edn.), p. 5.
89. *ibid.*, pp. 7, 14–15.
90. Senior, *Nation of Pirates*, p. 25.
91. Rediker, *Villains of All Nations*, p. 148.
92. Smith, *Atrocities*, p. 20.

93. Senior, *Nation of Pirates*, p. 24.
94. Cordingly, *Pirates*, p. 127.
95. Senior, *Nation of Pirates*, p. 30.
96. Rediker, *Villains of All Nations*, p. 36.
97. A. Smith, *The Atrocities of the Pirates: Being a Narrative of the Sufferings Endured by the Author During His Captivity Among the Pirates of the Island of Cuba* (1824), p. 75.
98. Taylor, 'Proletarians', p. 196.
99. D. Severn, 'The Bombardment of Algiers, 1816', *History Today* 28 (1978), pp. 31–9.
100. P. Johnson, *The Birth of the Modern: World Society 1815–1830* (1991), p. 352.
101. M.C. Hunter, 'Anglo-American Political and Naval Response to West Indian Piracy', *International Journal of Maritime History* 13 (2001), pp. 81–5, 90–1.

4   Slavers

1. R. Blackburn, *The Making of New World Slavery: From the Baroque to the Modern 1492–1800* (1997), pp. 222–9.
2. J. Walvin, *A Short History of Slavery* (Harmondsworth, 2007 pbk. edn.), pp. 51–4.
3. H.S. Klein, *The Atlantic Slave Trade* (Cambridge, 1999), pp. 97–80.
4. H. Thomas, *The Slave Trade: The Story of the Atlantic Slave Trade 1440–1870* (1997), pp. 240–1.
5. Eltis, 'Volume', table I, p. 42.
6. A. Games, 'Migration', in Armitage and Braddick (eds.), *British Atlantic World*, table 2.1, p. 41.
7. B. Bailyn, 'Considering the Slave Trade: History and Memory', *William and Mary Quarterly* 58 (2001), p. 246.
8. See S.D. Behrendt, 'Markets, Transaction Cycles, and Profits: Merchant Decision Making in the British Slave Trade' *William and Mary Quarterly* 58 (2001), pp. 174–5.
9. R. Anstey, *The Atlantic Slave Trade and British Abolition, 1760–1810* (1975), p. 15.
10. Klein, *Atlantic*, pp. 101–2.
11. W. St Clair, *The Grand Slave Emporium: Cape Coast Castle and the British Slave Trade* (2006), pp. 99–101.
12. E.J. Christopher, 'Another Head of the Hydra? Slave Trade Sailors and Militancy on the African Coast', *Atlantic Studies* 1 (2004), p. 147.
13. *idem.*, *Slave Ship Sailors*, p. 127.
14. Anstey, *Trade*, pp. 10, 24.
15. K. Morgan, 'James Rogers and the Bristol Slave Trade', *Historical Research* 76 (2003), p. 194.
16. Mann and Cowley, *Cargoes*, p. 104.
17. R.B. Sheridan, 'The Commercial and Financial Organisation of the British Slave Trade, 1750–1807', *Economic History Review* 11 (1958–59), pp. 250–1.
18. A. Falconbridge, *An Account of the Slave Trade on the Coast of Africa* (1788), p. 34.
19. J. Thornton, 'Cannibals, Witches, and Slave Traders in the Atlantic World', *William and Mary Quarterly* 60 (2003), pp. 274–5.
20. E. Williams, *Capitalism and Slavery* (1964 edn.), p. 105.

21. See the summary in D. Eltis and S.L. Engerman, 'The Importance of Slavery and the Slave Trade to Industrializing Britain', *Journal of Economic History* 60 (2000), p. 125.

22. Anstey, *Trade*, pp. 6–7.

23. M. Dresser, *Slavery Obscured: The Social History of the Slave Trade in an English Provincial Port* (2001), table 2, p. 24.

24. Anstey, *Trade*, p. 5.

25. D. Richardson, 'The Slave Trade, Sugar, and British Economic Growth 1748–1776', *Journal of Interdisciplinary History* 17 (1987), p. 744.

26. Anstey, *Trade*, table 1, p. 47, and p. 49.

27. B. Solow, 'Caribbean Slavery and British Growth: The Eric Williams Hypothesis', *Journal of Development Economics* 17 (1985), p. 105.

28. See the summary of this debate in W. Darity, Jr, 'The Numbers Game and the Profitability of the British Trade in Slaves', *Journal of Economic History* 45 (1985), table 3, p. 701, and p. 702.

29. K. Morgan, *Slavery, Atlantic Trade and the British Economy, 1660–1800* (Cambridge, 2000), pp. 47–8, 52–3, 59.

30. Dresser, *Slavery Obscured*, Fig. 14, p. 110.

31. Thomas, *Trade*, p. 297.

32. Eltis and Engerman, 'Importance', p. 129 and table 1, p. 134.

33. S.L. Engerman, 'The Slave Trade and British Capital Formation in the Eighteenth Century: A Comment on the Williams Thesis', *Business History Review* 46 (1972), pp. 434–5.

34. R.P. Thomas and R.N. Bean, 'The Fishers of Men: The Profits of the Slave Trade', *Journal of Economic History* 34 (1974), esp. pp. 887–8.

35. Richardson, 'Growth', p. 741 and pp. 757–60.

36. Blackburn, *Making*, table XII.1, p. 519.

37. S. Drescher, *Econocide: British Slavery in the Era of Abolition* (Pittsburgh, 1977), p. 68.

38. J.E. Inikori. *Africans and the Industrial Revolution in England: A Study in International Trade and Economic Development* (Cambridge, 2002), tables 4.2, 4.3, pp. 176, 178.

39. Blackburn, *Making*, pp. 540–2.

40. D. Eltis, 'Europeans and the Rise and Fall of African Slavery in the Americas: an Interpretation', *American Historical Review* 98 (1993), pp. 1399, 1403.

41. S. Drescher, *Capitalism and Antislavery: British Mobilization in Comparative Perspective* (Basingstoke, 1986), p. 5.

42. J.L. Ray, 'The Abolition of Slavery and the End of International War', *International Organization* 43 (1989), p. 409.

43. W.E. Minchinton, 'Characteristics of British Slaving Vessels, 1698–1775', *Journal of Interdisciplinary History* 20 (1989), tables 4–5, pp. 59–60.

44. Anstey, *Trade*, p. 9.

45. Thomas, *Trade*, p. 304.

46. D.P. Mannix and M. Cowley, *Black Cargoes: A History of the Atlantic Slave Trade, 1518–1865* (1962), p. 107.

47. Falconbridge, *Account*, p. 24.

48. Walvin, *History*, p. 73.

49. See some of the most recent estimates in H.S. Klein, S.L. Engerman, R. Haines and R. Shlomowitz, 'Transoceanic Mortality: The Slave Trade in Comparative Perspective', *William and Mary Quarterly* 58 (2001), table IV, p. 113, with given

death rates *per month* of 9.8 per cent in the late seventeenth century, declining to 4.6 per cent by the end of the eighteenth century.

50. E.R. Taylor, *If We Must Die: Shipboard Insurrections in the Era of the Atlantic Slave Trade* (Baton Rouge, La., 2006), pp. 43–55, and ft. 3, p. 215.
51. Klein, *Atlantic*, p. 84.
52. Mann and Cowley, *Cargoes*, p. 108.
53. J. Newton, *The Journal of a Slave Trader, 1750–1754* (1962 edn.), p. 104.
54. D. Richardson, 'Shipboard Revolts, African Authority, and the Atlantic Slave Trade', *William and Mary Quarterly* 58 (2001), p. 74.
55. Inikori, *Africans*, p. 256.
56. Richardson, 'Revolts', p. 73.
57. O. Equiano, *The Interesting Narrative and Other Writings* (Harmondsworth, 2003 pbk. edn.), p. 59.
58. Mann and Cowley, *Cargoes*, p. 118.
59. St Clair, *Emporium*, p. 105.
60. Mann and Cowley, *Caroges*, pp. 150–1.
61. Falconbridge, *Account*, p. 40.
62. Thomas, *Trade*, p. 311.
63. Anstey, *Trade*, p. 29.
64. Martin, *Newton*, p. 132; see also Newton, *Journal*, pp. 56–7, 80.
65. E.J. Christopher, 'The Sons of Neptune and the Sons of Ham: A History of Slave Ship Cargoes and their Captive Cargoes', University College London unpublished PhD Dissertation, 2003, p. 147.
66. Anstey, *Trade*, p. 33.
67. Newton, *Journal*, p. 104.
68. St Clair, *Emporium*, pp. 126–7.
69. J.R. Oldfield, *Popular Politics and British Anti-Slavery: The Mobilisation of Public Opinion Against the Slave Trade 1787–1807* (1998), pp. 42–5.
70. A. Hochschild, *Bury the Chains: The British Struggle to Abolish Slavery* (2006 pbk. edn.), pp. 127–30; Anstey, *Trade*, p. 257.
71. Drescher, *Antislavery*, pp. 70, 75, 80.
72. C. Midgley, *Women Against Slavery: The British Campaigns, 1780–1870* (1992), pp. 15–18.
73. L. Billington and R. Billington, ' "A Burning Zeal for Righteousness": Women in the British Anti-Slavery Movement, 1820–1870', in J. Rendall (ed.), *Equal or Different: Women's Politics 1800–1914* (Basingstoke, 1985), pp. 83–5, 94–5; see Oldfield, *Popular Politics*, pp. 133–5.
74. Ogborn, *Global Lives*, p. 271.
75. L.J. Bellot, 'Evangelicals and the Defense of Slavery in Britain's Old Colonial Empire', *Journal of Southern History* 37 (1971), pp. 20, 22.
76. A. Scherr, ' "Sambos" and "Black Cut-Throats": Peter Porcupine on Slavery and Race in the 1790s', *American Periodicals: A Journal of History, Criticism, and Bibliography* 13 (2003), pp. 10–12, 18.
77. S. White and G. White, 'Slave Clothing and African-American Culture in the Eighteenth and Nineteenth Centuries', *Past and Present* 148 (1995), p. 161.
78. H. Altink, 'Deviant and Dangerous: Pro-Slavery Representations of Jamaican Slave Women's sexuality, c. 1780–1834', *Slavery and Abolition* 26 (2005), p. 273.
79. D Lambert, 'The Counter-Revolutionary Atlantic: West Indian Petitions and Proslavery Networks', *Social and Cultural Geography* 6 (2005), pp. 409–10.

80. See D.B. Ryden, 'Does Decline Make Sense? The West Indian Economy and the Abolition of the British Slave Trade', *Journal of Interdisciplinary History* 31 (2000), figs. 4, 5, pp. 365, 371, the estate figures cited in Drescher, *Econocide*, p. 82, and the political comments in Oldfield, *Popular Politics*, pp. 63–4.

81. Anstey, *Trade*, p. 260.

82. M. Graton, J. Walvin and D. Wright, *Slavery, Abolition and Emancipation: Black Slaves and the British Empire* (1976), p. 249.

83. M. Wood, *Blind Memory: Visual Representations of Slavery in England and America* (Manchester, 2000), pp. 22–3.

84. S.P. Wainwright and C. Williams, 'Biography and Vulnerability: Loss, Dying and Death in the Romantic Paintings of J.M.W. Turner', *Auto/Biography* 13 (2005), p. 23. For more on the *Zong*, and on recent memorialisation, see J. Webster, 'The *Zong* in the Context of the Eighteenth-Century Slave Trade', *Journal of Legal History* 28 (2007), pp. 285–98, and A. Rupprecht, ' "A Limited Sort of Property": History, Memory and the Slave Ship *Zong*', *Slavery and Abolition* 29 (2008), pp. 265–77.

85. Colley, *Britons*, pp. 351, 358.

86. J. Pedro Marques, *The Sounds of Silence: Nineteenth-Century Portugal and the Abolition of the Slave Trade* (Eng. trans., Oxford, 2006), p. 42.

87. C.D. Kaufmann and R.A. Pape, 'Explaining Costly International Moral Action: Britain's Sixty-year Campaign Against the Atlantic Slave Trade', *International Organization* 53 (2003), pp. 634–7; D. Eltis, *Economic Growth and the Ending of the Transatlantic Slave Trade* (Oxford, 1987), table 2, pp. 92–3.

88. J. Postma, *The Atlantic Slave Trade* (Westport, CT, 2003), table 3.1, p. 36.

89. J.C. Dorsey, *Slave Traffic in the Age of Abolition: Puerto Rico, West Africa and the Non-Hispanic Caribbean 1815–1859* (Gainesville, Fla., 2003), pp. 41–2.

90. B. Semmel, *Liberalism and Naval Strategy: Ideology, Interest and Sea Power During the Pax Britannica* (1986), pp. 14–16, 33–4.

91. Thomas, *Trade*, pp. 741–3.

92. A Herman, *To Rule the Waves: How the Royal Navy Shaped the Modern World* (2005), pp. 421–2.

93. B. Hilton, *A Mad, Bad, and Dangerous People? England, 1783–1846* (Oxford, 2006), pp. 244–5, 292.

94. On 'psychological benefits' and 'imaginative constructs' of overseas possessions and investment cf. respectively A. Offer, 'The British Empire 1870–1914: A Waste of Money?', *Economic History Review* 46 (1993), pp. 232–3; and D. Cannadine, 'The Empire Strikes Back', *Past and Present* 147 (1995), p. 194.

95. M. Mason, 'The Battle of the Slaveholding Liberators: Great Britain, the United States, and Slavery in the Early Nineteenth Century', *William and Mary Quarterly* 59 (2002), pp. 665–96.

96. D. Robinson-Dunn, *The Harem, Slavery and British Imperial Culture: Anglo-Muslim Relations in the Late-Nineteenth Century* (Manchester, 2006), pp. 32–3.

97. D. Jordan and M. Walsh, *White Cargo: The Forgotten History of Britain's White Slaves in America* (Edinburgh, 2007), pp. 76–85, 120, 123.

98. Blackburn, *Making*, p. 248.

99. N. Matar, *Britain and Barbary 1589–1689* (Gainseville, Fla., 2005), pp. 49–63.

100. Colley, *Captives*, pp. 75–83.

101. Hochschild, *Chains*, p. 219.

102. C. Hall, *Civilising Subjects: Metropole and Colony in the English Imagination 1830–1867* (Cambridge, 2002), pp. 27, 424–33.

103. Colley, *Britons*, p. 360.
104. M. Sherwood, *After Abolition: Britain and the Slave Trade since 1807* (2007), p. 31.

5   Migrants

1. For life in early Jamestown, see most recently W.M. Kelso, *Jamestown: The Buried Truth* (Charlottesville, VA, 2006).
2. R. Daniels, *Coming to America: A History of Immigration and Ethnicity in American Life* (1991), p. 32.
3. E. Richards, *Britannia's Children: Emigration from England, Scotland, Wales and Ireland since 1600* (2004), p. 57.
4. D. Cressy, 'The Vast and Furious Ocean: The Passage to Puritan New England', *The New England Quarterly* 57 (1984), pp. 515, 521.
5. D.H. Fischer *Albion's Seed: Four British Folkways in America* (Oxford, 1989), pp. 14, 24–30.
6. A. Games, *Migration and the Origins of the English Atlantic World* (Cambridge, Mass., 2001 edn.), tables 2.2 and 2.4, pp. 47, 52.
7. A. Games, 'Migration', in D. Armitage and M.J. Braddick (eds.), *The British Atlantic World 1500–1800* (Basingstoke: 2002), table 2.1, p. 41.
8. J. Horn, 'British Diaspora: Emigration from Britain, 1680–1815', in P.J. Marshall (ed.), *The Oxford History of the British Empire Vol. II: The Eighteenth Century* (Oxford, 1998), table 2.1, p. 31.
9. L.P. Moch, *Moving Europeans: Migration in Western Europe since 1650* (Bloomington, Ind., 1992), pp. 2–3.
10. M.E. Ailes, *Military Migration and State Formation: The British Military Community in Seventeenth-Century Sweden* (2002), pp. 8–9.
11. T.M. Devine, 'Scotland', in R. Floud and P. Johnson (eds.), *The Cambridge Economic History of Modern Britain, Vol. II* (Cambridge, 2004), p. 391.
12. Games, 'Migration', p. 37.
13. D.F. Campbell and R.A. MacLean, *Beyond the Atlantic Roar: A Study of the Nova Scotia Scots* (Toronto, 1974), p. 20.
14. B. Bailyn, *The Peopling of British North America: An Introduction* (1986), p. 26.
15. Games, 'Migration', p. 31.
16. A. Murdoch, *British Emigration, 1603–1914* (Basingstoke, 2004), p. 33.
17. Bailyn, *Peopling*, p. 9.
18. K. Kenny, *The American Irish: A History* (Harlow, 2000), pp. 14–16.
19. P. Griffin, *The People with No Name: Ireland's Ulster Scots, America's Scots Irish, and the Creation of a British Atlantic World, 1689–1764* (Princeton, NJ, 2001), pp. 68–74, 88–94.
20. W.J. Smyth, 'Irish Emigration, 1700–1920', in P.C. Emmer and M. Mörner (eds.), *European Expansion and Migration: Essays on the Intercontinental Migration from Africa, Asia and Europe* (Oxford, 1992), p. 54.
21. Richards, *Britannia's Children*, p. 13.
22. P. Emmer, 'In Search of a System: The Atlantic Economy 1500–1800', in H. Pietschmann (ed.), *Atlantic History: A History of the Atlantic System 1580–1830* (Gottingen, 2002), p. 173; see P. Buckner, *English Canada: The Founding Generations* (1993), p. 4, on the migrants' 'Lilliputian' numbers.
23. B. Bailyn, *Voyagers to the West: Emigration from Britain to America on the Eve of the Revolution* (1987), pp. 24–5.

24. D. Eltis, 'Free and Coerced Transatlantic Migrations: Some Comparisons', *American Historical Review* 88 (1983), p. 252.
25. Richards, *Britannia's Children*, p. 11.
26. R. Haines, *Emigration and the Labouring Poor: Australian Recruitment in Britain and Ireland, 1831–60* (1997), appendix 1, pp. 261–3.
27. W.D. Borrie, *The European Peopling of Australasia: A Demographic History, 1788–1988* (Canberra, 1994), table 5.3, p. 110.
28. Richards, *Britannia's Children*, pp. 178, 211–12.
29. D. Baines, *Migration in a Mature Economy: Emigration and Internal Migration in England 1861–1900* (Cambridge, 1985), p. 45.
30. D. Hoerder, 'Migration in the Atlantic Economies: Regional European Origins and Worldwide Expansion', in D. Hoerder and L.P. Moch (eds.), *European Migrants: Global and Local Perspectives* (Boston, Mass., 1996), p. 36.
31. N.H. Carrier and J.R. Jeffery, *External Migration: A Study of the Available Statistics, 1815–1950* (1953), table 2, p. 14.
32. T.J. Hatton, 'A Model of U.K. Emigration, 1870–1913', *Review of Economics and Statistics* 77 (1995), table 1, p. 412.
33. D. Baines, 'European Emigration, 1815–1930: Looking at the Emigration Decision Again', *Economic History Review* 47 (1994), pp. 529, 532.
34. T.J. Hatton and J.G. Williamson, 'What Drove the Mass Migrations from Europe in the Late Nineteenth Century?', *Population and Development Review* 20 (1994), table 3, p. 548.
35. R.B. Stein, 'Seascape and the American Imagination: The Puritan Seventeenth Century', *Early American Literature* 7 (1972), p. 24.
36. D. Cressy, *Coming Over: Migration and Communication Between England and New England in the Seventeenth Century* (Cambridge, 1987), pp. 75–8, 83–4.
37. H. Kleinschmidt, *People on the Move: Attitudes Toward and Perceptions of Migration in Medieval and Modern Europe* (2003), p. 156.
38. P. Fitzgerald, 'A Sentence to Sail: The Transportation of Irish Convicts and Vagrants to America in the Eighteenth Century' in P. Fitzgerald and S. Ickringill (eds.), *Atlantic Crossroads: Historical Connections between Scotland, Ulster and North America* (Newtownards, 2001), pp. 115–17.
39. Daniels, *America*, p. 35.
40. P.W. Coldham, *Emigrants in Chains: A Social History of Forced Emigration to the Americas 1607–1776* (Stroud, 1992), pp. 1, 71, 79.
41. Richards, *Britannia's Children*, p. 85.
42. A. Roger Ekrich, *Bound for America: The Transportation of British Convicts to the Colonies, 1718–1775* (Oxford, 1987), pp. 100, 103.
43. Borrie, *Australasia*, tables 2.1–2.4, pp. 24–9.
44. O. Handlin, *The Uprooted: The Epic Story of the Great Migrations that Made the American People* (2nd edn., Boston, Mass., 1973), pp. 34–5.
45. For example, B. Thomas, *Migration and Economic Growth: A Study of Great Britain and the Atlantic Economy* (Cambridge, 1954); the citation is from M.L. Hansen, *The Atlantic Migration 1607–1860: A History of the Continuing Settlement of the United States* (Cambridge, Mass., 1940), p. 13.
46. N. Canny, 'English Migration Into and Across the Atlantic During the Seventeenth and Eighteenth Centuries', in N. Canny (ed.), *Europeans on the Move: Studies on European Migration, 1500–1800* (Oxford, 1994), p. 40.

47. Horn, 'Diaspora', p. 45.
48. M. McLean, *The People of Glengarry: Highlanders in Transition, 1745–1820* (Montreal, 1991), p. 80.
49. J. Prebble, *The Highland Clearances* (1963), pp. 248–50; Devine, *Scottish Nation*, pp. 468–9.
50. Bailyn, *Peopling*, pp. 12–14, 62–4; Bailyn, *Voyagers*, table 4.4, p. 111 and table 5.1, p. 128.
51. Horn, 'Diaspora', pp. 35–6.
52. Adams and M. Somerville, *Cargoes of Despair and Hope: Scottish Emigration to North America 1603–1803* (Edinburgh, 1993), pp. 35, 42–44.
53. C. Erickson, 'Emigration from the British Isles to the USA in 1831', *Population Studies* 35 (1981), pp. 186–8.
54. Devine, *Scottish Nation*, pp. 470–1.
55. Baines, *Migration*, pp. 279–81.
56. Haines, *Labouring Poor*, table 2.19, p. 70.
57. W.E. van Vugt, 'Running from Ruin? The Emigration of British Farmers to the USA in the Wake of the Repeal of the Corn Laws', *Economic History Review* 41 (1988), p. 418.
58. O.O. Winther, 'English Migration to the American West, 1865–1900', *The Huntington Library Quarterly* 27 (1964), p. 162.
59. D. Hollett, *Fast Passage to Australia: The History of the Black Ball, Eagle, and White Star Lines of Australian Packets* (1986), p. 12.
60. Bailyn, *Voyagers*, table 4.5, p. 115 and fig. 4.6, p. 123.
61. P. Taylor, *The Distant Magnet: European Emigration to the USA* (New York, 1971), pp. 145–6.
62. T. Coleman, *Passage to America: A History of Emigrants from Great Britain and Ireland to America in the Mid-Nineteenth Century* (1992), pp. 66–8.
63. K. Pescod, *Good Food, Bright Fires and Civility: British Emigrant Depots of the 19th Century* (Kew, Vic., 2003), p. 133.
64. R. Scally, 'Liverpool Ships and Irish Emigrants in the Age of Sail', *Journal of Social History* 17 (1983), p. 18.
65. O. MacDonagh, *A Pattern of Government Growth, 1800–1860: The Passenger Acts and Their Enforcement* (1961), p. 31.
66. B.D. Osborne, I. Quinn and D. Robertson, *Glasgow's River* (Glasgow, 1996), p. 51.
67. M. Brayshay, 'The Emigration Trade in Nineteenth Century Devon', in M. Duffy, S. Fisher, B. Greenhill, D. Starkey and J. Youings (eds.), *The New Maritime History of Devon, Vol. II: From the Late Eighteenth Century to the Present Day* (1994), p. 111.
68. B. Greenhill and A. Gifford, *Women under Sail* (1970), p. 125.
69. M. Prentis, 'Haggis on the High Seas: Shipboard Experiences of Scottish Emigrants to Australia, 1821–1897', *Australian Historical Studies* 36 (2004), p. 297.
70. P. Pennington, *William Wood's Diary: A Story of Nineteenth Century Emigration on Board the Sailing Ship 'Constance' in 1852* (Stansted, 2002), p. 84 (original author's italics).
71. E. Rushen, *Single and Free: Female Migration to Australia, 1833–1837* (Melbourne, 2003), p. 83.
72. E.C. Guillet, *The Great Migration: The Atlantic Crossing by Sailing Ship 1770–1860* (2nd edn., Toronto, 1963), p. 58.

73. N. Philbrick, *'Mayflower': A Voyage to War* (2006), p. 24.
74. Brayshay, 'Emigration Trade', pp. 111–12.
75. M.A. Jones, *Destination America* (1976), p. 26.
76. S. Fox, *The Ocean Railway: Isambard Kingdom Brunel, Samuel Cunard, and the Revolutionary World of the Great Atlantic Steamships* (2004 edn.), p. 10.
77. Coleman, *Passage*, p. 102.
78. Guillet, *Great Migration*, p. 66.
79. Greenhill and Gifford, *Women under Sail*, p. 126.
80. Rushen, *Single*, p. 83.
81. D. Hastings, *Over the Mountains of the Sea: Life on the Migrant Ships, 1870–1885* (Auckland, 2006), 74–5, 80–2.
82. Greenhill and Gifford, *Women under Sail*, p. 128.
83. Hastings, *Mountains*, p. 51.
84. Pennington, *Diary*, p. 90.
85. A. Hassam, *Sailing to Australia: Shipboard Diaries by Nineteenth-Century British Emigrants* (Manchester, 1994), pp. 75, 81.
86. *ibid.*, p. 105.
87. Guillet, *Great Migration*, p. 73.
88. H. Woolcock, *Rights of Passage: Emigration to Australia in the Nineteenth Century* (1986), p. 203.
89. S. Haines, *'No Trifling Matter': Being an Account of a Voyage by Emigrants from Sussex and Hampshire to Upper Canada on board the 'British Tar'* (Brighton, 1990), p. 26.
90. Fox, *Steamships*, p. 10.
91. Pennington, *Diary*, pp. 135, 147.
92. Prentis, 'Haggis', pp. 302–3.
93. M. Duffy, 'The Passage to the Colonies', *Mississippi Valley Historical Review* 38 (1951–52), pp. 23–4.
94. R. Haines, *Doctors at Sea: Emigrant Voyages to Colonial Australia* (Basingstoke, 2005), tables 3.2–3.3, pp. 44–5.
95. McLean, *Glengarry*, p. 87.
96. Coleman, *Passage*, p. 78.
97. M. Harper, 'Pains, Perils and Pastimes: Emigrant Voyages in the Nineteenth Century', in D. Killingray, M. Lincoln and N. Rigby (eds.), *Maritime Empires: British Imperial Maritime Trade in the Nineteenth Century* (Woodbridge, 2004), p. 167.
98. T.W. Page, 'The Transportation of Immigrants and Reception Arrangements in the Nineteenth Century', *Journal of Political Economy* 19 (1911), p. 741.
99. Most explicitly, cf. MacDonagh, *Pattern*, pp. 134–8, 144–5, 341.
100. P. Dunkley, 'Emigration and the State, 1803–1842: The Nineteenth-Century Revolution in Government Reconsidered', *Historical Journal* 23 (1980), pp. 357–8.
101. Eltis, 'Comparisons', p. 270.
102. Pescod, *Depots*, p. 140.
103. Haines, *Doctors at Sea*, pp. 8–9, 178–9.
104. R. Haines, *Life and Death in the Age of Sail: The Passage to Australia* (Sydney, 2003), pp. 46, 48.
105. *ibid.*, pp. 59, 70.
106. Page, 'Transportation', p. 737.
107. Fox, *Ocean Railway*, pp. 73–9.

108. S. Dugan, *Men of Iron: Brunel, Stephenson and the Inventions That Shaped the Modern World* (2003), pp. 81–7.

109. R.L. Cohn, 'The Transition from Sail to Steam in Immigration to the United States', *Journal of Economic History* 65 (2005), table 1, p. 472 and pp. 487–93.

110. R. Woodman, *The History of the Ship: The Comprehensive Story of Seafaring* (2005 edn.), pp. 228–9.

111. Taylor, *Distant Magnet*, p. 150.

112. Jones, *Destination America*, p. 44.

113. Woolcock, *Rights of Passage*, p. 180.

114. A. Hassam, *'Our Floating Home': Social Space and Group Identity on Board the Emigrant Ship* (1992), p. 1.

115. Hassam, *Sailing to Australia*, pp. 115, 120.

116. Hassam, *Social Space*, p. 5.

117. Prentis, 'Haggis', p. 305.

118. Haines, *'No Trifling Matter'*, p. 19.

119. Pennington, *Diary*, pp. 119, 128.

120. Hassam, *Social Space*, p. 76.

121. Prentis, 'Haggis', p. 308.

122. Guillet, *Great Migration*, p. 71.

123. Philbrick, *Mayflower*, pp. 30–1.

124. Cressy, 'Ocean', p. 524.

125. Jones, *Destination America*, p. 29.

126. J. Gothard, *Blue China: Single Female Migration to Colonial Australia* (Carlton South, Vic., 2001), p. 111.

127. Pennington, *Diary*, p. 153.

128. Hassam, *Sailing to Australia*, p. 81.

129. R.S. Kranidis, *The Victorian Spinster and Colonial Emigration: Contested Subjects* (Basingstoke, 1999), p. 134.

130. J.C. Myers, 'Performing the Voyage Out: Victorian Female Emigration and the Class Dynamics of Displacement', *Victorian Literature and Culture* 29 (2001), p. 130.

131. L. Chilton, *Agents of Empire: British Female Migration to Canada and Australia, 1860–1930* (Toronto, 2007), p. 54.

132. S. Maenpaa, 'Women Below Deck: Gender and Employment on British Passenger Liners, 1860–1938', *Journal of Transport History* 25 (2004), p. 61.

133. Hastings, *Mountains*, pp. 56–7.

134. S. Constantine, 'British Emigration to the Empire-Commonwealth since 1880: From Overseas Settlement to Diaspora', *Journal of Imperial and Commonwealth History* 31 (2003), p. 16.

135. A contemporary belief explained by, for example, D.S. King, *Making Americans: Immigration, Race, and the Origins of the Diverse Democracy* (Cambridge, Mass., 2000), p. 13, and recently critiqued in A. Behdad, *A Forgetful Nation: On Immigration and Cultural Identity in the United States* (Durham, NC, 2005).

136. J. Harland-Jacobs, ' "Hands across the Sea": The Masonic Network, British Imperialism, and the North Atlantic World', *Geographical Review* 89 (1999), p. 237.

137. Games, 'Migration', p. 32.

138. Cressy, *Coming Over*, p. 74.

139. Pennington, *Diary*, p. 77.

6   Warriors

1. G. Moorhouse, *Great Harry's Navy: How Henry VIII Gave England Seapower* (2005), pp. 11–12.
2. C. Ernest Fayle, *A Short History of the World's Shipping Industry* (1933), pp. 145–7.
3. N.A.M. Rodger, 'Queen Elizabeth and the Myth of Sea Power in English History',Transactions of the Royal Historical Society 14 (2004), pp. 157–8.
4. D.A. Baugh, 'Maritime Strength and Atlantic Commerce: The Uses of a "Grand Marine Empire"', in L. Stone (ed.), *An Imperial State at War: Britain 1689–1815* (1994), p. 189.
5. E. Milford, 'The Navy at Peace: The Activities of the Early Jacobean Navy, 1603–1618', *Mariner's Mirror* 26 (1990), esp. pp. 29–32.
6. Hebb, *Piracy and the English Government*, p. 234.
7. D. Loades, *England's Maritime Empire: Seapower, Commerce and Policy, 1490–1690* (2000), p. 167; J.D. Davies, 'The Birth of the Imperial Navy? Aspects of Maritime Strategy, c.1650–90', in M. Duffy (ed.), *Parameters of British Naval Power, 1650–1850* (Exeter, 1992), table 1, p. 15.
8. See H.W. Richmond, *The Navy as an Instrument of Policy 1558–1727* (Cambridge, 1953), pp. 95–6, 101, for the political motives behind the First Dutch War; on the economic motives see J. Israel, 'England's Mercantilist Response to Dutch World Trade Primacy, 1647–1674', in S. Groenveld and M. Wintle (eds.), *Britain and the Netherlands X: State and Trade* (Zutphen, 1992), esp. pp. 51–2, 54, 58.
9. R. Harding, *Seapower and Naval Warfare 1650–1830* (1999), pp. 41–2.
10. N.A.M. Rodger, *The Command of the Ocean: A Naval History of Britain, Vol. II: 1649–1815* (Harmondsworth, 2006 pbk. edn.), pp. 76–7.
11. P. Hore, *The Habit of Victory: The Story of the Royal Navy 1545 to 1945* (2005), p. 34.
12. G.E. Aylmer, 'Navy, State, Trade and Empire', in N. Canny (ed.), *The Oxford History of the British Empire, Vol. I: The Origins of Empire* (Oxford, 1998), pp. 468–9.
13. D.A. Baugh, 'Great Britain's "Blue Water" Policy, 1689–1815', *International History Review* 10 (1988), p. 37.
14. J.S. Wheeler, 'Prelude to Power: The Crisis of 1649 and the Foundation of English Naval Power', *Mariner's Mirror* 81 (1995), pp. 148–55; R. Harding, *The Evolution of the Sailing Navy, 1509–1815* (Basingstoke, 1995), pp. 69–70.
15. J.D. Davies, *Gentlemen and Tarpaulins: The Officers and Men of the Restoration Navy* (Oxford, 1991), p. 10.
16. J. Ehrman, *The Navy in the War of William III, 1689–1697: Its State and Direction* (Cambridge, 1953), pp. 350–1; Rodger, *Command*, pp. 145–6.
17. J.B. Hattendorf, 'The Struggle with France, 1690–1815', in Hill (ed.), *Illustrated History*, pp. 85–7.
18. D. French, *The British Way in Warfare 1688–2000* (2000), p. 32.
19. N. Tracy, *Navies, Deterrence and American Independence: Britain and Seapower in the 1760s and 1770s* (Vancouver, 1988), p. 2.
20. M.A. Palmer, *Command at Sea: Naval Command and Control since the Sixteenth Century* (2005), pp. 75–8.
21. P. Kennedy, *The Rise and Fall of British Naval Power* (Harmondsworth, 2004 pbk. edn.), pp. 72–88.

22. J. Black, 'Anglo–Baltic Relations 1714–1748', in W.E. Minchinton (ed.), *Britain and the Northern Seas* (Pontefract, 1988), pp. 67–71.

23. F. McLynn, *1759: The Year Britain Became Master of the World* (2005 pbk. edn.), pp. 354–87.

24. Baugh, ' "Blue Water" Policy', pp. 34–5, 43.

25. Baugh, 'Maritime Strength', p. 195.

26. Harding, *Evolution*, p. 117.

27. P. Woodfine, 'Ideas of Naval Power and the Conflict with Spain, 1737–1742', in J. Black and P. Woodfine (eds.), *The British Navy and the Use of Naval Power in the Eighteenth Century* (Leicester, 1988), p. 71.

28. G.S. Graham, *The Politics of Naval Supremacy: Studies in British Maritime Ascendancy* (Cambridge, 1965), p. 16.

29. The literature on Trafalgar is voluminous, but recent accessible texts include R. Adkins, *Trafalgar: The Biography of a Battle* (2005); N. Best, *Trafalgar: The Untold Story of the Greatest Sea Battle in History* (2005); T. Clayton and P. Craig, *Trafalgar: The Men, the Battle, the Storm* (2004); A. Nicolson, *Men of Honour: Trafalgar and the Making of the English Hero* (2005).

30. E. Ingram, 'Illusions of Victory: The Nile, Copenhagen and Trafalgar Revisited', *Military Affairs* 48 (1984), p. 140; E. Ingram, 'The Failure of British Sea Power in the War of the Second Coalition, 1798–1801', in E. Ingram (ed.), *In Defence of British India: Great Britain in the Middle East, 1775–1842* (1984), esp. pp. 68–9.

31. N. Mostert, *The Line Upon a Wind: An Intimate History of the Last and Greatest War Fought at Sea under Sail* (2007), p. 514.

32. G.S. Graham, *Empire of the North Atlantic: The Maritime Struggle for North America* (2nd edn., 1958), p. 196.

33. Hore, *Habit of Victory*, pp. 107–10.

34. D.A. Baugh, 'The Politics of British Naval Failure, 1775–1778', *American Neptune* 52 (1992), pp. 222–4; D.A. Baugh, 'Why Did Britain Lose Control of the Sea during the War for America?' in Black and Woodfine (eds.), *British Navy*, pp. 159–61.

35. J. Ferling, *'Almost a Miracle': The American Victory in the War of Independence* (Oxford, 2007), pp. 368–9.

36. D. Syrett, 'Home Waters or America? The Dilemma of British Naval Strategy in 1778', *Mariner's Mirror* 77 (1991), pp. 365–7.

37. D. Syrett, *The Royal Navy in American Waters 1775–1783* (Aldershot, 1989), p. 31.

38. Ferling, *'Almost a Miracle'*, pp. 361–4.

39. J.A. Tilley, *The British Navy and the American Revolution* (Columbia, SC, 1987), pp. 119–21.

40. D. Syrett, 'The Failure of the British Effort in North America, 1777', in Black and Woodfine (eds.), *British Navy*, pp. 173–5.

41. D. Syrett, 'The Methodology of British Amphibious Operations during the Seven Years' and American Wars', *Mariner's Mirror* 58 (1972), pp. 269–80.

42. M. Duffy, ' "Science and Labour": The Naval Contribution to Operations Ashore in the Great Wars with France', in P. Hore (ed.), *Seapower Ashore: 200 Years of Royal Navy Operations on Land* (2001), pp. 40–2.

43. C.D. Hall, 'The Royal Navy and the Peninsular War', *Mariner's Mirror* 79 (1993), pp. 409–17.

44. C.J. Fedorak, 'The Royal Navy and British Amphibious Operations during the Revolutionary and Napoleonic Wars', *Military Affairs* 52 (1988), p. 145.

45. A.W.H. Pearsall, 'The Royal Navy and Trade Protection 1688–1714', *Renaissance and Modern Studies* 30 (1986), pp. 113–23.

46. D. Syrett, 'The Organisation of British Trade Convoys during the American War, 1776–83', *Mariner's Mirror* 62 (1976), pp. 171–5.

47. N.A.M. Rodger, *The Safeguard of the Sea: A Naval History of Britain, Vol. I: 660–1649* (Harmondsworth, 2004 pbk. edn), pp. 228–9, 379–84.

48. A. Thrush, 'Naval Finance and the Origins and Development of Ship Money', in M.C. Fissel (ed.), *War and Government in Britain 1598–1650* (Manchester, 1991), pp. 135–7.

49. J.G. Coad, *The Royal Dockyards 1690–1850: Architecture and Engineering Works of the Sailing Navy* (Aldershot, 1989), p. 3; D.C. Coleman, 'Naval Dockyards under the Later Stuarts', *Economic History Review* 6 (1953–54), p. 140.

50. Ehrman, *William III*, p. 71.

51. Cf. S. Conway, *War, State and Society in Mid-Eighteenth Century Britain and Ireland* (Oxford, 2006), pp. 112–13.

52. B. Lavery, 'The Rebuilding of British Warships, 1690–1740: Part I', *Mariner's Mirror* 66 (1980), pp. 5–14.

53. R. Morriss, *The Royal Dockyards during the Revolutionary and Napoleonic Wars* (Leicester, 1983), pp. 13–14.

54. Morriss, *Naval Power and British Culture*, pp. 152–60.

55. R.G. Albion, *Forests and Sea Power: The Timber Problem of the Royal Navy, 1652–1862* (Cambridge, Mass., 1926), pp. 9, 29.

56. R.J.B. Knight, 'New England Forests and British Seapower: Albion Revisited', *American Neptune* 46 (1986), pp. 222–5; J.J. Malone, 'England and the Baltic Naval Stores Trade in the Seventeenth and Eighteenth Centuries', *Mariner's Mirror* 58 (1972), esp. pp. 383–5, 389–90.

57. Ehrman, *William III*, p. 39.

58. J. Brewer, *The Sinews of Power: War, Money and the English State 1688–1783* (1989), p. 34.

59. Ehrman, *William III*, p. 60.

60. Brewer, *Sinews*, p. 31.

61. K. Wilson, 'Empire, Trade and Popular Politics in Mid-Hanoverian Britain: The Case of Admiral Vernon', *Past and Present* 121 (1988), p. 81.

62. S. Conway, '"A Joy Unknown for Years Past": The American War, Britishness and the Celebration of Rodney's Victory at the Saints', *History* 86 (2001), p. 183.

63. M. Paris, *Warrior Nation: Images of War in British Popular Culture, 1850–2000* (2000), p. 18.

64. Jenks, *Naval Engagements*, pp. 194–200, 219–23.

65. T. Clayton, *Tars: The Men Who Made Britain Rule the Waves* (2007), p. 16.

66. Lincoln, *Representing*, pp. 141–2.

67. D. Cordingly, *Heroines and Harlots: Women at Sea in the Great Age of Sail* (2001), p. 78.

68. M. Lacy, *The Female Shipwright: or, the Life and Extraordinary Adventures of Mary Lacy, Written by Herself* (orig. pub. 1773; New York edn., 1807), pp. 7, 9.

69. P. Guillery, 'The Further Adventures of Mary Lacy: "Seaman", Shipwright, Builder', *History Workshop Journal* 49 (2000), pp. 213–14.

70. Lincoln, *Representing*, p. 24.

71. F. Crouzet, 'The Second Hundred Years War: Some Reflections', *French History* 10 (1996), p. 444.

72. B. Lavery (ed.), *The Line of Battle: Sailing Warships, 1650–1840* (1994), p. 11.

73. J.S. Bromley, 'The Second Hundred Years War', in J.S. Bromley (ed.), *Corsairs and Navies 1660–1760* (1987), pp. 495–6.

74. M. Adams, *Admiral Collingwood: Nelson's Own Hero* (2005), p. 147.

75. E. Grove, *The Royal Navy since 1815* (Basingstoke, 2005), p. 13.

76. N. Miller, *Broadsides: The Age of Fighting Sail, 1775–1815* (Chichester, 2000), pp. 93–4.

77. J. Sugden, *Nelson: A Dream of Glory* (2005 pbk. edn.), p. 562.

78. R. Knight, *The Pursuit of Victory: The Life and Achievement of Horatio Nelson* (2005), pp. 222–7.

79. Adams, *Collingwood*, pp. 149–50.

80. J. Masefield, *Sea Life in Nelson's Time* (1905), p. 157.

81. M. Lincoln, 'Mutinous Behaviour on Voyages to the South Seas and Its Impact on Eighteenth Century Civil Society', *Eighteenth Century Life* 31 (2007), p. 73.

82. D. Pope, *Life in Nelson's Navy* (1981), p. 221.

83. G. Dening, *Mr Bligh's Bad Language: Passion, Power and Theatre on the Bounty* (Cambridge, 1992), pp. 63–5.

84. W. Richardson, *A Mariner of England: An Account of the Career of William Richardson* (2000 edn.), pp. 292–3.

85. W.R. Nester, *The Great Frontier War: Britain, France, and the Imperial struggle for North America, 1607–1755* (2000), p. 135.

86. I. Land, 'Customs of the Sea: Flogging, Empire, and the "True British Seaman"', *Interventions: An International Journal of Post-Colonial Studies* 3 (2001), p. 175.

87. M. Eder, *Crime and Punishment in the Royal Navy of the Seven Years War, 1755–1763* (Aldershot, 2004), p. 41.

88. B. Capp, *Cromwell's Navy: The Fleet and the English Revolution 1648–1660* (Oxford, 1989), p. 57.

89. Davies, *Gentlemen*, p. 45.

90. Eder, *Crime and Punishment*, p. 45.

91. N.A.M. Rodger, *The Wooden World: An Anatomy of the Georgian Navy* (1986), pp. 205–6.

92. Pope, *Nelson's Navy*, p. 220.

93. C. Alexander, *The Bounty: The True Story of the Mutiny on the Bounty* (2004 pbk. edn.), p. 120.

94. A.N. Gilbert, 'The Changing Face of British Military Justice, 1757–83', *Military Affairs* 49 (1985), table III, p. 82.

95. D.A. Baugh, *British Naval Administration in the Age of Walpole* (Princeton, NJ, 1965), p. 166.

96. Lincoln, *Representing*, p. 14.

97. B. Greenhill and A. Giffard, *Steam, Politics and Patronage: The Transformation of the Royal Navy 1815–54* (1994), pp. 78–9.

98. J.S. Bromley, 'Away from Impressment: The Idea of a Royal Navy Reserve, 1696–1859', in A.C. Duke and C.A. Tamse (eds.), *Britain and the Netherlands VI: War and Society* (The Hague, 1977), pp. 172–6.

99. Greenhill and Giffard, *Politics and Patronage*, p. 60.

100. Davies, *Gentlemen*, pp. 17, 24–5.

101. N.A.M. Rodger, 'Devon Men and the Navy, 1688–1815', in M. Duffy, et al. (eds.), *The New Maritime History of Devon, Vol. I* (1992), pp. 210–12.

102. N.A.M. Rodger, ' "A Little Navy of Your Own Making": Admiral Boscawen and the Cornish Connection in the Royal Navy', in Duffy, *Parameters*, p. 89.

103. Greenhill and Giffard, *Politics and Patronage*, p. 77.

104. D. Howarth and S. Howarth, *Nelson: The Immortal Memory* (2004), p. 353.

105. Lincoln, *Representing*, p. 26.

106. E.L. Rasor, *Reform in the Royal Navy: A Social History of the Lower Deck, 1850–1880* (Hamden, Conn., 1976), pp. 42–55; for an American perspective on the contemporary anti-flogging campaign see M.C. Glenn, 'The Naval Reform Campaign Against Flogging, 1830–1850', *American Quarterly* 35 (1983), pp. 408–25.

107. Eder, *Crime and Punishment*, p. 64.

108. Rodger, *Wooden World*, p. 209.

109. Adams, *Collingwood*, p. 155.

110. C.J. Bartlett, *Great Britain and Sea Power, 1815–1853* (Oxford, 1963), pp. 13–14.

111. Grove, *Royal Navy*, pp. 30–1.

112. A. Herman, *To Rule the Waves: How the British Navy Shaped the Modern World* (2004), pp. 452–31.

113. J.F. Beeler, *British Naval Policy in the Gladstone-Disraeli Era* (Stanford, Cal., 1997), pp. 10–11.

114. P. Kennedy, 'Mahan versus Mackinder: Two Interpretations of British Sea Power', in P Kennedy (ed.), *Strategy and Diplomacy, 1870–1945: Eight Studies* (1983), pp. 46–8.

115. A. Lambert, 'The Shield of Empire, 1815–1895', in Hill (ed.), *Illustrated History*, p. 162.

116. J. Black, *The British Seaborne Empire* (2004), pp. 241–2; French, *Warfare*, p. 152.

117. R.K. Massie, *Dreadnought: Britain, Germany and the Coming of the Great War* (1992), pp. 180–1.

118. A.J. Marder, *From the Dreadnought to Scapa Flow: The Royal Navy in the Fisher era, 1904–1919* (Vol. 1, 1961), p. 9.

119. Beeler, *British Naval Policy*, pp. 18–19.

120. *ibid.*, p. 34.

121. P. Haggie, 'The Royal Navy and War Planning in the Fisher Era', *Journal of Contemporary History* 8 (1973), esp. p. 119.

122. A. Lambert, 'Strategic Command and Control for Manoeuvre Warfare: Creation of the Royal Navy's "War Room" System, 1905–1915', *Journal of Military History* 69 (2005), esp. pp. 376–83, 393.

123. French, *Warfare*, p. 165.

124. A.D. Harvey, *Collision of Empires: Britain in Three World Wars 1793–1945* (1992), p. 248.

125. Rüger, *Great Naval Game*, esp. pp. 217, 219.

126. N. Ferguson, *The Pity of War* (1998), pp. 71–2 and table 8, p. 85.

127. P.P. O'Brien, 'The Titan Refreshed: Imperial Overstretch and the British Navy Before the First World War', *Past and Present* 172 (2001), p. 160.

128. N. Ferguson, 'Public Finance and National Security: The Domestic Origins of the First World War Revisited', *Past and Present* 142 (1994), table 2, p. 154.

129. P. Clarke, *Hope and Glory: Britain 1900–1990* (Harmondsworth, 1997 pbk. edn.), pp. 56–7.

130. T. Zuber, 'The German Intelligence Estimates in the West, 1885–1914', *Intelligence and National Security* 21 (2006), p. 188.
131. D. Ormrod, *The Rise of Commercial Empires: England and the Netherlands in the Age of Mercantilism, 1650–1770* (Cambridge, 2003), pp. 273–84, 336–9, 350.
132. H.J. Newbolt, *Sea-Life in English Literature from the Fourteenth to the Nineteenth Century* (1925), p. vii.
133. G. Callender and F.H. Hinsley, *The Naval Side of British History* (1952 edn., 1924 orig. pub.), p. vi.
134. Graham, *Naval Supremacy*, p. 1.
135. S. Conway, *The British Isles and the War of American Independence* (Oxford, 2000), p. 186.
136. Davies, *Gentlemen*, p. 15.
137. Samuel, *Patriotism*, Vol. I, p. 49.
138. A. Law, 'Of Navies and Navels: Britain as A Mental Island', *Geografiska Annaler, Series B: Human Geography* 87 (2005), p. 270.
139. Lincoln, *Representing*, p. 7.
140. D. Armitage, *The Ideological Origins of the British Empire* (Cambridge, 2000), pp. 100–1, 124.

7 Victories?

1. G.R. Searle, *A New England? Peace and War, 1886–1918* (Oxford, 2004), p. 617.
2. D. Stevenson, *1914–1918: The History of the First World War* (Harmondsworth, 2005 pbk. edn.), p. 81.
3. A.D. Harvey, *Collision of Empires: Britain in Three World Wars* (1994 pbk. edn.), p. 281.
4. B.M. Gough, 'Maritime Strategy: The Legacies of Mahan and Corbett as Philosophers of Sea Power', *The RUSI Journal* 133 (1988), pp. 56–60.
5. Massie, *Dreadnought*, pp. 883–4.
6. R. Hough, *Former Naval Person: Churchill and the Wars at Sea* (1985), pp. 78–84.
7. E.J. Grove, *The Royal Navy since 1815: A New Short History* (Basingstoke, 2005), p. 115.
8. Herman, *To Rule the Waves*, p. 498.
9. R.F. Mackay, *Fisher of Kilverstone* (Oxford, 1973), pp. 482–7, 496–500.
10. J. Morris, *Fisher's Face* (2007 pbk. edn.), pp. 218–19.
11. M.D. Pugh, 'Asquith, Bonar Law and the First Coalition', *Historical Journal* 17 (1974), pp. 831–4.
12. J. Macleod, *Reconsidering Gallipoli* (Manchester, 2004), pp. 13, 23.
13. W. Churchill, *The World Crisis, 1911–1918* (Cambridge, 2005 pbk. edn.), p. 412.
14. E.J. Erickson, 'One More Push: Forcing the Dardanelles in March 1915', *Journal of Strategic Studies* 24 (2001), esp. pp. 169–75.
15. Herman, *To Rule the Waves*, pp. 503–6.
16. A. Gordon, *The Rules of the Game: Jutland and British Naval Command* (2005 pbk. edn.), pp. 449–63.
17. R.K. Massie, *Castles of Steel: Britain, Germany and the Winning of the Great War at Sea* (2005 pbk edn.), pp. 636–7.
18. Grove, *Royal Navy*, p. 126.

19. Massie, *Castles of Steel*, pp. 641, 648–50.
20. J.T. Sumida, 'British Capital Ship Design and Fire Control in the Dreadnought Era: Sir John Fisher, Arthur Hungerford Pollen, and the Battle Cruiser', *Journal of Modern History* 51 (1979), pp. 228–9.
21. N.A. Lambert, ' "Our Bloody Ships" or "Our Bloody System"? Jutland and the Loss of the Battle Cruisers, 1916', *Journal of Military History* 62 (1998), pp. 36–9, 52–5.
22. J.T. Sumida, 'Sir John Fisher and the Dreadnought: The Sources of Naval Mythology', *Journal of Military History* 59 (1995), pp. 625–6.
23. C. Barnett, *Engage the Enemy More Closely: The Royal Navy in the Second World War* (1991), p. 5.
24. Searle, *New England*, p. 689.
25. A. Lambert, *Admirals: The Naval Commanders Who Made Britain Great* (2008), pp. 373–5.
26. Gordon, *Rules*, pp. 508–10.
27. G. Bennett, *Naval Battles of the First World War* (Harmondsworth, 2001 pbk. edn.), p. 226.
28. Kennedy, *Rise and Fall*, p. 246.
29. Massie, *Castles of Steel*, pp. 682–4, 783–4.
30. See M. Ejrnæs, K.G. Persson and S. Rich, 'Feeding the British: Convergence and Market Efficiency in the Nineteenth-Century Grain Trade', *Economic History Review* 61 (2008), fig. 3, p. 146.
31. S. Broadberry and P. Howlett, 'The United Kingdom During World War I: Business as Usual?', in S.N. Broadberry and M. Harrison (eds.), *The Economics of World War I* (Cambridge, 2005), pp. 224–6.
32. A. Hurd, *A Merchant Fleet at War* (1920), p. 55.
33. R.M. MacLeod and E. Kay Andrews, 'Scientific Advice in the War at Sea, 1915–1917: The Board of Invention and Research', *Journal of Contemporary History* 6 (1971), p. 18.
34. A. Marder, 'The Influence of History on Sea Power: The Royal Navy and the Lessons of 1914–1918', *Pacific Historical Review* 41 (1972), p. 429.
35. J. Thompson, *Imperial War Museum Book of the War at Sea 1914–18* (2005), p. 192.
36. M.S. Neiberg, *Fighting the Great War: A Global History* (Cambridge, Mass., 2005), pp. 132–4.
37. Thompson, *War at Sea*, p. 196.
38. Stevenson, *First World War*, p. 257.
39. Hough, *Great War*, p. 301.
40. Stevenson, *First World War*, pp. 261, 321.
41. A.J. Marder, *From the Dreadnought to Scapa Flow, Vol. IV: 1917, Year of Crisis* (Oxford, 1969), p. 104.
42. P.G. Halpern, *A Naval History of World War I* (1994), p. 341.
43. Thompson, *War at Sea*, p. 326; Hough, *Great War*, p. 302.
44. J. Goldrick, 'The Battleship Fleet: The Test of War, 1895–1919', in Hill (ed.), *Illustrated History*, p. 311.
45. Marder, *Scapa Flow*, Vol. IV, p. 105.
46. J.T. Sumida, 'British Naval Operational Logistics, 1914–1918', *Journal of Military History* 57 (1993), p. 470.
47. T. Lane, 'The British Merchant Seaman at War', in H. Cecil and P.H. Liddle (eds.), *Facing Armageddon: The First World War Experienced* (1996), pp. 146–7.

48. R. Woodman, *The History of the Ship* (2005 edn.), p. 343.
49. Thompson, *War at Sea*, p. 328.
50. Marder, *Scapa Flow*, Vol. IV, pp. 118–19, 138, 140.
51. Barnett, *Enemy*, p. 9.
52. Hough, *Great War*, pp. 306–7.
53. Marder, *Scapa Flow*, Vol. IV, pp. 155–62.
54. Halpern, *Naval History*, p. 360.
55. Herman, *To Rule the Waves*, p. 513.
56. Marder, *Scapa Flow*, Vol. IV, p. 278.
57. Thompson, *War at Sea*, p. 330.
58. S.O. Rose, 'Sex, Citizenship, and the Nation in World War II Britain', *American Historical Review* 103 (1998), p. 1160.
59. H. Sebag-Montefiore, *Dunkirk: Fight to the Last Man* (Harmondsworth, 2007 pbk. edn.), p. 380.
60. Thompson, *Second World War*, p. 39.
61. Grove, 'A Service Vindicated, 1939–46', in Hill (ed.), *Illustrated History*, p. 353.
62. G.G. Connell, *Jack's War: Lower-Deck Recollections from World War II* (Bristol, rev. edn., 1995), pp. 65–6.
63. A. Gordon, 'Battle of Britain: The Naval Perspective: The Whale and the Elephant', *RUSI Journal Online*, http://www.rusi.org/research/militarysciences/history/commentary/, accessed 17 July 2008.
64. C. Goulter, A. Gordon and G. Sheffield, 'The Royal Navy Did Not Win the "Battle of Britain", But We Need a Holistic View of Britain's Defences in 1940', *The RUSI Journal* 151 (2006), p. 67.
65. B. James, 'Pie in the Sky?', *History Today* 56 (September 2006), p. 38.
66. J. Thompson, *The Imperial War Museum Book of the War At Sea: The Royal Navy in the Second World War* (1996), pp. 24–9.
67. Grove, 'Service Vindicated', p. 351.
68. A. Coles and T. Briggs, *Flagship Hood: The Fate of Britain's Mightiest Warship* (1985), pp. 215–16, 221.
69. P.C. Smith, *The Great Ships Pass: British Battleships at War 1939–1945* (1977), pp. 216–21.
70. R. Harrington, ' "The Mighty Hood": Navy, Empire, War at Sea and the British National Imagination, 1920–60', *Journal of Contemporary History* 38 (2003), pp. 172–4, 182.
71. For this theatre in general see most recently S. Ball, *The Bitter Sea: The Struggle for Mastery in the Mediterranean 1935–1949* (2009).
72. N.J.W. Goda, 'The Riddle of the Rock: A Reassessment of German Motives for the Capture of Gibraltar in the Second World War', *Journal of Contemporary History*, 28 (1993), pp. 303–6.
73. Herman, *To Rule the Waves*, p. 532.
74. Grove, 'Service Vindicated', p. 359.
75. A. Clark, *The Fall of Crete* (1962), pp. 168–73; D. Macintyre, *The Naval War Against Hitler* (1971), pp. 153–5.
76. P.K. Kemp, *Victory at Sea, 1939–1945* (1976 edn.), p. 192.
77. *ibid.*, p. 194.
78. J. Winton (ed.), *The War at Sea, 1939–1945: An Anthology of Personal Experience* (1994 edn.), pp. 221–5.
79. Barnett, *Enemy*, p. 503.
80. Macintyre, *Naval War*, pp. 177–8.

81. Barnett, *Enemy*, pp. 505–15.
82. P.C. Smith, *Pedestal: The Malta Convoy of August 1942* (2nd edn., 1987), pp. 53–6.
83. *ibid.*, pp. 172–98.
84. Barnett, *Enemy*, pp. 518–19, 523.
85. J. Holland, *Fortress Malta: An Island Under Siege* (2004 pbk. edn.), pp. 367–9.
86. Well summed up in G. Kennedy, 'Sea Denial, Interdiction and Diplomacy: The Royal Navy and the Role of Malta, 1939–43', in I. Spellar (ed.), *The Royal Navy and Maritime Power in the Twentieth Century* (2005), pp. 62–3.
87. For this view see M. Carver, *El Alamein* (2000 edn.), p. 180; P. Collier and D.M. Horner, *The Second World War: The Mediterranean 1940–1945* (2003), p. 41.
88. Smith, *Pedestal*, p. 224.
89. L.A. Rose, *Power at Sea, Vol. II: The Breaking Storm, 1919–1945* (Columbia, Mo., 2007), pp. 323–6.
90. S.W. Roskill, *The War at Sea, 1939–1945* (Vol. III, Part II, 1961), pp. 43, 45, 47.
91. C.J. Bruce, *Invaders: British and American Experience of Seaborne Landings, 1939–1945* (1997), p. 153.
92. M. Hastings, *Overlord: D-Day and the Battle for Normandy* (1989 rev. edn.), p. 80.
93. Bruce, *Invaders*, pp. 142, 169–70.
94. A. Jackson, *The British Empire and the Second World War* (2006), p. 293.
95. L.A. Rose, *Power at Sea, Vol. III: A Violent Peace, 1946–2006* (Columbia, Mo., 2007), p. 4.
96. M. Hastings, *Nemesis: The Battle for Japan 1944–45* (2007), pp. 434–6.
97. Smith, *Great Ships*, p. 82.
98. D.A. Rayner, *Escort: The Battle of the Atlantic* (1955), pp. 156–7.
99. D. Kahn, 'Codebreaking in World Wars I and II: The Major Successes and Failures, Their Causes and Their Effects', *Historical Journal* 23 (1980), p. 624.
100. Connell, *Jack's War*, pp. 56–7.
101. C. Whitham, 'On Dealing with Gangsters: The Limits of British "Generosity" in the Leasing of Bases to the United States, 1940–41', *Diplomacy and Statecraft* 7 (1996), pp. 589–630.
102. Barnett, *Enemy*, p. 184.
103. Connell, *Jack's War*, pp. 76–7.
104. A. Williams, *The Battle of the Atlantic* (2002), p. 60.
105. Barnett, *Enemy*, p. 266.
106. M. Schoenfeld, 'Winston Churchill as War Manager: The Battle of the Atlantic Committee, 1941', *Military Affairs* 52 (1988), p. 122.
107. Barnett, *Enemy*, p. 259, 263.
108. M. Milner, 'From Nelsonic to Newtonian: The Development of Anti-Submarine Warfare in the North Atlantic, 1939–45', *Mariner's Mirror* 92 (2006), esp. pp. 466–7.
109. D. Macintyre, *The Battle of the Atlantic* (2006 pbk. edn.), pp. 77–8.
110. Barnett, *Enemy*, p. 267.
111. Schoenfeld, 'Manager', pp. 124–6.
112. Barnett, *Enemy*, p. 269.
113. R. Lewin, *Ultra Goes to War* (1988 pbk. edn.), pp. 44–50.

114. W.J.R. Gardner, *Decoding History: The Battle of the Atlantic and Ultra* (Basingstoke, 1999), p. 15; see fig. 7.3, p. 143 for 1943 figures on decrypts read within 48 hours.

115. J. Terraine, *Business in Great Waters: The U-Boat Wars, 1916–1945* (1989), appendix D, p. 768.

116. S. Harper, *Capturing Enigma: How HMS Petard Seized the German Naval Codes* (Stroud, 2002), pp. 60–2, 76–7.

117. Terraine, *Great Waters*, pp. 529–31, 547–50.

118. L.E. Davis and S.L. Engerman, *Naval Blockades in Peace and War: An Economic History since 1750* (Cambridge, 2006), p. 281.

119. Kahn, 'Codebreaking', p. 625.

120. Terraine, *Great Waters*, appendix D, p. 768.

121. D. Redford, 'The March 1943 Crisis in the Battle of the Atlantic: Myth and Reality', *History* 95 (2007), pp. 67–8.

122. Gardner, *Decoding History*, p. 35.

123. Barnett, *Enemy*, p. 575.

124. A.G. Jamieson, *Ebb Tide in the British Maritime Industries: Change and Adaptation 1918–1990* (Exeter, 2003), p. 22.

125. A. Burton, *The Rise and Fall of British Shipbuilding* (1994), p. 200.

126. Barnett, *Enemy*, pp. 276, 600.

127. R. Goette, 'Britain and the Delay in Closing the Mid-Atlantic "Air Gap" During the Battle of the Atlantic', *Northern Mariner* 15 (2005), pp. 19–41.

128. Macintyre, *Atlantic*, pp. 71–3.

129. H. Guerlac and M. Boas, 'The Radar War Against the U-Boat', *Military Affairs* 14 (1950), p. 103.

130. J. Buckley, 'Air Power and the Battle of the Atlantic 1939–45', *Journal of Contemporary History* 28 (1993), pp. 146–56.

131. D. Syrett, *The Defeat of the German U-Boats: The Battle of the Atlantic* (Columbia, SC, 1994), p. 11.

132. Barnett, *Enemy*, pp. 603, 610–12.

133. For the post-war consequences of these debts see H. Mackenzie, 'Justice Denied: The Anglo-American Loan Negotiations of 1945', *Canadian Review of American Studies* 26 (1999), pp. 79–110.

134. J. Baylis and S. Marsh, 'The Anglo-American "Special Relationship": The Lazarus of International Relations', *Diplomacy and Statecraft* 17 (2006), p. 176.

135. Herman, *To Rule the Waves*, p. 548.

136. Jamieson, *Ebb Tide*, table 2.1, p. 12.

137. Kennedy, *Rise and Fall*, p. 314.

138. C. Barnett, *The Collapse of British Power* (1984 pbk. edn), p. 593.

139. C. Barnett, *The Audit of War: The Illusion and Reality of Britain as a Great Nation* (1987 pbk. edn.), p. 304.

140. See J. Tomlinson, 'The Decline of the Empire and the Economic "Decline" of Britain', *Twentieth Century British History* 14 (2003), pp. 201–21.

141. Harvey, *Collision*, pp. 592–3; see also J. Tomlinson, 'Correlli Barnett's History: The Case of Marshall Aid', *Twentieth Century British History* 8 (1997), pp. 222–38.

142. Barnett, *Enemy*, p. 21.

143. On these 'Bismarckian' assumptions see D. Edgerton, 'The Prophet Militant and Industrial: The Peculiarities of Correlli Barnett', *Twentieth Century British History* 2 (1991), pp. 360–79.

144. B.J.C. McKercher, *Transition of Power: Britain's Loss of Global Pre-eminence to the United States, 1930–1945* (Cambridge, 1999), pp. 21–2.

145. On this catastrophic and symbolic defeat see M. Middlebrook and P. Mahoney, *Battleship: The Loss of the Prince of Wales and the Repulse* (2001 edn.); A.J. Marder, *Old Friends, New Enemies: The Royal Navy and the Imperial Japanese Navy, Vol. I: Strategic Illusions, 1936–1941* (Oxford, 1981), esp. pp. 467–72; and C.M. Bell, 'The "Singapore Strategy" and the Deterrence of Japan: Winston Churchill, the Admiralty and the Dispatch of Force Z', *English Historical Review* 116 (2001), pp. 604–34.

146. D. Edgerton, *Warfare State: Britain, 1920–1970* (Cambridge, 2006), pp. 28–30.

147. G.C. Peden, *Arms, Economics and British Strategy: From Dreadnoughts to Hydrogen Bombs* (Cambridge, 2007), chapter 3, pp. 98–163.

148. Grove, *Royal Navy*, pp. 121, 212.

149. N. Moss, *Nineteen Weeks: America, Britain, and the Fateful Summer of 1940* (Boston, Mass., 2004), p. 287.

8 Immigrants

1. A point made by most writers: see, e.g., the entry in D. Dabydeen, J. Gilmore and C. Jones, *The Oxford Companion to Black British History* (Oxford, 2007), pp. 155–6.

2. J. Procter (ed.), *Writing Black Britain, 1948–1998: An Interdisciplinary Anthology* (Manchester, 2000), p. 16.

3. R. Winder, *Bloody Foreigners: The Story of Immigration to Britain* (2007 pbk. edn.), p. 347.

4. P. Hennessy, *Never Again: Britain 1945–51* (1992), pp. 299–302.

5. K. Lunn, *Race and Labour in Twentieth-Century Britain* (1985), p. 19.

6. C. Holmes, *John Bull's Island: Immigration and British Society* (1988), pp. 248–9.

7. C. Peach, *The Caribbean in Europe: Contrasting Patterns of Migration and Settlement in Britain, France and the Netherlands* (1986), p. 7 and figs. 2–3, pp. 8–9.

8. V. Robinson, *Transients, Settlers and Refugees: Asians in Britain* (Oxford, 1986), fig. 3.1, p. 28.

9. S.S. Thandi, 'Migrating to the "Mother Country", 1947–1980', in M. Fisher, S. Lahiri and S. Thandi (eds.), *A South-Asian History of Britain* (Oxford, 2007), pp. 163–4.

10. A view summarized, in Rochdale at least, by M. Anwar, *The Myth of Return: Pakistanis in Britain* (1979), pp. 216–17.

11. D. Robinson-Dunn, 'Lascar Sailors and English Converts: The Imperial Port and Islam in Late 19th-Century England', Paper presented at Conference on 'Seascapes, Littoral Cultures, and Trans-Oceanic Exchanges', Library of Congress, Washington DC, February 12–15, 2003.

12. C. Adams, *Across Seven Seas and Thirteen Rivers: Life Stories of Pioneer Sylhetti Settlers in Britain* (1987), pp. 15–30.

13. For these trends among students and intellectuals, see S. Lahiri, *Indians in Britain: Anglo-Indian Encounters, Race and Identity, 1880–1930* (2000), pp. 21–32.

14. R. Visram, *Ayahs, Lascars and Princes: The Story of Indians in Britain, 1700–1947* (1986), p. 191.

15. R. Visram, *Asians in Britain: 400 Years of History* (2002), pp. 343, 347.

16. C. Vassallo, 'Sailing under the Red Duster: Maltese Merchant Seafarers in the Twentieth Century', *Mariner's Mirror* 94 (2008), p. 448 and table 2, p. 449.

17. G. Balachandran, 'Crossing the Last Frontier: Transatlantic Movements of Asian Maritime Workers, c.1900–1945', *Research in Maritime History* 33 (2007), pp. 98–102.
18. Adams, *Across Seven Seas*, pp. 54, 64.
19. C. Peach, et al., 'Immigration and Ethnicity', in A.H. Halsey and J. Webb (eds.), *Twentieth-Century British Social Trends* (3rd edn., Basingstoke, 2000), table 4.1, p. 129.
20. E. Delaney, *The Irish in Post-War Britain* (Oxford, 2007), p. 2.
21. W. Webster, 'Immigration and Racism', in P. Addison and H. Jones (eds.), *A Companion to Contemporary Britain, 1939–2000* (Oxford, 2005), pp. 99–101.
22. Peach *et al.*, 'Immigration and Ethnicity', table 4.3, pp. 140–1.
23. G. Gmelch, *Double Passage: The Lives of Caribbean Migrants Abroad and Back Home* (Ann Arbor, MI, 1992), p. 43.
24. N. Deakin, *Colour, Citizenship and British Society* (1970), p. 50.
25. Hennessy, *Never Again*, pp. 442–3.
26. D.W. Dean, 'Conservative Governments and the Restriction of Commonwealth Immigration in the 1950s: The Problems of Constraint', *Historical Journal* 35 (1992), pp. 178–86.
27. M. Dawswell, 'The Pigmentocracy of Citizenship: Assimilation, Integration or Alienation?', in L. Black *et al.* (eds.), *Consensus or Coercion? The State, The People and Social Cohesion in Post-War Britain* (2001), p. 73.
28. J. Bailkin, 'Leaving Home: The Politics of Deportation in Postwar Britain', *Journal of British Studies* 47 (2008), esp. pp. 861–78.
29. R.G. Spencer, *British Immigration Policy since 1939* (1997), pp. 129–41.
30. Anwar, *Myth of Return*, p. 4.
31. P. Panayi, 'Immigration, Multiculturalism and Racism', in F. Carnevali and J-M. Strange (eds.), *Twentieth Century Britain: Economic, Cultural and Social Change* (2nd edn., 2007), p. 249.
32. A. Hennessy, 'Workers of the Night: West Indians in Britain', in M. Cross and H. Entzinger (eds.), *Lost Illusions: Caribbean Minorities in Britain and the Netherlands* (1988), table 2.1, p. 39.
33. Peach *et al.*, 'Immigration and Ethnicity', table 4.4, p. 143, and pp. 152–3, 157.
34. Peach, *Caribbean in Europe*, table 4, p. 13.
35. M. Phillips and T. Phillips, *Windrush: The Irresistible Rise of Multi-Racial Britain* (1998), p. 264.
36. R. Foulke, *The Sea Voyage Narrative* (2002), p. 169.
37. Cf. B. King, *Derek Walcott: A Caribbean Life* (Oxford, 2000), pp. 220–5, 502–22; B. Woodcock, 'Derek Walcott: *Omeros*', in N. Roberts (ed.), *A Companion to Twentieth Century Poetry* (Oxford, 2001), pp. 547–56.
38. D. Walcott, *Omeros* (1990), book III, chapter XXIX, p. 155.
39. D. Hinds, *Journey to an Illusion: The West Indian in Britain* (1966), pp. 7–8.
40. P. Fryer, *Staying Power: The History of Black People in Britain: Black People in Britain since 1504* (1984), p. 372.
41. Hinds, *Journey*, p. 36.
42. F. Dennis, 'Journeys Without Maps', in F. Dennis and N. Khan (eds.), *Voices of the Crossing* (2000), p. 39.
43. Gmelch, *Double Passage*, pp. 69, 89.
44. Hinds, *Journey*, p. 38.
45. W. Collins, *Jamaican Migrant* (1965), pp. 54–6.

46. S. Patterson, *Dark Strangers: A Sociological Study of the Absorption of a Recent West Indian Migrant Group* (1963), p. 40.
47. Hinds, *Journey*, pp. 36, 49.
48. Richards, *Britannia's Children*, pp. 236, 246.
49. S. Constantine, 'Migrants and Settlers', in W.R. Louis *et al.* (eds.), *The Oxford History of the British Empire: Volume IV: The Twentieth Century* (Oxford, 1999), table 7.4, p. 167.
50. M. Flinn *et al.*, *Scottish Population History from the Seventeenth Century to the 1930s* (Cambridge, 1977), table 6.1.1, p. 441; table 6.1.4, p. 447; and table 6.1.5, p. 449.
51. I. Lindsay, 'Migration and Motivation: A Twentieth-Century Perspective', in T.M. Devine (ed.), *Scottish Emigration and Scottish Society* (Edinburgh, 1992), p. 155.
52. Devine, *Scottish Nation*, pp. 479, 484–5.
53. Richards, *Britannia's Children*, pp. 257, 260.
54. P. Clarke, *Hope and Glory: Britain 1900–1990* (Harmondsworth, 1996), p. 321.
55. Constantine, 'British Emigration', p. 25.
56. T. Hatton, 'Emigration from the UK, 1870–1913 and 1950–1998', *European Review of Economic History* 8 (2004), pp. 163–7.
57. M. Roe, *Australia, Britain and Migration 1915–1940: A Study of Desperate Hopes* (Cambridge, 1995), p. 200.
58. A. McCarthy, *Personal Narratives of Scottish and Irish Migration* (Manchester, 2007), p. 23.
59. S. Constantine, 'Immigration and the Making of New Zealand, 1918–1939', in S. Constantine (ed.), *Emigrants and Empire: British Settlement in the Dominions Between the Wars* (Manchester, 1990), p. 136.
60. J.A. Schultz, '"Leaven for the Lump": Canada and Empire Settlement, 1918–1939', in Constantine (ed.), *Emigrants and Empire*, pp. 159–62.
61. Richards, *Britannia's Children*, pp. 243–5.
62. Constantine, 'British World', p. 22.
63. Richards, *Britannia's Children*, p. 262.
64. W. Webster, *Imagining Home: Gender, 'Race', and National Identity, 1945–64* (1998), p. 31.
65. A. Hassam, 'The "Bring out a Briton" Campaign of 1957 and British Migration to Australia in the 1950s', *History Compass* 5 (2007), p. 822.
66. R. Parker, *Uprooted: The Shipment of Poor Children to Canada, 1867–1917* (Bristol, 2008), table 8, p. 135.
67. S. Constantine, 'Child Migration: Philanthropy, the State and the Empire', *History in Focus* 14 (2008), http://www.history.ac.uk/ihr/Focus/welfare/articles/constantines.html, accessed 3 February 2008.
68. S. Constantine, 'The British Government, Child Welfare and Child Migration to Australia after 1945', *Journal of Imperial and Commonwealth History* 30 (2002), p. 105.
69. House of Commons, *Select Committee on Health, Third Report* (Session 1997/98), paras. 1, 10, 44.
70. J. Cavell, 'The Imperial Race and the Immigration Sieve: The Canadian Debate on Assisted British Migration and Empire Settlement, 1900–30', *Journal of Imperial and Commonwealth History* 34 (2006), pp. 347, 352–6.
71. Schultz, 'Leaven', p. 168.

72. M. Goodwin, J. Gregory and B. Balmer, 'The Anatomy of the Brain Drain Debate, 1950–1970s', *Contemporary British History* iFirst content, http://www.informaworld.com/smpp/title~content=g769536214~db=all, accessed 23 January 2009.

73. Lindsay, 'Migration', p. 164.

74. Hatton, 'Emigration', pp. 157–8.

75. J. Wilkie, *Metagama: A Journey from Lewis to the New World* (Edinburgh, 1987), pp. 79–80.

76. Roe, *Migration*, p. 213.

77. R. Appleyard, *The Ten Pound Immigrants* (1988), p. 66.

78. McCarthy, *Personal Narratives*, p. 20.

79. Roe, *Migration*, p. 212.

80. M. Hutching, *Long Journey for Sevenpence: Assisted Immigration to New Zealand from the United Kingdom, 1947–1975* (Wellington, 1999), pp. 102, 114, 117, 120–1.

81. B. Zamoyska, *The Ten Pound Fare: Experiences of British People Who Emigrated to Australia in the 1950s* (1998), p. 35.

82. McCarthy, *Personal Narratives*, p. 93.

83. Appleyard, *Ten Pound Immigrants*, p. 65.

84. Hutching, *Long Journey*, p. 108.

85. *ibid.*, p. 112.

86. McCarthy, *Personal Narratives*, pp. 85–7.

87. Zamoyska, *Ten Pound Fare*, p. 42.

88. Hutching, *Long Journey*, p. 111.

89. McCarthy, *Personal Narratives*, p. 89.

90. Foot, *Immigration*, p. 9.

91. Heffer, *Roman*, p. 450.

92. Richards, *Britannia's Children*, p. 264.

93. A.J. Hammerton and A. Thomson, *'Ten Pound Poms': Australia's Invisible Migrants* (Manchester, 2005), p. 115.

94. McCarthy, *Personal Narratives*, p. 99.

95. Zamoyska, *Ten Pound Fare*, p. 43.

96. Roe, *Migration*, p. 216.

97. A. Thomson, ' "My Wayward Heart": Homesickness, Longing and the Return of British Post-War Immigrants From Australia', in M. Harper (ed.), *Emigrant Homecomings: The Return Movement of Migrants, 1600–2000* (Manchester, 2005), p. 111.

98. Zamoyska, *Ten Pound Fare*, p. 53.

99. R.E.G. Davies, *A History of the World's Airlines* (Oxford, 1967), pp. 480, 482, table 45, p. 485.

100. *Annual Abstract of Statistics* (hereafter *AAS*) 97 (1960), table 36, p. 39; *AAS* 105 (1968), table 259, p. 222; *AAS* 115 (1978), table 10.81, p. 298; Department of Transport, *Transport Statistics, Great Britain, 1964–1974* (1976), table 122, p. 161.

101. W.H. Miller, *British Ocean Liners: A Twilight Era, 1960–85* (1986), pp. 52–62.

102. T. Coleman, *The Liners: A History of the North Atlantic Crossing* (New York, 1976), pp. 177, 179, 188.

103. Hutching, *Long Journey*, p. 106.

104. Woodman, *History*, pp. 362–4.

105. Coleman, *Liners*, p. 187.

106. T.A. Heppenheimer, *Turbulent Skies: The History of Commercial Aviation* (New York, 1995), pp. 192–5.

107. I. Dear, *Great Ocean Liners: The Heyday of Luxury Travel* (1991), p. 25.

108. P.S. Dawson, *British Superliners of the Sixties* (1990), pp. 112–29, 142–3.

109. Richards, *Britannia's Children*, p. 267.

110. J. Jupp, *The English in Australia* (Cambridge, 2004), p. 138.

111. Constantine, 'Child Migration to Australia', pp. 123–4.

112. Hammerton and Thomson, *'Ten Pound Poms'*, p. 118.

113. Thomson, 'Wayward Heart', p. 120.

114. *AAS* 105 (1968), table 259, p. 222; *AAS* 115 (1979), table 10.81, p. 298.

115. Procter, *Black Britain*, p. 16.

116. Patterson, *Dark Strangers*, pp. 40–1.

117. See the vivid account by the US Ambassador and his wife in T.P. Melady and M.B. Melady, *Uganda: The Asian Exiles* (1978), pp. 14, 22.

118. Winder, *Foreigners*, pp. 381–2.

119. E.N. Swinerton, *Ugandan Asians in Great Britain* (1975), pp. 39–40.

120. Commission on the Future of Multi-Ethnic Britain (Parekh Report), *The Future of Multi-Ethnic Britain: Report of the Commission on the Future of Multi-Ethnic Britain* (2000), pp. 18, 103–5.

121. D. Dabydeen, *Turner: New and Selected Poems* (1994), 'Turner', XII, p. 17.

122. N. Lunt, 'Boats, Planes and Trains: British Migration, Mobility and Transnational Experience', *Migration Letters* 5 (2008), p. 157.

123. D. Sriskandaraajah and C. Drew, *Brits Abroad: Mapping the Scale and Nature of British Emigration* (2006), appendix A, p. 104, and p. 15.

124. *ibid.*, pp. 45–7, 64–5 and fig. 3.3, p. 15.

125. Richards, *Britannia's Children*, p. 271.

126. Thomson, 'Wayward Heart', p. 106.

127. McCarthy, *Personal Narratives*, p. 16.

128. Lunt, 'Boats, Planes and Trains', pp. 153, 157.

9 Collapse

1. A. Booth, *The British Economy in the Twentieth Century* (Basingstoke, 2001), pp. 105–6.

2. C. Lee, 'Scotland, 1860–1939: Growth and Poverty', in R. Floud and P. Johnson (eds.), *The Cambridge Economic History of Modern Britain, Vol. III* (Cambridge, 2004), p. 438.

3. L.H. Powell, *The Shipping Federation: A History of the First Sixty Years, 1890–1950* (1950), p. 8.

4. E.H. Lorenz and F. Wilkinson, 'The Shipbuilding Industry', in B. Elbaum and W. Lazonick (eds.), *The Decline of the British Economy* (Oxford, 1986), p. 114.

5. B. Stråth, *The Politics of De-Industrialisation: The Contraction of the West European Shipbuilding Industry* (1987), pp. 116–17.

6. G. Owen, *From Empire to Europe: The Decline and Revival of British Industry since the Second World War* (1999), p. 93.

7. D. Greasley and L. Oxley, 'Discontinuities in Competitiveness: The Impact of the First World War on British Industry', *Economic History Review* 94 (1996), pp. 94, 98–9.

8. Jamieson, *Ebb Tide*, pp. 54, 57.

9. For a contemporary view of this see Sir A. Hurd, *British Maritime Policy: The Decline of Shipping and Shipbuilding* (1938), pp. 27–35.

10. B.W.E. Alford, *Britain in the World Economy since 1880* (1996), p. 140.

11. Booth, *British Economy*, p. 109.

12. Owen, *Empire to Europe*, pp. 95–6.

13. S. Bowden and D.M. Higgins, 'British Industry in the Inter-War Years', in R. Floud and P. Johnson (eds.), *The Cambridge Economic History of Modern Britain, Vol. III* (Cambridge, 2004), table 14.1, p. 375.

14. S. Pollard, *The Development of the British Economy 1914–1990* (4th edn., 1992), pp. 71–2.

15. E. Green, 'Very Private Enterprise: Ownership and Finance in British Shipping, 1825–1940', in T. Yui and K. Nakagawa (eds.), *Business History of Shipping: Strategy and Structure* (Tokyo, 1985), pp. 235–41.

16. Pollard, *Development*, pp. 87–96.

17. J. Phillips, 'Class and Industrial Relations in Britain: The "Long" Mid-century and the Case of Port Transport, *c.*1920–70', *Twentieth Century British History* 16 (2005), pp. 56–61.

18. S. Glynn and A. Booth, *Modern Britain: An Economic and Social History* (1996), p. 252.

19. Stråth, *De-Industrialisation*, p. 119.

20. Jamieson, *Ebb Tide*, p. 60 and table 3.2, p. 65.

21. Lorenz and Wilkinson, 'Shipbuilding Industry', p. 119 and table 5, p. 120.

22. A. Burton, *The Rise and Fall of British Shipbuilding* (1994), p. 201.

23. E.H. Lorenz, *Economic Decline in Britain: The Shipbuilding Industry, 1890–1970* (Oxford, 1991), table 4.3, p. 81.

24. L. Johnman and H. Murphy, *British Shipbuilding and the State since 1918: A Political Economy of Decline* (Exeter, 2002), pp. 133–4.

25. A. Cairncross, *Economic Ideas and Government Policy: Contributions to Contemporary Economic History* (1996), p. 134; Johnman and Murphy, *Political Economy*, pp. 138–9.

26. Cmnd. 2937 (Geddes Report), *Shipbuilding Inquiry Committee, 1965–66: Report* (March 1966), p. 9.

27. Burton, *Rise and Fall*, pp. 204–7.

28. P. Pagnamenta and R. Overy, *All Our Working Lives* (1984), pp. 141, 148.

29. Cmnd. 2937, *Shipbuilding*, pp. 151–6.

30. J.F. Wilson, *British Business History 1720–1994* (Manchester, 1995), table 6.2, p. 196.

31. Booz-Allen and Hamilton International, *British Shipbuilding 1972: A Report to the Department of Trade and Industry* (1973), exhibit 28, p. 86.

32. Johnman and Murphy, *Political Economy*, p. 161.

33. L. Johnman and H. Murphy, *Scott Lithgow, Déjà vu All Over Again! The Rise and Fall of a Shipbuilding Company* (St John's, Newfoundland, 2005), p. 207.

34. B.W. Hogwood, *Government and Shipbuilding: The Politics of Industrial Change* (Farnbrough, 1979), pp. 194–6.

35. Stråth, *De-Industrialisation*, pp. 132–5.

36. M. Davies, *Belief in the Sea: State Encouragement of British Merchant Shipping and Shipbuilding* (1992), pp. 259–60.

37. R. Hope, *A New History of British Shipping* (1990), p. 445.

38. Stråth, *De-Industrialisation*, p. 119.

39. Johnman and Murphy, *Political Economy*, pp. 231–2.

40. K. Warren, *Steel, Ships and Men: Cammell Laird, 1824–1993* (Liverpool, 1998), pp. 299–300.
41. Johnman and Murphy, *Political Economy*, pp. 235–6.
42. Cmnd. 4337 (Rochdale Report), *Committee of Inquiry into Shipping, Report* (May 1970), pp. 14, 16.
43. S.G. Sturmey, *British Shipping and World Competition* (1962), table 33, p. 212.
44. A.W. Cafruny, *Ruling the Waves: The Political Economy of International Shipping* (Berkeley, CA, 1987), p. 92.
45. Davies, *Belief in the Sea*, p. 204.
46. Jamieson, *Ebb Tide*, p. 26.
47. I. Cafruny, *Ruling the Waves*, tables 7–8, pp. 101–2.
48. I. Friel, *A Maritime History of Britain and Ireland, c.400–2001* (2003), p. 281.
49. Jamieson, *Ebb Tide*, p. 49.
50. Hope, *New History*, figs. 16–17, pp. 428, 430 and pp. 449–50.
51. P. Hennessy, *Having It So Good: Britain in the Fifties* (2006), pp. xiv–xvi.
52. G.S. Cross and J.K. Walton, *The Playful Crowd: Pleasure Places in the Twentieth Century* (2005), p. 153.
53. J. Walvin, *Beside the Seaside: A Social History of the Popular Seaside Holiday* (1978), pp. 129–31.
54. J.A.R. Pimlott, *The Englishman's Holiday: A Social History* (Sussex, 1976 edn.), pp. 239–40.
55. For the background to and history of this concept see R.W. Butler, 'The Origins of the Tourism Area Life Cycle', in R.W. Butler (ed.), *The Tourism Area Life Cycle: Conceptual and Theoretical Issues* (Bristol, 2000), pp. 13–26.
56. C. Cooper, 'Parameters and Indicators of the Decline of the British Seaside Resort', in G. Shaw and A. Williams (eds.), *The Rise and Fall of British Coastal Resorts: Cultural and Economic Perspectives* (1997), table 4.1, pp. 80–1.
57. V.T.C. Middleton, *British Tourism: The Remarkable Story of Growth* (2005), p. 28.
58. S. Wright, 'Sun, Sea, Sand and Self-Expression: Mass Tourism as an Individual Experience', in H. Berghof (ed.), *The Making of Modern Tourism* (Basingstoke, 2002), p. 193.
59. R.W. Butler, 'Introduction', in R.W. Butler and D. Pearce (eds.), *Change in Tourism: People, Places, Processes* (1995), pp. 1, 7–8.
60. Urry, *Tourist Gaze*, pp. 7–11.
61. Cross and Walton, *Playful Crowd*, p. 141.
62. Pimlott, *Holiday*, pp. 244–5.
63. Morgan and Pritchard, *Power and Politics at the Seaside*, p. 35.
64. C. Cooper, 'The Environmental Consequences of Declining Destinations', in C. Cooper and S. Wanhill (eds.), *Tourism Development: Environment and Community Issues* (Chichester, 1997), p. 130.
65. T. Gale, 'Modernism, Post-Modernism and the Decline of British Seaside Resorts as Long Holiday Destinations: A Case Study of Rhyl, North Wales', *Tourism Geographies* 7 (2005), pp. 91–5.
66. N.J. Morgan and A. Pritchard, *Power and Politics at the Seaside: The Development of Devon's Resorts in the Twentieth Century* (Exeter, 1999), table 3.1, p. 39 and pp. 42–3.
67. P. Thornton, 'Coastal Tourism in Cornwall since 1900', in S. Fisher (ed.), *Recreation and the Sea* (Exeter, 1997), p. 78.

68. C. Beatty and S. Fothergill, 'Economic Change and the Labour Market in Britain's Seaside Towns', *Regional Studies* 38 (2004), table 4, p. 468; table 7, p. 471; and table 8, p. 472.
69. S. Agarwal and P. Brunt, 'Social Exclusion and English Seaside Resorts', *Tourism Management* 27 (2006), pp. 656, 662.
70. House of Commons Communities and Local Government Committee, *Coastal Towns: The Government's Second Response* (2007), annex. 1, p. 14.
71. House of Commons Communities and Local Government Committee, *Coastal Towns, First Report* (2007), pp. 8–9, 16–21.
72. J. McCormick, *British Politics and the Environment* (1991), pp. 16–18.
73. A. Burges and R.J. Eden, 'Ashby, Eric, Baron Ashby (1904–1992)', *Oxford Dictionary of National Biography*, http://www.oxforddnb.com/view/article/50791, accessed 29 September 2008.
74. J. Hassan, *The Seaside, Health and the Environment in England and Wales since 1800* (Aldershot, 2003), pp. 193, 198–9, 204–5.
75. Walton, *British Seaside*, p. 138.
76. S. Allen, 'British Cinema at the Seaside – the Limits of Liminality', *Journal of British Cinema and Television* 5 (2008), pp. 55–65.
77. N. Danziger, *Danziger's Britain: A Journey to the Edge* (1996), p. 143.
78. Ministry of Reconstruction, *British Fishermen and the Nation 1, Sea Fisheries* (1919), p. 1.
79. R.H. Mottram, *About Britain No. 4: East Anglia* (1951), pp. 12–13. I am grateful to Lyndsay Grant for this reference.
80. Girling, *Sea Change*, p. 139.
81. Prime Minister's Strategy Unit, *Net Benefits: A Sustainable and Profitable Future for UK Fishing* (2004), fig. 3.9, p. 31.
82. D. Whitmarsh, 'Adaptation and Change Within the Fishing Industry since the 1970s', in D.J. Starkey, C. Reid and N. Ashcroft (eds.), *England's Sea Fisheries: The Commercial Sea Fisheries of England and Wales since 1300* (2000), table 24.2, p. 228.
83. C. Reid, 'From Boom to Bust: The Herring Industry in the Twentieth Century', in Starkey, Reid and Ashcroft (eds.), *England's Sea Fisheries*, pp. 194–5.
84. C. Clover, *The End of the Line: How Overfishing Is Changing the World and What We Eat* (2005 pbk. edn.), p. 55.
85. European Environment Agency, 'Late Lessons From Early Warnings: The Precautionary Principle, 1896–2000', *Environmental Issue Report* 22 (2001), pp. 17–18.
86. J. Ramster, 'Fisheries Research in England and Wales, 1850–1980', in Starkey, Reid and Ashcroft (eds.), *England's Sea Fisheries*, p. 179.
87. M. Kurlansky, *The Last Fish Tale: The Fate of the Atlantic and Our Disappearing Fisheries* (2008), p. xvii.
88. Roberts, *Unnatural History*, p. 163.
89. J.M. Knauss, 'The Growth of British Fisheries during the Industrial Revolution', *Ocean Development and International Law* 36 (2005), pp. 5, 7.
90. Girling, *Sea Change*, pp. 122–3.
91. R. Carson, *The Sea Around Us* (1952 edn.), pp. 150, 186–7, 216.
92. E.S. Russell, *The Overfishing Problem* (Cambridge, 1942), p. 98.
93. G.M. Graham, *The Fish Gate: On the English Fishing Industry* (1943), pp. 155, 162–3.

94. Ramster, 'Fisheries Research', in Starkey, Reid and Ashcroft (eds.), *Sea Fisheries*, p. 186.
95. R. Ellis, *The Empty Ocean* (Washington DC, 2003), p. 12.
96. H.M. Rozwadowski, *The Sea Knows No Boundaries: A Century of Marine Science Under ICES* (Seattle, WA., 2002), pp. 158–64.
97. M. Leigh, *European Integration and the Common Fisheries Policy* (1983), p. 38.
98. A. Menon, 'Britain and European Integration: The View from Within', *Political Quarterly* 75 (2004), p. 289.
99. Leigh, *Common Fisheries Policy*, pp. 46–7.
100. *ibid.*, pp. 75–6.
101. Girling, *Sea Change*, p. 130.
102. Kurlansky, *Last Fish*, p. 168.
103. World Wildlife Fund, 'How Can Europe Tackle the Problem of Discard?', Press Briefing, 8 December 2008.
104. Clover, *End of the Line*, p. 64.
105. 'Skippers in the Dock as Cornwall's Last Great Fishing Town Awaits Fate', *The Guardian*, 28 August 2007.
106. Girling, *Sea Change*, p. 131.
107. Clover, *End of the Line*, p. 151.
108. Prime Minister's Strategy Unit, *Net Benefits*, pp. 41–2.
109. European Commission, *Reform of the Common Fisheries Policy* (2009), esp. pp. 11–13; 'EU Invites Public to Join Fishing Reform Debate', *The Guardian*, 26 May 2009.
110. Cm. 6392, Royal Commission on Environmental Pollution, 24th Report, *Turning the Tide: Addressing the Impact of Fisheries on the Marine Environment* (December 2004), p. 39.
111. Prime Minister's Strategy Unit, *Net Benefits*, fig. 3.13, p. 35, and pp. 23, 129.
112. Cm. 6392, *Turning the Tide*, pp. 254–5.
113. Roberts, *Unnatural History*, pp. 376–7, 383.
114. D. Preikshot and D. Pauly, 'Global Fisheries and Marine Conservation: Is Coexistence Possible?', in E.A. Norse and L.B. Crowder (eds.), *Marine Conservation Biology: the Science of Maintaining the Sea's Biodiversity* (2005), pp. 185–97.
115. Cm. 7047, *A Sea Change: A Marine Bill White Paper* (March 2007), pp. 70, 118–21.
116. 'Marine Bill Newsletter', DEFRA, September 2008, http://www.defra.gov.uk/marine/pdf/legislation/marine-news8.pdf, accessed 7 October 2008.
117. Grove, *Royal Navy*, pp. 214–17.
118. J.R. Hill, 'The Realities of Medium Power: 1946 to the Present', in Hill (ed.), *Illustrated History*, table 13.1, p. 398.
119. The standard text is M.H. Murfett, *Hostage on the Yangtze: Britain, China, and the Amethyst Crisis of 1949* (1991).
120. C.J Bartlett, *The Long Retreat: A Short History of British Defence Policy, 1945–1970* (1972), p. 49.
121. L. Johnman and H. Murphy, 'The Rationalization of Warship Building in the United Kingdom, 1945–2000', *Journal of Strategic Studies* 24 (2001), p. 110.
122. E.J. Grove, *Vanguard to Trident: British Naval Policy since World War Two* (1987), pp. 219–20, 229.
123. The classic work on 'broken-backed warfare' is L.W. Martin, 'The Market for Strategic Ideas in Britain: The "Sandys Era"', *American Political Science Review* 56 (1962), esp. pp. 25, 32.

124. See R. Jackson, *Suez 1956: Operation Musketeer* (1980), pp. 14–23 on the dispatch of the carriers.

125. I. Speller, 'The Seaborne/Airborne Concept: Littoral Manoeuvre in the 1960s?', *Journal of Strategic Studies* 29 (2006), pp. 57–9.

126. Cmnd. 124, *Defence: Outline of Future Policy* (March 1957), pp. 1–4.

127. D. Wettern, *The Decline of British Seapower* (1982), p. 137.

128. Grove, *Royal Navy*, p. 229.

129. M.S. Navis, ' "Vested Interests and Vanished Dreams": Duncan Sandys, the Chiefs of Staff and the 1957 White Paper', in P. Smith (ed.), *Government and the Armed Forces in Britain, 1856–1990* (1996), pp. 232–3.

130. J. Baylis, *Ambiguity and Deterrence: British Nuclear Strategy, 1945–1964* (Oxford, 1995), pp. 171–78, 218–27.

131. K. Young, 'The Royal Navy's Polaris Lobby, 1955–62', *Journal of Strategic Studies* 25 (2002), pp. 61–4.

132. R. Moore, *The Royal Navy and Nuclear Weapons* (2001), pp. 162–6.

133. W. Loth, *Europe: Cold War and Coexistence, 1953–1965* (2004), pp. 147–8.

134. Grove, *Vanguard to Trident*, p. 242.

135. Johnman and Murphy, 'Rationalization', pp. 115–18.

136. J. Colman, *A 'Special Relationship'? Harold Wilson, Lyndon B. Johnson and Anglo-American Relations 'At the Summit', 1964–68* (Manchester, 2004), p. 76.

137. S. Dockrill, *Britain's Retreat from East of Suez: The Choice Between Europe and the World?* (Basingstoke, 2002), pp. 138–9.

138. D. Healey, *The Time of My Life* (Harmondsworth, pbk. edn., 1990), pp. 275–6.

139. S.C. Smith, 'Power Transferred? Britain, the United States and the Gulf, 1956–71', *Contemporary British History* 21 (2007), pp. 5–6.

140. I. Speller, 'Naval Diplomacy: Operation Vantage, 1961', in I. Speller (ed.), *The Royal Navy and Maritime Power in the Twentieth Century* (2005), pp. 170–1.

141. A. Gorst, 'CVA-01', in R. Harding (ed.), *The Royal Navy, 1930–2000: Innovation and Defence* (2000), p. 170.

142. Dockrill, *Britain's Retreat*, pp. 114–4.

143. For his views see C. Mayhew, *Britain's Role Tomorrow* (1967), p. 92.

144. J. Pickering, 'Politics and "Black Tuesday": Shifting Power in the Cabinet and the Decision to Withdraw from East of Suez, November 1967–January 1968', *Twentieth Century British History* 13 (2002), pp. 156–63, 167–8.

145. P. Catterall, 'The East of Suez Decision: Witness Seminar', *Contemporary British History* 7 (1993), pp. 612–14.

146. Grove, *Vanguard to Trident*, pp. 282–3.

147. A. Ellner, 'Carrier Airpower in the Royal Navy during the Cold War: The International Strategic Context', *Defense and Security Analysis* 22 (2006), p. 31.

148. A. Benvenuti, 'The Heath Government and British Defence Policy in South East Asia at the End of Empire', *Twentieth Century British History* 20 (2009), p. 71; A. Jackson, 'The Royal Navy and the Indian Ocean Region since 1945', *The RUSI Journal* 151 (2006), p. 82.

149. A. Jackson, 'Empire and Beyond: The Pursuit of Overseas Interests in the Late Twentieth Century', *English Historical Review* 122 (2007), p. 1353.

150. Grove, *Vanguard to Trident*, pp. 307, 311, 321–4, 341, 350.

151. Ellner, 'Carrier Airpower', p. 34.

152. S. Croft, *British Security Policy: The Thatcher Years and the End of the Cold War* (1991), pp. 93–4.

153. This mix of motives is most closely analysed in J. Arquilla and M.M. Rasmussen, 'The Origins of the South Atlantic War', *Journal of Latin American Studies* 33 (2001), esp. pp. 750–8.

154. B. Conekin, *The Autobiography of a Nation: The 1951 Festival of Britain* (Manchester, 2003), p. 127

155. F.M. Leventhal, ' "A Tonic to the Nation": The Festival of Britain, 1951', *Albion* 27 (1995), p. 452.

156. I. Cox, *Festival Ship Campania: A Guide to the Story It Tells* (1951), pp. 16–17.

157. Friel, *Maritime History*, p. 285.

158. Kurlansky, *Last Fish*, p. xiii.

159. Owen, *Empire to Europe*, p. 90.

160. The classic statement of this case is M. Abromavitz, 'Catching Up, Forging Ahead, and Falling Behind', *Journal of Economic History* 46 (1986), pp. 385–406.

161. 'South Korea: The Export Juggernaut', *The Economist*, 27 September 2008.

162. See J.H.B. Tew, 'Policies Aimed at Improving the Balance of Payments', in F.T. Blackaby (ed.), *British Economic Policy 1960–74: Demand Management* (Cambridge, 1978), table 7.1, p. 305.

10   Afterglow

1. L. Freedman, *The Official History of the Falklands Campaign* (2005 edn.), vol. I, pp. 3–8, 12–16.

2. A. Dabat and L. Lorenzano, *Argentina, The Malvinas and the End of Military Rule* (Eng., trans., 1984), pp. 33–5, 64–70, 76–9.

3. Cmnd. 8787, *The Falkland Islands Review* (1983; 1992 Pimlico pbk. reprint), paras. 114–18, pp. 33–4.

4. M. Hastings and S. Jenkins, *The Battle for the Falklands* (1983), p. 71.

5. *ibid.*, pp. 61–3.

6. P. Pugh, ' "The Empire Strikes Back": The Falklands/Malvinas Campaigns of 1982', *Mariner's Mirror* 93 (2007), p. 310.

7. Herman, *To Rule the Waves*, pp. 560–1.

8. G.M. Dillon, *The Falklands, Politics and War* (Basingstoke, 1989), p. 34.

9. S. Woodward, *One Hundred Days: The Memoirs of the Falklands Battle Group Commander* (1992), pp. 81–2, 148–9.

10. D.G. Boyce, *The Falklands War* (Basingstoke, 2005), p. 106.

11. Hastings and Jenkins, *Battle*, p. 148.

12. P. Eddy and M. Linklater, *The Falklands War* (1982), pp. 159–60.

13. Boyce, *Falklands War*, pp. 142–6.

14. H. Bicheno, *Razor's Edge: The Unofficial History of the Falklands War* (2006), p. 118.

15. Bicheno, *Razor's Edge*, p. 131.

16. Freedman, *Official History*, vol. II, pp. 466–8, 475.

17. M. Parsons, *The Falklands War* (Stroud, 2000), pp. 62–5.

18. R. Harris, *Gotcha! The Media, The Government and the Falklands Crisis* (1983), p. 38.

19. A. Barnett, *Iron Britannia: Why Parliament Fought Its Falklands War* (1982), pp. 30, 36–7.

20. R. Hamilton, ' "When the Seas Are Empty, So Are the Words": Representations of the Task Force', in J. Aulich (ed.), *Framing the Falklands War: Nationhood, Culture and Identity* (Milton Keynes, 1992). p. 134.

21. J. Aulich, 'Wildlife in the South Atlantic: Graphic Satire, Patriotism and the Fourth Estate', in Aulich (ed.), *Framing the Falklands*, figs. 29–30, p. 99.

22. K.E. Lane, *Blood and Silver: A History of Piracy in the Caribbean and Central America* (1999), preface, v.

23. Harris, *Gotcha!*, p. 148.

24. E. Grove, 'The Falklands War and British Defence Policy', *Defense and Security Analysis* 18 (2002), pp. 307–11.

25. Ellner, 'Carrier Airpower', p. 36.

26. W. Chin, 'Operations in a War Zone: The Royal Navy in the Persian Gulf in the 1980s', in Speller (ed.), *Maritime Power*, esp. pp. 189–93.

27. E. Grove, 'The Discovery of Doctrine: British Naval Thinking at the Close of the Twentieth Century', in G. Till (ed.), *The Development of British Naval Thinking: Essays in Memory of Bryan McLaren Ranft* (2006), pp. 187, 189.

28. I. Speller, 'Delayed Reaction: UK Maritime Expeditionary Capabilities and the Lessons of the Falklands Conflict', *Defense and Security Analysis* 18 (2002), p. 373.

29. I. Ballantyne, *Strike from the Sea: The Royal Navy and US Navy at War in the Middle East* (2004), pp. 97–101, 109, 129.

30. I. Finlan, *The Royal Navy in the Falklands Conflict and the Gulf War: Culture and Strategy* (2004), pp. 124–5.

31. On the 'Wrens' see M.H. Fletcher, *The WRNS: A History of the Women's Royal Naval Service* (1989).

32. C. Dandeker and M.W. Segal, 'Gender Integration in Armed Forces: Recent policy Developments in the United Kingdom', *Armed Forces and Society* 23 (1996), pp. 34–5.

33. Ballantyne, *Strike from the Sea*, p. 111.

34. A. Dorman, 'From Peacekeeping to Peace Enforcement: The Royal Navy and Peace Support Operations', in Speller (ed.), *Royal Navy and Maritime Power*, pp. 202–5.

35. J. Black, 'A Post-Imperial Power? Britain and the Royal Navy', *Orbis* 49 (2005), pp. 358–9.

36. J. Kampfner, *Blair's Wars* (2003), pp. 65–73.

37. J.L. Hirsch, *Sierra Leone: Diamonds and the Struggle for Democracy* (Boulder, CO, 2001), pp. 87–8.

38. Black, 'Post-Imperial Power', p. 359–60.

39. W. Murray and R.H. Scales, *The Iraq War: A Military History* (Cambridge, Mass., 2003), pp. 131–2.

40. M. Dickinson, 'New Aircraft Carriers Delayed', *The Independent*, 11 December 2008.

41. J. Prescott, *My Story: Pulling No Punches* (2008), pp. 37–48, 220.

42. Cm. 3950, *British Shipping: Charting a New Course* (1998), action 23, p. 28.

43. HM Treasury, *Independent Enquiry into a Tonnage Tax: A Report by The Lord Alexander of Weedon QC* (1999), paras. 20–41, 92.

44. National Audit Office, *The Maritime and Coastguard Agency's Response to Growth in the UK Merchant Fleet: Report by the Comptroller and Auditor General, Session 2008–2009* (2009), p. 5 and charts 3–4, p. 13.

45. D. Yergin, *The Prize: The Epic Quest for Oil, Money and Power* (1991), p. 670.

46. A. Sampson, *The Seven Sisters: The Great Oil Companies and the World They Made* (1975), pp. 181–2.

47. C. Harvie, *Fool's Gold: The Story of North Sea Oil* (Harmondsworth, 1995), pp. 164–5.
48. Alvarez, *Offshore: A North Sea Journey* (1986), p. 126.
49. R. Middleton, *Government Versus the Market: The Growth of the Public Sector, Economic Management and British Economic Performance c.1890–1979* (Cheltenham, 1996), pp. 465–6.
50. Glynn and Booth, *Modern Britain*, pp. 231, 234.
51. R. Toye, 'The New Commanding Height: Labour Party Policy on North Sea Oil and Gas, 1964–74', *Contemporary British History* 16 (2002), pp. 107–10.
52. C. Robinson and J. Morgan, *North Sea Oil in the Future: Economic Analysis and Government Policy* (1978), table 1.7, p. 12.
53. S. Howarth, *A Century in Oil: The Shell Transport and Trading Company, 1897–1997* (1997), p. 317.
54. DTI, *Digest of United Kingdom Energy Statistics 2000* (2000), pp. 80–1.
55. C. Bean, *The Macroeconomic Consequences of North Sea Oil* (1986), p. 2 and table 1, p. 42.
56. S.J. Reso, 'Finding the Oil: Techniques, Costs and Risks', in Bank of Scotland Information Services, *Understanding North Sea Oil* (1977), p. 10; M.J.W. Lofting, 'Development Planning', in *ibid.*, pp. 14–17.
57. Howarth, *Century in Oil*, p. 319.
58. M. Jenkin, *British Industry and the North Sea: State Intervention in a Developing Industrial Sector* (1981), pp. 26–33.
59. L. Johnman and H. Murphy, 'A Triumph of Failure: The British Shipbuilding Industry and the Offshore Structures Market, 1960–1990: A Case Study of Scott Lithgow Limited', *International Journal of Maritime History* 14 (2002), pp. 79, 83, 88–90.
60. A.G. Jamieson, 'British OSV companies in the North Sea, 1964–1997', *Maritime Policy and Management* 25 (1998), esp. pp. 307, 309–10.
61. K. Adams and K. Macdonald-Wallis, 'UK Oil Imports since 1920', *Energy Trends* (2007), chart 1, p. 26.
62. C. Nakhle, 'Do High Oil Prices Justify an Increase in Taxation in a Mature Oil Province? The Case of the UK Continental Shelf', *Energy Policy* 35 (2007), p. 4306.
63. R. Dafter and I. Davidson, 'North Sea Oil and Gas and British Foreign Policy', *Chatham House Papers* 10 (1980), table 5, p. 14.
64. 'Making the most of the North Sea', *The Economist*, 12 July 2007.
65. Robinson and Morgan, *Future*, p. 52.
66. Department for Business, Enterprise and Regulatory Reform, 'Press Release: Increased Oil Production Starts at Home', 28 May 2008.
67. T. Smit, M. Junginger and R. Smits, 'Technological Learning in Offshore Wind Energy: Different Roles of the Government', *Energy Policy* 35 (2007), table 1, p. 6434.
68. Department of Energy and Climate Change, 'Environment Study to Inform Location of Future Offshore Energy Developments', press release, 26 January 2009.
69. Department of Energy and Climate Change, *UK Offshore Energy Strategic Environmental Assessment* (2009), non-technical summary, ii, xx.
70. S.A. Jay, *At the Margins of Planning: Offshore Windfarms in the United Kingdom* (Aldershot, 2008), pp. 12–18.
71. Cm. 3950, *British Shipping*, p. 3.

72. Jamieson, *Ebb Tide*, pp. 121–5, 157.
73. G. Shaw and T. Coles, 'The Resort Economy: Changing Structures and Management Issues in British Resorts', in Agarwal and Shaw (eds.), *Managing Coastal Tourism*, pp. 40–1.
74. T. Mason, *Shifting Sands: Design and the Changing Image of English Seaside Towns* (2003), p. 4.
75. Walton, *British Seaside*, p. 69.
76. S. Agarwal, 'Global-Local Interactions in English Coastal Resorts: Theoretical Perspectives', *Tourism Geographies* 7 (2005), pp. 351–2.
77. P. Theroux, *The Kingdom by the Sea* (1983), p. 202.
78. T. Gale, 'The Problems and Dilemmas of Northern European Post-Mature Coastal Tourism Resorts', in Agarwal and Shaw (eds.), *Managing Coastal Tourism Resorts: A Global Perspective*, p. 33.
79. S. Agarwal, 'Institutional Change and Resort Capacity: The Case of Southwest English Coastal Resorts', in Agarwal and Shaw (eds.), *Managing Coastal Tourism*, pp. 56–7.
80. Walton, *British Seaside*, p. 117.
81. Mason, *Shifting Sands*, pp. 5, 10–13.
82. D. St John Thomas, *Journey Through Britain: Landscape, People and Books* (New edn., 2004), pp. 487–8.
83. C. Desmoulins, *Living by the Sea: 25 International Examples* (Basel, Eng. trans., 2008), pp. 112–15.
84. P. Williams, *The English Seaside* (Swindon, 2005), pp. 34–51, and p. 7.
85. Walton, *British Seaside*, p. 118.
86. Association of District Councils, *Making the Most of the Coast* (1993), p. 21.
87. English Tourist Board, *Turning the Tide: A Heritage and Environment Strategy for a Seaside Resort* (1993), esp. pp. 14–21.
88. North West Development Agency, *Blackpool: An Action Plan for Sustainable Growth* (2007), table 2.1, pp. 4–5; table 3.5, pp. 10–11.
89. Walton, *British Seaside*, p. 158.
90. 'Riding the Rogue Wave: Booming Resort Bucks the Trend as City Surfers Flock In', *The Guardian*, 7 July 2008.
91. Shaw and Coles, 'Resort Economy', p. 48 and table 3.5, p. 49.
92. On 'new social movements', see P.W. Sutton, *Nature, Environment and Society* (Basingstoke, 2004), pp. 29–35.
93. C. Rootes, 'Environmental Protest in Britain, 1988–1997', in B. Seel, M. Paterson and B. Doherty (eds.), *Direct Action in British Environmentalism* (2000), pp. 55–6.
94. D. Booth, 'Surfing: From One (Cultural) Extreme to Another', in B. Wheaton (ed.), *Understanding Lifestyle Sports: Consumption, Identity and Difference* (2004). pp. 94–8.
95. B. Wheaton, 'Identity, Politics, and the Beach: Environmental Activism in Surfers Against Sewage', *Leisure Studies* 26 (2007), pp. 284–9.
96. Walton, *British Seaside*, p. 139.
97. J. Benidickson, *The Culture of Flushing: A Social and Legal History of Sewage* (pbk. edn., Vancouver, BC, 2007), pp. 298–9, 313–14, 320–1.
98. Hassan, *Health and the Environment*, table 8.2, p. 209, pp. 235, 237; Time Out Guides, *Seaside: Discover the Best of Britain's Best Beaches* (2008), p. 6.
99. F. Gray, *Designing the Seaside: Architecture, Society and Nature* (2006), pp. 221–7.

100. P. Gogarty, *The Coast Road: A 3,000-mile Journey Round the Edge of England* (Rev. edn., 2007), p. 48.
101. Mason, *Shifting Sands*, p. 5.
102. NWDA, *Blackpool*, p. 1.
103. B.T. Robinson, 'Turning the Tide: Regeneration and Seaside Towns', Unpublished Oxford Brookes MSc Thesis, 2007, pp. 38–53.
104. N. Triggle, 'The Return of the British Seaside', BBC News Online, 10 April 2004, http://news.bbc.co.uk/1/hi/uk/3612329.stm, accessed 19 March 2009.
105. House of Commons, *Coastal Towns*, p. 3.
106. Time Out Guides, *Seaside*, p. 7.
107. C. Beatty and S. Fothergill, *The Seaside Economy: The Final Report of the Seaside Towns Research Project* (Sheffield, 2003), pp. 5, table 2.10, p. 46, and pp. 99, 105.
108. G.S. Burgess, W. Raymond and J. Barron, *The Voyage of Saint Brendan: Representative Versions of the Legend in English Translation* (Exeter, 2005), pp. 66–7.
109. M. Fuller, *Remembering the Early Modern Voyage: English Narratives in the Age of European Expansion* (Basingstoke, 2008), pp. 21–31.
110. J.G. Singh, 'History or Colonial Ethnography? The Ideological Formation of Edward Terry's *A Voyage to East-India* (1655 and 1665)', in I. Camps and J.G. Singh (eds.), *Travel Knowledge: European 'Discoveries' in the Early Modern Period* (Basingstoke, 2001), pp. 200–2.
111. H. Cooper, *The English Romance in Time: Transforming Motifs from Geoffrey of Monmouth to the Death of Shakespeare* (Oxford, 2004), pp. 106–13.
112. P. Edwards, *Sea-Mark: The Metaphorical Voyage, Spenser to Milton* (Liverpool, 1997), pp. 179–80.
113. P. Edwards, *The Story of the Voyage: Sea-Narratives in Eighteenth-Century England* (Cambridge, 1994), pp. 21–32, 187–8.
114. R. Davenport-Hines, *Auden* (1995), pp. 146–55.
115. W.H. Auden, *Collected Shorter Poems, 1927–57* (1966), pp. 99, 123.
116. W.H. Auden, *The Sea and the Mirror: A Commentary on Shakespeare's 'The Tempest'* (Oxford, 2003 edn.), pp. 20–1.
117. W.H. Auden, *The Enchaféd Flood: Or, The Romantic Iconography of the Sea* (1951), p. 26.
118. V. Sackville-West, *No Signposts in the Sea* (1985 Virago edn.), p. 147.
119. I. Murdoch, *The Sea, The Sea* (1999 pbk. edn.), p. 19.
120. I. McEwan, *On Chesil Beach* (2007), pp. 18, 166.
121. S. Basnett, 'Cabin'd Yet Unconfined: Heroic Masculinity in English Seafaring Novels', in B. Klein (ed.). *Fictions of the Sea: Critical Perspectives on the Ocean in British Literature and Culture* (Aldershot, 2002), pp. 180–1, 184–5.
122. C.S. Forester, *Mr. Midshipman Hornblower* (1950), p. 190.
123. P.K. O'Brian, *Master and Commander* (2007 pbk. edn.), pp. 65, 67, 77.
124. T. Williams, *Structures of Desire: British Cinema, 1939–1955* (New York, 2000), p. 73.
125. A. Aldgate, *Best of British: Cinema and Society from 1930 to the Present* (2002), pp. 59, 136.
126. J. Richards, *Films and British National Identity: From Dickens to 'Dad's Army'* (Manchester, 1997), pp. 144–5.
127. S. Harper, *British Cinema of the 1950s: The Decline of Deference* (Oxford, 2003), pp. 59–60.
128. C. Geraghty, *British Cinema in the Fifties: Gender, Genre and the 'New Look'* (2000), pp. 180–1.

129. J. Rayner, *The Naval War Film: Genre, History, National Cinema* (Manchester, 2007), pp. 55–7.
130. Gogarty, *Coast Road*, p. 28.
131. R. Wymer, *Derek Jarman* (Manchester, 2005), pp. 132–3.
132. D. Jarman and H. Sooley, *Derek Jarman's Garden* (1995), pp. 47–8.
133. K. Worpole, *Last Landscapes: The Architecture of the Cemetery in the West* (2003), pp. 60–1.
134. Jarman and Sooley, *Garden*, p. 136.
135. S. Dillon, *Derek Jarman and Lyric Film: The Mirror and the Sea* (Austin, Tex., 2004), pp. 34–40, 76–8, 90–2.
136. M. O'Pray, *Derek Jarman: Dreams of England* (1996), p. 102.
137. D. Martin, 'The Sound of England', in S.E. Grosby and A.S. Leoussi (eds.), *Nationalism and Ethnosymbolism: History, Culture and Ethnicity in the Formation of Nations* (Edinburgh, 2007), pp. 78–9.
138. On Vaughan Williams and the sea, see e.g. Harvie, *Floating Commonwealth*, pp. 1–3.
139. For instance, C. Bartolovich, ' "Baseless Fabric": London as a "World City" ', in P. Hulme and W.H. Sherman (eds.), *The Tempest and Its Travels* (2000), pp. 13–26.
140. B. Ashcroft, *On Post-Colonial Futures: Transformations of Colonial Culture* (2001), pp. 81, 93–7.
141. A. Byatt, A. Fothergill and M. Holmes, *The Blue Planet: A Natural History of the Oceans* (2001), pp. 19, 21.
142. C. Somerville, *Coast: A Celebration of Britain's Coastal Heritage* (2005), p. 6.
143. B. Lavery, *The Island Nation: A History of Britain and the Sea* (2005), p. 162.

11   Conclusions: A Star to Steer By?

1. For instance, in Stanley Baldwin's famous May 1924 speech 'On England', see D. Cannadine, *In Churchill's Shadow: Confronting the Past in Modern Britain* (2002), p. 167.
2. Cf. J.M. Winter, *Remembering War: The Great War Between Memory and History in the Twentieth Century* (New Haven, CT, 2006), p. 244.
3. A. Gregory, *The Silence of Memory: Armistice Day 1919–1946* (Oxford, 1994), pp. 99ff.
4. A. King, *Memorials of the Great War in Britain* (Oxford, 1998), p. 45.
5. On the great post-war monuments see J. Winter, *Sites of Memory, Sites of Mourning: The Great War in European Cultural History* (Cambridge, 1995), pp. 85–108. For the later importance of personal narratives over monuments see S. Hynes, 'Personal Narratives and Commemoration', in J. Winter and E. Sivan (eds.), *War and Remembrance in the Twentieth Century* (1999), pp. 206–7.
6. RAF personnel's view of the 'old-fashioned' Navy and Army, and their own unpopularity leading up to the 'finest hour', is covered in M. Francis, *The Flyer: British Culture and the Royal Air Force 1939–1945* (Oxford, 2008), esp. pp. 16–20.
7. T. Clayton and P. Craig, *Finest Hour* (2001), pp. 317–8.
8. K. Jefferys, *Finest and Darkest Hours: The Decisive Events in British Politics from Churchill to Blair* (2003), p. 31.
9. J. Baxendale, *Priestley's England: J.B. Priestley and English Culture* (Manchester, 2007), pp. 148–9.

10. For the former, see M.A. Conley, *From Jack Tar to Union Jack: Representing Naval Manhood in the British Empire, 1870–1918* (Manchester, 2009), pp. 127–8, 165–6, 193–4; on the latter, P. Baker and J. Stanley, *Hello Sailor! The Hidden History of Gay Life at Sea* (2003); and M. Houlbrook, *Queer London: Perils and Pleasures in the Sexual Metropolis, 1918–1957* (Chicago, 2005), esp. pp. 72–3.

11. J. Stanley, 'Women at Sea: An Other Category', *Gender and History* 15 (2003), p. 137.

12. Very selectively, see J. Winch, *A Gentleman of Color: The Life of James Forten* (Oxford, 2003); G. Horne, *Red Seas: Ferdinand Smith and Radical Black Sailors in the United States and Jamaica* (New York, 2005); A.G. Cobley, 'Black West Indian Seamen in the British Merchant Marine in the Mid Nineteenth Century', *History Workshop Journal* 58 (2004), esp. pp. 263–4; and J.N. Brown, *Dropping Anchor, Setting Sail: Geographies of Race in Black Liverpool* (Princeton, NJ, 2005).

13. K.G. Persson, 'Mind the Gap! Transport Costs and Price Convergence in the Nineteenth Century Atlantic Economy', *European Review of Economic History* 8 (2004), esp. figs. 5–6, pp. 134–5; Cohn, 'Transition from Sail to Steam', *passim.*

14. Rodger, 'Recent Books', pp. 683–4.

15. Rodger, *Safeguard*; Rodger, *Command*; *passim.*

16. J. Glete, *Warfare at Sea, 1500–1650: Maritime Conflicts and the Transformation of Europe* (2000), p. 9.

17. E. Childers, *The Riddle of the Sands* (Oxford, 1998 pbk. edn.), p. 89.

18. P. Waller, *Writers, Readers, and Reputations: Literary Life in Britain 1870–1918* (Oxford, 2006), pp. 280–1.

19. B. Klein, 'Britain and the Sea', in Klein (ed.), *Fictions of the Sea: Critical Perspectives on the Ocean in British Literature and Culture* (Aldershot, 2002), p. 4.

20. J. Allen, *The Sea Years of Joseph Conrad* (1967), pp. 113–14, 118–19, 175.

21. J. Conrad, *The Mirror of the Sea* (1968 edn.), pp. 7, 24, 28.

22. J. Conrad, *Heart of Darkness* (1994 pbk. edn.), p. 5.

23. D. Cordingly, *Ships and Seascapes: An Introduction to Maritime Prints, Drawings and Watercolours* (1997), pp. 77–8, 92–4.

24. C. Payne, *Where the Sea Meets the Land: Artists on the Coast in Nineteenth-Century Britain* (Bristol, 2007), pp. 13–14.

25. Cf. also C.F. Behrman, *Victorian Myths of the Sea* (Athens, OH, 1977), esp. pp. 24–37.

26. T.R. Gourvish, *The Official History of Britain and the Channel Tunnel* (2006), p. 364.

27. P. Hall, 'Magic Carpets and Seamless Webs: Opportunities and Constraints for High-Speed Trains in Europe', *Built Environment* 35 (2009), pp. 59–69.

28. K.M. Wilson, *Channel Tunnel Visions, 1850–1945: Dreams and Nightmares* (1994), pp. 6, 18–19; see I.F. Clarke, *Voices Prophesying War, 1763–1984* (Oxford, 1966), p. 110.

29. J. Parry, *The Politics of Patriotism: English Liberalism, National Identity and Europe, 1830–1886* (Cambridge, 2006), pp. 355–6.

30. R.S. Peckham, 'The Uncertain State of Islands: National Identity and the Discourse of Islands in Nineteenth-Century Britain and Greece', *Journal of Historical Geography* 29 (2003), p. 504.

31. P. Crimmin, 'The Channel's Strategic Significance: Invasion Threat, Line of Defence, Prison Wall, Escape Route', in J. Falvey and W. Brooks (eds.), *The Channel in the Eighteenth Century: Bridge, Barrier and Gateway* (Oxford, 1991), p. 69.

32. Gourvish, *Channel Tunnel*, pp. 369, 371.
33. Department for Transport, *Maritime Statistics 2007* (2008), table 31 (b), p. 59.
34. Admiral Sir Alan West, 'Midweek', BBC Radio 4, 21 December 2005.
35. F. Broeze, *Island Nation: A History of Australians and the Sea* (St Leonard's, NSW, 1998), p. 223.
36. B. Labaree *et al.*, *America and the Sea: A Maritime History* (Mystic, CT, 1999), p. 9.
37. D.G. Kirby and M-J. Hinkkanen, *The Baltic and the North Seas* (2000), p. 276.
38. For this phrase see C. Connery, '*There Was No More Sea*: The Supersession of the Ocean, From the Bible to Cyberspace', *Journal of Historical Geography* 32 (2006), p. 496.
39. One call for a 'holistic approach' can be found in H. Driessen, 'Review Article: *Seascapes* and *Mediterranean Crossings*', *Journal of Global History* 3 (2008), p. 448.

Bibliography of works cited

Place of publication is London unless otherwise stated

C. Adams, *Across Seven Seas and Thirteen Rivers: Life Stories of Pioneer Sylhetti Settlers in Britain* (1987).

K. Adams and K. Macdonald-Wallis, 'UK Oil Imports since 1920', *Energy Trends* (2007), pp. 26–31.

M. Adams, *Admiral Collingwood: Nelson's Own Hero* (2005).

I. Adams and M. Somerville, *Cargoes of Despair and Hope: Scottish Emigration to North America 1603–1803* (Edinburgh, 1993).

R. Adkins, *Trafalgar: The Biography of a Battle* (2005).

R. Adkins and L. Adkins, *The War for All the Oceans: From Nelson at the Nile to Napoleon at Waterloo* (2005).

J. Agar, S. Green and P. Harvey, 'Cotton to Computers: From Industrial to Information Revolutions', in S. Woolgar (ed.), *Virtual Society? Technology, Cyberbole, Reality* (Oxford, 2002), pp. 264–85.

S. Agarwal, 'Global-Local Interactions in English Coastal Resorts: Theoretical Perspectives', *Tourism Geographies* 7 (2005), pp. 351–72.

———, 'Institutional Change and Resort Capacity: The Case of Southwest English Coastal Resorts', in S. Agarwal and G. Shaw (eds.), *Managing Coastal Tourism Resorts: A Global Perspective* (Clevedon, 2006), pp. 56–72.

———, and P. Brunt, 'Social Exclusion and English Seaside Resorts', *Tourism Management* 27 (2006), pp. 654–70.

P. Aghion and J.G. Williamson, *Growth, Inequality and Globalization: Theory, History and Policy* (Cambridge, 1998).

M.E. Ailes, *Military Migration and State Formation: The British Military Community in Seventeenth-Century Sweden* (2002).

R.G. Albion, *Forests and Sea Power: The Timber Problem of the Royal Navy, 1652–1862* (Cambridge, Mass., 1926).

A. Aldgate, *Best of British: Cinema and Society from 1930 to the Present* (2002).

D. Aldridge, 'The Navy as Handmaid for Commerce and High Policy 1680–1720', in J. Black and P. Woodfine (eds.), *The British Navy and the Use of Naval Power in the Eighteenth Century* (Leicester, 1988), pp. 51–69.

J. Allen, *The Sea Years of Joseph Conrad* (1967).

S. Allen, 'British Cinema at the Seaside – the Limits of Liminality', *Journal of British Cinema and Television* 5 (2008), pp. 53–71.

H. Altink, 'Deviant and Dangerous: Pro-Slavery Representations of Jamaican Slave Women's sexuality, c. 1780–1834', *Slavery and Abolition* 26 (2005), pp. 271–88.

A. Alvarez, *Offshore: A North Sea Journey* (1986).

O. Anderson, 'The Establishment of British Supremacy at Sea and the Exchange of Naval Prisoners of War, 1689–1783', *English Historical Review* 75 (1960), pp. 77–89.

————, 'Emigration and Marriage Break-Up in Mid-Victorian England', *Economic History Review* 50 (1997), pp. 104–09.

K.R. Andrews, *Elizabethan Privateering: English Privateering During the Spanish War* (Cambridge, 1964).

————, 'The Aims of Drake's Expedition of 1577–1580', *American Historical Review* (1968), pp. 724–41.

————, 'Sir Robert Cecil and Mediterranean Plunder', *English Historical Review* (1972), pp. 513–32.

————, *Ships, Money and Politics: Seafaring and Naval Enterprise in the Reign of Charles I* (Cambridge, 1991).

R. Anstey, *The Atlantic Slave Trade and British Abolition, 1760–1810* (1975).

M. Anwar, *The Myth of Return: Pakistanis in Britain* (1979).

J.C. Appleby, 'A Nursery of Pirates: The English Pirate Community in Ireland in the Early 17th Century', *International Journal of Maritime History* (1990), pp. 1–27.

R. Appleyard, *The Ten Pound Immigrants* (1988).

D. Armitage, *The Ideological Origins of the British Empire* (Cambridge, 2000).

J. Armstrong and D.M. Williams, 'The Steamship as an Agent of Modernisation, 1812–1840', *International Journal of Maritime History* 19 (2007), pp. 145–60.

B. Ashcroft, *On Post-Colonial Futures: Transformations of Colonial Culture* (2001).

S. Ashley, 'How Navigators Think: The Death of Captain Cook Revisited', *Past and Present* 194 (2007), pp. 107–37.

Association of District Councils, *Making the Most of the Coast* (1993).

S-E. Astrom, *From Cloth to Iron: The Anglo-Baltic Trade in the Late Seventeenth Century* (Helsingfors, 2 vols., 1963–65).

W.H. Auden, *The Enchaféd Flood: Or, The Romantic Iconography of the Sea* (1951).

————, *Collected Shorter Poems, 1927–57* (1966).

————, *The Sea and the Mirror: A Commentary on Shakespeare's 'The Tempest'* (Oxford, 2003 edn.).

J. Aulich, 'Wildlife in the South Atlantic: Graphic Satire, Patriotism and the Fourth Estate', in J. Aulich (ed.), *Framing the Falklands War: Nationhood, Culture and Identity* (Milton Keynes, 1992), pp. 84–116.

G.E. Aylmer, 'Navy, State, Trade and Empire', in N. Canny (ed.), *The Oxford History of the British Empire, Vol. I: The Origins of Empire* (Oxford, 1998), pp. 467–81.

J.H. Baer, ' "Captain John Avery" and the Anatomy of a Mutiny', *Eighteenth Century Life* 18 (1994), pp. 1–26.

J. Bailkin, 'Leaving Home: The Politics of Deportation in Postwar Britain', *Journal of British Studies* 47 (2008), pp. 852–82.

B. Bailyn, *The Peopling of British North America: An Introduction* (1986).

————, *Voyagers to the West: Emigration from Britain to America on the Eve of the Revolution* (1987).

————, 'Considering the Slave Trade: History and Memory', *William and Mary Quarterly* 58 (2001), pp. 245–52.

————, 'Introduction', in D. Armitage and M. Braddick (eds.), *The British Atlantic World, 1500–1800* (Basingstoke, 2002), pp. xiv–xx.

————, *Atlantic History: Concept and Contours* (Cambridge, Mass., 2005).

D. Baines, *Migration in a Mature Economy: Emigration and Internal Migration in England 1861–1900* (Cambridge, 1985).

————, 'European Emigration, 1815–1930: Looking at the Emigration Decision Again', *Economic History Review* 47 (1994), pp. 525–44.

P. Baker and J. Stanley, *Hello Sailor! The Hidden History of Gay Life at Sea* (2003).

G. Balachandran, 'Crossing the Last Frontier: Transatlantic Movements of Asian Maritime Workers, c.1900–1945', *Research in Maritime History* 33 (2007), pp. 97–112.

S. Ball, *The Bitter Sea: The Struggle for Mastery in the Mediterranean 1935–1949* (2009).

I. Ballantyne, *Strike from the Sea: The Royal Navy and US Navy at War in the Middle East* (2004).

P. Banbury, *Shipbuilders of the Thames and Medway* (Newton Abbot, 1971).

V. Barbour, 'Privateers and Pirates of the West Indies', *The American Historical Review* 16 (1911), pp. 529–66.

———, 'Dutch and English Merchant Shipping in the Seventeenth Century', in E.M. Carus-Wilson (ed.), *Essays in Economic History, Vol. I* (1954), pp. 227–53.

A. Barnett, *Iron Britannia: Why Parliament Fought Its Falklands War* (1982).

C. Barnett, *The Audit of War: The Illusion and Reality of Britain as a Great Nation* (pbk. edn., 1987).

———, *Engage the Enemy More Closely: The Royal Navy in the Second World War* (1991).

J.M. Barrie, *Peter Pan* (1906; Harmondsworth, 1995 edn.).

C.J. Bartlett, *Great Britain and Sea Power, 1815–1853* (Oxford, 1963).

———, *The Long Retreat: A Short History of British Defence Policy, 1945–1970* (1972).

C. Bartolovich, ' "Baseless Fabric": London as a "World City" ', in P. Hulme and W.H. Sherman (eds.), *The Tempest and Its Travels* (2000), pp. 13–26.

S. Basnett, 'Cabin'd Yet Unconfined: Heroic Masculinity in English Seafaring Novels', in B. Klein (ed.). *Fictions of the Sea: Critical Perspectives on the Ocean in British Literature and Culture* (Aldershot, 2002), pp. 176–87.

D.A. Baugh, *British Naval Administration in the Age of Walpole* (Princeton, NJ, 1965).

———, 'Great Britain's "Blue Water" Policy, 1689–1815', *International History Review* 10 (1988), pp. 33–58.

———, 'Why Did Britain Lose Control of the Sea During the War for America?' in Black and Woodfine (eds.), *British Navy*, pp. 149–69.

———, 'The Politics of British Naval Failure, 1775–1778', *American Neptune* 52 (1992), pp. 221–46.

———, 'Maritime Strength and Atlantic Commerce: The Uses of a "Grand Marine Empire" ', in L. Stone (ed.), *An Imperial State at War: Britain 1689–1815* (1994), pp. 185–223.

———, 'The Eighteenth Century Navy as a National Institution', in J.R. Hill (ed.), *The Oxford Illustrated History of the Royal Navy* (Oxford, 1995), pp. 120–60.

J. Baxendale, *Priestley's England: J.B. Priestley and English Culture* (Manchester, 2007).

C. Bean, *The Macroeconomic Consequences of North Sea Oil* (1986).

R.N. Bean, 'The British Trans-Atlantic Slave Trade 1650–1775', *Journal of Economic History* 32 (1972), pp. 409–11.

C. Beatty and S. Fothergill, *The Seaside Economy: The Final Report of the Seaside Towns Research Project* (Sheffield, 2003).

———, 'Economic Change and the Labour Market in Britain's Seaside Towns', *Regional Studies* 38 (2004), pp. 461–80.

J.V. Beckett, *Coal and Tobacco: The Lowthers and the Economic Development of West Cumberland, 1660–1760* (1981).

J.F. Beeler, *British Naval Policy in the Gladstone-Disraeli Era* (Stanford, Cal., 1997).

A. Behdad, *A Forgetful Nation: On Immigration and Cultural Identity in the United States* (Durham, NC, 2005).

S.D. Behrendt, 'Markets, Transaction Cycles, and Profits: Merchant Decision Making in the British Slave Trade' *William and Mary Quarterly* 58 (2001), pp. 171–204.

C.F. Behrman, *Victorian Myths of the Sea* (Athens, Ohio, 1977).

C.M. Bell, 'The "Singapore Strategy" and the Deterrence of Japan: Winston Churchill, the Admiralty and the Dispatch of Force Z', *English Historical Review* 116 (2001), pp. 604–34.

L.J. Bellot, 'Evangelicals and the Defense of Slavery in Britain's Old Colonial Empire', *Journal of Southern History* 37 (1971), pp. 19–40.

G. Bennett, *Naval Battles of the First World War* (Harmondsworth, 2001 pbk. edn.).

J. Benidickson, *The Culture of Flushing: A Social and Legal History of Sewage* (Vancouver, BC, 2007 pbk. edn.).

L. Benton, 'Legal Spaces of Empire: Piracy and the Origins of Ocean Regionalism', *Comparative Studies in Society and History* 47 (2005), pp. 700–24.

A. Benvenuti, 'The Heath Government and British Defence Policy in South East Asia at the End of Empire', *Twentieth Century British History* 20 (2009), pp. 53–73.

M. Berg and P. Hudson, 'Rehabilitating the Industrial Revolution', *Economic History Review* 45 (1992), pp. 24–50.

———, *Luxury and Pleasure in Eighteenth Century England* (Oxford, 2005).

N. Best, *Trafalgar: The Untold Story of the Greatest Sea Battle in History* (2005).

L.M. Bethell, 'Britain, Portugal and the Suppression of the Brazilian Slave Trade: The Origin of the Palmerston Act of 1839', *English Historical Review* 80 (1965), pp. 761–84.

A. Bialuschewski, 'Between Newfoundland and the Malacca Strait: A Survey of the Golden Age of Piracy, 1695–1725', *Mariner's Mirror* 90 (2004), pp.167–86.

H. Bicheno, *Razor's Edge: The Unofficial History of the Falklands War* (2006).

L. Billington and R. Billington, ' "A Burning Zeal for Righteousness": Women in the British Anti-Slavery Movement, 1820–1870', in J. Rendall (ed.), *Equal or Different: Women's Politics 1800–1914* (Basingstoke, 1985), pp. 82–111.

J. Black, 'Anglo-Baltic Relations 1714–1748', in W.E. Minchinton (ed.), *Britain and the Northern Seas* (Pontefract, 1988), pp. 67–74.

———, *The British Seaborne Empire* (2004).

———, 'A Post-Imperial Power? Britain and the Royal Navy', *Orbis* 49 (2005), pp. 353–65.

R. Blackburn, *The Making of New World Slavery: From the Baroque to the Modern 1492–1800* (1997).

M. Bogucka, 'Scots in Gdansk (Danzig) in the Seventeenth Century', in A.I. Macinnes, T. Riis and F. Pedersen (eds.), *Ships, Guns and Bibles in the North Sea and Baltic States, c.1350–1700* (East Linton, 2000), pp. 39–46.

W.J. Bolster, 'Opportunities in Marine Environmental History', *Environmental History* 11 (2006), pp. 567–97.

———, 'Putting the Ocean in Atlantic History: Maritime Communities and Marine Ecology in the Northwest Atlantic, 1500–1800', *American Historical Review* 113 (2008), pp. 19–47.

D.W. Bone, *Merchantmen-At-Arms: The British Merchant Service in the War* (1929).

D. Booth, 'Surfing: From One (Cultural) Extreme to Another', in B. Wheaton (ed.), *Understanding Lifestyle Sports: Consumption, Identity and Difference* (2004), pp. 94–109.

Booz-Allen and Hamilton International, *British Shipbuilding 1972: A Report to the Department of Trade and Industry* (1973).

M.D. Bordo and E.N. White, 'A Tale of Two Currencies: British and French Finance During the Napoleonic Wars', *Journal of Economic History* 51 (1991), pp. 303–16.

W.D. Borrie, *The European Peopling of Australasia: A Demographic History, 1788–1988* (Canberra, 1994).

D.H. Boteler, 'The Super Storms of August/September 1859 and Their Effects on the Telegraph System', *Advances in Space Research* 38 (2006), pp. 159–72.

H.R. Fox Bourne, *English Merchants: Memoirs in Illustration of the Progress of British Commerce* (1886).

D.G. Boyce, *The Falklands War* (Basingstoke, 2005).

F. Braudel, *The Mediterranean and the Mediterranean World in the Age of Philip II* (Eng. trans., 1972 edn.).

M. Bravo, 'Geographies of Exploration and Improvement: William Scoresby and Arctic Whaling, 1782–1822', *Journal of Historical Geography* 32 (2006), pp. 512–38.

M. Brayshay, 'The Emigration Trade in Nineteenth Century Devon', in M. Duffy, et al. (eds.), *The New Maritime History of Devon, Vol. II: From the Late Eighteenth Century to the Present Day* (Exeter, 1994), pp. 108–18.

K. Breen, 'Divided Command: The West Indies and North America, 1780–1781', in Black and Woodfine (eds.), *British Navy*, pp. 191–206.

R. Brenner, 'The Social Basis of English Commercial Expansion, 1550–1650', *Journal of Economic History* 32 (1972), pp. 361–84.

J. Brewer, *The Sinews of Power: War, Money and the English State 1688–1783* (1989).

C. Bridenbaugh and R. Bridenbaugh, *No Peace Beyond the Line: The English in the Caribbean, 1624–1690* (1972).

A. Briggs, *The Age of Improvement 1783–1867* (2nd edn., 2000).

Brighton Fishing Community Project Team, *Catching Stories: Voices from the Brighton Fishing Community* (Brighton, 1996).

F. Broeze, *Island Nation: A History of Australians and the Sea* (St Leonard's, NSW, 1998).

J.S. Bromley, 'The British Navy and Its Seamen after 1688: Notes Towards an Unwritten History', in S. Palmer and G. Williams (eds.), *Charted and Uncharted Waters: Proceedings of a Conference on the Study of British Maritime History* (Greenwich, 1981), pp. 125–60.

———, 'Outlaws at Sea', in F. Krantz (ed.), *History from Below: Studies in Popular Protest and Popular Ideology* (1985), pp. 293–318.

———, 'The Second Hundred Years War', in J.S. Bromley (ed.), *Corsairs and Navies 1660–1760* (1987), pp. 495–503.

C. Broodbank, *An Island Archaeology of the Early Cyclades* (Cambridge, 2000).

D.K. Brown, 'The Form and Speed of Sailing Warships', *Mariner's Mirror* 84 (1998), pp. 298–307.

J.N. Brown, *Dropping Anchor, Setting Sail: Geographies of Race in Black Liverpool* (Princeton, NJ, 2005).

C.J. Bruce, *Invaders: British and American Experience of Seaborne Landings, 1939–1945* (1997).

J. Buckley, 'Air Power and the Battle of the Atlantic 1939–45', *Journal of Contemporary History* 28 (1993), pp. 143–161.

P. Buckner, *English Canada: The Founding Generations* (1993).

G.S. Burgess, W. Raymond and J. Barron, *The Voyage of Saint Brendan: Representative Versions of the Legend in English Translation* (Exeter, 2005).

J. Burnett and P. Burnett, *Plenty and Want: A Social History of Food in England from 1815 to the Present Day* (rev. edn., 1979).

A. Burton, *The Rise and Fall of British Shipbuilding* (1994).

J. Bush, ' "The Right Sort of Woman": Female Emigrators and Emigration to the British Empire, 1890–1910', *Women's History Review* 3 (1994), pp. 385–409.

———, *Edwardian Ladies and Imperial Power* (2000).

R.W. Butler, 'Introduction', in R.W. Butler and D. Pearce (eds.), *Change in Tourism: People, Places, Processes* (1995), pp. 1–11.

———, 'The Origins of the Tourism Area Life Cycle', in R.W. Butler (ed.), *The Tourism Area Life Cycle: Conceptual and Theoretical Issues* (Bristol, 2000), pp. 13–26.

A. Byatt, A. Fothergill and M. Holmes, *The Blue Planet: A Natural History of the Oceans* (2001).

A.W. Cafruny, *Ruling the Waves: The Political Economy of International Shipping* (Berkeley, CA, 1987).

P.J. Cain and A.G. Hopkins, *British Imperialism 1688–2000* (2nd edn., Harlow, 2002).

G. Callender and F.H. Hinsley, *The Naval Side of British History* (1924 orig.; 1952 edn.).

D.F. Campbell and R.A. MacLean, *Beyond the Atlantic Roar: A Study of the Nova Scotia Scots* (Toronto, 1974).

M.C. Campbell, 'St George's Cay: Genesis of the British Settlement of Belize', *Journal of Caribbean History* 37 (2003), pp. 171–203.

D. Cannadine, 'The Empire Strikes Back', *Past and Present* 147 (1995), pp. 180–94.

———, *In Churchill's Shadow: Confronting the Past in Modern Britain* (2002).

———, 'Introduction', in D. Cannadine (ed.), *Empire, the Sea and Global History: Britain's Maritime World, c.1763–c.1840* (Basingstoke, 2007), pp. 1–5.

N. Canny, 'Migration and Opportunity: Britain, Ireland the New World', *Irish Economic and Social History* 12 (1985), pp. 7–32.

———, 'English Migration into and Across the Atlantic During the Seventeenth and Eighteenth Centuries', in N. Canny (ed.), *Europeans on the Move: Studies on European Migration, 1500–1800* (Oxford, 1994), pp. 39–75.

B. Capp, *Cromwell's Navy: The Fleet and the English Revolution 1648–1660* (Oxford, 1989).

N.H. Carrier and J.R. Jeffery, *External Migration: A Study of the Available Statistics, 1815–1950* (1953).

S.L. Carruthers, *The Media at War: Communication and Conflict in the Twentieth Century* (Basingstoke, 2000).

R.L. Carson, *The Sea Around Us* (1951).

M. Castells, 'Information, Networks and the Network Society: A Theoretical Blueprint', in M. Castells (ed.), *The Network Society: A Cross-Cultural Perspective* (Cheltenham, 2004), pp. 3–48.

P. Catterall, 'The East of Suez Decision: Witness Seminar', *Contemporary British History* 7 (1993), pp. 612–53.

J. Cavell, 'The Imperial Race and the Immigration Sieve: The Canadian Debate on Assisted British Migration and Empire Settlement, 1900–30', *Journal of Imperial and Commonwealth History* 34 (2006), pp. 345–67.

K.N. Chaudhuri, 'The English East India Company's Shipping c.1660–1760', in J.R. Bruijn and F.S. Gaastra (eds.), *Ships, Sailors and Spices: East India Companies and Their Shipping in the Sixteenth, Seventeenth and Eighteenth Centuries* (The Hague, 1987), pp. 49–80.

———, *The English East India Company: The Study of an Early Joint-Stock Company 1600–1640* (1999 edn.)

J. Child, *A New Discourse on Trade* (1668; 3rd edn., 1693).

E. Childers, *The Riddle of the Sands* (1903; Oxford, 1998 pbk. edn.).

L. Chilton, *Agents of Empire: British Female Migration to Canada and Australia, 1860s–1930* (Toronto, 2007).

W. Chin, 'Operations in a War Zone: The Royal Navy in the Persian Gulf in the 1980s', in I. Speller (ed.), *The Royal Navy and Maritime Power in the Twentieth Century* (2005), pp. 181–96.

G.E. Chortareas and T. Pelagidis, 'Trade Flows: A Facet of Regionalisation or Globalisation?', *Cambridge Journal of Economics* 28 (2004), pp. 253–71.

E.J. Christopher, 'Another Head of the Hydra? Slave Trade Sailors and Militancy on the African Coast', *Atlantic Studies* 1 (2004), pp. 145–57.

———, *Slave Ship Sailors and Their Captive Cargoes* (Cambridge, 2006).

A.C. Clarke, *Voice Across the Sea* (2nd edn., 1974).

I.F. Clarke, *Voices Prophesying War, 1763–1984* (Oxford, 1966).

P. Clarke, *Hope and Glory: Britain 1900–1990* (Harmondsworth, 1996).

T. Clayton, *Tars: The Men Who Made Britain Rule the Waves* (2007).

T. Clayton and P. Craig, *Finest Hour* (2001).

———, *Trafalgar: The Men, the Battle, the Storm* (2004).

S. Clissold, 'Christian Renegades and Barbary Corsairs', *History Today* 26 (1976), pp. 508–15.

W.L. Clowes, *The Royal Navy: A History from the Earliest Times to the Present* (1997 edn.), Vol. VII.

C. Clover, *The End of the Line: How Overfishing Is Changing the World and What We Eat* (2005).

Cm. 3950, *British Shipping: Charting a New Course* (1998).

Cm. 6392, Royal Commission on Environmental Pollution, 24th Report, *Turning the Tide: Addressing the Impact of Fisheries on the Marine Environment* (2004).

Cmnd. 124, *Defence: Outline of Future Policy* (1957).

Cmnd. 2937, *Shipbuilding Inquiry Committee, 1965–66: Report* (1966).

Cmnd. 4337, *Committee of Inquiry into Shipping, Report* (1970).

Cmnd. 8787, *The Falkland Islands Review* (1983; 1992 Pimlico pbk. reprint).

J.G. Coad, *The Royal Dockyards 1690–1850: Architecture and Engineering Works of the Sailing Navy* (Aldershot, 1989).

A.G. Cobley, 'Black West Indian Seamen in the British Merchant Marine in the Mid Nineteenth Century', *History Workshop Journal* 58 (2004), pp. 259–74.

L.E. Cochran, *Scottish Trade with Ireland in the Eighteenth Century* (Edinburgh, 1985).

R. Cock, '"The Finest Invention in the World": The Royal Navy's Early Trials of Copper Sheathing, 1708–1770', *Mariner's Mirror* 87 (2001), pp. 446–59.

P.A. Coclanis, 'Atlantic World or Atlantic/World?', *William and Mary Quarterly* 63 (2006), pp. 675–92.

R.L. Cohn, 'The Transition from Sail to Steam in Immigration to the United States', *Journal of Economic History* 65 (2005), pp. 469–95.

P.W. Coldham, *Emigrants in Chains: A Social History of Forced Emigration to the Americas 1607–1776* (Stroud, 1992).

D.C. Coleman, 'Naval Dockyards under the Later Stuarts', *Economic History Review* 6 (1953–54), pp. 134–55.

T. Coleman, *The Liners: A History of the North Atlantic Crossing* (New York, 1976).

A. Coles and T. Briggs, *Flagship Hood: The Fate of Britain's Mightiest Warship* (1985).

T. Coleman, *Passage to America: A History of Emigrants from Great Britain and Ireland to America in the Mid-Nineteenth Century* (1992).

L. Colley, *Britons: Forging the Nation 1707–1837* (1992).

———, *Captives: Britain, Empire and the World 1600–1850* (2002).

V. Collingridge, *Captain Cook* (2000).

W. Collins, *Jamaican Migrant* (1965).

R. Colls, *Identity of England* (Oxford, 2002).

Commission on the Future of Multi-Ethnic Britain (Parekh Report), *The Future of Multi-Ethnic Britain: Report of the Commission on the Future of Multi-Ethnic Britain* (2000).

M.A. Conley, *From Jack Tar to Union Jack: Representing Naval Manhood in the British Empire, 1870–1918* (Manchester, 2009).

G.G. Connell, *Jack's War: Lower-Deck Recollections from World War II* (Bristol, rev. edn., 1995).

C. Connery, '*There Was No More Sea*: The Supersession of the Ocean, From the Bible to Cyberspace', *Journal of Historical Geography* 32 (2006), pp. 494–511.

J. Conrad, *The Mirror of the Sea* (1906; 1968 edn.).

———, *Heart of Darkness* (1899; pbk. edn., 1994).

S. Constantine, 'Immigration and the Making of New Zealand, 1918–1939', in S. Constantine (ed.), *Emigrants and Empire: British Settlement in the Dominions between the Wars* (Manchester, 1990), pp. 121–49.

———, 'Empire Migration and Social Reform, 1880–1950', in C.G. Pooley and I.D. White (eds.), *Migrants, Emigrants and Immigrants: A Social History of Migration* (1991), pp. 62–85.

———, 'Migrants and Settlers', in W.R. Louis *et al.* (eds.), *The Oxford History of the British Empire: Volume IV: The Twentieth Century* (Oxford, 1999), pp. 163–87.

———, 'The British Government, Child Welfare and Child Migration to Australia after 1945', *Journal of Imperial and Commonwealth History* 30 (2002), pp. 99–132.

———, 'British Emigration to the Empire-Commonwealth since 1880: >From Overseas Settlement to Diaspora?', *Journal of Imperial and Commonwealth History* 31 (2003), pp. 16–35.

S. Conway, *The British Isles and the War of American Independence* (Oxford, 2000).

———, ' "A Joy Unknown for Years Past": The American War, Britishness and the Celebration of Rodney's Victory at the Saints', *History* 86 (2001), pp. 180–99.

———, *War, State and Society in Mid-Eighteenth Century Britain and Ireland* (Oxford, 2006).

T.P. Coogan, *Wherever Green Is Worn: The Story of the Irish Diaspora* (2001).

C. Cooper, 'The Environmental Consequences of Declining Destinations', in C. Cooper and S. Wanhill (eds.), *Tourism Development: Environment and Community Issues* (Chichester, 1997), pp. 129–37.

H. Cooper, *The English Romance in Time: Transforming Motifs from Geoffrey of Monmouth to the Death of Shakespeare* (Oxford, 2004).

D. Cordingly, *Ships and Seascapes: An Introduction to Maritime Prints, Drawings and Watercolours* (1997).

———, *Life Among the Pirates: The Romance and the Reality* (2000 edn.).

———, *Heroines and Harlots: Women at Sea in the Great Age of Sail* (2001).

———, *Billy Ruffian: The Bellerophon and the Downfall of Napoleon* (pbk. edn., 2004).

P. Corfield, *The Impact of English Towns, 1700–1800* (Oxford, 1982).

L. Cormack, *Charting an Empire: Geography at the English University 1580–1620* (1997).

J.R. Coull, *The Sea Fisheries of Scotland* (Edinburgh, 1996).

C. Coultass, 'British Feature Films and the Second World War', *Journal of Contemporary History* 19 (1984), pp. 7–22.

D. Coyle, *The Weightless World* (Oxford, 1999 pbk. edn.).

N. Crafts, *British Economic Growth During the Industrial Revolution* (Oxford, 1985).

J. Craik, 'The Culture of Tourism', in C. Rojek and J. Urry (eds.), *Touring Cultures: Transformations of Travel and Theory* (1997), pp. 113–36.

M. Craton, J. Walvin and D. Wright, *Slavery, Abolition, and Emancipation: Black Slaves and the British Empire* (1976).

D. Cressy, 'The Vast and Furious Ocean: The Passage to Puritan New England', *The New England Quarterly* 57 (1984), pp. 511–32.

———, *Coming Over: Migration and Communication between England and New England in the Seventeenth Century* (Cambridge, 1987).

P. Crimmin, 'The Channel's Strategic Significance: Invasion Threat, Line of Defence, Prison Wall, Escape Route', in J. Falvey and W. Brooks (eds.), *The Channel in the Eighteenth Century: Bridge, Barrier and Gateway* (Oxford, 1991), pp. 67–81.

P. Croft, 'Trading with the Enemy, 1585–1604', *Historical Journal* 32 (1989), pp. 281–302.

A.W. Crosby, *Ecological Imperialism: The Biological Expansion of Europe, 900–1900* (Cambridge, 1986).

G.S. Cross and J.K. Walton, *The Playful Crowd: Pleasure Places in the Twentieth Century* (2005).

F. Crouzet, 'The Second Hundred Years War: Some Reflections', *French History* 10 (1996), pp. 432–50.

L.M. Cullen, 'The Irish Diaspora of the Seventeenth and Eighteenth Centuries', in Canny (ed.), *Europeans on the Move*, pp. 113–49.

P.D. Curtin, *The Rise and Fall of the Plantation Complex: Essays in Atlantic History* (2nd edn., Cambridge, 1998).

A. Dabat and L. Lorenzano, *Argentina, The Malvinas and the End of Military Rule* (Eng. trans., 1984).

D. Dabydeen, *Turner: New and Selected Poems* (1994).

D. Dabydeen, J. Gilmore and C. Jones, *The Oxford Companion to Black British History* (Oxford, 2008 pbk. edn.).

R. Dafter and I. Davidson, 'North Sea Oil and Gas and British Foreign Policy', *Chatham House Papers* 10 (1980).

C. Dandeker and M.W. Segal, 'Gender Integration in Armed Forces: Recent policy Developments in the United Kingdom', *Armed Forces and Society* 23 (1996), pp. 29–47.

R. Daniels, *Coming to America: A History of Immigration and Ethnicity in American Life* (1991).

W. Darity, Jr., 'The Numbers Game and the Profitability of the British Trade in Slaves', *Journal of Economic History* 45 (1985), pp. 693–703.

M. Daunton, *Progress and Poverty: An Economic and Social History of Britain 1700–1850* (Oxford, 1995).

R. Davenport-Hines, *Auden* (1995).

C.S.L. Davies, 'The Alleged "Sack of Bristol": International Ramifications of Breton Privateering 1484–5', *Historical Research* 67 (1994), pp. 230–9.

J.D. Davies, *Gentlemen and Tarpaulins: The Officers and Men of the Restoration Navy* (Oxford, 1991).

———, 'The Birth of the Imperial Navy? Aspects of Maritime Strategy, c. 1650–90', in M. Duffy (ed.), *Parameters of British Naval Power, 1650–1850* (Exeter, 1992), pp. 14–38.

R.E.G. Davies, *A History of the World's Airlines* (Oxford, 1967).

R. Davis, *The Rise of the English Shipping Industry in the Seventeenth and Eighteenth Centuries* (1962).

———, 'English Foreign Trade, 1700–1774', *Economic History Review* 15 (1962), pp. 285–303.

———, *English Overseas Trade, 1500–1700* (1973).

———, *English Merchant Shipping and Anglo-Dutch Rivalry in the Seventeenth Century* (1975).

———, 'Maritime History: Progress and Problems', in S. Marriner (ed.), *Business and Businessmen: Studies in Business, Economic and Accounting History* (Liverpool, 1978), pp. 169–97.

P.S. Dawson, *British Superliners of the Sixties* (1990).

M. Dawswell, 'The Pigmentocracy of Citizenship: Assimilation, Integration or Alienation?', in L. Black *et al.* (eds.), *Consensus or Coercion? The State, The People and Social Cohesion in Post-War Britain* (2001), pp. 66–81.

N. Deakin, *Colour, Citizenship and British Society* (1970).

D.W. Dean, 'Conservative Governments and the Restriction of Commonwealth Immigration in the 1950s: The Problems of Constraint', *Historical Journal* 35 (1992), pp. 171–94.

I. Dear, *Great Ocean Liners: The Heyday of Luxury Travel* (1991).

D. Defoe, *Captain Singleton* (1719; 1963 edn.).

———, *Robinson Crusoe* (1720; Harmondsworth, 1994 edn.).

E. Delaney, *The Irish in Post-War Britain* (Oxford, 2007).

J.M. Delombard, 'Turning Back the Clock: Black Atlantic Literary Studies', *The New England Quarterly* 75 (2002), pp. 647–55.

G. Dening, *Mr Bligh's Bad Language: Passion, Power and Theatre on the Bounty* (Cambridge, 1992).

F. Dennis and N. Khan (eds.), *Voices of the Crossing* (2000).

Department for Environment, Food and Rural Affairs (DEFRA), *Making Space for Water: Developing a New Government Strategy for Flood and Coastal Erosion Risk Management in England* (2004).

———, *Making Space for Water: Taking Forward a New Government Strategy for Flood and Coastal Erosion Risk in England* (2005).

Department of Energy and Climate Change (DECC), 'Environment Study to Inform Location of Future Offshore Energy Developments', available at http://www.decc.gov.uk/.

———, *UK Offshore Energy Strategic Environmental Assessment* (2009).

Department of Trade and Industry, *Digest of United Kingdom Energy Statistics 2000* (2000).

Department of Transport, *Transport Statistics, Great Britain, 1964–1974* (1976).

———, *Maritime Statistics* (1997).

C. Desmoulins, *Living by the Sea: 25 International Examples* (Basel, Eng. trans., 2008).

T.M. Devine, *The Scottish Nation, 1700–2000* (Harmondsworth, 1999).

———, *Scotland's Empire 1600–1815* (Harmondsworth, 2004).

T.M. Devine, 'Scotland', in R. Floud and P.A. Johnson (eds.), *The Cambridge Economic History of Modern Britain* (Cambridge, 2004 edn.).

G.M. Dillon, *The Falklands, Politics and War* (Basingstoke, 1989).

S. Dillon, *Derek Jarman and Lyric Film: The Mirror and the Sea* (Austin, Tex., 2004).

S. Dockrill, *Britain's Retreat from East of Suez: The Choice between Europe and the World, 1945–1968* (2002).

A. Dorman, 'From Peacekeeping to Peace Enforcement: The Royal Navy and Peace Support Operations', in Speller (ed.), *Royal Navy and Maritime Power*, pp. 197–208.

S. Drescher, *Capitalism and Antislavery: British Mobilization in Comparative Perspective* (Basingstoke, 1986).

M. Dresser, *Slavery Obscured: The Social History of the Slave Trade in an English Provincial Port* (2001).

J.C. Dorsey, *Slave Traffic in the Age of Abolition: Puerton Rico, West Africa and the Non-Hispanic Caribbean 1815–1859* (Gainseville, FL, 2003).

B. Douglas, 'Voyages, Encounters, and Agency in Oceania: Captain Cook and Indigenous People', *History Compass* 6 (2008), pp. 712–37.

R. Drayton, *Nature's Government: Science, Imperial Britain, and the 'Improvement' of the World* (2000).

H. Driessen, '*Seascapes* and *Mediterranean Crossings*', *Journal of Global History* 3 (2008), pp. 445–9.

F. Driver, 'Distance and Disturbance: Travel, Exploration and Knowledge in the Nineteenth Century', *Transactions of the Royal Historical Society* VIth Series, 14 (2004), pp. 73–92.

M. Duffy, 'The Passage to the Colonies', *Mississippi Valley Historical Review* 38 (1951–52), pp. 21–38.

M. Duffy, ' "Science and Labour": The Naval Contribution to Operations Ashore in the Great Wars with France', in P. Hore (ed.), *Seapower Ashore: 200 Years of Royal Navy Operations on Land* (2001), pp. 39–52.

D. Dugaw, *Warrior Women and Popular Balladry, 1650–1850* (Chicago, 1996).

P. Dunkley, 'Emigration and the State, 1803–1842: The Nineteenth-Century Revolution in Government Reconsidered', *Historical Journal* 23 (1980), pp. 353–80.

P. Earle, *A City Full of People: Men and Women of London, 1650–1750* (1994).

———, *Sailors: English Merchant Seamen 1650–1775* (1998).

———, *The Pirate Wars* (2003).

P. Eddy and M. Linklater, *The Falklands War* (1982).

M. Eder, *Crime and Punishment in the Royal Navy of the Seven Years War, 1755–1763* (Aldershot, 2004).

D. Edgerton, *Warfare State: Britain, 1920–1970* (Cambridge, 2006).

B. Edwards, *The Fighting Tramps: The Merchant Navy Goes to War* (1989).

P. Edwards, *The Story of the Voyage: Sea-Narratives in Eighteenth-Century England* (Cambridge, 1994).

———, *Sea-Mark: The Metaphorical Voyage, Spenser to Milton* (Liverpool, 1997).

J. Ehrman, *The Navy in the War of William III, 1689–1697: Its State and Direction* (Cambridge, 1953).

G. Eley, 'Finding the People's War: Film, British Collective Memory, and World War II', *American Historical Review* 106 (2001), pp. 818–38.

R. Ellis, *The Empty Ocean* (Washington DC, 2003).

A. Ellner, 'Carrier Airpower in the Royal Navy during the Cold War: The International Strategic Context', *Defense and Security Analysis* 22 (2006), pp. 23–34.

D. Eltis, 'Free and Coerced Transatlantic Migrations: Some Comparisons', *American Historical Review* 88 (1983), pp. 251–80.

———, *Economic Growth and the Ending of the Transatlantic Slave Trade* (Oxford, 1987).

———, 'Europeans and the Rise and Fall of African Slavery in the Americas: An Interpretation', *American Historical Review* 98 (1993), pp. 1399–1423.

D. Eltis and S.L. Engerman, 'The Importance of Slavery and the Slave Trade to Industrializing Britain', *Journal of Economic History* 60 (2000), pp. 123–44.

———, 'The Volume and Structure of the Transatlantic Slave Trade: A Reassessment', *William and Mary Quarterly* 58 (2001), pp. 17–46.

P. Emmer, 'In Search of a System: The Atlantic Economy 1500–1800', in H. Pietschmann (ed.), *Atlantic History: A History of the Atlantic System 1580–1830* (Gottingen, 2002), pp. 169–78.

S. L. Engerman, 'The Slave Trade and British Capital Formation in the Eighteenth Century: A Comment on the Williams Thesis', *Business History Review* 46 (1972), pp. 430–43.

English Tourist Board, *Turning the Tide: A Heritage and Environment Strategy for a Seaside Resort* (1993).

O. Equiano, *The Interesting Narrative and Other Writings* (Harmondsworth, 2003 edn.).

C. Erickson, 'Emigration from the British Isles to the USA in 1831', *Population Studies* 35 (1981), pp. 175–97.

———, *Leaving England: Essays on British Emigration in the Nineteenth Century* (Ithaca, NY, 1994).

C. Ernest Fayle, *A Short History of the World's Shipping Industry* (1933).

European Commission, *Reform of the Common Fisheries Policy* (2009).

European Environment Agency, 'Late Lessons from Early Warnings: The Precautionary Principle, 1896–2000', *Environmental Issue Report* 22 (2001).

E.J. Evans, *The Forging of the Modern State: Early Industrial Britain 1783–1870* (1983).

J.J. Ewald, 'Crossers of the Sea: Slaves, Freedmen, and Other Migrants in the Northwestern Indian Ocean, c. 1750–1914', *American Historical Review* 105 (2000), pp. 69–91.

C. Ewan, 'The Emancipation Proclamation and British Public Opinion', *The Historian* 67 (2005), pp. 1–19.

J. Exquemeling, *The Buccaneers of America* (1898; Harmondsworth, 1969 edn.).

A. Farrington, *The English Factory in Japan, 1613–1623, Vol. II* (1991).

C.J. Fedorak, 'The Royal Navy and British Amphibious Operations During the Revolutionary and Napoleonic Wars', *Military Affairs* 52 (1988), pp. 141–6.

N. Ferguson, 'Public Finance and National Security: The Domestic Origins of the First World War Revisited', *Past and Present* 142 (1994), pp. 141–68.

———, *The Pity of War* (1999).

A. Finlan, *The Royal Navy in the Falklands Conflict and the Gulf War: Culture and Strategy* (2004).

C.H. Firth, *Naval Songs and Ballads* (1908).

G. Fisher, *Barbary Legend: War, Trade and Piracy in North Africa, 1415–1830* (Oxford, 1957).

P. Fitzgerald, 'A Sentence to Sail: The Transportation of Irish Convicts and Vagrants to America in the Eighteenth Century' in P. Fitzgerald and S. Ickringill (eds.), *Atlantic Crossroads: Historical Connections between Scotland, Ulster and North America* (Newtownards, 2001), pp. 114–32.

M.H. Fletcher, *The WRNS: A History of the Women's Royal Naval Service* (1989).

M. Flinn *et al.*, *Scottish Population History from the Seventeenth Century to the 1930s* (Cambridge, 1977).

D.O. Flynn and A. Giràldez, 'Cycles of Silver: Global Economic Unity through the Mid-Eighteenth Century', *Journal of World History* 13 (2002), pp. 391–427.

C.S. Forrester, *Mr. Midshipman Hornblower* (1950).

R. Foulke, *The Sea Voyage Narrative* (2002).

F.L. Fox, 'The English Naval Shipbuilding Programme of 1664', *Mariner's Mirror* 78 (1992), pp. 277–92.

———, 'Hired Men-of-War, 1664–67', *Mariner's Mirror* 84 (1998), pp. 13–25 and pp. 152–72.

M. Francis, *The Flyer: British Culture and the Royal Air Force 1939–1945* (Oxford, 2008).

L. Freedman, *The Official History of the Falklands Campaign* (2005 edn.).

D. French, *The British Way in Warfare 1688–2000* (2000).

I. Friel, *A Maritime History of Britain and Ireland, c.400–2001* (2003).

P. Fryer, *Staying Power: The History of Black People in Britain* (1984).

B. Fuchs, 'Faithless Empires: Pirates, Renegadoes and the English Nation', *English Literary History* 67 (2000), pp. 45–69.

M. Fuller, *Remembering the Early Modern Voyage: English Narratives in the Age of European Expansion* (Basingstoke, 2008).

T. Gale, 'Modernism, Post-Modernism and the Decline of British Seaside Resorts as Long Holiday Destinations: A Case Study of Rhyl, North Wales', *Tourism Geographies* 7 (2005), pp. 86–112.

———, 'The Problems and Dilemmas of Northern European Post-Mature Coastal Tourism Resorts', in Agarwal and Shaw (eds.), *Managing Coastal Tourism*, pp. 12–39.

L.E. Gallaway and R.K. Vedder, 'Emigration from the United Kingdom to the United States: 1860–1913', *Journal of Economic History* 31 (1971), pp. 885–97.

P.R. Galvin, *Patterns of Pillage: A Geography of Caribbean-Based Piracy in Spanish America, 1536–1718* (New York 1999).

A. Games, *Migration and the Origins of the English Atlantic World* (Cambridge, Mass., 1999).

———, 'Migration', in Armitage and Braddick (eds.), *British Atlantic World*, pp. 31–50.

———, 'Atlantic History: Definitions, Challenges, and Opportunities', *American Historical Review* 111 (2006), pp. 741–57.

J.S. Gardiner, 'Geography of British Fisheries', *Geographical Journal* 45 (1915), pp. 472–91.

W.J.R. Gardner, *Decoding History: The Battle of the Atlantic and Ultra* (Basingstoke, 1999).

N. Gash, *Sir Robert Peel: The Life of Sir Robert Peel after 1830* (pbk. edn., 1986).

D. Geggus, 'The Enigma of Jamaica in the 1790s: New Light on the Causes of Slave Rebellions', *William and Mary Quarterly* 44 (1987), pp. 274–99.

———, 'Sex Ratio and Ethnicity: A Reply to Paul E. Lovejoy', *Journal of African History* 30 (1989), pp. 395–7.

C. Geraghty, *British Cinema in the Fifties: Gender, Genre and the 'New Look'* (2000).

A.N. Gilbert, 'The Changing Face of British Military Justice, 1757–83', *Military Affairs* 49 (1985), pp. 80–4.

J.R. Gillis, 'Islands in the Making of an Atlantic Oceania, 1500–1800', in J.H. Bentley, R. Bridenthal and K. Wigen (eds.), *Seascapes: Maritime Histories, Littoral Cultures, and Transoceanic Exchanges* (Honolulu, 2007), pp. 21–37.

R. Girling, *Sea Change: Britain's Coastal Catastrophe* (2008 pbk. edn.).

R.E. Glass, 'The Image of the Sea Officer in English Literature, 1660–1710', *Albion* 26 (1994), pp. 583–99.

M.C. Glenn, 'The Naval Reform Campaign Against Flogging, 1830–1850', *American Quarterly* 35 (1983), pp. 408–25.

J. Glete, *Warfare at Sea, 1500–1650: Maritime Conflicts and the Transformation of Europe* (2000).

G. Gmelch, *Double Passage: The Lives of Caribbean Migrants Abroad and Back Home* (Ann Arbor, MI, 1992).

N.J.W. Goda, 'The Riddle of the Rock: A Reassessment of German Motives for the Capture of Gibraltar in the Second World War', *Journal of Contemporary History* 28 (1993), pp. 297–314.

P. Gogarty, *The Coast Road: A 3,000-mile Journey Round the Edge of England* (Rev. edn., 2007).

J. Goldrick, 'The Battleship Fleet: The Test of War, 1895–1919', in Hill (ed.), *Illustrated History*, pp. 280–318.

M. Goodwin, J. Gregory and B. Balmer, 'The Anatomy of the Brain Drain Debate, 1950–1970s', *Contemporary British History* iFirst online content, available at http://www.tandf.co.uk/journals/titles/13619462.asp.

A. Gordon, 'Battle of Britain: The Naval Perspective: The Whale and the Elephant', *RUSI Journal Online*, http://www.rusi.org/research/militarysciences/history/commentary.

A. Gorst, 'CVA-01', in R. Harding (ed.), *The Royal Navy, 1930–2000: Innovation and Defence* (2000), pp. 170–92.

J. Gothard, *Blue China: Single Female Migration to Colonial Australia* (Carlton South, Vic., 2001).

B.M. Gough, 'Maritime Strategy: The Legacies of Mahan and Corbett as Philosophers of Sea Power', *The RUSI Journal* 133 (1988), pp. 55–62.

C. Goulter, A. Gordon and G. Sheffield, 'The Royal Navy Did Not Win the "Battle of Britain", But We Need a Holistic View of Britain's Defences in 1940', *The RUSI Journal* 151 (2006), pp. 66–7.

T.R. Gourvish, *The Official History of Britain and the Channel Tunnel* (2006).

L. Gragg, 'The Port Royal Earthquake of 1692', *History Today* 50 (2000), pp. 28–34.

G.M. Graham, *The Fish Gate: On the English Fishing Industry* (1943).

G.S. Graham, *Empire of the North Atlantic: The Maritime Struggle for North America* (2nd edn., 1958).

———, *The Politics of Naval Supremacy: Studies in British Maritime Ascendancy* (Cambridge, 1965).

———, *The China Station: War and Diplomacy 1830–1860* (Oxford, 1978).

F. Gray, *Designing the Seaside: Architecture, Society and Nature* (2006).

P. Gray, ' "Shovelling out Your Paupers": The British State and Irish Famine Migration 1846–50', *Patterns of Prejudice* 33 (1999), pp. 47–65.

D. Greasley and L. Oxley, 'Discontinuities in Competitiveness: The Impact of the First World War on British Industry', *Economic History Review* 94 (1996), pp. 82–100.

E. Green, 'Very Private Enterprise: Ownership and Finance in British Shipping, 1825–1940', in T. Yui and K. Nakagawa (eds.), *Business History of Shipping: Strategy and Structure* (Tokyo, 1985), pp. 219–48.

M. Greenberg, *British Trade and the Opening of China 1800–42* (Cambridge, 1951).

J.P. Greene, 'Transatlantic Colonization and the Redefinition of Empire in the Early Modern Era', in C. Daniels (ed.), *Negotiated Empires: Centres and Peripheries in the New World, 1500–1820* (2001), pp. 267–82.

B. Greenhill and A. Gifford, *Women under sail* (1970).

———, *Steam, Politics and Patronage: The Transformation of the Royal Navy 1815–54* (1994).

B. Greenhill and M. Nix, 'North Devon Shipping, Trade and Ports, 1786–1939', in Duffy *et al.* (eds.), *New Maritime History of Devon, Vol. II*, pp. 48–59.

A. Gregory, *The Silence of Memory: Armistice Day 1919–1946* (Oxford, 1994).

A. Grenfell Price, *The Western Invasions of the Pacific and Its Continents* (Oxford, 1963).

P. Griffin, *The People with No Name: Ireland's Ulster Scots, America's Scots Irish, and the Creation of a British Atlantic World, 1689–1764* (Princeton, NJ, 2001).

E.J. Grove, *Vanguard to Trident: British Naval Policy since World War Two* (1987).

———, 'A Service Vindicated, 1939–1946', in Hill (ed.), *Illustrated History*, pp. 348–80.

——— (ed.), *The Defeat of the Enemy Attack on Shipping, 1939–1945* (Aldershot, 1997).

———, 'The Falklands War and British Defence Policy', *Defense and Security Analysis* 18 (2002), pp. 307–17.

———, *The Royal Navy Since 1815* (Basingstoke, 2005).

———, 'The Discovery of Doctrine: British Naval Thinking at the Close of the Twentieth Century', in G. Till (ed.), *The Development of British Naval Thinking: Essays in Memory of Bryan McLaren Ranft* (2006), pp. 182–91.

R.H. Grove, *Green Imperialism: Colonial Expansion, Tropical Island Edens and the Origins of Environmentalism, 1600–1868* (Cambridge, 1996).

H. Guerlac and M. Boas, 'The Radar War Against the U-Boat', *Military Affairs* 14 (1950), pp. 99–111.

E.C. Guillet, *The Great Migration: The Atlantic Crossing by Sailing Ship 1770–1860* (2nd edn., 1963, Toronto).

J.M. Haas, 'The Royal Dockyards: The Earliest Visitations and Reform 1749–1778', *Historical Journal* 13 (1970), pp. 191–215.

P. Haggie, 'The Royal Navy and War Planning in the Fisher Era', *Journal of Contemporary History* 8 (1973), pp. 113–31.

R. Haines, *Emigration and the Labouring Poor: Australian Recruitment in Britain and Ireland, 1831–60* (1997).

———, *Life and Death in the Age of Sail: The Passage to Australia* (Sydney, 2003).

———, *Doctors at Sea: Emigrant Voyages to Colonial Australia* (Basingstoke, 2005).

S. Haines, *'No Trifling Matter': Being an Account of a Voyage by Emigrants from Sussex and Hampshire to Upper Canada on Board the 'British Tar'* (Brighton, 1990).

C. Hall, *Civilising Subjects: Metropole and Colony in the English Imagination* (Chicago, 2002).

C.D. Hall, 'The Royal Navy and the Peninsular War', *Mariner's Mirror* 79 (1993), pp. 403–18.

P. Hall, 'Magic Carpets and Seamless Webs: Opportunities and Constraints for High-Speed Trains in Europe', *Built Environment* 35 (2009), pp. 59–69.

P.G. Halpern, *A Naval History of World War I* (1994).

C.I. Hamilton, 'Naval Hagiography and the Victorian Hero', *Historical Journal* 23 (1980), pp. 381–98.

H. Hamilton, *An Economic History of Scotland in the Eighteenth Century* (Oxford, 1963).

R. Hamilton, ' "When the Seas are Empty, So Are the Words": Representations of the Task Force', in Aulich (ed.), *Framing the Falklands*, pp. 129–39.

A.J. Hammerton and A. Thomson, *'Ten Pound Poms': Australia's Invisible Migrants* (Manchester, 2005).

O. Handlin, *The Uprooted: The Epic Story of the Great Migrations That Made the American People* (2nd edn., Boston, Mass., 1973).

M.L. Hansen, *The Atlantic Migration 1607–1860: A History of the Continuing Settlement of the United States* (Cambridge, Mass., 1940).

R. Harding, *The Evolution of the Sailing Navy, 1509–1815* (Basingstoke, 1995).

———, *Seapower and Naval Warfare 1650–1830* (1999).

R. Hargreaves, *The Narrow Seas: A History of the English Channel 400 BC–1945* (1959).

J. Harland-Jacobs, ' "Hands across the Sea": The Masonic Network, British Imperialism, and the North Atlantic World', *Geographical Review* 89 (1999), pp. 237–53.

V.T. Harlow, *The Founding of the Second British Empire, 1763–93, Vol. I: Discovery and Revolution* (1954).

L.A. Harper, *The English Navigation Laws: A Seventeenth Century Experiment in Social Engineering* (New York, 1939).

R. Harrington, ' "The Mighty Hood": Navy, Empire, War at Sea and the British National Imagination, 1920–60', *Journal of Contemporary History* 38 (2003), pp. 171–85.

R. Harris, *Gotcha! The Media, The Government and the Falklands Crisis* (1983).

M. Harper, 'Pains, Perils and Pastimes: Emigrant Voyages in the Nineteenth Century', in D. Killingray, M. Lincoln and N. Rigby (eds.), *Maritime Empires: British Imperial Maritime Trade in the Nineteenth Century* (Woodbridge, 2004), pp. 159–72.

S. Harper, *Capturing Enigma: How HMS Petard Seized the German Naval Codes* (Stroud, 2002).

———, *British Cinema of the 1950s: The Decline of Deference* (Oxford, 2003).

A.D. Harvey, *Collision of Empires: Britain in Three World Wars, 1793–1945* (1994 pbk. edn.).

D. Harvey, *Spaces of Capital: Towards a Critical Geography* (2001).

C. Harvie, *Fool's Gold: The Story of North Sea Oil* (Harmondsworth, 1995).

———, *A Floating Commonwealth: Politics, Culture, and Technology on Britain's Atlantic Coast, 1860–1930* (Oxford, 2008).

A. Hassam, *'Our Floating Home': Social Space and Group Identity on Board the Emigrant Ship* (1992).

———, *Sailing to Australia: Shipboard Diaries by Nineteenth-Century British Emigrants* (Manchester, 1994).

———, 'The "Bring out a Briton" Campaign of 1957 and British Migration to Australia in the 1950s', *History Compass* 5 (2007), pp. 818–44.

J. Hassan, *The Seaside, Health and the Environment in England and Wales since 1800* (Aldershot, 2003).

D. Hastings, *Over the Mountains of the Sea: Life on the Migrant Ships, 1870–1885* (Auckland, 2006).

M. Hastings and S. Jenkins, *The Battle for the Falklands* (1983).

J.B. Hattendorf, 'The Struggle with France, 1690–1815', in Hill (ed.), *Illustrated History*, pp. 80–119.

T.J. Hatton and J.G. Williamson, 'What Drove the Mass Migrations from Europe in the Late Nineteenth Century?', *Population and Development Review* 20 (1994), pp. 533–59.

———, 'A Model of U.K. Emigration, 1870–1913', *Review of Economics and Statistics* 77 (1995), pp. 407–15.

———, 'Emigration from the UK, 1870–1913 and 1950–1998', *European Review of Economic History* 8 (2004), pp. 149–69.

T.J. Hatton and J.G. Williamson 'After the Famine: Emigration from Ireland, 1850–1913', *Journal of Economic History* 53 (1993), pp. 575–600.

D. Healey, *The Time of My Life* (pbk. edn., 1989).

D.D. Hebb, *Piracy and the English Government, 1616–1642* (Aldershot, 1994).

N. Heertz, *The Silent Takeover: Global Capitalism and the Death of Democracy* (2001).

D. Held, A. McGrew, D. Goldblatt and J. Perraton, *Global Transformations: Politics, Economics and Culture* (Cambridge, 1999).

A. Hennessy, 'Workers of the Night: West Indians in Britain', in M. Cross and H. Entzinger (eds.), *Lost Illusions: Caribbean Minorities in Britain and the Netherlands* (1988), pp. 36–53.

P. Hennessy, *Never Again: Britain 1945–51* (1992).

T.A. Heppenheimer, *Turbulent Skies: The History of Commercial Aviation* (New York, 1995).

A. Herman, *To Rule the Waves: How the British Navy Shaped the Modern World* (2004).

E.S. Herman and R.S. McChesney, *The Global Media: The New Missionaries of Contemporary Capitalism* (1997).

J.R. Hill, 'The Realities of Medium Power: 1946 to the Present', in Hill (ed.), *Illustrated History*, pp. 381–408.

B. Hilton, *A Mad, Bad, and Dangerous People? England, 1783–1846* (Oxford, 2006).

D. Hinds, *Journey to an Illusion: The West Indian in Britain* (1966).

R.W.K. Hinton, *The Eastland Trade and the Common Weal in the Seventeenth Century* (Cambridge, 1959).

J.L. Hirsch, *Sierra Leone: Diamonds and the Struggle for Democracy* (Boulder, CO, 2001).

A. Hochschild, *Bury the Chains: The British Struggle to Abolish Slavery* (2006 pbk. edn.).

A.A. Hoehling, *The Great War at Sea: A History of Naval Action, 1914–18* (1965).

D. Hoerder, 'Migration in the Atlantic Economies: Regional European Origins and Worldwide Expansion', in D. Hoerder and L.P. Moch (eds.), *European Migrants: Global and Local Perspectives* (Boston, Mass., 1996), pp. 21–51.

B.W. Hogwood, *Government and Shipbuilding: The Politics of Industrial Change* (Farnbrough, 1979).

D. Hollett, *Fast Passage to Australia: The History of the Black Ball, Eagle, and White Star Lines of Australian Packets* (1986).

C. Holmes, *John Bull's Island: Immigration and British Society* (1988).

J. Horn, ' "To Parts Beyond the Seas": Free Emigration to the Chesapeake in the Seventeenth Century', in I. Altman and J. Horn (eds.), *'To Make America': European Emigration in the Early Modern Period* (Berkley, 1991), pp. 85–130.

———, 'British Diaspora: Emigration from Britain, 1680–1815', in P.J. Marshall (ed.), *The Oxford History of the British Empire Vol. II: The Eighteenth Century* (Oxford, 1998), pp. 28–52.

G. Horne, *Red Seas: Ferdinand Smith and Radical Black Sailors in the United States and Jamaica* (New York, 2005).

R. Hope, *A New History of British Shipping* (1990).

A.G. Hopkins, 'Globalization – An Agenda for Historians', in A.G. Hopkins (ed.), *Globalization in World History* (2002), pp. 1–21.

P. Horden and N. Purcell, 'The Mediterranean and "the New Thalassology" ', *American Historical Review* 111 (2006), pp. 722–40.

P. Hore, *The Habit of Victory: The Story of the Royal Navy 1545–1945* (2005).

R. Hough, *Former Naval Person: Churchill and the Wars at Sea* (1985).

M. Houlbrook, *Queer London: Perils and Pleasures in the Sexual Metropolis, 1918–1957* (Chicago, 2005).

House of Commons, *Select Committee on Health, Third Report* (Session 1997/98).

House of Commons Communities and Local Government Committee, *Coastal Towns, First Report* (2007).

———, *Coastal Towns, Second Report* (2007).

D. Howarth and S. Howarth, *Nelson: The Immortal Memory* (2004).

S. Howarth, *A Century in Oil: The Shell Transport and Trading Company, 1897–1997* (1997).

P. Hudson, *Regions and Industries: A Perspective on the Industrial Revolution in Britain* (Cambridge, 1989).

J. Donald Hughes, *An Environmental History of the World: Humankind's Changing Role in the Community of Life* (2002).

M. Hughes-Warrington, 'World and Global History', *Historical Journal* 51 (2008), pp. 753–61.

M.C. Hunter, 'Anglo-American Political and Naval Response to West Indian Piracy', *International Journal of Maritime History* 13 (2001), pp. 63–93.

A. Hurd, *A Merchant Fleet at War* (1920).

——, *British Maritime Policy: The Decline of Shipping and Shipbuilding* (1938).

M. Hutching, *Long Journey for Sevenpence: Assisted Immigration to New Zealand from the United Kingdom, 1947–1975* (Wellington, 1999).

F.E. Hyde, *Liverpool and the Mersey: An Economic History of a Port, 1700–1970* (1971).

S. Hynes, 'Personal Narratives and Commemoration', in J. Winter and E. Sivan (eds.), *War and Remembrance in the Twentieth Century* (1999), pp. 205–20.

A.H. Imlah, *Economic Elements in the Pax Britannica* (New York, 1958).

E. Ingram, 'The Failure of British Sea Power in the War of the Second Coalition, 1798–1801', in E. Ingram (ed.), *In Defence of British India: Great Britain in the Middle East, 1775–1842* (1984), pp. 67–77.

——, 'Illusions of Victory: The Nile, Copenhagen and Trafalgar Revisited', *Military Affairs* 48 (1984), pp. 140–3.

J.E. Inikori, *Africans and the Industrial Revolution: A Study in International Trade and Economic Development* (Cambridge, 2002).

H.A. Innis, *The Cod Fisheries: The History of an International Economy* (Toronto, 1954 rev. edn.).

——, *The Fur Trade in Canada: An Introduction to Canadian Economic History* (Toronto, 1956 rev. edn.).

A. Iriye, 'Environmental History and International History', *Diplomatic History* 32 (2008), pp. 643–6.

J. Israel, 'England's Mercantilist Response to Dutch World Trade Primacy, 1647–1674', in S. Groenveld and M. Wintle (eds.), *Britain and the Netherlands X: State and Trade* (Zutphen, 1992), pp. 50–61.

A. Jackson, *The British Empire and the Second World War* (2006).

——, 'The Royal Navy and the Indian Ocean Region since 1945', *The RUSI Journal* 151 (2006), pp. 78–82.

——, 'Empire and Beyond: The Pursuit of Overseas Interests in the Late Twentieth Century', *English Historical Review* 122 (2007), pp. 1350–66.

G. Jackson, *Hull in the Eighteenth Century: A Study in Economic and Social History* (Oxford, 1972).

——, *The British Whaling Trade* (1978).

G. Jackson and C. Munn, 'Trade, Commerce and Finance', in W. Hamish Fraser and I. Maver (eds.), *Glasgow, Vol. II: 1830 to 1912* (Manchester, 1996), pp. 52–95.

R. Jackson, *Suez 1956: Operation Musketeer* (1980).

B. James, 'Pie in the Sky?', *History Today* 56 (September 2006), pp. 38–40.

W.M. James, *The Influence of Sea Power on the History of the British People* (Cambridge, 1948).

A.K. Jameson, 'Some New Spanish Documents Dealing with Drake', *English Historical Review* 49 (1934), pp. 14–31.

A.G. Jamieson, 'British OSV Companies in the North Sea, 1964–1997', *Maritime Policy and Management* 25 (1998), pp. 305–12.

———, *Ebb Tide in the British Maritime Industries: Change and Adaptation 1918–1990* (Exeter, 2003).

D. Jarman and H. Sooley, *Derek Jarman's Garden* (1995).

S.A. Jay, *At the Margins of Planning: Offshore Windfarms in the United Kingdom* (Aldershot, 2008).

K. Jefferys, *Finest and Darkest Hours: The Decisive Events in British Politics from Churchill to Blair* (2003).

M. Jenkin, *British Industry and the North Sea: State Intervention in a Developing Industrial Sector* (1981).

H.J.K. Jenkins, 'Privateers, Picaroons, Pirates: West Indian Commerce Raiders, 1793–1801', *Mariner's Mirror* 73 (1987), pp. 181–6.

T. Jenks, *Naval Engagements: Patriotism, Cultural Politics, and the Royal Navy, 1793–1815* (Oxford, 2006).

G. Jenner, 'A Spanish Account of Drake's Voyages', *English Historical Review* 16 (1901), pp. 46–66.

G.T. Jóhannesson, 'How "Cod War" Came: The Origins of the Anglo-Icelandic Fisheries Dispute, 1958–61', *Historical Research* 77 (2004), pp. 543–74.

L. Johnman and H. Murphy, 'The Rationalization of Warship Building in the United Kingdom, 1945–2000', *Journal of Strategic Studies* 24 (2001), pp. 107–27.

———, 'A Triumph of Failure: The British Shipbuilding Industry and the Offshore Structures Market, 1960–1990: A Case Study of Scott Lithgow Limited', *International Journal of Maritime History* 14 (2002), pp. 63–92.

———, *British Shipbuilding and the State since 1918: A Political Economy of Decline* (Exeter, 2002).

———, *Scott Lithgow, Déjà vu All Over Again! The Rise and Fall of a Shipbuilding Company* (St John's, Newfoundland, 2005).

C. Johnson, *A General History of the Pyrates* (1724; New York, 1999 edn.).

P. Johnson, *The Birth of the Modern: World Society 1815–1830* (1991).

E.T. Jones, 'Illicit Business: Accounting for Smuggling in Mid-Sixteenth Century Bristol', *Economic History Review* 54 (2001), pp. 17–38.

———, 'The *Matthew* of Bristol and the Financiers of John Cabot's 1497 Voyage to North America', *English Historical Review* 121 (2006), pp. 778–95.

L.R. Jones, 'The British Fisheries', *Economic Geography* 2 (1926), pp. 70–85.

M.A. Jones, *Destination America* (1976).

D. Jordan and M. Walsh, *White Cargo: The Forgotten History of Britain's White Slaves in America* (Edinburgh, 2007).

T.E. Jordan, ' "Stay and Starve, or Go and Prosper!" Juvenile Emigration from Great Britain in the Nineteenth Century', *Social Science History* 9 (1985), pp. 145–66.

G.M. Joseph, 'John Coxon and the Role of Buccaneering in the Settlement of the Yucatan Colonial Frontier', *Terrae Incognitae* 12 (1980), 65–84.

C. Jowitt, 'Piracy and Politics in Heywood and Rowley's *Fortune by Land and Sea*', *Renaissance Studies* 16 (2002), pp. 217–33.

J. Jupp, *The English in Australia* (Cambridge, 2004).

M. Kale, *Fragments of Empire: Capital, Slavery, and Indian Indentured Labour Migration in the British Caribbean* (Philadelphia, Penn., 1998).

J. Kampfner, *Blair's Wars* (2003).

P.J. Kastor, 'Toward "the Maritime War Only": The Question of Naval Mobilization, 1811–1812', *Journal of Military History* 61 (1997), pp. 455–80.

C.D. Kaufmann and R.A. Pape, 'Explaining Costly International Moral Action: Britain's Sixty-Year Campaign Against the Atlantic Slave Trade', *International Organization* 53 (2003), pp. 631–68.

H. Kelsey, *Sir Francis Drake: The Queen's Pirate* (1998).

W.M. Kelso, *Jamestown: The Buried Truth* (Charlottesville, VA, 2006).

P.K. Kemp, *Victory at Sea, 1939–1945* (1976 edn.).

G. Kennedy, 'Sea Denial, Interdiction and Diplomacy: The Royal Navy and the Role of Malta, 1939–1943', in Speller (ed.), *Royal Navy and Maritime Power*, pp. 50–66.

P. Kennedy, 'Mahan versus Mackinder: Two Interpretations of British Sea Power', in P. Kennedy (ed.), *Strategy and Diplomacy, 1870–1945: Eight Studies* (1983), pp. 41–85.

———, *The Rise and Fall of British Naval Mastery* (1991 pbk. edn).

K. Kenny, *The American Irish: A History* (Harlow, 2000).

D. Killingray, 'Military and Labour Recruitment in the Gold Coast During the Second World War', *The Journal of African History* 23 (1982), pp. 83–95.

A. King, *Memorials of the Great War in Britain* (Oxford, 1998).

B. King, *Derek Walcott: A Caribbean Life* (Oxford, 2000).

D.S. King, *Making Americans: Immigration, Race, and the Origins of the Diverse Democracy* (Cambridge, Mass., 2000).

D.G. Kirby and M-J. Hinkkanen, *The Baltic and the North Seas* (2000).

P. Kirby, *Ireland and Latin America: Links and Lessons* (1992).

A.W. Kirkaldy, *British Shipping: Its History, Organisation and Significance* (1919).

B. Klein, 'Britain and the Sea', in Klein (ed.), *Fictions of the Sea*, pp. 1–12.

H.S. Klein, *The Atlantic Slave Trade* (Cambridge, 1999).

H.S. Klein, S.L. Engerman, R. Haines and R. Shlomowitz, 'Transoceanic Mortality: The Slave Trade in Comparative Perspective', *William and Mary Quarterly* 58 (2001), pp. 93–118.

N. Klein, *No Logo* (rev. edn., 2001).

H. Kleinschmidt, *People on the Move: Attitudes Toward and Perceptions of Migration in Medieval and Modern Europe* (2003).

J.M. Knauss, 'The Growth of British Fisheries during the Industrial Revolution', *Ocean Development and International Law* 36 (2005), pp. 1–11.

R.J.B. Knight, 'The Introduction of Copper Sheathing into the Royal Navy, 1779–1786', *Mariner's Mirror* 59 (1973), pp. 299–309.

———, 'New England Forests and British Seapower: Albion Revisited', *American Neptune* 46 (1986), pp. 221–9.

———, *The Pursuit of Victory: The Life and Achievements of Horatio Nelson* (2005).

R.S. Kranidis, *The Victorian Spinster and Colonial Emigration: Contested Subjects* (Basingstoke, 1999).

J.C. Kunich, *Killing Our Oceans: Dealing with the Mass Extinction of Maritime Life* (2006).

M. Kurlansky, *Cod: A Biography of the Fish That Changed the World* (1999).

———, *Salt: A World History* (2003).

———, *The Last Fish Tale: The Fate of the Atlantic and Our Disappearing Fisheries* (2008).

B. Labaree *et al.*, *America and the Sea: A Maritime History* (Mystic, CT, 1999).

S. Lahiri, *Indians in Britain: Anglo-Indian Encounters, Race and Identity, 1880–1930* (2000).

A. Lambert, 'The Shield of Empire, 1815–1895', in Hill (ed.), *Illustrated History*, pp. 161–99.

————, *Admirals: The Naval Commanders Who Made Britain Great* (2008).

D. Lambert, 'The Counter-Revolutionary Atlantic: West Indian Petitions and Proslavery Networks', *Social and Cultural Geography* 6 (2005), pp. 405–20.

N.A. Lambert, ' "Our Bloody Ships" or "Our Bloody System"? Jutland and the Loss of the Battle Cruisers, 1916', *Journal of Military History* 62 (1998), pp. 29–55.

————, 'Strategic Command and Control for Manoeuvre Warfare: Creation of the Royal Navy's "War Room" System, 1905–1915', *Journal of Military History* 69 (2005), pp. 361–410.

C. Lamberta, L. Martins and M. Ogborn, 'Currents, Visions and Voyages: Historical Geographies of the Sea', *Journal of Historical Geography* 32 (2006), pp. 479–93.

I. Land, 'Eighteenth Century Masculinity', *Journal of British Studies* 39 (2000), pp. 518–26.

————, 'Customs of the Sea: Flogging, Empire, and the "True British Seaman" ', *Interventions: An International Journal of Post-Colonial Studies* 3 (2001), pp. 169–85.

————, 'Tidal Waves: The New Coastal History', *Journal of Social History* 40 (2007), pp. 731–43.

K.E. Lane, *Blood and Silver: A History of Piracy in the Caribbean and Central America* (1999).

T. Lane, 'The British Merchant Seaman at War', in H. Cecil and P.H. Liddle (eds.), *Facing Armageddon: The First World War Experienced* (1996), pp. 146–59.

P. Langford, *Englishness Identified: Manners and Character, 1650–1850* (Oxford, 2005).

B. Lavery, 'The Rebuilding of British Warships, 1690–1740', *Mariner's Mirror* 66 (1980), pp. 5–14.

————, *The Line of Battle: Sailing Warships, 1650–1840* (1994).

————, *The Island Nation: A History of Britain and the Sea* (2005).

A. Law, 'Of Navies and Navels: Britain as a Mental Island', *Geografiska Annaler, Series B: Human Geography* 87 (2005), pp. 267–77.

P. Legrain, *Open World: The Truth About Globalisation* (2002).

M. Leigh, *European Integration and the Common Fisheries Policy* (1983).

B. Lemire, *Fashion's Favourite: The Cotton Trade and the Consumer in Britain, 1660–1800* (Oxford, 1991).

D.M. Levy, *How the Dismal Science Got Its Name: Classical Economics and the Ur-Text of Racial Politics* (Ann Arbor, 2001).

M. Lincoln, *Representing the Royal Navy: British Sea Power 1750–1815* (Aldershot, 2002).

————, 'Mutinous Behaviour on Voyages to the South Seas and Its Impact on Eighteenth Century Civil Society', *Eighteenth Century Life* 31 (2007), pp. 62–80.

I. Lindsay, 'Migration and Motivation: A Twentieth-Century Perspective', in T.M. Devine (ed.), *Scottish Emigration and Scottish Society* (Edinburgh, 1992), pp. 154–74.

P. Linebaugh and M. Rediker, *The Many-Headed Hydra: Sailors, Slaves, Commoners, and the Hidden History of the Revolutionary Atlantic* (2000).

B. Little, *The City and County of Bristol: A Study of Atlantic Civilisation* (1954).

C. Lloyd, 'Captain John Ward: Pirate', *History Today* 29 (1979), pp. 751–5.

————, *English Corsairs on the Barbary Coast* (1981).

D. Loades, *England's Maritime Empire: Seapower, Commerce and Policy, 1490–1690* (2000).

M.J.W. Lofting, 'Development Planning', in Bank of Scotland Information Services, *Understanding North Sea Oil* (1977), pp. 14–17.

E.H. Lorenz, *Economic Decline in Britain: The Shipbuilding Industry, 1890–1970* (Oxford, 1991).

E.H. Lorenz and F. Wilkinson, 'The Shipbuilding Industry', in B. Elbaum and W. Lazonick (eds.), *The Decline of the British Economy* (Oxford, 1986), pp. 109–34.

P.E. Lovejoy, 'The Volume of the Atlantic Slave Trade: A Synthesis', *Journal of African History* 23 (1982), pp. 473–501.

———, 'The Impact of the Atlantic Slave Trade on Africa: A Review of the Literature', *Journal of African History* 30 (1989), pp. 365–94.

———, 'Autobiography and Memory: Gustavus Vassa, alias Olaudah Equiano, the African', *Slavery and Abolition* 27 (2006), pp. 317–47.

P.E. Lovejoy and D. Richardson, 'Trust, Pawnship and Atlantic History: The Institutional Foundations of the Old Calabar Slave Trade', *American Historical Review* 104 (1999), pp. 333–55.

K. Lunn, *Race and Labour in Twentieth-Century Britain* (1985).

K. Lunn and A. Day, 'Britain as Island: National Identity and the Sea', in H. Brocklehurst and R. Phillips (eds.), *History, Nationhood and the Question of Britain* (Basingstoke, 2004), pp. 124–36.

N. Lunt, 'Boats, Planes and Trains: British Migration, Mobility and Transnational Experience', *Migration Letters* 5 (2008), pp. 151–65.

C. MacCrossa, 'New Journeys through Old Voyages: Literary Approaches to Richard Hakluyt and Early Modern Travel Writing', *Literature Compass* 6 (2009), pp. 97–112.

O. MacDonagh, *A Pattern of Government Growth, 1800–1860: The Passenger Acts and Their Enforcement* (1961).

J. Macdonald, *Feeding Nelson's Navy: The True Story of Food at Sea in the Georgian Era* (2004).

D. MacGregor, 'The Use, Misuse, and Non-Use of History: The Royal Navy and the Operational Lessons of the First World War', *Journal of Military History* 56 (1992), pp. 603–16.

D. Macintyre, *The Naval War Against Hitler* (1971).

E. Mackie, 'Welcome the Outlaw: Pirates, Maroons, and Caribbean Countercultures', *Cultural Critique* 59 (2005), pp. 24–62.

R.M. MacLeod and E. Kay Andrews, 'Scientific Advice in the War at Sea, 1915–1917: The Board of Invention and Research', *Journal of Contemporary History* 6 (1971), pp. 3–40.

S. Maenpaa, 'Women Below Deck: Gender and Employment on British Passenger Liners, 1860–1938', *Journal of Transport History* 25 (2004), pp 57–74.

J.A. Maiolo, *The Royal Navy and Nazi Germany, 1933–39: A Study in Appeasement* (1998).

H.L. Malchow, 'Trade Unions and Emigration in Late Victorian England: A National Lobby for State Aid', *Journal of British Studies* 15 (1976), pp. 92–116.

J.J. Malone, 'England and the Baltic Naval Stores Trade in the Seventeenth and Eighteenth Centuries', *Mariner's Mirror* 58 (1972), pp. 375–95.

P.C. Mancall, *Hakluyt's Promise: An Elizabethan's Obsession for an English America* (New Haven, CT, 2007).

E. Mancke, 'Early Modern Expansion and the Politicization of Oceanic Space', *Geographical Review* 89 (1999), pp. 225–36.

G.J. Marcus, *Heart of Oak: A Survey of British Sea Power in the Georgian Era* (Oxford, 1975).

A.J. Marder, *From the Dreadnought to Scapa Flow: The Royal Navy in the Fisher Era, 1904–1919* (Oxford, 5 vols., 1961–70).

————, *Old Friends, New Enemies: The Royal Navy and the Imperial Japanese Navy* (Oxford, 2 vols., 1981–90).

P.J. Marshall, 'British Immigration into India in the Nineteenth Century', in P.C. Emmer and M. Mörner (eds.), *European Expansion and Migration: Essays on the Intercontinental Migration from Africa, Asia and Europe* (Oxford, 1992), pp. 179–96.

D. Martin, 'The Sound of England', in S.E. Grosby and A.S. Leoussi (eds.), *Nationalism and Ethnosymbolism: History, Culture and Ethnicity in the Formation of Nations* (Edinburgh, 2007), pp. 68–83.

L.W. Martin, 'The Market for Strategic Ideas in Britain: The "Sandys Era"', *American Political Science Review* 56 (1962), pp. 23–41.

J. Masefield, *Sea Life in Nelson's Time* (1905).

T. Mason, *Shifting Sands: Design and the Changing Image of English Seaside Towns* (2003).

R.K. Massie, *Dreadnought: Britain, Germany and the Coming of the Great War* (1992).

————, *Castles of Steel: Britain, Germany and the Winning of the Great War at Sea* (pbk. edn., 2005).

P. Mathias, 'Risk, Credit and Kinship in Early Modern Enterprise', in J.I. McCusker and K. Morgan (eds.), *The Early Modern Atlantic Economy* (Cambridge, 2000), pp. 15–35.

C. Matson, 'The Atlantic Economy in an Era of Revolutions: An Introduction', *William and Mary Quarterly* 62 (2005), pp. 357–64.

C. Mayhew, *Britain's Role Tomorrow* (1967).

A. McCarthy, *Personal Narratives of Scottish and Irish Migration* (Manchester, 2007).

J.J. McCusker, *Essays in the Economic History of the Atlantic World* (1997).

I. McEwan, *On Chesil Beach* (2007).

S. McGrail, 'The Sea and Archaeology', *Historical Research* 76 (2003), pp. 1–17.

M. McLean, *The People of Glengarry: Highlanders in Transition, 1745–1820* (Montreal, 1991).

F. McLynn, *1759: The Year Britain Became Master of the World* (2005 pbk. edn.).

J. McNeill, *Something New Under the Sun: An Environmental History of the Twentieth Century* (Harmondsworth, 2000).

T.P. Melady and M.B. Melady, *Uganda: The Asian Exiles* (1978).

A. Menon, 'Britain and European Integration: The View from Within', *Political Quarterly* 75 (2004), pp. 285–317.

W.R. Meyer, 'English Privateering in the War of 1688 to 1697', *Mariner's Mirror* 67 (1981), pp. 259–72.

————, 'English Privateering in the War of the Spanish Succession, 1702–13', *Mariner's Mirror* 69 (1983), pp. 259–72.

M. Middlebrook and P. Mahoney, *Battleship: The Loss of the Prince of Wales and the Repulse* (2001 edn.).

R. Middleton, 'British Naval Strategy 1755–62: The Western Squadron', *Mariner's Mirror* 75 (1989), pp. 349–67.

————, 'The Visitation of the Royal Dockyards, 1749', *Mariner's Mirror* 77 (1991), pp. 21–30.

R. Middleton, *Government Versus the Market: The Growth of the Public Sector, Economic Management and British Economic Performance c.1890–1979* (Cheltenham, 1996).

V.T.C. Middleton, *British Tourism: The Remarkable Story of Growth* (2005).

C. Midgley, *Women Against Slavery: The British Campaigns, 1780–1870* (1992).

E. Milford, 'The Navy at Peace: The Activities of the Early Jacobean Navy, 1603–1618', *Mariner's Mirror* 26 (1990), pp. 23–39.

N. Miller, *Broadsides: The Age of Fighting Sail, 1775–1815* (Chichester, 2000).

W.H. Miller, *British Ocean Liners: A Twilight Era, 1960–85* (1986).

W.E. Minchinton, 'Bristol – Metropolis of the West in the Eighteenth Century', in P. Clark (ed.), *The Early Modern Town* (1976), pp. 297–313.

———, 'Characteristics of British Slaving Vessels, 1698–1775', *Journal of Interdisciplinary History* 20 (1989), pp. 53–81.

Ministry of Reconstruction, *British Fishermen and the Nation 1, Sea Fisheries* (1919).

L.P. Moch, *Moving Europeans: Migration in Western Europe since 1650* (Bloomington, Ind., 1992).

R. Moore, *The Royal Navy and Nuclear Weapons* (2001).

A. Moorehead, *The Fatal Impact: An Account of the Invasion of the South Pacific* (1966).

G. Moorhouse, *Great Harry's Navy: How Henry VIII Gave England Sea Power* (2006 pbk. edn.).

K. Morgan, *Bristol and the Atlantic Trade in the Eighteenth Century* (1993).

———, *Slavery, Atlantic Trade and the British Economy, 1660–1800* (Cambridge, 2000).

———, 'James Rogers and the Bristol Slave Trade', *Historical Research* 76 (2003), pp. 189–216.

N.J. Morgan and A. Pritchard, *Power and Politics at the Seaside: The Development of Devon's Resorts in the Twentieth Century* (Exeter, 1999).

R. Morriss, *The Royal Dockyards During the Revolutionary and Napoleonic Wars* (Leicester, 1983).

———, *Naval Power and British Culture, 1760–1850: Public Trust and Government Ideology* (Aldershot, 2004).

N. Mostert, *The Line Upon a Wind: An Intimate History of the Last and Greatest War Fought at Sea under Sail* (2007).

A. Murdoch, *British Emigration, 1603–1914* (Basingstoke, 2004).

I. Murdoch, *The Sea, The Sea* (1978; 1999 pbk. edn.).

S. Murdoch, 'Children of the Diaspora: The "Homecoming" of the Second Generation Scot in the Seventeenth Century', in M. Harper (ed.), *Emigrant Homecomings: The Return Movement of Emigrants, 1600–2000* (Manchester, 2005), pp. 55–76.

M.H. Murfett, *Hostage on the Yangtze: Britain, China, and the Amethyst Crisis of 1949* (1991).

W. Murray and R.H. Scales, *The Iraq War: A Military History* (Cambridge, Mass., 2003).

A.E. Musson, *The Growth of British Industry* (pbk. edn., 1981).

J.C. Myers, 'Performing the Voyage Out: Victorian Female Emigration and the Class Dynamics of Displacement', *Victorian Literature and Culture* 29 (2001), pp. 129–46.

R.A. Myers and B. Worm, 'Rapid Worldwide Depletion of Predatory Fish Communities', *Nature* 423 (2003), pp. 280–3.

C. Nakhle, 'Do High Oil Prices Justify an Increase in Taxation in a Mature Oil Province? The Case of the UK Continental Shelf', *Energy Policy* 35 (2007), pp. 4305–18.

National Audit Office, *The Maritime and Coastguard Agency's Response to Growth in the UK Merchant Fleet: Report by the Comptroller and Auditor General, Session 2008–2009* (2009).

A. Neill, 'Buccaneer Ethnography: Nature, Culture and Nation in the Journals of William Dampier', *Eighteenth-Century Studies* 33 (2000), pp. 165–80.

W.R. Nester, *The Great Frontier War: Britain, France, and the Imperial struggle for North America, 1607–1755* (2000).

H.J. Newbolt, *Sea-Life in English Literature from the Fourteenth to the Nineteenth Century* (1925).

A. Nicolson, *Men of Honour: Trafalgar and the Making of the English Hero* (2005).

North West Development Agency, *Blackpool: An Action Plan for Sustainable Growth* (2007).

P. O'Brian, *Master and Commander* (1970; 2007 pbk. edn.).

P.K. O'Brien, 'Fiscal Exceptionalism: Great Britain and Its European Rivals', in D. Winch and P.K. O'Brien (eds.), *The Political Economy of British Historical Experience 1688–1914* (Oxford, 2002), pp. 245–65.

P.P. O'Brien, 'The Titan Refreshed: Imperial Overstretch and the British Navy Before the First World War', *Past and Present* 172 (2001), pp. 146–69.

A. Offer, 'The British Empire 1870–1914: A Waste of Money?', *Economic History Review* 46 (1993), pp. 215–38.

M. Ogborn, *Global Lives: Britain and the World, 1550–1800* (Cambridge, 2008).

G. O'Hara, ' "The Sea Is Swinging into View": Modern British Maritime History in a Globalised World', *English Historical Review* CXXIV (2009), forthcoming.

J.R. Oldfield, *Popular Politics and British Anti-Slavery: The Mobilisation of Public Opinion against the Slave Trade 1787–1807* (1998).

J. Oldham, 'New Light on Mansfield and Slavery', *Journal of British Studies* 27 (1988), pp. 45–68.

M. O'Pray, *Derek Jarman: Dreams of England* (1996).

B.D. Osborne, I. Quinn and D. Robertson, *Glasgow's River* (Glasgow, 1996).

G. Owen, *From Empire to Europe: The Decline and Revival of British Industry since the Second World War* (1999).

D. Oxley, *Convict Maids: The Forced Migration of Women to Australia* (Cambridge, 1996).

T.W. Page, 'The Transportation of Immigrants and Reception Arrangements in the Nineteenth Century', *Journal of Political Economy* 19 (1911), pp. 732–49.

P. Pagnamenta and R. Overy, *All Our Working Lives* (1984).

M.A. Palmer, *Command at Sea: Naval Command and Control since the Sixteenth Century* (2005).

P. Panayi, 'Immigration, Multiculturalism and Racism', in F. Carnevali and J-M. Strange (eds.), *Twentieth Century Britain: Economic, Cultural and Social Change* (2nd edn., 2007), pp. 247–61.

M. Paris, *Warrior Nation: Images of War in British Popular Culture, 1850–2000* (2000).

R. Parker, *Uprooted: The Shipment of Poor Children to Canada, 1867–1917* (Bristol, 2008).

G.B. Parks, *Richard Hakluyt and the English Voyages* (1928).

G. Parratt, *The Royal Navy, The Sure Shield of the Empire* (1930).

J. Parry, *The Politics of Patriotism: English Liberalism, National Identity and Europe, 1830–1886* (Cambridge, 2006).

M. Parsons, *The Falklands War* (Stroud, 2000).

S. Patterson, *Dark Strangers: A Sociological Study of the Absorption of a Recent West Indian Migrant Group* (1963).

C. Payne, *Where the Sea Meets the Land: Artists on the Coast in Nineteenth Century Britain* (Bristol, 2007).

C. Peach, *The Caribbean in Europe: Contrasting Patterns of Migration and Settlement in Britain, France and the Netherlands* (1986).

C. Peach, et al., 'Immigration and Ethnicity', in A.H. Halsey and J. Webb (eds.), *Twentieth-Century British Social Trends* (3rd edn., Basingstoke, 2000), pp. 128–75.

A.W.H. Pearsall, 'The Royal Navy and Trade Protection 1688–1714', *Renaissance and Modern Studies* 30 (1986), pp. 109–23.

M. Pearson and D. Buisseret, 'A Pirate at Port Royal in 1679', *Mariner's Mirror* 57 (1971), pp. 303–6.

R.S. Peckham, 'The Uncertain State of Islands: National Identity and the Discourse of Islands in Nineteenth-Century Britain and Greece', *Journal of Historical Geography* 29 (2003), pp. 499–515.

J. Pedro Marques, *The Sounds of Silence: Nineteenth-Century Portugal and the Abolition of the Slave Trade* (Eng. trans., Oxford, 2006).

C.R. Pennell, 'Dealing with Pirates: British, French and Moroccans, 1834–56', *Journal of Imperial and Commonwealth History* 22 (1994), pp. 54–83.

———, 'Brought to Book: Reading About Pirates', in C.R. Pennell (ed.), *Bandits at Sea: A Pirates Reader* (New York, 2001), pp. 3–23.

P. Pennington, *William Wood's Diary: A Story of Nineteenth Century Emigration on Board the Sailing Ship 'Constance' in 1852* (Stansted, 2002).

R. Perren, 'The Nineteenth-Century Economy', in W. Hamish and C.H. Lee (eds.), *Aberdeen 1800–2000: A New History* (East Lothian, 2000), pp. 75–94.

K.G. Persson, 'Mind the Gap! Transport Costs and Price Convergence in the Nineteenth Century Atlantic Economy', *European Review of Economic History* 8 (2004), pp. 125–47.

K. Pescod, *Good Food, Bright Fires and Civility: British Emigrant Depots of the 19th Century* (Kew, Vic., 2003).

N. Philbrick, *'Mayflower': A Voyage to War* (2006).

J. Phillips, '*Oceanspan*: Deindustrialisation and Devolution in Scotland, c.1960–1974', *Scottish Historical Review* 84 (2005), pp. 63–84.

M. Phillips and T. Phillips, *Windrush: The Irresistible Rise of Multi-Racial Britain* (1998).

J. Pickering, 'Politics and "Black Tuesday": Shifting Power in the Cabinet and the Decision to Withdraw from East of Suez, November 1967–January 1968', *Twentieth Century British History* 13 (2002), pp. 144–70.

S. Pollard, 'The Decline of Shipbuilding on the Thames', *Economic History Review* 3 (1950–51), pp. 72–89.

J. Pollock, *William Wilberforce* (1977).

J. Postma, *The Atlantic Slave Trade* (Westport, CT, 2003).

A. Potkay, 'Olaudah Equiano and the Art of Spiritual Autobiography', *Eighteenth-Century Studies* 27 (1994), pp. 677–92.

A. Prakash and J.A. Hart, 'Globalization and Governance', in Prakash and Hart (eds.), *Globalization and Governance* (1999), pp. 1–24.

J. Prebble, *The Highland Clearances* (1963).

M. Prentis, 'Haggis on the High Seas: Shipboard Experiences of Scottish Emigrants to Australia, 1821–1897', *Australian Historical Studies* 36 (2004), pp. 294–311.

J. Prescott, *My Story: Pulling No Punches* (2008).

J.M. Price, 'What Did Merchants Do? Reflections on British Overseas Trade, 1660–1790', *Journal of Economic History* 49 (1989), pp. 267–84.

———, 'The Imperial Economy 1700–1776', in Marshall (ed.), *British Empire, Vol. II*, pp. 78–104.

Prime Minister's Strategy Unit, *Net Benefits: A Sustainable and Profitable Future for UK Fishing* (2004).

J. Procter (ed.), *Writing Black Britain, 1948–1998: An Interdisciplinary Anthology* (Manchester, 2000).

P. Pugh, ' "The Empire Strikes Back": The Falklands/Malvinas Campaigns of 1982', *Mariner's Mirror* 93 (2007), pp. 307–24.

S. Purchas, *Hakluytus Posthumus, or Purchas his Pilgrimes: Contayning a History of the World in Sea Voyages and Lande Travells by Englishmen and Others* (1625; 1905–07 edn.)

D. Quinn and A.N. Ryan, *England's Sea Empire 1550–1642* (1983).

T.K. Rabb, *Enterprise and Empire: Merchant and Gentry Investment in the Expansion of England, 1575–1630* (Cambridge, Mass., 1967).

———, *Jacobean Gentleman: Sir Edwin Sandys 1561–1629* (Princeton, NJ, 1998).

P. Rainbird, *The Archaeology of Micronesia* (Cambridge, 2004).

———, *The Archaeology of Islands* (Cambridge, 2007).

G.D. Ramsay, 'The Smugglers' Trade: A Neglected Aspect of English Commercial Development', *Transactions of the Royal Historical Society* Vth Series, 2 (1952), pp. 131–57.

J. Ramsden, 'Refocusing "The People's War": British War Films of the 1950s', *Journal of Contemporary History* 33 (1998), pp. 35–63.

J. Ramster, 'Fisheries Research in England and Wales, 1850–1980', in D.J. Starkey, C. Reid and N. Ashcroft (eds.), *England's Sea Fisheries: The Commercial Sea Fisheries of England and Wales since 1300* (2000), pp. 179–87.

E.L. Rasor, *Reform in the Royal Navy: A Social History of the Lower Deck, 1850–1880* (Hamden, Conn., 1976).

J.L. Ray, 'The Abolition of Slavery and the End of International War', *International Organization* 43 (1989), pp. 405–39.

D.A. Rayner, *Escort: The Battle of the Atlantic* (1955).

J. Rayner, *The Naval War Film: Genre, History, National Cinema* (Manchester, 2007).

M. Reckord, 'The Colonial Office and the Abolition of Slavery', *Historical Journal* 14 (1971), pp. 723–34.

D. Redford, 'The March 1943 Crisis in the Battle of the Atlantic: Myth and Reality', *History* 95 (2007), pp. 64–83.

M. Rediker, ' "Under the Banner of King Death": The Social World of Anglo-American Pirates, 1716 to 1726', *William and Mary Quarterly* 38 (1981), pp. 203–27.

———, *Between the Devil and the Deep Blue Sea: Merchant Seamen, Pirates, and the Anglo-American Maritime World 1700–1750* (Cambridge, 1987).

———, 'When Women Pirates Sailed the Seas', *Wilson Quarterly* 17 (1993), pp. 102–10.

———, *Villains of all Nations: Atlantic Pirates in the Golden Age* (2004).

C. Reid, 'From Boom to Bust: The Herring Industry in the Twentieth Century', in Starkey, Reid and Ashcroft (eds.), *England's Sea Fisheries*, pp. 188–96.

S.J. Reso, 'Finding the Oil: Techniques, Costs and Risks', in Bank of Scotland, *North Sea Oil*, pp. 9–13.

E. Richards, *Britannia's Children: Emigration from England, Scotland, Wales and Ireland since 1600* (2004).

J. Richards, *Films and British National Identity: From Dickens to 'Dad's Army'* (Manchester, 1997).

D. Richardson, 'The Slave Trade, Sugar, and British Economic Growth 1748–1776', *Journal of Interdisciplinary History* 17 (1987), pp. 739–69.

———, 'Shipboard Revolts, African Authority, and the Atlantic Slave Trade', *William and Mary Quarterly* 58 (2001), pp. 69–92.

H.W. Richardson, 'British Emigration and Overseas Investment, 1870–1914', *Economic History Review* 25 (1972), pp. 99–113.

W. Richardson, *A Mariner of England: An Account of the Career of William Richardson* (2000 edn.).

H.W. Richmond, *Statesmen and Sea Power* (Oxford, 1947 edn.).

———, *The Navy as an Instrument of Policy 1558–1727* (Cambridge, 1953).

K. Robbins, *Great Britain: Identities, Institutions and the Idea of Britishness* (1998).

C. Roberts, *The Unnatural History of the Sea: The Past and the Future of Man and Fishing* (2007).

L. Robin, 'Ecology: A Science of Empire?', in T. Griffiths and L. Robin (eds.), *Ecology and Empire: Environmental History of Settler Societies* (Edinburgh, 1997), pp. 63–75.

B.T. Robinson, 'Turning the Tide: Regeneration and Seaside Towns', Unpublished Oxford Brookes MSc Thesis, 2007.

C. Robinson and J. Morgan, *North Sea Oil in the Future: Economic Analysis and Government Policy* (1978).

R. Robinson, *Trawling: The Rise and Fall of the British Trawl Fishery* (Exeter, 1996).

V. Robinson, *Transients, Settlers and Refugees: Asians in Britain* (Oxford, 1986).

D. Robinson-Dunn, 'Lascar Sailors and English Converts: The Imperial Port and Islam in Late 19th-Century England', Paper presented at Conference on 'Seascapes, Littoral Cultures, and Trans-Oceanic Exchanges', Library of Congress, Washington DC, February 12–15, 2003.

———, *The Harem, Slavery and British Imperial Culture: Anglo-Muslim Relations in the Late-Nineteenth Century* (Manchester, 2006).

N.A.M. Rodger, *The Wooden World: An Anatomy of the Georgian Navy* (1981).

———, 'Devon Men and the Navy, 1688–1815', in M. Duffy, et al. (eds.), *The New Maritime History of Devon, Vol. I: From Early Times to the Late Eighteenth Century* (Exeter, 1992), pp. 209–15.

———, ' "A Little Navy of Your Own Making": Admiral Boscawen and the Cornish Connection in the Royal Navy', in Duffy (ed.), *Parameters*, pp. 82–92.

———, 'Recent Books on the Royal Navy of the Eighteenth Century', *Journal of Military History* 63 (1999), pp. 683–703.

———, *The Safeguard of the Sea: A Naval History of Britain, Vol. I: 660–1649* (Harmondsworth, 2004 pbk. edn.).

———, 'Queen Elizabeth and the Myth of Sea Power in English History', *Transactions of the Royal Historical Society* VIth series, 14 (2004), pp. 153–74.

———, *The Command of the Ocean: A Naval History of Britain, Vol. II: 1649–1815* (Harmondsworth, 2006 pbk. edn.)

M. Roe, *Australia, Britain and Migration 1915–1940: A Study of Desperate Hopes* (Cambridge, 1995).

W. Rogers, *A Cruising Voyage Round the World* (1712; 1970 edn.).

C. Rootes, 'Environmental Protest in Britain, 1988–1997', in B. Seel, M. Paterson and B. Doherty (eds.), *Direct Action in British Environmentalism* (2000), pp. 25–61.

L.A. Rose, *Power at Sea, Vol. II: The Breaking Storm, 1919–1945* (Columbia, MO, 2007).

———, *Power at Sea, Vol. III: A Violent Peace, 1946–2006* (Columbia, MO, 2007).

S.O. Rose, 'Sex, Citizenship, and the Nation in World War II Britain', *American Historical Review* 103 (1998), pp. 1147–76.

S.W. Roskill, *The War at Sea, 1939–1945* (3 vols., 1954–61).

H.M. Rozwadowski, *The Sea Knows No Boundaries: A Century of Marine Science Under ICES* (Seattle, WA, 2002).

J. Rüger, *The Great Naval Game: Britain and Germany in the Age of Empire* (Cambridge, 2007).

A. Rupprecht, ' "A Limited Sort of Property": History, Memory and the Slave Ship Zong', *Slavery and Abolition* 29 (2008), pp. 265–77.

E. Rushen, *Single and Free: Female Migration to Australia, 1833–1837* (Melbourne, 2003).

E.S. Russell, *The Overfishing Problem* (Cambridge, 1942).

D.B. Ryden, 'Does Decline Make Sense? The West Indian Economy and the Abolition of the British Slave Trade', *Journal of Interdisciplinary History* 31 (2000), pp. 347–74.

V. Sackville-West, *No Signposts in the Sea* (1961; 1985 Virago edn.).

P. Salmon, ' "Between the Sea Power and the Land Power": Scandinavia and the Coming of the First World War', *Transactions of the Royal Historical Society* VIth Series, 3 (1993), pp. 23–49.

A. Sampson, *The Seven Sisters: The Great Oil Companies and the World They Made* (1975).

R. Samuel, *Patriotism: The Making and Unmaking of British National Identity* (1989), Vol. I.

R. Scally, 'Liverpool Ships and Irish Emigrants in the Age of Sail', *Journal of Social History* 17 (1983), pp. 5–30.

S. Schama, *The Embarrassment of Riches: An Interpretation of Dutch Culture in the Golden Age* (1987).

———, *Rough Crossings: Britain, the Slaves, and the American Revolution* (2005).

A. Scherr, ' "Sambos" and "Black Cut-Throats": Peter Porcupine on Slavery and Race in the 1790s', *American Periodicals: A Journal of History, Criticism, and Bibliography* 13 (2003), pp. 3–30.

M. Schoenfeld, 'Winston Churchill as War Manager: The Battle of the Atlantic Committee, 1941', *Military Affairs* 52 (1988), pp. 122–7.

J.A. Schultz, ' "Leaven for the Lump": Canada and Empire Settlement, 1918–1939', in Constantine (ed.), *Emigrants and Empire*, pp. 150–73.

D.M. Schurman, *The Education of a Navy: The Development of British Naval Strategic Thought, 1867–1914* (1965).

———, *Julian S. Corbett, 1854–1922: Historian of British Maritime Policy from Drake to Jellicoe* (1981).

G.R. Searle, *A New England? Peace and War, 1886–1918* (Oxford, 2004).

B. Semmel, *Liberalism and Naval Strategy: Ideology, Interest and Sea Power During the Pax Britannica* (1986).

C.M. Senior, *A Nation of Pirates* (Exeter, 1976).

D. Severn, 'The Bombardment of Algiers, 1816', *History Today* 28 (1978), pp. 31–9.

G. Shaw and T. Coles, 'The Resort Economy: Changing Structures and Management Issues in British Resorts', in Agarwal and Shaw (eds.), *Managing Coastal Tourism*, pp. 40–55.

J.F. Shepherd and G.M. Walton, *Shipping, Maritime Trade and the Economic Development of Colonial North America* (Cambridge, 1972).

R.B. Sheridan, 'The Commercial and Financial Organisation of the British Slave Trade, 1750–1807', *Economic History Review* 11 (1958–59), pp. 249–63.

B. Simms, *Three Victories and a Defeat: The Rise and Fall of the First British Empire, 1714–1783* (2007).

J.G. Singh, 'History or Colonial Ethnography? The Ideological Formation of Edward Terry's *A Voyage to East-India* (1655 and 1665)', in I. Camps and J.G. Singh (eds.), *Travel Knowledge: European 'Discoveries' in the Early Modern Period* (Basingstoke, 2001), pp. 197–207.

L. Sklair, *Globalization: Capitalism and Its Alternatives* (Oxford, 2002).

J. Slader, *The Red Duster At War: A History of the Merchant Navy during the Second World War* (1988).

A. Slaven, *The Development of the West of Scotland 1750–1960* (1975).

J. Smail, 'Credit, Risk and Honour in Eighteenth Century Commerce', *Journal of British Studies* 44 (2005), pp. 439–56.

T. Smit, M. Junginger and R. Smits, 'Technological Learning in Offshore Wind Energy: Different Roles of the Government', *Energy Policy* 35 (2007), pp. 6431–44.

A. Smith, *The Atrocities of the Pirates* (1824; 1997 edn.).

G. Smith, *Smuggling in the Bristol Channel, 1700–1850* (1989).

P.C. Smith, *The Great Ships Pass: British Battleships at War 1939–1945* (1977).

S. Smith, 'Piracy in Early British America', *History Today* 46 (1996), pp. 29–37.

S.C. Smith, 'Power Transferred? Britain, the United States and the Gulf, 1956–71', *Contemporary British History* 21 (2007), pp. 1–23.

W.J. Smyth, 'Irish Emigration, 1700–1920', in Emmer and Mörner (eds.), *European Expansion and Migration*, pp. 49–78.

B.L. Solow, 'Caribbean Slavery and British Growth: The Eric Williams Hypothesis', *Journal of Development Economics* 17 (1985), pp. 99–115.

B.L. Solow and S.L. Engerman (eds.), *British Capitalism and Caribbean Slavery: The Legacy of Eric Williams* (Cambridge, 1987).

C. Somerville, *Coast: A Celebration of Britain's Coastal Heritage* (2005).

M.K. Søndergaard, 'The Rise and Fall of the North European Mackerel Fisheries in the Nineteenth Century', *International Journal of Maritime History* 20 (2008), pp. 115–32.

B. Southam, *Jane Austen and the Navy* (2000).

I. Speller, 'Delayed Reaction: UK Maritime Expeditionary Capabilities and the Lessons of the Falklands Conflict', *Defense and Security Analysis* 18 (2002), pp. 363–78.

———, 'Naval Diplomacy: Operation Vantage, 1961', in I. Speller (ed.), *The Royal Navy and Maritime Power in the Twentieth Century* (2005), pp. 164–80.

———, 'The Seaborne/Airborne Concept: Littoral Manoeuvre in the 1960s?', *Journal of Strategic Studies* 29 (2006), pp. 53–82.

R.G. Spencer, *British Immigration Policy since 1939* (1997).

H. Sprout and M. Sprout, 'The Dilemma of Rising Demands and Insufficient Resources', *World Politics* 20 (1968), pp. 660–93.

D. Sriskandaraajah and C. Drew, *Brits Abroad: Mapping the Scale and Nature of British Emigration* (2006).

J. Stanley, 'The Company of Women', *The Northern Mariner* 9 (1999), pp. 69–86.

———, Women at Sea: An Other Category', *Gender and History* 15 (2003), pp. 135–9.

D.J. Starkey, *British Privateering Enterprise in the Eighteenth Century* (Exeter, 1990).

———, 'Pirates and Markets', in C.R. Pennell (ed.), *Bandits at Sea: A Pirates Reader* (New York, 2001), pp. 107–23.

B.M. Stave, J.F. Sutherland and A. Salerno, *From the Old Country: An Oral History of the European Migration to America* (New York, 1994).

I.K. Steele, *The English Atlantic, 1675–1740: An Exploration of Communication and Community* (Oxford, 1986).

N. Steensgaard, 'European Shipping to Asia, 1497–1700', *Scandinavian Economic History Review* 18 (1970), pp. 1–11.

R.B. Stein, 'Seascape and the American Imagination: The Puritan Seventeenth Century', *Early American Literature* 7 (1972), pp. 17–37.

D. Stevenson, *1914–1918: The History of the First World War* (Harmondsworth, 2005 pbk. edn.).

R.L. Stevenson, *Treasure Island* (1883; Oxford, 1998 edn.).

J.C. Stewart, *The Sea Our Heritage: British Maritime Interests Past and Present* (rev. edn., 1995).

J. Stiglitz, *Making Globalization Work* (2006).

D. St John Thomas, *Journey Through Britain: Landscape, People and Books* (New edn., 2004).

A.E. Stone, 'Sea and the Self: Travel as Experience and Metaphor in Early American Autobiography', *Genre* 7 (1974), pp. 279–306.

N.R. Stout, 'Manning the Royal Navy in North America, 1763–1775', *American Neptune* 23 (1963), pp. 174–85.

B. Stråth, *The Politics of De-Industrialisation: The Contraction of the West European Shipbuilding Industry* (1987).

S.G. Sturmey, *British Shipping and World Competition* (1962).

J. Sugden, *Nelson: A Dream of Glory* (2005 pbk. edn.).

J.T. Sumida, 'British Capital Ship Design and Fire Control in the Dreadnought Era: Sir John Fisher, Arthur Hungerford Pollen, and the Battle Cruiser', *Journal of Modern History* 51 (1979), pp. 206–30.

———, 'British Naval Operational Logistics, 1914–1918', *Journal of Military History* 57 (1993), pp. 447–80.

———, 'Sir John Fisher and the Dreadnought: The Sources of Naval Mythology', *Journal of Military History* 59 (1995), pp. 619–37.

J. Sutton, *Lords of the East: The East India Company and Its Ships* (1981).

P.W. Sutton, *Nature, Environment and Society* (Basingstoke, 2004).

E.N. Swinerton, *Ugandan Asians in Great Britain* (1975).

D. Syrett, 'The Methodology of British Amphibious Operations during the Seven Years' and American Wars', *Mariner's Mirror* 58 (1972), pp. 269–80.

———, 'The Organisation of British Trade Convoys during the American War, 1776–83', *Mariner's Mirror* 62 (1976), pp. 169–81.

———, 'The Failure of the British Effort in North America, 1777', in Black and Woodfine (eds.), *British Navy*, pp. 171–90.

———, *The Royal Navy in American Waters 1775–1783* (Aldershot, 1989).

———, 'Home Waters or America? The Dilemma of British Naval Strategy in 1778', *Mariner's Mirror* 77 (1991), pp. 365–77.

———, *The Defeat of the German U-Boats: The Battle of the Atlantic* (Columbia, SC, 1994).

E.R. Taylor, *If We Must Die: Shipboard Insurrections in the Era of the Atlantic Slave Trade* (Baton Rouge, LA, 2006).

J. Taylor, *I Was Born a Slave: An Anthology of Classic Slave Narratives, 1770–1849* (Chicago, 2 vols., 1999).

P. Taylor, *The Distant Magnet: European Emigration to the USA* (New York, 1971).

M. Teorey, 'Pirates and State-Sponsored Terrorism in Eighteenth Century England', *Perspectives on Evil and Human Wickedness* (2003), pp. 53–63.

S.S. Thandi, 'Migrating to the "Mother Country", 1947–1980', in M. Fisher, S. Lahiri and S. Thandi (eds.), *A South-Asian History of Britain* (Oxford, 2007), pp. 159–81.

P. Theroux, *The Kingdom by the Sea* (1983).

J. Thirsk and J.P. Cooper (eds.), *Seventeenth Century Economic Documents* (Oxford, 1972).

H. Thomas, *The Slave Trade: The Story of the Atlantic Slave Trade 1440–1870* (1997).

R.P. Thomas and R.N. Bean, 'The Fishers of Men: The Profits of the Slave Trade', *Journal of Economic History* 34 (1974), pp. 885–914.

A. Thomson, ' "My Wayward Heart": Homesickness, Longing and the Return of British Post-War Immigrants From Australia', in Harper (ed.), *Emigrant Homecomings*, pp. 105–30.

J. Thompson, *The Imperial War Museum Book of the War At Sea: The Royal Navy in the Second World War* (1996).

———, *Imperial War Museum Book of the War at Sea 1914–18* (2005).

J.E. Thomson, *Mercenaries, Pirates, and Sovereigns: State Building and Extra-Territorial Violence in Early Modern Europe* (Princeton, NJ, 1996).

H. Thornton, 'John Selden's Response to Hugo Grotius: The Argument for the Closed Seas', *International Journal of Maritime History* 18 (2006), pp. 105–27.

J. Thornton, 'Cannibals, Witches, and Slave Traders in the Atlantic World', *William and Mary Quarterly* 60 (2003), pp. 273–94.

A. Thrush, 'Naval Finance and the Origins and Development of Ship Money', in M.C. Fissel (ed.), *War and Government in Britain 1598–1650* (Manchester, 1991), pp. 133–62.

G. Till, 'Retrenchment, Rethinking, Revival, 1919–1939', in Hill (ed.), *Illustrated History*, pp. 319–47.

J.A. Tilley, *The British Navy and the American Revolution* (Columbia, SC, 1987).

Time Out Guides, *Seaside: Discover the Best of Britain's Best Beaches* (2008).

M. Todd, 'A Captive's Story: Puritans, Pirates and the Drama of Reconciliation', *Seventeenth Century* 12 (1997), pp. 37–56.

R. Toye, 'The New Commanding Height: Labour Party Policy on North Sea Oil and Gas, 1964–74', *Contemporary British History* 16 (2002), pp. 89–118.

N. Tracy, *Navies, Deterrence and American Independence: Britain and Seapower in the 1760s and 1770s* (Vancouver, BC, 1988).

B. Traister, 'Review: *Unchained Voices: An Anthology of Black Authors in the English-Speaking World of the Eighteenth Century*', *Eighteenth Century Fiction* 18 (2005), pp. 131–3.

HM Treaury, *Independent Enquiry into a Tonnage Tax: A Report by the Lord Alexander of Weedon QC* (1999).

F. Trentmann, *Free Trade Nation: Commerce, Consumption and Civil Society in Modern Britain* (Oxford, 2008).

A. Trodd, 'Collaborating in Open Boats: Dickens, Collins, Franklin and Bligh', *Victorian Studies* 42 (1999), pp. 210–25.

H. Turley, *Rum, Sodomy and the Lash: Piracy, Sexuality and Masculine Identity* (1999).

R. Unger (ed.), *Conway's History of the Ship: Cogs Caravels and Galleons, The Sailing Ship 1000–1650* (1994).

J. Urry, *The Tourist Gaze: Leisure and Travel in Contemporary Societies* (1990).

R.G. Usher, 'Royal Navy Impressment During the American Revolution', *Mississippi Valley Historical Review* 37 (1951), pp. 673–88.

W.E. van Vugt, 'Prosperity and Industrial Emigration from Britain during the Early 1850s', *Journal of Social History* 22 (1988), pp. 339–54.

————, 'Running from Ruin? The Emigration of British Farmers to the USA in the Wake of the Repeal of the Corn Laws', *Economic History Review* 41 (1988), pp. 411–28.

C. Vassallo, 'Sailing under the Red Duster: Maltese Merchant Seafarers in the Twentieth Century', *Mariner's Mirror* 94 (2008), pp. 446–60.

F. Vigier, *Change and Apathy: Liverpool and Manchester during the Industrial Revolution* (Cambridge, Mass., 1970).

R. Visram, *Ayahs, Lascars and Princes: The Story of Indians in Britain, 1700–1947* (1986).

————, *Asians in Britain: 400 Years of History* (2002).

S.P. Wainwright and C. Williams, 'Biography and Vulnerability: Loss, Dying and Death in the Romantic Paintings of J.M.W. Turner', *Auto/Biography* 13 (2005), pp. 16–32.

D. Walcott, *Omeros* (1990).

A. Waley, *The Opium War Through Chinese Eyes* (1958).

P. Waller, *Writers, Readers, and Reputations: Literary Life in Britain 1870–1918* (Oxford, 2006).

J.K. Walton, *Fish and Chips and the British Working Class, 1870–1940* (1992).

————, *The British Seaside: Holidays and Resorts in the Twentieth Century* (Manchester, 2000).

J. Walvin, *Beside the Seaside: A Social History of the Popular Seaside Holiday* (1978).

————, *A Short History of Slavery* (Harmondsworth, 2007).

O. Wambu, *Empire Windrush: Fifty Years of Writing About Black Britain* (1999 pbk. edn.).

J.R. Ward, 'The British West Indies in the Age of Abolition, 1748–1815', in Marshall (ed.), *British Empire Vol. II*, pp. 415–39.

P. Ward, *Britishness since 1870* (2004).

K. Warren, *Steel, Ships and Men: Cammell Laird, 1824–1993* (Liverpool, 1998).

S. Watson, ' "England Expects": Nelson as a Symbol of Local and National Identity within the Museum', *Museum and Society* 4 (2006), pp. 129–51.

D.C. Watt, 'The Anglo-German Naval Agreement of 1935: An Interim Judgment', *Journal of Modern History* 28 (1956), pp. 155–75.

J. Webster, 'The *Zong* in the Context of the Eighteenth-Century Slave Trade', *Journal of Legal History* 28 (2007), pp. 285–98.

W. Webster, *Imagining Home: Gender, 'Race', and National Identity, 1945–64* (1998).

————, 'Immigration and Racism', in P. Addison and H. Jones (eds.), *A Companion to Contemporary Britain, 1939–2000* (Oxford, 2005), pp. 93–109.

R. Weight, *Patriots: National Identity in Britain 1940–2000* (pbk. edn., 2002).

D. Wettern, *The Decline of British Seapower* (1982).

B. Wheaton, 'Identity, Politics, and the Beach: Environmental Activism in Surfers Against Sewage', *Leisure Studies* 26 (2007), pp. 279–302.

J.S. Wheeler, 'Prelude to Power: The Crisis of 1649 and the Foundation of English Naval Power', *Mariner's Mirror* 81 (1995), pp. 148–55.

S. White and G. White, 'Slave Clothing and African-American Culture in the Eighteenth and Nineteenth Centuries', *Past and Present* 148 (1995), pp. 149–86.

C. Whitham, 'On Dealing with Gangsters: The Limits of British "Generosity" in the Leasing of Bases to the United States, 1940–41', *Diplomacy and Statecraft* 7 (1996), pp. 589–630.

D. Whitmarsh, 'Adaptation and Change in the Fishing Industry since the 1970s', in Starkey, Reid and Ashcroft (eds.), *England's Sea Fisheries*, pp. 227–34.

W.M. Wiecek, 'Somerset: Lord Mansfield and the Legitimacy of Slavery in the Anglo-American World', *University of Chicago Law Review* 42 (1974), pp. 86–146.

K. Wigen, 'Oceans of History', *American Historical Review* 111 (2006), pp. 717–21.

———, 'Introduction', in Bentley, Bridenthal and Wigen (eds.), *Seascapes*, pp. 1–18.

A. Wiles (ed.), *Migration: An Economic and Social Analysis* (2000).

J. Wilkie, *Metagama: A Journey from Lewis to the New World* (Edinburgh, 1987).

E. Williams, *Capitalism and Slavery* (1964).

J.B. Williams, *British Commercial Policy and Trade Expansion 1750–1850* (Oxford, 1972).

N. Williams, *Contraband Cargoes: Seven Centuries of Smuggling* (1959).

P. Williams, *The English Seaside* (Swindon, 2005).

T. Williams, *Structures of Desire: British Cinema, 1939–1955* (New York, 2000).

S.B.A. Willis, 'Fleet Performance and Capability in the Eighteenth-Century Royal Navy', *War in History* 11 (2004), pp. 373–92.

C. Wilson, *England's Apprenticeship, 1603–1763* (2nd edn., 1984).

J.F. Wilson, *British Business History 1720–1994* (Manchester, 1995).

K. Wilson, 'Empire, Trade and Popular Politics in Mid-Hanoverian Britain: The Case of Admiral Vernon', *Past and Present* 121 (1988), pp. 74–109.

K.M. Wilson, *Channel Tunnel Visions, 1850–1945: Dreams and Nightmares* (1994).

J. Winch, *A Gentleman of Color: The Life of James Forten* (Oxford, 2003).

R. Winder, *Bloody Foreigners: The Story of Immigration to Britain* (2007 pbk. edn.).

J. Winter, *Sites of Memory, Sites of Mourning: The Great War in European Cultural History* (Cambridge, 1995).

———, *Remembering War: The Great War between Memory and History in the Twentieth Century* (New Haven, CT, 2006).

O.O. Winther, 'English Migration to the American West, 1865–1900', *The Huntington Library Quarterly* 27 (1964), pp. 159–73.

J. Winton (ed.), *The War at Sea, 1939–1945: An Anthology of Personal Experience* (1994 edn.).

S.M. Wise, *Though the Heavens May Fall: The Landmark Trial That Led to the End of Human Slavery* (2005).

M. Wood, *Blind Memory: Visual Representations of Slavery in England and America* (Manchester, 2000).

B. Woodcock, 'Derek Walcott: *Omeros*', in N. Roberts (ed.), *A Companion to Twentieth Century Poetry* (Oxford, 2001), pp. 547–56.

P. Woodfine, 'Ideas of Naval Power and the Conflict with Spain, 1737–1742', in Black and Woodfine (eds.), *British Navy*, pp. 71–90.

R. Woodman, *The Sea Warriors: Fighting Captains and Frigate Warfare in the Age of Nelson* (2001).

———, *The History of the Ship: The Comprehensive Story of Seafaring* (2005 edn.).

S. Woodward, *One Hundred Days: The Memoirs of the Falklands Battle Group Commander* (1992).

H. Woolcock, *Rights of Passage: Emigration to Australia in the Nineteenth Century* (1986).

B. Woolley, *The Queen's Conjurer: The Science and Magic of Dr John Dee, Advisor to Queen Elizabeth I* (2001).

B. Worm, H.K. Lotze and R.A. Myers, 'Predator Diversity Hotspots in the Blue Ocean', *Proceedings of the National Academy of Science of the United States* 100 (2003), pp. 9884–8.

K. Worpole, *Last Landscapes: The Architecture of the Cemetery in the West* (2003).

E.A. Wrigley, 'The Divergence of England: The Growth of the English Economy in the Seventeenth and Eighteenth Centuries', *Transactions of the Royal Historical Society* VIth Series, 10 (2000), pp. 117–41.

R. Wymer, *Derek Jarman* (Manchester, 2005).

D. Yergin, *The Prize: the Epic Quest for Oil, Money and Power* (1991).

N. Zahedieh, 'Trade, Plunder and Economic Development in Early English Jamaica, 1655–1689', *Economic History Review* 39 (1986), pp. 213–22.

———, ' "A Frugal, Prudential and Hopeful Trade": Privateering in Jamaica, 1655–89', *Journal of Imperial and Commonwealth History* 18 (1990), pp. 145–68.

B. Zamoyska, *The Ten Pound Fare: Experiences of British People Who Emigrated to Australia in the 1950s* (1998).

T. Zuber, 'The German Intelligence Estimates in the West, 1885–1914', *Intelligence and National Security* 21 (2006), pp. 177–201.

Index